This pioneer volume brings together for the first time a range of essays on the anthropology of food in Oceania and Southeast Asia. The essays reflect current research in the field, particularly that undertaken by Australian scholars.

The volume focuses on four main concerns. First, it examines the ecological, economic, social, and political factors that influence the production of food, food choice, and dietary behavior. It then explores the way in which people think and speak about food, diet, nutrition, and eating, including discussions of concepts of hunger and the classification of foods. Next follow accounts of infant feeding practices in Southeast Asia and the South Pacific. These include descriptions of traditional feeding and the changes that are taking place in it, specifically in response to the promotion of bottle feeding. The roles of government agencies and of multinational corporations are also discussed. Finally, the book raises questions about methods and research directions for nutritional anthropologists.

The regional focus of the volume allows for an examination of differences in food systems and uses within a single area, as well as for discussion of common trends, especially those that have arisen as a result of societies in the region having been incorporated into the world economy. Much that is discussed in the volume is applicable elsewhere in the world, and the collection therefore offers a basis for a comparative analysis of food in culture and society.

Shared wealth and symbol

*Food, culture, and society
in Oceania and Southeast Asia*

Shared wealth and symbol

Food, culture, and society
in Oceania and Southeast Asia

Edited by
LENORE MANDERSON

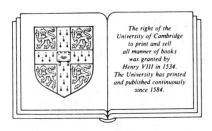

The right of the
University of Cambridge
to print and sell
all manner of books
was granted by
Henry VIII in 1534.
The University has printed
and published continuously
since 1584.

Cambridge University Press

Cambridge
London   New York   New Rochelle
Melbourne   Sydney

Editions de la Maison des Sciences de l'Homme

Paris

Published by the Press Syndicate of the University of Cambridge
The Pitt Building, Trumpington Street, Cambridge CB2 1RP
32 East 57th Street, New York, NY 10022, USA
10 Stamford Road, Oakleigh, Melbourne 3166, Australia
and

Editions de la Maison des Sciences de l'Homme
54 Boulevard Raspail, 75720 Paris, Cedex 06

First published 1986

Printed in the United States of America

Sponsored by the International Commission on the Anthropology of Food

Library of Congress Cataloging in Publication Data
Main entry under title:
Shared wealth and symbol.
Bibliography: p.
1. Food habits – Oceania – Addresses, essays, lectures.
2. Ethnology – Oceania – Addresses, essays, lectures.
3. Nutrition – Oceania – Social aspects – Addresses,
essays, lectures.   4. Food habits – Asia, Southeastern –
Addresses, essays, lectures.   5. Ethnology – Asia,
Southeastern – Addresses, essays, lectures.   7. Oceania –
Social life and customs – Addresses, essays, lectures.
8. Asia, Southeastern – Social life and customs – Addresses,
essays, lectures.   I. Manderson, Lenore.
GN663.S49   1986   306'.099   85-29957

British Library Cataloguing in Publication Data
Shared wealth and symbol: food, culture, and
society in Oceania and Southeast Asia.
1. Food habits – Oceania   2. Food habits – Asia,
Southeastern
I. Manderson, Lenore
306'.3   GT2853.03

ISBN 0 521 32354 1

Contents

Part III   Infant feeding practice

Part IV   Research method and direction

Tables and figures

Contributors

THOMAS K. FITZGERALD, Professor of Anthropology at the University of North Carolina at Greensboro, is editor of the nutritional anthropology text, *Nutrition and Anthropology in Action* (1977), as well as author of numerous nutrition–anthropology articles in journals such as *Ecology of Food and Nutrition, Nutrition Today,* and *The South Pacific Bulletin*. Dr. Fitzgerald has served on the Scientific Board of Directors of the N.C. Nutrition Institute, has taught graduate courses in nutrition and behavior at the University of North Carolina at Chapel Hill, and in 1977 was awarded a Certificate of Distinguished Service by the N.C. Institute of Nutrition for his contributions to the improvement of nutrition in North Carolina. His research in nutrition has been in the Pacific and in North Carolina.

VALERIE J. HULL is currently a Research Fellow in the Department of Demography, the Australian National University. Her academic career began with the study of anthropology, and she obtained her B.A. at the University of Michigan and M.A. at the University of Hawaii, specializing in applied anthropology. While in Hawaii, she also obtained a Certificate of Population Studies from the East West Center, and continued her study in demography at the Australian National University, completing her Ph.D. with a thesis on "Fertility, Socioeconomic Status and the Position of Women in a Javanese Village," based in fieldwork on Yogyakarta. From 1975 to 1979, she worked as Research Associate at the Population Institute, Gadjah Mada University in Yokyakarta, and was involved in several research projects including the longitudinal study on which the chapter in this current volume is based.

DAVID HYNDMAN is a graduate of the University of Colorado and the University of Queensland, where he is currently Lecturer in the Department of Anthropology and Sociology. His research interests are focused on Papua New Guinea, particularly in the Ok Tedi region of the Upper Fly River drainage system. From 1972 to 1977, he made four visits to this region, equalling one and a half years of fieldwork, and has returned to the region regularly since that time. His research interests include human ecology, medical and nutritional anthropology, ethnobiology, environmental perception, and assessing the cultural and ecological impact of development.

LENORE MANDERSON is a graduate in Asian Studies from the Australian National University, and lectures in anthropology in the School of Sociology, the University of New South Wales. Her research interests include demography, the position of women, and the anthropology of food. She has undertaken fieldwork in Malaysia in 1974, 1976–7, and 1978–9, and has also worked with the Vietnamese and Turkish immigrant communities in Australia. She is the author of *Overpopulation in Java: Problems and Reactions* (1974) and *Women, Politics, and Change* (1980), and editor of *Women's Work and Women's Roles* (1983) and *Australian Ways* (1985). She is presently on secondment to the Australian National University, where she is writing a book on health care and medical services in colonial Malaya.

NANCY POLLOCK received her B.A. in Anthropology from Colorado College and her M.A. and Ph.D. in Anthropology from the University of Hawaii. Her doctoral research examined changing food habits on an atoll in the Marshall Islands. She has continued this topic of research with Polynesian populations and is author of several articles on social aspects of food habits of Pacific Islanders. She is currently engaged in research into the food habits of the Pacific Island migrants living in Wellington, New Zealand. She is Senior Lecturer in Anthropology at Victoria University of Wellington, New Zealand.

GRAHAM H. PYKE is currently a Research Fellow at the Australian Museum. He has a B.Sc. in Mathematical Statistics from the University of Sydney and a Ph.D. in Biology from the University of Chicago. His principal research interests have been the feeding ecology of nonhuman animals, especially bees and nectar-feeding birds. Although having maintained a general interest in human behavior for many years, the paper in this book is his first written venture into the realm of humans. This paper was inspired by lively discussion and debate between the author and various anthropologists, especially Lenore Manderson and Janice Reid.

JANICE REID is Associate Professor in Medical Anthropology at the Commonwealth Institute of Health, the University of Sydney. Originally a science graduate, she taught in Papua New Guinea before leaving to study anthropology at the University of Hawaii (M.A.) and Stanford (M.A., Ph.D.). For a period of 15 months during 1974–5, 1978, and 1979 she undertook research among the Yolngu of Yirrkala, northeastern Arnhem Land, on change in the indigenous medical system and sociocultural factors affecting the utilization of health services. The chapter in this volume is based on field data collected in association with that project.

KATHY ROBINSON teaches anthropology in the School of Behavioral Sciences, Macquarie University. She holds a Ph.D. from the Department of Anthropology, Research School of Pacific Studies, at the Australian National University, on the transformation of a rural subsistence economy consequent to the development of a mining and mineral processing industry in a formerly remote part of Indonesia. She has recently returned from serving as Academic Consultant at the Social Science Research Training Station in Ujung Pandang, Indonesia.

BARRY SHAW is Visiting Fellow at the Development Studies Centre, Australian National University. He has a Ph.D. in economics from this university and was earlier on the staff of Victoria University, Wellington, New Zealand, where he gained degrees in history and economics as well as studying anthropology, sociology, and medicine. He is particularly interested in the complex linkages between all aspects of rural life and society in the Third World and has done fieldwork in New Zealand, Fiji, Papua New Guinea, India, and Thailand. After living in Papua New Guinea for many years, he became First Assistant Secretary for Primary Industry. He currently directs courses in rural development at the Development Studies Centre.

MARIANNE SPIEGEL holds a Master of Social Work degree from Adelphi University and is completing her doctoral dissertation in anthropology at Columbia University. Her thesis is concerned with the effects of rapid modernization on women's roles and status in Taipei, Taiwan. She has also worked extensively in home-based, mother-centered early childhood programs among various cultural groups in the United States.

JULIE WADDY is a graduate of the University of Sydney (B.Sc.) and of Macquarie University (B.A. Dip. Ed.). She has just completed a Ph.D. in Anthropology at Macquarie University. She has been working at Angurugu on Groote Eylandt, collecting and classifying plants and animals and obtaining their names and uses and associated stories. Her work was carried out at the request of the local Aboriginal council who wanted the information recorded from the old people before it was lost. Her thesis covers biological, food, totemic, and linguistic classification of plants and animals from a Groote Eylandt Aboriginal point of view. Her chapter in this volume is based on part of her thesis. She is currently working at Angurugu as a linguist, with the Church Missionary Society with whom she has been associated throughout her work on the island.

CHRISTINE S. WILSON received her B.A. in biology from Brown University (1950) and her Ph.D. in human nutrition from the University of California, Berkeley (1970). Her research has combined techniques of nutrition and anthropology in field studies of diet and health within the culture, including among Malay fishing villagers and urban Mexican Americans. She is affiliated with the Department of Epidemiology and International Health, University of California, San Francisco, is an editor of *Nutrition Reviews* and a member of the editorial advisory board of *Ecology of Food and Nutrition*.

MICHAEL W. YOUNG was born in Manchester, England. He is a graduate of the University of London and the Australian National University, where he is a Senior Fellow in the Research School of Pacific Studies. He has done anthropological fieldwork in Papua New Guinea, Indonesia, and most recently Vanuatu, and has taught at the University of Cambridge. His best-known works are *Fighting with Food* (1971) and *Magicians of Manumanua* (1983).

Introduction: the anthropology of food in Oceania and Southeast Asia

Lenore Manderson

The production and provision of food is a major aspect of human endeavor everywhere. In small-scale subsistence societies, food getting dominates everyday life, and people of all ages may participate in hunting, gathering, or horticulture. But even in complex social formations, the need for food underpins economic activity, with wages for labor directed first to meet subsistence needs, then to other commodities.

In the first instance, food is important simply to sustain biological life. However, because of its essentiality, food largely features as the matter and symbol of social life, as a means by which people communicate with each other, and as an embodiment of the communication itself. The matter – items of food – is subject to various constraints, including ecological and environmental factors that determine the initial range of potential foods. But beyond this, cultural, social, and economic factors shape food choice, thus diet and nutrition. A basic distinction is made by all people between food and nonfood from the range of possible alternative edibles. Systems of production and the technology for production constrain food availability and accessibility. Changes in the mode of production may reduce indigenous food resources while offering new items, resulting in dietary changes. The marking, enactment, and elaboration of key cultural and life-cycle events through the use of food further determine dietary variation seasonally and throughout the life-span. The differential allocation of food within the domestic sphere and in the larger community; the style and elaborateness or simplicity of the preparation and presentation of food, and the particular responsibilities of individuals in these activities; the act of eating, in the absence or presence of select others – all provide keys to social life and to the role and status of members of a given society. At both micro- and macrocosmic levels, within the family, in the community, and in an international economic context, food is also matter for manipulation: to censure or reward, encourage or control.

Developments in nutritional anthropology

Food has always been a focus of anthropological inquiry, precisely because of the necessity of food to survival and hence the pivotal role of food in productive activity, and as a result of the richness of symboling through food items. Nutritional anthropology, and in more general terms the anthropology of food, has developed relatively recently as a discrete subdiscipline. It has, however, a long heritage. It is not my intention here to offer a general history of the field, but some attention to the early direction of nutritional anthropological studies provides a context against which to view more recent developments, including the contributions to this volume.

Audrey Richards's study of the Bemba, resulting first in the publication of *Hunger and Work in a Savage Tribe* (1932) and subsequently of *Land, Labour and Diet in Northern Rhodesia* (1939), demonstrates the central role of food production and distribution in social structure, and provides the conventional start to this brief overview. Although Freedman (1977:2) noted a number of earlier dietary and food habit studies dating from 1890, Richards's work has pioneer status in the anthropological study of food. She was also probably the first anthropologist to collaborate with a biochemist-nutritionist, resulting in a joint paper in 1936 which examines the nutritive value of foods eaten by the Bemba, as well as methods of preparation and attitudes toward foodstuffs (Richards and Widdowson 1936). A number of other papers reflecting collaboration between anthropologists and nutritionists appeared around this time, in part as a result of the appointment of a Diet Committee of the British International African Institute (Freedman 1977:3). Fortes and Fortes (1936), for example, published a paper on food production, exchange and distribution, and the sexual division of labor among the Tallensi; other related publications include those of Hellman (1936), Read (1938), and Ashton (1939). But in the same year that *Hunger and Work in a Savage Tribe* appeared, Hortense Powdermaker published an article on the role of food and feasting in the economic and social life of New Ireland (Powdermaker 1932). Three years later, Malinowski's massive ethnography and linguistic analysis, *Coral Gardens and Their Magic,* appeared (1935) (of which more below). By the end of the 1930s, a number of British social anthropologists other than those associated with the Diet Committee were undertaking research on food and nutrition, Rosemary Firth's study of household expenditure and domestic economics among Malays in Kelantan (Firth 1943/1966) being but one example.

It was British-trained anthropologists, then, who dominated the broad area of the anthropology of food in the 1930s. This related at least in part to government concern with the nutritional status of subject peoples within the colonial empire, leading to the establishment of a Committee on Nutrition within the Colonial Office (see Great Britain Economic Advisory Council 1939), and to a measure of collaboration and dialogue between the Colonial Office and prominent anthropologists, of whom Fortes was one (Files of the Colonial Office CO 859/78). The United States lacked colonial domains as extensive as those of Britain. Not surprisingly then, nutritional anthropological studies by United States scholars date slightly later and were concerned particularly with internal circumstance. In 1940, a Committee on Food Habits was established by the United States National Research Council, directed to explore ways to improve physical fitness through improved nutrition. It involved a number of anthropologists such as Ruth Benedict and Margaret Mead, and led to several publications, including two major volumes by the committee itself – *The Problem of Changing Food Habits* (U.S. National Research Council 1943) and *Manual for the Study of Food Habits* (U.S. National Research Council 1945), and by committee members (e.g., Mead 1943, on changing food habits within the United States, and her later comparative volume in 1955). During this same period, a series of food habit studies were undertaken among both Indian and Spanish-American communities in the Southwest, under the direction of Fred Eggan of the Department of Anthropology, the University of Chicago. In various articles, participants in this project drew attention to the importance of the social and economic context of nutrition (Eggan and Pijoan 1943) and to the effect on diet of changes in the mode of production (Pijoan 1942a; Eggan and Pijoan 1943; Hawley, Pijoan, and Elkin 1943), as well as on specific nutritional questions (Pijoan 1942b) and infant feeding practice (Pijoan and Elkin 1943). Also of note in this period are two other United States studies, one undertaken in the rural Midwest – southern Illinois – and the other in the rural Southeast, both concerned with dietary change. The former study included documentation of differences in dietary behavior in different subcultures (Bennett, Smith, and Passin 1942) and drew attention to the use of food as a prestige commodity and the special status of store-bought, refined, and tinned products (Bennett 1943). Cussler and de Give also explored the prestige value of food in their study, but paid particular attention to the implications of cash cropping, and the effect of tenancy and social relations between tenants and landlords, on diet (see *'Twixt the Cup and the Lip,'* Cussler and de Give 1952; but also de Give and Cussler 1941; Cussler and de Give 1942, 1943).

Although not discounting intellectual interest as a factor in the motivation of individual scholars to undertake nutritional anthropological studies, practical and instrumental concerns clearly provided much of the impetus, certainly where governments were involved. In Britain, the concern was to ensure a labor force sufficiently healthy to allow the economic exploitation of the colonies; in the United States the interest was in defense. Following World War II, the practical implications of food habit studies remained important. This was especially so as medical and food science professionals recognized the importance of understanding the interrelationship between diet and culture in explaining particular nutritional problems and in introducing dietary changes through health and nutrition programs. Publications in the 1950s and later reflect the application of anthropological expertise to nutritional problems (e.g., Cassel 1955, 1957; Wellin 1955a, 1955b).

Under the canopy of the anthropology of food, a broad range of issues relevant to scholarly inquiry had already been set out by the mid-1940s. And although anthropologists continued to work in the area, it was not until the early 1970s that there was an expansion of interest and major developments in the field, inspired in part by general developments in anthropological theory and the use of food as subject matter in both materialist and cognitive analyses. In the latter realm, the works of Simoons (1961), Douglas (1966, 1975), and Lévi-Strauss (1969) are of note. With respect to the former, world political and economic events as well as disciplinary developments had certain impact. Popular publications such as those of George (1976), Lappé and Collins (1977), and Tudge (1979), following from an earlier concern with world hunger and population, sharpened an awareness among anthropologists, as among others, of the social, economic, and political context of food availability, diet, and nutrition. Two fine monographs from the 1970s reflect the divergent interests of cognitive and materialist studies: Michael Young's *Fighting with Food* (1971), a study of the social meaning and political uses of food among the Kalauna of Goodenough Island in Melanesia; and Bernard Nietschmann's *Between Land and Water* (1973), which exposes the nutritional price paid by the Miskito of Nicaragua for their incorporation into the world economy.

The appearance of the journal *Ecology of Food and Nutrition* in 1971 provided a necessary venue for the expanding number of studies of diet and culture of interdisciplinary interest if not execution. Since that time, the published literature within scholarly journals, representing both the social and medical sciences, has expanded rapidly (see the bibliographies of Wilson 1973a, 1979). Most recently, a number of edited collections have also appeared, including those by Arnott (1975), Fitzgerald (1977a), and Jerome, Kandel, and Pelto (1980), each offering considerable variety within the collections in terms of theory, method, and ethnographic area. In addition, a few area-specific collections have been published, notably Chang's volume on China (1977) and Forster and Ranum's collection concerned primarily with Western Europe (1979), each including contributions from both historians and anthropologists. This volume is equally diverse in terms of method and theory, representing recent research interests of both professional anthropologists and other scholars concerned with food and nutrition; anthropological perspectives range from those of a formally trained nutritionist-cum-anthropologist (Christine Wilson) to those whose interest in food derives from a prior interest in ideation and cognition. Geographically the volume falls between the two, neither global in coverage nor focused on a single cultural area. The regional specificity of the collection, with chapters that deal with Southeast Asia, the South Pacific, and Aboriginal Australia, reflects in part the interests of Australian scholars, whose work dominates this volume. Yet regional specificity serves two contrasting purposes: On the one hand, it emphasizes differences in food systems and uses between cultures within a single, if large, area; on the other hand, it points to common trends, particularly as a result of the incorporation of various societies within the region into industrial or industrializing nation-states and a world market economy. Individual cultures are subject to broader, now international, forces, and this is reflected in patterns of food production and use. Finally, much of what is said in the contributing chapters to this volume may be applied elsewhere in the world; this collection then offers a basis for a comparative analysis of food in culture and society.

None of the chapters offers an overview of food within a particular culture or society. Rather, each explores a particular area of inquiry: nutritional returns to labor in a subsistence society; national strategies of food production; infant feeding practice and the commercial marketing of milk; food prescriptions and proscriptions. It is useful, then, prior to introducing the chapters, to provide an overview of food in Southeast Asia and Oceania, drawing out certain common themes while highlighting again the differences within the region.

Food and culture in Oceania and Southeast Asia: an overview

Physical and cultural diversity rather than unity distinguishes the societies of Oceania and Southeast Asia and determines food resources and use. Topography, climate, soil, animal and plant reserves, social structure and organization, economic and political systems, and history all have influenced the exploitation of the environment and the utilization of its products. The differential use and perceptions of these products highlights the individuality of each society. Yet diversity notwithstanding, the very significance of food stands out as a common theme across cultures. Tikopians believe that their island "does not exist without food...It is nothing...There is no life on the island without food" (Firth 1959: 84). This, as an expression of social rather than biological existence, is a sentiment still echoed throughout the region. As in any other culture, food in Southeast Asian and Oceanic societies is both nutrient and symbol, central and fundamental to social survival and to cultural identity.

The significance of food in culture is perhaps most explicit in Melanesia, partly because until recently small-scale subsistence societies predominated in this region; it is therefore not surprising that the ethnographic record is richest here. The pioneer work of Malinowski, particularly *Coral Gardens and Their Magic* (1935), provides an enduring record of the centrality of food to society, as do the later articles of Bell (1946–8). More recent ethnographies make this same point: Rappaport's analysis of ritual and ecology (1968), Young's study of leadership and social control (1971), Strathern's monograph on women's roles (1972), Schieffelin's work on reciprocity and ceremony (1977) are all also finally ethnographies of food and are only a few of the many publications that illustrate the importance of food in Melanesian culture. For Polynesia, Australia, and Southeast Asia, the record is less complete, in part because the relationship of people to food is less explicit as a consequence of the earlier incorporation of the peoples of the regions into national agrarian and industrial states. Even so, ethnographies again provide detailed descriptions of the production, distribution, consumption, and symbolism of food. The special issue of *Asie du Sud-Est et Monde Insulindien* (1978), with articles dealing with the preparation, presentation, and vocabulary of food for a number of Southeast Asian societies (see also Martin 1978 and Pagezy 1978); the publications on Thai food habits and nutrition by Hauck and others (1956, 1958, 1959); Rosemary Firth's *Housekeeping Among Malay Peasants* (1943/1966); Hanks's *Rice and Man* (1972); and Ruddle, Johnson, Townsend, and Rees's book *Palm Sago* (1978) stand out, but they are not alone. Golomb's study of ethnic adaptation (1978), for example, explores the ways by which Thais and Malays in rural Malaysia are able to live adjacently in a spirit of relative cooperation and harmony, despite the fact that the former produce, eat, and use as a prime symbol of group identity and allegiance the very food, pork, which is most abhorred by and considered antipathetical to Malay society. And virtually every ethnography for the region deals to some extent with food: To not do so would be to ignore a vital and essential element of both everyday and ceremonial life.

Food serves to distinguish humanness. Choice and definition of food from a wide range of available plant and animal resources, the preparation of selected and acceptable resources prior to consumption, and ideas regarding the appropriate consumption of foods according to time of day and in association with other foods differentiate people from their potential and actual nonhuman competitors for food, and between each other, within groups, and with other groups. Meal composition of the Semai of the Malay Peninsula demonstrates this difference: Meat, fish, fowl, or fungus is an essential element of a "real meal," but a meal by definition includes a starch, either rice or tapioca: "What do you think we are, cats?" (Dentan 1968:50). The production and distribution of food similarly serves to denote humanity: Kalauna people thus perceive their ability to garden as a symbol of civilization: "If we did not grow yams we would be like dogs...You think we are birds or dogs and can't plant food?" (Young 1971:195–8).

Food classification systems provide a shorthand to distinguish food and nonfood, edible and inedible plants and animals. Following the first distinction between humans (edible or inedible, depending on the culture) and animals and plants (edible or inedible), Thai folk taxonomy, for instance, designates like resources further into edible and inedible subcategories. Accordingly the animal kingdom is first differentiated into insects (inedible), birds (edible), and animals; animals are further categorized into those of the water and those of the land, with the latter group then classified as domestic, field, or forest dwellers. Within this system, animals that are unaffiliated, or that are ambiguously or anomalously classified by virtue of their habitat, behavior, or physical appearance, tend to be classed as nonfood. According to Tambiah (1969), Thais do not eat animals that are not readily classified, such as animals that may be either of the land or of the water (e.g., snakes, monitors); animals that are classified and yet are exceptional and therefore ambiguous as food (e.g., the otter, which lives in the water but looks like a dog); or other unaffiliated animals that leave their habitat and invade, ominously, human environs (toads enter houses, vultures rest on roofs). Further taboos here include animals that are metaphorically and/or metonymically linked with human society. The dog, living in the house and in close association with humans, has a metonymical relationship to them, and at the same time its dirty and incestuous behavior provides an analogy with human conduct: A dog therefore cannot be eaten or incorporated into human society because it is already part of it. Monkeys likewise may not be eaten, for although they have a nonmetonymical relation with humans, they bear a metaphoric resemblance and are believed to have descended from humans. Bulmer similarly has argued that among the Kalam of Papua New Guinea, the controlled killing and consumption of cassowary relates not simply to its anomalous and thus unaffiliated position within folk taxonomy, but to its metaphorical cross-cousin relationship to humans. Dogs are avoided absolutely because they are seen as distant potential affines and adopted children; but pigs are edible even though they share human habitat and eat human food (including human milk) and even though, on the other hand, they are dirty (e.g., eat feces), for they are considered not metaphorical humans but rather "sub-human or non-human members of the human family" (Bulmer 1967:20). In the first instance, then, people determine which animals are edible and which are not edible both on the basis of the animal's environment and behavior and on the perceived relationship of the animal to humans.

Yet humans, while apart from the natural world, are also of it. Food allows and sustains human existence both literally and symbolically. Fetal development and maternal diet are frequently associated directly. Kaberry reported (1939:56) that Aboriginal women in the Kimberleys in Western Australia believe that the fetus is nourished by the food eaten by the mother, and hence she abstains from ceremonial food throughout pregnancy and until the child is over a year old. Thai villagers explain that "babies grow within their mother's stomach where they sit eating the food the mother eats. Tissue is made of rice because it derives from rice" (Hanks 1972:22). Throughout Southeast Asia and Oceania, women avoid a range of foods during pregnancy for sympathetic magical reasons, believing that the foods they eat will physically affect the infant, and eat other foods to ensure the healthy growth of the child. Beyond birth, food continues to contribute directly to physical being. An Arapesh father "grows" his son, providing food for him from which he himself must abstain: "Piece by piece he has built his son's body. The Arapesh father does not say to his son: 'I am your father, I begot you, therefore you must obey me'.... Instead he says: 'I grew you. I grew the yams, I worked the sago, I hunted the meat, I laboured for the food that made your body...'" (Mead 1935/1963:77). In the same way, a man's claim to his wife is also that he has "grown" her, contributed the food that has become her flesh and bone. Covarrubias (1936/1973:71) has recounted that Balinese similarly believe that a person's body and soul are built from the rice that is eaten; central Thai villagers maintain that "man's body itself is rice, and eating rice renews the body directly...Thus the rice grower's image of man becomes rice itself; perhaps, according to this vision, man differs slightly from other living creatures, largely because of the diet that sustains him" (Hanks 1972:22). Malay villagers again believe that life itself is dependent on eating rice (McArthur 1962:127). Thus not only economically and socially but quite literally, food creates, sustains, and is "the bones of the people" (Moerman 1968:16).

Conversely, or perhaps in consequence, mythology frequently relates the origin of food to human or superhuman union. Southeast Asian and Papua New Guinea myths explain the origins of sago often either from a culture heroine by birth, vaginal secretion, or defecation; from the corpse of a culture heroine; or from a substance scattered by a culture hero. In West Seram myth, for example, the corpse of a grandmother gave rise to various palms, *arenga* from her head, coconut palm from her genitals, sago palm from her body. In myth from the Humboldt Bay area of Irian Jaya, a woman gave birth to sago starch and thence the sago palm; animals originated from her placenta (Ruddle et al. 1978:71, 75). In Balinese myth, rice was born from the cosmic union of the divine male and female creative forces: Wisnu, God of Water, raped and impregnated Mother Earth to give birth to rice for human consumption (Covarrubias 1936/1973:70). Agricultural ritual frequently involves offerings to personified spirits; the growth of the plant is likened to human pregnancy. Thus both Balinese and the Semai of the Malay Peninsula not only refer to rice in the field as pregnant, but offer or sprinkle the crop with sour or acidic foods favored by pregnant women (Dentan 1968:45; Covarrubias 1936/1973:77). Humans and food, then, are inextricably linked: Food originates from and is produced by humans; humans originate from and are sustained by food.

Thus humans are the food they eat, and are defined and recognized accordingly. Individual and general, temporary and permanent proscriptions of certain foods may express a person's relationship to his or her environment, and identify kin affiliation, family status, age, sex, physiological condition, ritual status, class position, rank, or ethnicity. Totemic associations with particular animals, thereby taboo as a food resource, serve to identify the individual by kinship, subclan, or clan affiliation by what he or she does not eat; religious proscriptions similarly provide a medium for the articulation of cultural identity. Regional cuisine and food preference serve a similar purpose. In Thailand, for example, glutinous and nonglutinous rice are regarded in such a way: Central Thais eat ordinary rice and associate the consumption of glutinous rice with stolidness, sloth, and sluggish thought. Government officials in northern Thailand express their class position vis-à-vis the local rice farmers by eating central Thai food, or minimize class difference by choosing to eat, and being seen to eat, local food (Moerman 1968: 11). In Malaysia, the distinction is one of ethnicity and is a barrier all but immutable: In Malay eyes, Chinese and Thais are pork eaters by definition and regardless of actual dietary practice, and as such exist in a state of permanent ritual contamination. The state of pollution may be revoked only by conversion to Islam, whereby the converts in effect "become Malay" and assume the Malay/Muslim taboo on pork and other ritually tabooed flesh.[1] For Malays, the grossest vituperation is pig or dog; Malay fishermen avoid the very mention of these animals while at sea, lest their catch be unsuccessful (Raymond Firth 1946/1966:115). Chinese historically have exploited Malay abhorrence of pork especially during periods of interethnic tension.[2] But Golomb's monograph on ethnic adaptation in northeast rural Malaysia demonstrates the resolution of the seemingly irreconcilable difference between pork-eating Thais and pork-avoiding Malays: In a spirit of reciprocity, Malays, forbidden to handle let alone eat taboo flesh, kill wild pigs and other animals that desecrate their gardens, whereas the Thai Buddhists, forbidden to slaughter but not to eat the animals, remove and consume the offensive flesh. Thus ethnic, class, or clan conflict may be resolved by the manipulation of food.

As taboos distinguish between groups, so too they may distinguish individuals within their own society. Taboos applied differentially to men, women, or children, for example, underline both ritually and practically the importance of age and sex. In ancient Tahiti, taboos prevented women generally from eating pigs, dogs, turtles, albacore, shark, dolphin, whale, and porpoise, highly esteemed foods which were in short supply either seasonally or throughout the year. Neither could women eat food prepared in the *marae* precincts where contact was made between men and the spirit world (Oliver 1974:224ff). In this society, food taboos operated to disadvantage women nutritionally – what Lindenbaum has referred to as the "politics of protein" (1977:148) – whereby foodstuffs symbolically represent and in actuality explicitly define women's subordination to men.[3] Among the Kaluli of the

1 The Malay term for conversion to Islam is *masuk Melayu*, literally "to enter [thus become] Malay."
2 During the period immediately after World War II, for example, Chinese guerillas were alleged to have taken revenge on Malay informers by desecrating mosques with pigs, forcing Malays to eat pork, feeding their bodies to pigs, and wrapping their corpses in pig skin (Burridge 1957:163-5).
3 See O'Laughlin (1974) for the elaboration of the interrelationship of food taboos and the status of women. Others prefer to explain taboos that direct prime protein sources to men as a resource allocation strategy (see Ross 1978).

Southern Highlands of Papua New Guinea, only unmarried men and the very old may eat freely fresh meat. Young children avoid certain birds and snakes, considered to be "too strong" for them; women from the time of menstruation to menopause may eat only cassowary, domestic pig, and dry or smoked meat; at marriage men must also assume their wives' taboos. In addition, women and children may not eat food found in supernaturally dangerous areas (Schieffelin 1977:66). By contrast, men rather than women in Maring society carry the burden of taboo: "Fight magic men" and other men involved in warfare avoid a variety of marsupials and snakes, eels, catfish, lizards, and frogs which might deplete their magical, ritual, and physical strength. Although there are no explicit restrictions for men against eating rats, small birds, or insects, these foods are generally considered suitable only for women and children. In addition, pigs killed in connection with the festivals of other local populations may not always be eaten by adult or adolescent men, although they may be eaten by women and children. Accordingly, Rappaport has argued (1968:79ff, 150–1) that here food taboos function to divert protein to those who are nutritionally the most vulnerable while at the same time preserving scarce resources, even though men in fact may circumvent the bans.

Food taboos operate also to recognize and define the ritual status of men, in a similar way that taboos, instituted largely for sympathetic magical reasons, govern young male initiands and women at menarche and during pregnancy and lactation; such taboos during rite of passage are observed throughout the region. Taboos during mourning again acknowledge ritual status as well as loss. Aboriginal women in Kaberry's study (1939:214) could eat only their own vegetable food while in mourning; Maring and Kaluli people avoid a number of specified foods and additionally may for sentimental reasons declare as taboo, foods that were particularly favored by the deceased.

Taboos operate also with regard to the production, preparation, and distribution of food, either generally or as a result of individual ritual status. The Kaluli people invoke food taboos during planting time, prohibit certain food combinations, and avoid entering gardens after eating pork, in order to ensure the fertility of the soil and the abundancy of the harvest (Schieffelin 1977:65). In Polynesia, crops of fruit groves may be declared taboo by demarcation of the area with a coconut front, in order to allow the food to mature and to conserve potential scarce resources (Firth 1939/1967:202ff). Although both women and men may eat common foods, in some cases taboos operate to control consumption according to the ownership of resources. In ancient Tahiti, women could eat pork only if they owned the pig or provided from their own gardens the food it ate; eat fish only if they caught it themselves or if it was caught by a man not designated ritually as having full male status; eat breadfruit paste only if the fruit came from their trees and was fermented in their own pits (Oliver 1974:224–6). Moreover, women's cooking utensils touched by men had to be replaced. In addition to the taboo against "male-touched" food, there appears also to have been a taboo affecting commensality which related to the pollution of women: It was necessary ritually to allow the male kin of a new bride to eat food touched by her husband, who by his sexual contact with her was a source of pollution (Oliver 1974:437).

Typically, however, it is women who pollute and contaminate food, by virtue of menstruation and childbirth. In some societies the taboo on women's handling, preparing, cooking, or sharing of food during menstruation is elaborate and absolute; elsewhere it is today nominal. Thus in contemporary Malay society, people believe that rice cooked by menstruating women will go gluggy and that fruit will fail to ripen if they enter an orchard, although in practice, menstruating taboos affect religious observance primarily. In Tikopia in the 1930s at least, women could enter the cooking house and sit there, but could not fill waterbottles or handle food at the ovenside (Firth 1936/1963:476). In parts of New Guinea, in contrast, women are secluded for the duration of menstruation. Bell noted (1936:311) that in Tanga, female pollution extended beyond menstruation, and the very presence of a woman at a fishing reef was believed sufficient to drive the fish away; among the Melpa, a woman who is menstruating is referred to euphemistically as one who "cooks bad food" (Strathern 1972:166). In Aboriginal society, the seclusion of menstruating women to prevent their contact with food caught by men also conversely prevents men from contact with the food the women have gathered and prepared.

The concept of pollution and the associated controls on food handling and consumption extend also in many cases to sexual intercourse, and affect gardening and hunting activities as well as cooking. Further, where a food is associated symbolically with sex, then taboos that relate to its distribution may provide an articulation and elaboration of the relationships between kin and affines. McKnight (1973), for example, has argued that among the Wik-Mungkan Aborigines, taboos that govern the gift and receipt of particular foods are explicable because the foods are likened to male or female genitalia. By appearance and linguistically, synonymously or metaphorically, eggs are associated with testicles, mudshells with the vagina, yams with the penis, sugarbag (wild honey) with either male or female genitals depending on the type, the spear – and thus speared food – with the penis again. Food speared by a wife's brother may not be eaten by his sister's husband, for "to eat from one's wife's brother's spear is the same as eating from his penis or even eating his penis." But sex of the animal is also important: "To eat a male swamp turtle caught by one's wife's brother would be like eating him. But it would be permissible to eat a female swamp turtle that he had caught, for this would be like eating his sister, which in a sense one has already done by marrying her" (McKnight 1973:202). Even where food itself may not be perceived explicitly as a sexual symbol, the taking of food may be synonymous with coitus and therefore governed by incest and related kinship regulations. Thus Arapesh prescriptions on yam surplus and pigs designated for ceremonial purpose are linked analogously to incest taboos: Men may not eat their own surplus in the same way that they may not "eat" their own sisters or mothers (Mead 1935/1963:83); the people of the Tor Valley of Irian Jaya forbid men to accept sago from specified women because the offering of sago mash is synonymous with sexual intercourse (Ruddle et al. 1978:90).[4]

Because food is closely associated with sexuality, commensality is frequently a public statement of a sexual relationship and, in effect, the consummation of marriage. A woman marries, not by the assumption of sexual relations alone, because lovers are thus defined also, but by participating in the production of food for her husband as well as for herself, by processing and cooking the food, and by sharing with him his meals. In Burma, the most important indication of common-law marriage is commensality: By eating at the same dish, the hand of the husband and wife come together. In the past, evidence of commensality was sufficient to compel a man and woman to live together as husband and wife. Colloquially, a parent gives his daughter to a husband for eating, a son to a wife for eating; the word "to eat" (*sade*) is also used colloquially for "to copulate" (Spiro 1977:186–7). Among the Kaluli, intention to consummate the marriage, which may be one or two months after the wedding day, is indicated when the wife offers her husband some food; a day or two later the couple go to a secluded sago camp, make sago together for the first time, and begin sexual relations (Schieffelin 1977:61–2). Similarly, Kaberry's early study of Aboriginal Australia recounts that a "proper marriage" for a woman, as distinct from a liaison, "involves a union with a man generally in the correct relationship who will hand over gifts to her parents and with whom she will share food and a common fireplace" (Kaberry 1939:104). Wedding ceremonies throughout the region often include the joint meal of husband and wife: In the Fijian wedding ceremony, a ritual meal – *kanavata* ("eating together") – symbolically celebrates the new union (Sahlins 1962:181).[5]

Woman's role in the preparation of food is a major duty and symbol of the marriage. A woman is expected to prepare food for her husband whether or not he chooses to dine with her. Cowives in Mount Hagen, for instance, sharing a common fireplace, should both prepare and present to their husband a meal (Strathern 1972:47). In Burma, according to Spiro (1977:274),

---

4 In Tanga society, according to Bell (1948), a woman could accept food only from her husband or from close, nontaboo kin. Women who indiscriminately accepted food were considered to have loose morals, because the acceptance of food was taken as consent to sexual intercourse. A "loose" woman was termed "one who accepts food on the road from any man" (Bell 1948:54).

5 In the Trobriands also, during the period between the commencement of shared residence and the completion of the payment of bridewealth, a new husband and wife are secluded and eat together, without company, from the same plate. At the end of a year, when exchange is complete, the marriage is final; thereafter they never again eat from the same dish (Weiner 1977:184).

"what is particularly singled out...is (woman's) role as provider of food. The wife should have her husband's meals prepared whenever he wishes and as soon as he returns from work. It is expected that he receive the first and best portion of whatever food is in the pot." In Java, the process of adjustment to marriage is signified by the term *atut*, connoting firstly and particularly sexual compatibility but also a woman's willingness to cook for and serve her husband (Geertz 1961:73). A woman's participation in gardening activities and, in Papua New Guinea, her role in caring for and feeding her husband's pigs are further integral aspects of her role as a wife.

But with marriage, women bring to men not only their labor as producers and preparers of food, but also capital: their knowledge of food. Kaberry's comments regarding Aboriginal women from the Kimberleys express this succinctly, and remain applicable today for a woman of any society:

> Her knowledge acquired during childhood and puberty is capital on which she can always draw successfully even in times of drought. It places a premium on her as a food-gatherer, and makes her eligible as a marital partner... Her economic skill is not only a weapon for subsistence, but also a means of enforcing good treatment and justice... her co-operation in economics is a necessity, and enables her on the basis of this to demand rights in marriage. (1939:36-8)

Food, in consequence, becomes also a means by which marital disharmony may be expressed and the union repudiated. At the time of a quarrel, a Burmese woman simply stops cooking for and eating with her husband; reconciliation may be effected when she invites him to join her for a meal. Melpa and Kaluli women, provoked by their husbands, deliberately step over the food, exposing it to their genitals and thus rendering it unfit for consumption. In Tikopia, where in the past women and men together gardened, collected food, prepared and cooked it, and shared the meal, areca nut, and tobacco, a husband wooed his wife to return when she left the marital home by sending her a gift of food (Firth 1936/1963:134). Finally, a woman's laziness or reluctance to garden or to cook may provide a husband with sufficient grounds for divorce: A Mount Hagen woman who pushes her grievance by refusing to cook for her husband may provoke him to divorce her (Strathern 1972:45). A Kalauna man may first resort to shame his wife to mend her ways: Young has provided an example of a Kalauna man who publicly presented his wife with a *ketowai* gift of food, designated specifically to insult, criticize, or shame, because of her refusal to cook a meal for him on one occasion (1971:246).

Commensality similarly provides for the expression of friendship and goodwill outside marriage relationships. In New Guinea in particular, where eating is very much a private activity, women and men, by sharing food with others, express to each other affection and alliance. Food sharing may identify and affirm kinship or clan allegiance, or cut across kin and clan. In the

Trobriands, clan membership is manifested in behavior: Clanspeople, "people like us," share cooked food; people outside the clan do not share (Weiner 1977:53–4). A Melpa woman may share food with friends, husband's brother, or husband's brother's wives; they use a common "food name" thereafter to address each other to symbolize their bond (Strathern 1972:29–30). Similarly among the Kaluli people, men signify their sharing of food through a food name, thereby proclaiming their friendship and identification (Schieffelin 1977:50). Kalauna men may establish *aveyau* relationships with men from neighboring hamlets, eating companionships without the formal obligations that typify other adult relationships; in addition politically significant *fofofo* relations are established across clan boundaries which operate as food exchange partnerships: Partners assist each other in their external food exchanges and eat the food prohibited to the other through exchange (Young 1971:46–7, 69ff). Customary practice regarding interdining may be suspended to express friendship. Thai and Malay villagers as a rule almost never enter each other's kitchens, particularly when food is being prepared or eaten, and generally Malays refrain from accepting even a cup of coffee from a Thai for fear of pollution. However, particularly close friendships may develop, wherein Malays "would graciously partake of any dish specially prepared by close Buddhist-Thai friends, who were trusted to omit any ingredients tabooed by Islam" (Golomb 1978:8), although without their interdining being made known to more orthodox villagers. Commensality may be contingent, however, as in *kula* exchange, when *kula* partners eat alone until the exchange has been successful and finalized, at which point the partners sit and eat together (Weiner 1977:184). Finally, commensality need not be an integral or continued feature of marriage or friendship. Trobriand husbands and wives eat from the same plate only at the time of their marriage; thereafter other men and unmarried boys join the husband in his meal (Weiner 1977:184). In much of Asia, women are expected to eat only after the men have had their fill, and in the presence of guests they may be segregated from men. In Fijian society, women and children sit at the "lower" end of the mat and wait until the men have eaten before partaking of the meal (Sahlins 1962:107); in ancient Tahiti, at least in chiefly society, women and men were segregated at mealtimes (Oliver 1974:226).

Hospitality need not necessarily be commensurate with interdining. Eating is private in Southeast Asia and Oceania, and uninvited guests and fellow villagers or camp members make themselves scarce at meal times: To remain is to beg to be invited, and generally this is considered inappropriate behavior. Cooking areas may be shared, but typically the domestic unit eats alone and discretely. Hence when a meal is shared, intimacy is implied: Moerman noted that in Thailand, "when someone from another village...is invited to join a circle around a tray or a low table, he is often told, 'We are all eating together; therefore we are kinsmen'" (1968:10). On the other hand, a host properly should offer a guest refreshment; failure to do so implies that the visitor is not welcome, and inability to provide a guest with food in sufficient quality will cause extreme embarrassment. Provision of food in this context assures the host of reciprocal generosity. In addition, as Oliver has noted (1974:230), excessive hospitality by the host may function, in Polynesia at least, to intentionally embarrass a guest known to be unable to reciprocate (see also Bell 1931). Generous hospitality may also afford the host considerable prestige.

Conversely, withdrawal of hospitality and taboos on interdining function to express enmity. Among the Maring, for example, interpersonal conflict as a result of personal insult, dispute over a pig, homicide, or any other personal or property misdemeanor may be expressed by the refusal of the antagonists to eat food from the same hearth or grown by each other, even if in other respects they maintain communication and cooperation. Taboos arising from warfare again may involve the avoidance of food grown or cooked at the fire of the opponents, and full abrogation of the taboos is not until the fourth generation, the great-grandchildren of the original enemies. In addition, natal parties must make a choice: Thus, "if the natal groups of the wives of brothers become enemies, either the brothers must choose between eating with each other or with their respective wives, or one or both wives must refuse to adopt the inter-dining taboos of her natal group" (Rappaport 1968:206–7).

But it is in the exchange and public display of food at feasts and festivals that the politics of food comes into full force.

Rites of passage – at birth, initiation, and particularly marriage – involve the preparation of large quantities of food either for a single or series of celebratory feasts, or for intergroup exchange without shared dining also. Among Aboriginal Australians, for example, infant betrothal is marked by the presentation of food to the parents of the girl by the father of the boy. In rural Southeast Asia, wedding ceremonies publicly announce the marriage, and the preparation and consumption of food provides a focus for village attention. Depending on both the society and the intended size of the ceremony, close kin or also other neighbors and friends may be involved for several days in advance, preparing ritual food for display, dishes for consumption at the feast, food gifts – in Malay society, wrapped or otherwise elaborately decorated hard-boiled eggs – for presentation to the guests, food for preliminary ceremonial meals, and sufficient food also to feed a stream of visitors to the house, the helpers, and the household itself. Labor provided is reciprocated eventually within the village as each laborer in turn holds a special feast. To some extent, the cost of the feast may be shared: In Javanese and Malay society, for instance, guests attending a wedding or other feast typically contribute money to defray costs.[6] But in addition, a lavish ceremony confers on the hosts considerable prestige: The larger the

6 See Geertz (1960: Chapter 5) for details of the elaborate *slametan* cycles associated with circumcision and marriage in Javanese society.

feast, the more money or resources spent on food and entertainment, the greater the derived status. Further, in the case of marriage, an elaborate ceremony provides insurance of a successful union and allows for the public statement of the bride's chastity and family honor. By implication, a modest or hasty ceremony implies suspect circumstance: "Well she behaves properly now, but do you think she had a proper wedding? Not at all, it was just a matter of serving *bubor kachang* (sweet bean porridge)" (Djamour 1965:78). Ceremonies, including marriage celebrations, are no less ostentatious in the Pacific than they are in Asia. In Fiji, for example, wedding ceremonies may extend over several days, with four days of feasting marked also by major food exchanges between the bride's and groom's kin (Sahlins 1962:179–82). Feasts in Polynesia involve the exchange of food and the close cooperation of kin; guests at feasts assume an obligation to reciprocate later; they confer considerable prestige on the host, reflecting, among other things, his or her ability to command and control considerable resources; and at the same time affirm kinship ties and extend goodwill: "Feasts are the movement of the needle which sews together the parts of our reed roofs, making of them a single roof, one single word" (Mauss 1969:19).

In Melanesia, by contrast, marriage and other life-cycle events are not typically celebrated by elaborate ceremony and festivity, but food is no less the vehicle by which kin and affinal bonds are affirmed or established. With marriage, this is effected through bridewealth payments. Timing of the commencement and cessation of these payments, and the nature of the goods exchanged between kin groups, varies according to resources and tradition. In the Highlands, pearlshells and in recent times money as well as live and cooked pigs may be used; in coastal areas, garden produce, pigs, and cash may be exchanged. But bridewealth is but one occasion for the exchange of food in Melanesia. Countless minor exchanges occur as everyday expressions not only of affection and friendship, but also of obligation, reinforcing kin and affinal ties; similarly the exchange of food may establish new networks and allegiances. Frequently, the major ceremonial occasions coincide with and celebrate large-scale intergroup presentation and mark the preparatory stages of these exchanges. As Mauss pointed out in his classic essay, presentations of food, hospitality, and valuables are loaded with moral, political, and economic implications; "through the imperative of reciprocity, presentation enriches both donor and recipient with the same produce" (1969:55). Moreover, individual and group food exchange, together with the exchange of other valuables, is by no means peculiar to the Melanesian region. Among Aborigines of northwest Australia, a *bulba* (ring), reminiscent of the *kula* ring of Melanesia, involves the exchange of prized durable items but also, particularly for women whose access to valuables is limited, the exchange of wild honey, flour, and other foodstuffs (Kaberry 1939:168–9).

But food exchange and its ceremonial context is not only and is much more than a medium to express friendship, cooperation, alliance, and mutual obligation: It allows also for the elaboration of animosity and conflict. Food, through its use or its withdrawal, can punish, shame, repudiate, and indict. I have noted above that among the Maring people, taboos governing garden produce and shared cooking facilities allow for the expression of hostility and enmity without necessarily causing further disruption of social and economic life; that in Polynesia, hospitality may intentionally embarrass a guest unable to reciprocate with like largess.

Michael Young, in *Fighting with Food*, has provided the most complete analysis of the use of food for aggression and control, both at a personal and intravillage level and as a prime means of articulating and resolving interclan and intervillage conflict and competition. In Kalauna, everyday food-related activities demand considerable discretion and manipulation to avoid offense, jealousy, or insult: Improper or unequal distribution of food, refusing requests for food, hoarding or theft of food, damage to pigs or gardens, boasting about food, any display of produce, queries regarding production or supply – all may provoke quarrels or give offense, in turn resolvable by the aggressive gift of food. Kalauna people use as a sanction what Young refers to as "food-giving-to-shame": "patterned, purposive behaviour, triggered by a delict and pursued as a course of redress" (1971:207). The simplest offense is punished by food given with intent to shame: A villager prying on his neighbor's food supply, for example, will be presented with one of the largest yams, and a scathing comment that that was what he was looking for (Young 1971:157). Major festivals, overtly occasions for pleasure and happiness, provide also an opportunity to embarrass and shame, and to assert dominance and power: The climax of festivities, *aidabana*, provides explicit opportunity for insult and sanction with the presentation of *ketowai* food gifts, with the wrongs of the recipient publicly elaborated in response to any query regarding the purpose of the gift. The major institution of food competition, however, is the *abutu*. *Abutu* provides a surrogate to warfare and blood feuds: Principal combatants aim to shame their opponents by giving more and larger yams, pigs, and other produce than can be reciprocated, thereby demonstrating their superiority. The visitor holds political and moral power over his debtor until the time that all debts have been repaid: The debtor in turn seeks to repay as quickly as possible, commonly overpaying to cast back shame on his erstwhile creditor.

Typically, food exchanges and feasts involve the distribution and/or consumption of prestige foods rather than foods that constitute an everyday component of the diet. Pig raising in the Papua New Guinea Highlands, for instance, is important primarily because of the value of pigs in presentation and exchange, although through exchange participants eat (each other's) pigs. Among Australian Aboriginal communities such as the Pitjandjara, the most prestigious food, kangaroo, is available variably and contributes little to the daily diet: Small game, insects and larvae, and a wide variety of vegetables provide the major foods.[7] Elsewhere, however, the most valued and prestigious food is also the staple. In the Trobriands and on Goodenough Island, for instance, yams are part of the everyday diet and are the medium of personal wealth and exchange. Throughout Southeast Asia, although a variety of special dishes play an important role in feasts, the prestige food is again also the staple – rice. The everyday and cultural value of staples may be expressed lexically. For Balinese, the word for "rice," *nasi*, is synonymous with food; in Malay and in Thai, "to eat" is "to eat rice," "to be hungry" is "to hunger for rice." Similarly, among the Kaluli of New Guinea, for whom the staple is sago, the word for "sago," *maen*, is used generically for food.

The production and preparation of food, both the staple and supplementary and prestige items, dominates the lives of people throughout Oceania and Southeast Asia. The rhythm of everyday life, the passing of time, is reckoned by the provision of food and the changing availability of resources. It is hardly surprising then that in the Trobriands the agricultural cycle serves to reckon both seasons and the passing of years (Malinowski 1935:52–5).

The analysis of production provides us with a final appreciation of the importance of food in the region. Again, there is sufficient diversity to deny generalization regarding the interrelationship of the economics of food and the status of its producers and their products. In some cultures – in Polynesia and among Aboriginal Australians, for instance – prestige foods are also, significantly, food hunted, fished, or cultivated by men. In the Papua New Guinea Highlands, men own and control the distribution of pigs, but pig rearing is women's work: "Her work in raising pigs, a major exchange valuable, is the point at which a woman's economic role most clearly feeds into her status as an intermediary in the exchange system" (Strathern 1972:132). In Southeast Asia, in particular, agricultural tasks are distributed on the basis of sex, but in many areas women are the sole rice producers either in the absence of men during periods of seasonal migration or with their deployment in other traditional or commercial production activities. Arguably, the status of men and women is linked to production. Women's political status may increase concordantly with her participation in economic life: Southeast Asian women farmers certainly enjoy considerable authority and autonomy, albeit largely within the confines of the domestic sphere and in any case controlled by class.

Throughout the region, then, gender determines the participation of individuals in production; the relationship of the individual to the means of production designates her or his status within society. Among Aboriginal

---

7 The variety is wide. Irvine (1957), for example, lists 106 species of fruit with several subspecies, 43 species of roots, and numerous edible berries, seeds, grasses, fungi, seaweed, nuts, etc.

Australians in general, men hunt and women gather, although women's gathering includes the collection of reptiles and small game, whereas men may collect other edibles for their own use when in pursuit of large game animals. In coastal areas, men and women may both fish or gather molluscs and crustacea, although typically women and men pursue different seafood and their contributions to the domestic food supply vary (e.g., see Meehan 1977). Moreover the relative contribution of women and men overall in supplying food may be widely discrepant. Gould, for example, has estimated that among Western Desert Aborigines, 70–80 percent of diet by bulk is provided by women, who spend one-third more time than men in the preparation and production of food: Women are, he argues, "the mainstay of the subsistence economy" (1969:263). Peterson (1978:22) has reported that in the Arnhem Land group with which he lived, up to 90 percent of all food, animal and vegetable, was provided by women. The predominant role of women in production serves to free men to participate in art and ritual, although the exclusion of women from secret rites, and their perceived general subordination to men in politics and religion, incorrectly implies their general subservience. Elsewhere, too, women in hunter–gatherer societies have enjoyed considerable personal if not political or ritual power and authority. Karen Endicott (1979), for instance, has argued that Batek society, in the Malay Peninsula, is effectively egalitarian. Typically men hunt and women gather, but both sexes participate in all food foraging activities, including blowpipe and other hunting, fishing, gathering tubers, collecting other fruit and vegetables, collecting honey, and providing rattan as a trade items for cash with which to buy rice, flour, and sugar. Women produce staple goods whereas men diversify to collect less constant supplies, but male-produced foods are not especially prestigious. Both sexes produce both for immediate use and for exchange, and both are equal contributors and recipients in the distribution of food.

In horticultural and in agricultural societies, production activities may involve both women and men or fall to either women or men. Tsembaga women and men, for example, cooperate to prepare garden land; both men and women fire the ground for the first time, although women are responsible for the second firing. Women plant taro, yam, sweet potato, and green vegetables, whereas men plant bananas, sugar cane, and *manap* (*Saccharum edule*). Generally, weeding and harvesting are women's work; planting and harvesting fruit trees fall to the men. Women are responsible for caring for pigs; men occasionally hunt and thereby supplement the diet. Although a woman is primarily responsible for her husband's garden and pigs, she may also garden for her father, unmarried brothers, husband's brothers, or her widowed father-in-law; a man may also garden for his unmarried sisters or widowed mother (Rappaport 1968). Melpa women similarly play a predominant role in gardening and pig raising, though men also garden – women planting "women's crops," men tending "men's crops." Women are dependent on men for the allocation of land and its preparation; they do not have rights to the land but do have the right to work and thus also have control over produce (Strathern 1972). Again, it is women's participation in production that allows men to participate in political and ritual life: Strathern characterizes this by referring to women as producers and men as transactors. Among the Tor people of Irian Jaya, by contrast, where sago is symbolic both of female sexuality and of vitality and life itself, women have both property rights to and responsibility for the production of sago (Ruddle et al. 1978:90).

In Fiji, agriculture is the domain of men; women's major role in the production of food involves the collection of vegetable greens and of molluscs, sea slugs, and fishing. But at the same time, work is distributed on the basis of age, with adolescents and young daughters-in-law undertaking the most onerous tasks of production (Sahlins 1962:120-2). And, as noted above, in Southeast Asia, women frequently are the major producers of rice, at the same time caring for domestic vegetable gardens and animals, and in coastal areas collecting shellfish while men fish offshore. Within rice production, tasks are allocated according to sex: Men prepare the land and assume responsibility for the building and maintenance of irrigation dykes; women tend the nurseries, transplant seedlings, and do the weeding. Harvesting may be a community activity, with contributed labor finally reciprocated as each village plot reaches maturity. The threshing and winnowing of rice is typically women's work; men or women may undertake to sell the harvest surplus.

The processing and cooking of food provides further elaboration of gender. In general, women carry produce to their camp or village; grind, grate, pound, leach, or in other ways prepare the food for cooking; carry water and firewood; cook; distribute the food; and clear away after the meal. Animal flesh, on the other hand, may rather be butchered, divided, and cooked by men, and feast food may be prepared by men also: in Bali, whereas women cook everyday meals, men are the chefs who prepare pork and turtle meat for ritual occasions; in Fiji, again men assume full responsibility for the food and the ovens used for ceremonial and other major meals. Further, these divisions are not immutable: In Tikopia, for instance, men and women share together the tasks associated with everyday cooking (Firth 1936/1963:94).

Economic and political changes, particularly recently, have profoundly affected production. Today most Aborigines in rural Australia retain some links with traditional life, but depend largely on European foodstuffs – white flour, sugar, tea – through outlets at missions, settlements, and outstations, with often serious nutritional problems in consequence (Hetzel and Firth 1978). Those who live in urban and periurban areas have little knowledge of, and far less opportunity to acquire, traditional foods. Hunter–gatherers in the Malay Peninsula have lost significant forest reserves to development projects and increasingly have been forced to settle; their opportunities to trap, hunt, and fish diminished and their diet changed radically and to their detriment (Kirk Endicott 1979). Shifting cultivators in Sarawak over nearly two centuries have been alienated from prime farmland, forced further into the jungle to cultivate inferior soil. In Papua New Guinea, development projects such as the Ok Tedi gold and copper mining project have and will radically affect the social organization and production of peoples previously outside the cash economy; in areas of Papua New Guinea today, cases of beer bought with cash earned from wage labor supplement or displace traditional food items in exchange and presentation. In Polynesia, imported rice and tinned fish have become components of the diet, as economic development and the commercialization of agriculture have eroded the subsistence economy and left people with little choice but to work for wages and buy their food. Frequently urbanization and migration have hastened changes in food habits and diet. And everywhere, development has created a fourth world of poverty and deprivation, and, in Boulding's terms (1977), a fifth world of women whose critical roles with men as the producers, traders, and decision makers have been overlooked.

But economic development appears not to have eroded the core of values surrounding food, nor its centrality to social and ritual life. Food, in abundance, remains a community wealth, a resource to be shared, a prime symbol of humanity, culture, and identity.

Shared Wealth and Symbol: prefatory remarks

The chapters that follow are organized into four parts. Part I is concerned with the ecological, economic, social, and political contexts of diet, all of which might determine systems of food production and so influence food choice and dietary behavior. The first chapter, by David Hyndman, is concerned with food getting in a low-technology society, that of the Wopkaimin of the Papua New Guinea Highland Fringe. Traditional collector–hunter and horticultural food systems tend to be highly effective in exploiting the environment and meeting the society's nutritional requirements, while maintaining harmony with the environment. As Pimental et al. have demonstrated (1973), these systems are also highly cost and energy efficient, in contrast to high-technology agriculture in the industrialized and developing world. However, Schlegel and Guthrie (1973) have argued that nutritional gains accompany economic development: Their comparison of Tiruray farming systems in the Philippines suggests that plow farmers in the modern sector of the economy enjoy some nutritional advantages over traditional swidden farmers. Hyndman demonstrates both the energy efficiency and the nutritional adequacies of Wopkaimin subsistence food production activities. Labor demands, time and distance factors, and the expenditure of energy are analyzed to evaluate nutritional returns.

The chapters by Janice Reid and Thomas Fitzgerald are each concerned with the impact of contact between peoples of different cultures, including the changes in mode of production. Janice Reid is concerned, like Hyndman, with a small-scale society, the Yolngu of northern Australia. Until recently, food was hunted and collected; today, storebought European food dominates the diet. But traditional food resources continue to be highly valued. With social change, traditionally available foods have assumed new meanings, providing the vocabulary for statements about Aboriginality, identity, and integrity. The author demonstrates the ways in which food is used in contemporary contexts, including those that involve both Aboriginal and European Australians.

Thomas Fitzgerald deals with the food habits and attitudes toward foods and eating of Cook Islanders who have migrated to urban New Zealand. With development, industrialization, and urbanization, there has been considerable rural–urban and intercountry migration in search of work. Lack of land for gardening in cities; employment in the modern sector; access to manufactured and refined foods, often with a lack of fresh alternatives; and the increased availability of "fast" food or precooked meals all have contributed to changes in eating patterns and food choice. Cost of fuel and time in addition to the cost of raw food items may also influence diet. However, immigrants may be able to maintain some elements of a premigration diet. Fitzgerald's chapter highlights the flexibility and adaptability of the immigrants, a finding that is surprising only because of the ignorance of Western health workers with regard to migrant dietary practice.

Economic and dietary changes are inevitable for most peoples in Southeast Asia and the Pacific. For many countries in the region, the critical issue is the provision of an adequate food supply in the future. Nancy Pollock discusses the problems of future food supplies at a macro level: She is concerned with the Pacific region as a whole, within the world market economy. Her chapter queries conventionally understood alternatives to the maintenance of a subsistence economy. She rejects an assumption that involvement in the wider economy need result in food shortages and dependence on food aid. She argues for limited development of forestry and the continuation of shifting agriculture, which would allow both the provision of subsistence foods and sufficient cash to enable the purchase of supplementary foodstuffs and other commodities.

Part II is concerned with cognition and ideation: The chapters focus on the ways in which people conceptualize food and eating. The section starts with Michael Young's chapter on hunger. In many societies, rituals operate to assure the society of prosperity and to avoid famine and hunger. Among Trobriand Islanders, for example, garden magic, and magic at harvest time and prior to the storage of the yams, is performed to ensure an abundant crop, then to make the yams last, to continue to reflect plenty, prosperity, wealth, and security. Magic acts not only on the food itself, but also on the appetites of the members of the society (Malinowski 1935, vol 1:239). Food for the Kalauna people of Goodenough Island again serves as a prime symbol of the society and as a medium for the expression of kinship, community, and conflict. In his chapter, Young demonstrates the converse, that lack of food represents social destruction; hunger, the collapse of moral values and social order (see also Schneider 1957). He demonstrates that hunger, like food, "can be ideologically exploited, politically and ritually, as a potent symbolic idiom."

The chapters by Lenore Manderson and Julie Waddy are concerned with the classification of food. Lenore Manderson examines the bipolar classification of foods into hot and cold categories. This system is widely used throughout the world, particularly in Asia and Latin America, influenced by, when not derived directly from, classical humoral medical theory. In Malaysia, the system is supplemented by other classifications – windy, sharp, itchy, poison – all of which, like hot and cold, relate to the presumed effect of the food on the body. In Manderson's chapter, the classification of food and the dietary restrictions that flow from it are related to physical states that might be considered closer to nature than to culture. Food precautions and behavioral restrictions provide a cultural means for the reestablishment of order and control over nature. Julie Waddy is concerned with taxonomic classification of food, which, she demonstrates, is related to but not coincidental with a biological taxonomic system. She explores the complex and dynamic system of classification used by Groote Eylandt Aborigines, developed from the primary differentiation between flesh and nonflesh foods. She notes that this system relates to and is determined by people's attitudes toward food. For Groote Eylandt Aborigines, the first distinction between flesh and nonflesh reflects a desire for contrast and balance in diet.

Part III is concerned with infant feeding practice in Southeast Asia and the Pacific. The chapters therein provide descriptions of traditional feeding and changes to these practices, and discuss the role of multinational corporations and government agencies in the promotion of bottle feeding. The section opens with Marianne Spiegel's chapter on infant feeding practice in Malaysia, in which she examines the broad context within which infant feeding decisions are made. These include economic and social organization, labor force participation among women, kinship, and domestic structure and authority, all of which may influence a woman's decision to breast- or bottle-feed her infant. Her chapter questions the uncompromising advocation of breast feeding. Although not supporting the role of the multinational corporations in their often indiscriminate advertisement and sale of tinned milk, she argues for an understanding of the complexity of factors that might encourage women to choose between breast and bottle.

Barry Shaw's paper considers infant feeding in a cultural, ecological, and health context. Focusing on the Kyaka Enga of the Papua New Guinea Highlands during 1950–60, he argues for the importance of human milk as a critical element of the child's diet to the age of four or five years. Breast milk provided them with significant nutrients, fluid to prevent dehydration, and immunological protection in an environment where health risks were manifold. At the same time, lactation played an important role in child spacing. He argues for the importance of studying the period of mixed consumption of human milk and other foods, as a distinct phase of dietary behavior.

Kathy Robinson's chapter returns to the issue of artificial feeding. The high cost of infant formula, the failure to explain its preferability over other tinned and powdered milk, and advertising campaigns that have implied the suitability of any milk product for infant feeding have led to the purchase and use of milk unsuitable for infants. This has caused nutritional and gastrointestinal complaints and at times early death (Jelliffe and Jelliffe 1978; Raphael 1979). Criticisms of the promotion of artificial feeding in the Third World have been directed mainly at major multinational corporations, and in particular Nestle. But they are not alone. Kathy Robinson discusses the activities of an Australian Government statutory authority, the Australian Dairy Corporation. She provides us with a powerful example of the nature of the activities of capitalist enterprise in developing countries, through her discussion of the activities of the Australian Dairy Corporation in Indonesia.

The final part of the volume presents three distinct chapters, each of which raises questions of method or research direction for nutritional anthropologists. Valerie Hull argues that our knowledge of actual food behavior – as opposed to ideal practices – is limited. She discussed Javanese food taboos, and identifies various misconceptions or "myths" and "mysteries" that surround food habits and diet. She suggests that region, economic class, and gender might all affect the consumption of food. Her chapter calls for further research on actual eating patterns and their nutritional implications, to provide a sound basis for future nutritional policies and programs.

Christine Wilson again draws attention to the need for accurate documentation of the foods eaten in any given society. She is concerned in this chapter with foods that are indigenous to the study region or are especially prepared or processed following local recipes. These foods tend to be highly valued socially, but they are seasonally available only and supplementary to the diet. They are consumed then, outside the regular diet, yet are important and should be considered for both nutritional and cultural consequence.

Finally, Graham Pyke queries the extent of our knowledge of dietary behavior and the relative effect of culture and genes. He argues that food choice and eating patterns are determined both culturally and genetically for all animals including humans. Animal feeding behavior is influenced by genetically based differences, by hunger and health status, including nutritional deficiencies, and by the color, taste, and odor of foods. In addition, social interaction influences foraging behavior and the quantity of food consumed. Pyke recognizes that for humans, culture masks the influence of genes, but he suggests that genetic and biological factors remain of considerable importance. He argues the need for further research to understand possible genetically based components of human dietary behavior, both in terms of individual eating habits and with respect to the proper management of the world food supply.

Part I

THE CONTEXT OF DIET

1. Men, women, work, and group nutrition in a New Guinea Mountain Ok society

David Hyndman

Maintenance of a human population requires a regular flow of energy. Shifting cultivation, silviculture, gathering, pig raising, hunting, fishing, and collecting are all components of the Wopkaimin subsistence system, and they are the main activities through which energy and materials are channeled to the Wopkaimin. Variables such as labor inputs, time and distance factors, foodstuff yields, and nutrient returns are used to illustrate energetics, productivity, and nutritional adaptation in the subsistence system.

The Wopkaimin

The Wopkaimin are hunter–horticulturalists living near the Fly River headwaters in Papua New Guinea (Figure 1.1). They are one of several small groups of Mountain Ok-speaking peoples occupying the center of the island adjacent to the headwaters of the Fly and Sepik rivers. Mountain Ok people are part of the ecologically and culturally distinctive region known as the Highland Fringe (Brown 1978:272–4). Ethnographic studies of the Mountain Ok began in the late 1960s and still continue.

There are about 700 Wopkaimin people (Figure 1.2), and they are divided into five autonomous parish groups, which range in size from 108 to 250 members. Each local parish group consists of two or more cognatic descent groups. Parish endogamy is strongly favored. Iralim, the largest parish, has three cognatic descent groups. The Fikkalinmin are the core members of the Kam Basin neighborhood. Brown and Podelefsky's (1976) comparative study of the Highland region shows the population size to range from 1.8 to 5.4 persons per square-kilometer. By comparison, the Kam Basin neighborhood of the Wopkaimin numbers 76, and they are part of the larger Iralim parish political unit with 250 members. The Kam Basin spans 46 square-kilometers, and the Iralim parish extends over 160 square-kilometers.

Wopkaimin socioeconomic organization is an interrelated, largely undifferentiated system. Social and economic relationships cannot be separated. Interpersonal behavior is organized in a kinship idiom. The Wopkaimin have cognatic, named descent groups with overlapping membership. The Wopkaimin, along with the Tifalmin, Urapmin, and Telefolmin (see Figure 1.1)

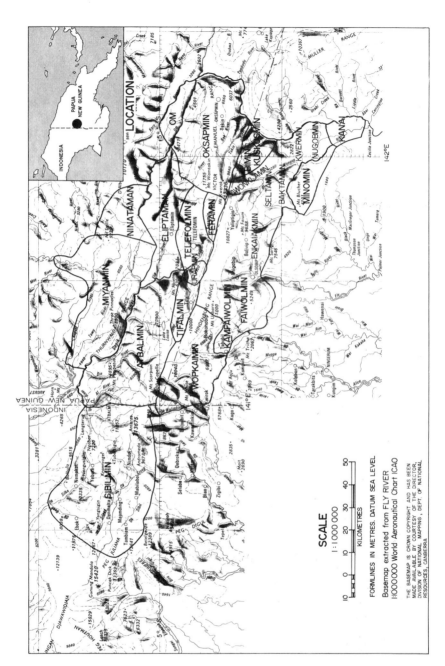

Figure 1.1. Major territories of the Mountain Ok.

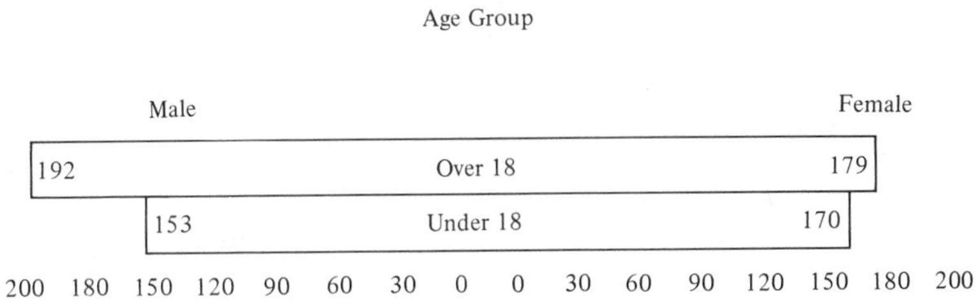

Age Group

Male		Female
192	Over 18	179
153	Under 18	170

200 180 150 120 90 60 30 0   0 30 60 90 120 150 180 200

Figure 1.2. Gross distribution of Wopkaimin population by age and sex. (After Ransley 1975.)

form a central clustering of Mountain Ok speakers that are distinguished by bilaterally oriented social systems. Patrilocal residence as well as parish endogamy is commonly practiced; access to land is a use right for parish residents. Nuclear families are independent working units for property using and daily work routine. They do not function as part of an extended family nor are they a commensal unit because men take their meals in the men's house. The prohibition of incest is extended bilaterally, and the exogamous unit becomes the close group of bilateral kin based on nuclear family and sibling relationships.

The Wopkaimin obtain their subsistence from cultivating taro, *Colocasia esculenta*, and from procuring numerous wild resources that take them to a great variety of resource areas and several residential sites within a large territory of over 1,000 square-kilometers. Low-intensity agriculture based on taro, spatial diversity of food resources, and exceedingly complex male initiation ceremonies involving game animals are commonly shared features among the Mountain Ok.

Food-getting strategies

Plant procurement systems

Shifting cultivation. Shifting cultivation is the mainstay of the Wopkaimin subsistence system. Wopkaimin agriculture is so rudimentary that all techniques accounting for variability in New Guinea cultivation practices are absent. Gardens are not even differentiated by crop composition, as is common in other localities in the Highland Fringe. Taro is the staple crop and occupies about 75 percent of garden space; twenty-two other cultigens are planted in the remaining space. Gardens average about 6,700 taro plants per hectare.

The Wopkaimin establish their gardens between 1,200 and 1,750 meters above sea level in secondary forest that has been fallowed for 25–30 years. About 90 percent of the 7.5 hectares under cultivation in the Kam Basin is represented by three aggregate gardens. Cultivated land averages .11 hectares per person, which is within the .08- to .12-hectare per person average for Melanesian rain forest peoples (Barrau 1958:25). Gardens are never fenced because feral pigs tend to forage below 1,000 meters in the Foothill Rainforest. Cloud, rain, elevation, terrain, and cropping techniques delay harvesting in the Kam Basin. Taro matures after 12 months and is harvested over a six-month period. Over the final 18–24 months, only *Xanthosoma, Hibiscus,* and *Musa* continue to produce.

I mapped the three aggregate gardens and visited them during periods of slashing, tree killing, planting, weeding, and harvesting to measure and record a sample of time expenditures. The Wopkaimin average 1,600 hours per hectare under their system of shifting cultivation. Travel accounts for some seven percent of gardening time because the 900 hectares of secondary forest in the Kam Basin are widely distributed and gardens are sometimes two hours away from hamlets. Because of variations in family size, responsibilities of pig raising, and commitment to other subsistence activities, individual gardeners work between 635 and 950 work hours per year.

Silviculture. The Wopkaimin own land from 300 meters to over 3,000 meters above sea level and cultivate tree crops characteristic of Lowland, Highland Fringe, and Highland New Guinea. Sago (*Metroxylon*) is common to the Lowlands (Lea 1972; Ohtsuka 1977a, 1977b), whereas fruit pandanus (*Pandanus conoideus*), breadfruit (*Artocarpus altilis*), and banana (*Musa*) are common to the Highland Fringe (Barrau 1958:53–54, 55–60), and nut pandanus (*Pandanus julianettii*) is common to the Highlands (Bowers 1968; Waddell 1972). All Wopkaimin tree crops except bananas are planted in groves.

Pandanus conoideus is grown in small groves of 5–10 trees at 700 to 1,300 meters above sea level. Individual men own each tree. Twelve varietal names are distinguished by the tree height, color of syncarp and ripening time. Drupes, the edible portion of the syncarp, are baked and made into a sauce, which undiluted is an important source of fat (Clarke 1971: 237).

Pandanus julianettii is always planted separately from fruit pandanus. Five to 10 nut pandanus are planted in groves between 1,500 and 2,000 meters above sea level. Tenure is strictly individual; each male owner has *julianettii* planted in various groves. Eighteen varietals are distinguished by tree height, configuration of prop roots, and size and shape of nut sheath and kernals.

Pandanus conoideus is harvested yearly, but *Pandanus julianettii* yields only every other year. Location of *Pandanus* groves, intensity of labor inputs, and yields are influenced by distance from the hamlet. Elsewhere in the Highland Fringe, Clarke (1971:139, 174) estimates that Maring men spend 45 minutes silviculture labor per *Pandanus* per year. Wopkaimin silviculture techniques are similar to those of the Maring, but they maintain fewer *Pandanus*; about 10 fruit and 10 nut pandanus per male owner. Each Wopkaimin man spends about 15 work hours per year in *Pandanus* silviculture.

Metroxylon is more important in Wopkaimin silviculture than is *Pandanus*. Sago is culturally valued, is greatly esteemed as a food, and is considered a staple food second only to taro. Nine varieties are distinguished according to the presence or absence of spines, dimensions of the bole, and the color of the starch. Sago palms are owned by those who plant them and also by their descendents. Up to 12 palms are carefully managed in groves located in the Foothill Rainforest between 700 and 1,000 meters above sea level.

A sago palm produces maximum starch content when it flowers around the fifteenth year of growth (Cobley 1956). The manufacture of sago starch is a straining process, which is remarkably similar across the Highland Fringe (Townsend 1969:26-33; Dornstreich 1973:208-11, 331-4). The sexual division of labor in sago manufacture involves men and women in (1) traveling to the sago grove, (2) felling and splitting, (3) pulverizing, and (4) constructing the straining apparatus; and involves women in (5) washing, and (6) transporting of finished starch. There is no comparable division of labor or technological complexity in *Pandanus* silviculture.

The Wopkaimin wash about 15.6 kilograms of sago per hour. They take about 15 work hours to produce around 28.5 kilograms of edible starch. Raw sago is not channeled to pigs, nor are palms felled to encourage sago grub colonization. Sago introduces flexibility to Wopkaimin subsistence because it provides reliable bulk food to sustain movement into the Foothill Rainforest for gathering, hunting, fishing, and collecting. Each subsistence producer spends on average 25 work hours per year on sago and 40 work hours per year on silviculture.

Gathering. Gathering is a system for acquiring wild plant foods. It is a supplementary food-getting activity undertaken by women. Ferns, leafy greens, nuts, fruits, roots, grass stems, palm stems, vines, and fungi are the types of wild plants eaten by the Wopkaimin. Edible ferns (*Athyrium, Dennstaedtia, Dicksonia, Cyathea,* and *Microlepia*) are termed *taton.* They constitute the most important group of wild plants, and they are gathered daily by women and children. Edible ferns and leafy greens occur in secondary forests and in abandoned gardens and hamlets. Roots, nuts, fruits, palm stems, and fungi are gathered from various elevational zones of rain forest. *Finchia* and *Pandanus* nuts are dependable and regularly consumed wild plant foods. *Finchia* is a canopy tree of the Foothill Rainforest, nut *Pandanus* occurs at much higher elevations in Moss Forest, and Upper Montane Rainforest.

From June to August 1975, over 3,000 kilograms of cultivated and wild plant foods were consumed in Bakonabip. Wild plants amounted to 62.7 kilograms and equaled two percent by weight of all plant food. Ninety percent of gathered plant food consisted of edible ferns and leafy greens. Elsewhere in the Highland Fringe, the Gadio (Dornstreich 1973:227-30) expend 165 hours to gather 375 kilograms of edible ferns and leafy greens. These wild plants are easily obtained by the Gadio and the Wopkaimin, and they involve little diversion in time or distance from a normal day's gardening. Average gathering time spent by each Wopkaimin woman is about five hours per year. Gathering is important to subsistence because it (1) requires no special technology, (2) has high food value, (3) complements a carbohydrate-based diet, and (4) reduces subsistence risk because the exploited resources occur at known places at known times (Nietschmann 1973:152).

Meat procurement systems

Pig raising. The contribution of domestic pigs to the Wopkaimin diet is important and domestic pigs are considered absolutely essential sacrificial animals for initiation and curing ceremonies. The Wopkaimin pattern of mobility and settlement dispersion is not compatible with the pattern of food and care required in pig raising. The problem is resolved by fostering pigs in a system of communal management in residentially separate pig houses away from hamlets. The demands of bedding, food, and care of pigs fall exclusively to women. It is quite common across the Highland Fringe for domestic pigs to be wild, semidomestic, and domestic during different parts of their life cycle (Dornstreich 1973:236). The communal pig population is increased through piglet capture, purchase, and trade and through the uncertainties of sow breeding associated with newborn mortality and feral boar availability.

Wopkaimin families foster out one or two domestic pigs. Eleven domestic pigs were in Kam Basin in June 1975. All fodder comes from *Colocasia* gardens, and each pig consumes an amount equivalent to the daily produce ration of humans. About 90–125 work hours per year, 14 percent of gardening time, is channeled to domestic pigs. In the Kam Basin from June to July 1975, six domestic pigs weighing over 400 kilograms were killed. Based on the foodstuff yield of 385 kilograms, Wopkaimin subsistence producers expend about 2.5 to 3.5 hours per kilogram of edible pork.

Hunting. The core of Wopkaimin life revolves around hunting. Meat has tremendous cultural value, and hunting surpasses pig raising in emotional and social importance and nutritional significance. The dog is important to hunting returns and is as culturally important to men as the domestic pig is to women (see Clarke 1971:89). The favored hunting strategy is to use the dog while stalking, besetting, and chasing. It is common for up to five or six men to hunt together. Hunting partnerships are loosely structured and typically center around the presence of an acknowledged skillful hunting dog and his owner.

All 12 economically productive men in the Kam Basin hunted. Economic constraints of gardening, silviculture, and pig raising tend to fall more heavily upon the 30- to 40-years age group, leaving the younger men more mobile for hunting. Nonetheless, every adult male hunts because it has such positive emotional and social value, and there is no other food-getting activity that yields such a large quantity of protein in such a short period of time.

Wopkaimin men use the same hunting equipment complex wherever they hunt. Black palm bows are traded from the Ningerum people south of the Ok Kirok and Ok Maani (Figure 1.1). The bow is strung with shaved rattan (*Calamus*). Arrows are fashioned from cane grass (*Miscantus floridulus*). Projectile points made from bamboo (*Bambusa*) are used in hunting feral pigs; those made from palm wood (*Hydriastele, Nengella, Caryota*) are used in hunting game mammals. Multipronged and blunted projectile points are used in hunting birds and in fishing. Other hunting equipment includes the ax, a braided tree-climbing ring (*makar*), and the hunting dog.

The two most time-consuming hunting activities are putting distance between hamlet and hunter and stalking. Every hunter integrates his knowledge of game animal microenvironment preference, feeding habits, and topographic features to guide his stalking activity. The Wopkaimin possess accurate ecological and animal behavioral knowledge necessary for successful and intensive rain forest hunting. The Wopkaimin direct their hunting efforts primarily at four animals that offer the least subsistence risk in terms of cultural meat preferences and recognition of habits and habitats: the cassowary, feral pig, cuscus (*Phalanger vestitus*), and ringtail (*Pseudocheirus cupreus*). Cultural and nutritional significance of hunting is reflected in the necessity of game animals for sacrificial provisioning in the cult system and in the public decorum of meat sharing. From June to August 1975, there were two hunts in the Upper Montane Rainforest, one hunt in the Kam Basin, and one hunt in the Foothill Rainforest. From these hunting expeditions, estimates are made of yearly game animal yield in terms of time expenditure in traveling and stalking.

Table 1.1 summarizes inputs and outputs from 400 hours of Wopkaimin hunting. Hunting is their major means of obtaining meat, and by New Guinea standards they are very successful at it. Four hundred hours of hunting returned an edible weight of 150,364 grams. In the more densely populated Eastern Highlands, returns from 500 hours of Rofaifo hunting amounted to only 9,700 grams (Dwyer 1974:290). On average, the Rofaifo obtain one game animal for every 25 work hours of effort and expend 25 work hours for one kilogram bag weight of game. By comparison, the Wopkaimin obtain one game animal for every 5.8 hours and on average expend only 2.1 hours for one kilogram bag weight of game. Game animal hunting returned 1,370 calories for every 100 calories expended whereas mammal hunting returned 580 calories for 100 calories expended. In the 400-hour sample, 56 percent of the total yield came from the two large terrestrial game animals: feral pig (27 percent) and cassowary (29 percent), which took 18 percent of the hunting time and required an average round-trip distance of over 16 kilometers. Game mammals were 44 percent of the yield, with *Phalanger*

Table 1.1. *Inputs and outputs from 400 hours of Wopkaimin hunting*

Location	People[a] present	Returns (kg)	Hunting strategy (daylight) & bag wt return (kg)					Hunting strategy (nocturnal) & bag wt return (kg)			
			Solitary stalking	Solitary stalking & dog	Group stalking & dog	Ambush	Chase	Solitary stalking	Solitary stalking & dog	Group stalking & dog	Ambush
Bansikin	5 M 3 F 1 C	26.6	9.1		14.1	3.5	1.6				
Finimterr	5 M 2 F	39.5				9.6		3.7	12.7	6.8	4.6
Ulatem	4 M 7 F 4 C	109.5	109.5								
Bleilimal	4 M	12.2		2.6	4.3					5.1	
Totals		188	118.6	2.6	18.4	13.1	1.6	3.7	12.7	11.9	4.6

[a] Male (M), female (F), children (C).

vestitus 8 percent and *Pseudocheirus cupreus* 11 percent. Game mammals took 82 percent of the hunting time and required an average round trip distance of five kilometers. Extrapolating from the 400-hour sample, each hunter spends about 500 work hours per year in hunting for a yearly game animal bag weight return of around 160 kilograms and an edible weight return of around 38,900 grams.

Fishing. Wopkaimin fishing techniques are sex specific. Women primarily pursue fishing because of the behavioral outcome of folk taxonomy and food prohibitions. Men are prohibited from catching and consuming fish during initiation ceremonies. Fully initiated men rarely eat fish, and cult house leaders (*awen kinum*) observe a complete food taboo on fish.

Number of game animals killed	Hours hunted	Hours per 1 kg	Edible weight return (g)	Where consumed	Efficiency ratio
12	88.5	3.3	21,312	Bansikin	7.2:1
43	188	4.7	31,700	Finimterr Bakonabip	5:1
4	70	0.6	87,560	Ulatem	37.5:1
9	54.5	4.5	9,792	Bleilimal	5.4:1
68	401	2.13 (total average) 4.1 (av. mammals only)	150,364		13.7:1 (total average) 5.8:1 (av. mammals)

Hand probing and erecting small stone weirs in steams are two fishing techniques used by women. Almost all women's fishing is focused on the rough-scaled loter, *Oxyeleotris fimbriatus*, found in Mid-mountain Rainforest streams, and on the spotted mountain goby (*Glossogobius celebius*), and dusky mountain goby (*Glossogobius brunnoides*), found in Foothill Rainforest streams. Hand probing and small stone weirs are integrated women's fishing techniques appropriate to catching these small, 100-gram fish. Previously men fished with poison, basket traps (*warap*) made from climbing palm (*Korthalsia*) and fish spears. Today they still spear fish but prefer to use steel hooks and monfilament line. Men fish for the large catfish, *Neosilurus equinus* and *Neosilurus gjellerupi*, found in the Ok Tedi and its tributaries below 650 meters.

Fishing is associated with temporary settlement shifts to alternate living sites. The two fishing trips to the Ok Tedi River in Foothill Rainforest, observed from June to August 1975, returned 20 kilograms for 100 work hours expended. The return of 600 calories for every 100 calories expended equals a ratio of 6:1, which is remarkably similar to the ratio of 5.8:1 for game mammal hunting. By extrapolating from the 100-hour sample fishing period, the yearly return from catfish is estimated to be 170 kilograms, and the yearly return from loters and gobies is estimated to be 780 kilograms. On average, each man fishes about 70 work hours per year, and each woman fishes about 150 work hours per year for an approximate return of 3.8 kilograms per hour per subsistence producer.

Collecting. Collecting refers to the acquisition of small animals as food. The large python (*Chondropython viridis*) and the agamid lizard (*Goniocephalus modestus*) are collected by men. These larger animals are generally cooked and consumed at the hamlet. Collecting small animals such as frogs (25 species), lizards and skinks (15 species), snakes (5 species), insects (several species), and mammals (several species) is a food-getting activity of women and children. Collecting is reliable and regularly followed in conjunction with gardening and gathering. When obtained in small quantities, these collected animals are consumed away from hamlets.

Certain collecting techniques return sufficient quantities of small animals to justify transporting them back to hamlets. Women's combined fishing and frogging trips regularly return the highest yield of small animals. The collecting activity involves temporary shelter for one or two nights in a frog house (*kulam*). At night, using torches made of split *Pandanus* prop roots, the women collect streambank-dwelling Microhylidae and tree-dwelling Hylidae. At low elevations where the frugivorous gecko (*Cyrtodactylus mimikanus*) lays its eggs in streamside sand, both the gecko and its eggs are collected on frogging trips. An ingenious skink-collecting technique is the litter trap, *atim moon*, which is constructed of leaf humus along trailsides and in abandoned gardens. *Sphenomorphus nigriventus* and *Emoia baudini* colonize under the litter, and women later collect the skinks and their eggs.

Small collected animals are routinely distributed according to a system of food prohibitions based on the age, physical condition, social status, and kinship of those present. Collecting returns are important for women and children because they are the only wild animal foods specifically channeled to them in a cultural system that otherwise disadvantages them in the pattern of meat distribution. On the basis of several comparative observations, women spend about 50 work hours per year collecting, which is 10 times the amount spent on gathering. The return from one hour of collecting returns a bag weight of approximately five kilograms of small animals. This is an average of 300 calories for every 100 calories expended. Collecting is marginally efficient energetically, but as a system of acquiring quality protein, it does have the advantages of no waste, abundance, reliability, and occasional avoidance of sharing (see Dornstreich 1973:271).

Wopkaimin men, as shown in Table 1.2, expend 1,245 work hours per year in subsistence activities, and females expend 1,307 work hours per year in subsistence activities. These inputs and outputs are estimates, but they do generally represent the relative contributions men and women make to subsistence production. Men are less committed to shifting cultivation than are women. In all, men work in only three additional subsystems of subsistence. There is little difference in labor input and weight of foodstuff yield between men and women in the subsistence system. Men produce approximately 760 grams of foodstuff yield per hour of labor, and women produce approximately 670 grams of foodstuff yield per hour of labor.

The chief concern of this section on food-getting strategies has been with the patterned effects of space and time on human activity in the Wopkaimin subsistence system. Elsewhere in the Highland Fringe, the Wopkaimin average of 1,245 work hours for men and 1,307 work hours for women compares to 1,150 work hours for the Maring gardener (Clarke 1971:174). In the diversified subsistence of the Lowland Oriomo Papuans, the average time spent on subsistence per year is 1,356–1,539 hours (Ohtsuka 1977a:255; 1977b:472).

The appearance of relatively equal work expenditure for weight of food return between the sexes does not, however, reveal that nutritionally women's work produces 64 percent of the calories. Men produce approximately 3,515 calories per day, and women produce approximately 6,375 calories per day. Consideration of space, time, and food weight yield, therefore, cannot produce a balanced view of subsistence ecology. Detailed consideration must also be given to nutrient return.

Nutrient returns

Most dietary analyses initially carried out in the Highland Fringe have been the work of human ecologists (Rappaport 1968; Townsend 1969; Clarke 1971; Buchbinder 1973, 1977; Dornstreich 1973; Townsend, Liao, and Konlande 1973). McArthur (1974, 1977) cautions that the collection of food production and nutritional status data for subsistence-oriented populations such as the Wopkaimin is fraught with both theoretical and practical difficulties for human ecologists, especially for the lone fieldworker. Estimates provided in the following section are undoubtedly founded on some questionable values and therefore should not be accepted uncritically. Although it is true that there are certain inadequacies inherent in conducting food consumption surveys and in assigning nutritional values to local foods, the fact remains that it is the lone human ecologist who usually undertakes extended periods of fieldwork among remote subsistence-oriented peoples. This protracted fieldwork commitment has been necessary to place subsistence ecological data in contextual and comparative perspective. I have attempted to provide sufficient

Table 1.2. *Estimated yearly work input and food yield per subsistence producer*

Subsistence subsystem	Men			Women		
	Work-hour inputs	Kilogram yield	Kilocalorie yield	Work-hour inputs	Kilogram yield	Kilocalorie yield
Shifting cultivation	635	700	749,000	950	700	749,000
Silviculture	40	80	260,000	40	80	260,000
Gathering				5	11.2	4,200
Pig raising				90–135	40	1,080,000
Hunting	500	160	162,500			
Fishing	70	14.2	115,200	150	30	230,400
Collecting				50	5	3,120
Total yearly average	1,245	954.2	1,286,700	1,285–1,330 1,307	866.2	2,326,720
Total daily average	3.4	2.6	3,515	3.6	2.4	6,375

quantitative data to allow for cross-cultural comparison and for revision as better estimates of nutritional values and status become available. For example, the Papua New Guinea Institute of Medical Research collaborated in collecting clinical, biochemical, and anthropometric information among the Wopkaimin people in 1975, but as of writing this paper, none of the data has eventuated.

In this section, foods and nutrients are analyzed together in order to understand how foodstuff yields are converted into edible food. Nutritional returns substantiate the diversified nature of the Wopkaimin dietary pattern. Wopkaimin diet and nutrition reflect the interrelationship between environmental heterogeneity and subsistence diversity. The primary aim of this dietary analysis is to demonstrate through nutritional percentages how subsistence subsystems articulate, and to provide a qualitative and quantitative comprehension of food consumption per person.

Bakonabip residents of the Kam Basin were the focus of a three-month diet study from June to August of 1975. Complete daily records were kept of food returns and of the age and sex composition of the resident population. A food book with the headings cultivated plant food, wild plant food, domestic pigs, and wild animal food was used to record daily food returns. Table 1.3 shows the cumulative totals from the daily weighing of all food returns. All food was weighed fresh, and a sample was made of cooked food proportions.

Food was received and distributed during the initial months of fieldwork. The diet study was conducted during the final months of fieldwork when my own garden and store-purchased food was used to minimize consumption of Wopkaimin food. I worked alone in the field. My assistant and interpreter came from the community and fed himself from his own subsistence efforts and from my provisions. The Wopkaimin did not accommodate their subsistence activities to my presence and activities, except for one hunting trip in 1977. The Wopkaimin occasionally place ritual restrictions on public acquisition and consumption of game animals. Ritual activities were not dropped while I lived with the Wopkaimin, and my familiarity with the men was such that they kept me informed of ritual hunting returns.

Unfortunately, there are no analyses of Wopkaimin foods nor are there any comparable ones for other Highland Fringe foods. Dornstreich's (1973:422) table of nutritional values of 56 Gadio foods is compiled from 25 sources. I have retained all of Dornstreich's Gadio food values to analyze the Wopkaimin diet because the dietaries of these groups are similarly diverse and there are minimal variations in taxonomic identification, food preparation, bag weight:edible weight ratios, and wastage from cooking.

Nutritional returns from Wopkaimin food-getting activities

Wopkaimin food-getting strategies are integrated with nutritional returns in Table 1.4. It is unsatisfactory to use only food weight returns to determine

Table 1.3. *Raw weight foodstuff returns from Wopkaimin food-getting activities, June–August 1975*

Cultivated vegetable foods		Wild vegetable foods		Domestic animal foods		Wild animal foods			
						Game (hunting)		Small vertebrates (collecting)	
Colocasia esculenta	2368.8	Asplenium	0.1	Sus scorfa papuensis	190.0	Large game (hunting)		Fish	
Cucumis sativus	11.0	Baccaurea papuana	1.9			Casuarius spp.	38.20	Neosilurus equinus	6.23
Cucurbita moschata	92.6	Cissus	0.3			Sus scorfa papuensis	36.25	Oxyeleotris fimbriatus	1.92
Dioscorea	20.2	Cyathea	22.9			Small game (hunting)			
Hibiscus manihot	105.5	Dennstaedia	0.8			Dactylonax palpator	0.2	Snakes	
Ipomoea batatas	2.5	Dioscorea	2.4			D. moluccensis	6.63	Amphiesma mairii	0.05
Metroxylon	57.0	Diplazium esculentum	14.8			Gymnophaps albertsii	2.0		
Musa	27.0	Fungus	1.8			Eudromicia caudata	0.6	Frogs	6.48
Saccharum officinarum	21.8	Oenanthe javanica	5.2			Mallomys rothschildi	1.8	Litoria	
Sechium edule (fruit)	80.8	Peperonia	0.2			Melomys rubex	0.06	L. angiana	
(leaves)	8.8	Rungia klossii	18.3			Melipotes fumigatus	1.0	L. arfakiana	
Setaria palmifolia	90.9	Trichosanthes	0.3			Myzomela rosenbergii	0.2	L. dorsinena	
Xanthosoma	28.2					Neophascogale lorentzi	0.2	L. iris	
						Opopsitta diophthalma	0.3	Phrynomantis eurydactyla	
								Rana grisea	
								Sphenophryne macrophyncha	

Melidectes rufocrissalis	0.3
Peroryctes longicauda	0.77
Pseudocheirus cupreus	14.51
Pseudocheirus corinnae	1.02
Phalanger atrimaculatus	5.45
Phalanger carmelitae	5.7
Phalanger gymnotis	4.1
Phalanger interpositus	4.63
Phalanger vestitus	11.24

Lizards	0.43
Emoia	
Cyrtodactylus mimicanus	
Sphenomorphus cinereus	
S. leptofasciatus	
S. nigriventria	

Totals	2,914.6 kg	69.0 kg	190.0 kg	150.47 kg

group subsistence patterns because all foods are not nutritionally equal. The relative importance of a food-getting strategy can be calculated by its relationship to nutritional returns. In Table 1.4 Wopkaimin subsistence is analyzed in terms of nutrient return percentages derived from each food-getting strategy from June to August 1975.

The bulk of nutrient returns are provided by plant food-getting activities. Shifting cultivation is the significant subsistence strategy because it provides the greatest percentages of all nutrients except proteins and fats. Gathering is a good source of iron, vitamin A, and vitamin C. Silviculture provides calories that complement the nutrients obtained from gathering.

In the Wopkaimin diet, 95 percent of the fats and half of the protein comes from animal food-getting activities. Pig raising contributes the bulk of dietary fat. Hunting provides over 23 percent of total dietary protein and is the greatest contributor of protein from animal food-getting strategies. Collecting is negligible in overall dietary terms except for protein and phosphorus. Likewise, fishing is nutritionally insignificant except for protein and calcium.

The Wopkaimin staple food is taro (*Colocasia esculenta*), which provides 66 percent of all calories. Taro is a high-calorie food and is eaten in large quantities every day. Although *Colocasia* taro has more protein than any other New Guinea staple food (Oomen 1971), it contributes in combination with other foods. This improves the amino acid balance of daily meals, especially because the sulfur-containing amino acid methionine is limited in taro (Oomen 1971:10). Miller, Baner, and Denning (1952:437) indicate that taro is an excellent source of thiamine. Over 60 percent of dietary thiamine comes from the daily taro staple.

Leafy greens *Hibiscus manihot, Sechium edule, Oenanthe javanica, Rungia klossii,* and *Peperonia* and edible ferns *Cyathea, Dennstaedtia,* and *Diplazium* are seven percent by weight of all foodstuffs. The Wopkaimin gather together tender upper shoots of these plants which contain the highest protein content (Rogers and Miner 1963; Terra 1964; Whiting and Morton 1966; Stanley and Lewis 1969; Schuphan 1970). Leafy greens and edible ferns are also quite good providers of vitamin A, vitamin C, thiamine, riboflavin, and niacin. New Guineans generally receive adequate thiamine, carotene, calcium, iron, vitamin C, and potassium in their diet (Oomen 1971:16–17), as do the Wopkaimin with their very diversified diet.

Fat is the nutrient most lacking in New Guinean diets (Oomen 1971:16–17). Fat makes food more palatable, and it enables the body to use other nutrients. Vitamins A, D, E, and K are fat soluble and require the presence of fat for their complete utilization (Deuel 1955; Sebrell and Harris 1967; Rajalakshmi 1969). Whiting and Morton (1966:10) state that diets dependent upon leafy greens require at least seven percent of dietary calories from fat in order for vitamin A to be fully utilized. The Wopkaimin derive two percent of their dietary calories from fat and may not be fully absorbing the

Table 1.4. *Percent of nutrients supplied by subsistence activities, Kam Basin, June–August 1975*

Percent of nutrient supplied

Food-getting activities	Edible (g%)	Calories	Proteins	Fat	Calcium	Iron	Vit. A	Vit. B$_1$ (thiamine)	Vit. B$_2$ (riboflavin)	Vit. C (ascorbic acid)	Phosphorus	Potassium
1. Shifting cultivation	87.2	71.2	51.9	4.7	94.1	77.5	87.3	64.7	60.8	90.8	89.8	93.0
2. Silviculture	2.2	5.7			0.7	1.0						
3. Gathering	2.1	0.8	3.2	0.3	2.6	11.5	12.6	2.5	5.0	9.2	1.9	7.0
Plant food-getting	91.5	77.7	55.1	5.0	97.4	90.0	99.9	67.2	65.8	100.0	91.7	100.0
4. Pig raising	4.5	15.8	18.6	73.2	0.7	4.8		16.0	9.9		5.8	
5. Hunting	3.6	6.2	23.6	21.5	0.8	4.8		16.7	23.1		0.8	
6. Fishing	0.2	0.2	1.5	0.2	1.0	0.2	0.1	0.1	0.8		0.8	
7. Collecting	0.2	0.1	1.2	0.1	0.1	0.2	0.1		0.4		1.7	
Animal food-getting	8.5	22.3	44.9	95.0	2.6	10.0	0.1	32.8	34.2		8.3	
Total	100.0	100.0	100.0	100.0	100.0	100.0	100.0	100.0	100.0	100.0	100.0	100.0

large quantity of vitamin A they regularly eat. Fat is generally limiting to the Wopkaimin. Pork provides 87 percent; birds and game animals, another 8 percent; and *Finchia* and *Pandanus* nuts, the remaining 5 percent of dietary fat.

Animals contribute eight percent by weight of foods eaten by the Wopkaimin, which is very high by New Guinea standards. Highland diets consist almost entirely of plants (Sinnett 1977:70). Lowland diets, even where fish is available, are 2.2 percent animal food weight (Norgan, Ferro-Luzzi, and Durnin, 1974:323). Elsewhere in the Highland Fringe, the Gadio and Sanio-Hiowe consume about as much weight in animals as do the Wopkaimin. Five percent by weight of the Gadio diet is animals (Dornstreich 1973:366), and eight percent by weight of the Sanio-Hiowe diet is animals (Townsend 1969:62). Animals are important in the Wopkaimin diet because they contribute high-quality protein. Animals provide a daily protein intake of 22.3 grams per person per day.

Conclusion

A total of 1,607 Wopkaimin were in residence in the Kam Basin from June to July 1975. As shown in Table 1.5, 3,250,284 calories, 76,081 grams of protein, and 70,424 grams of fat provided 2,022.5 calories, 47.3 grams of protein, and 43.7 grams of fat for every person every day.

Nutritional requirements set by Langley (1947), Venkatachalam (1962), and the FAO/WHO (1973) are the authorities widely used to evaluate diet and subsistence in Papua New Guinea. The values chosen for Wopkaimin nutritional requirements strongly influence any conclusions reached about their diet. The average weight and height for Wopkaimin men are 48.3 kilograms and 153.3 centimeters; the average for women are 44.3 kilograms and 148.6 centimeters. The nutritional requirement baseline determined by Dornstreich (1973:430) for the Highland Fringe Gadio is taken as the basis for this analysis because the two populations closely resemble one another. Calorie and protein intake in the Wopkaimin population is adequate when considered as a daily per capita average. Fat intake is low. A protein intake of 47.3 grams per person per day is favorably high by New Guinean standards. As a group the Wopkaimin are satisfactorily nourished with respect to calories, protein, vitamins, and minerals, especially when one considers the diversity of plant and animal foods in their diet. The heterogeneous nature of the Wopkaimin diet is demonstrated by the interaction between availability, acquisition, and adequacy of local foods. Nutritional returns further substantiate a diversified dietary pattern capable of providing adequate daily per capita nutrition for the Wopkaimin.

The Highland Fringe, noted for its rugged terrain, high rainfall, infertile soils, biotic diversity, and endemic malaria, is a distinctive regional zone in New Guinea where human adaptation is possible through diversified hunter–

Table 1.5. *Per capita nutritional returns, Kam Basin, June–August 1975*

	Edible (g)	Fat (g)	Calories	Calcium (mg)	Phosphorus (mg)	Vit. A (IU)	Vit. B$_2$ (mg)	Vit. C (mg)
Grand total	2,603.99	70,424.9	3,250,284.0	1,234,649.0	2,100,842.7	7,913,083.70	1,616.70	282,578.0
Average per capita per day consumption		43.7	2,022.5	768.3		4,924.00	1.00	161.0

	H$_2$O (g)	Protein (g)	Carbohy-drate (g)	Iron (mg)	Potassium (mg)	Vit. B$_1$ (mg)	Niacin (mg)	Fiber (g)	Ash (g)
Grand total	1,664.73	76,081.2	4,259,547.3	38,124.3	449,935.8	3,571.70	25,670.90	25,333.9	30,319.6
Average per capita per day consumption		47.3		23.7		2.20	16.00		

horticulturalist subsistence. Eight percent by weight of all foods consumed by the Wopkaimin comes from animals. Men's work is primarily responsible for this high percentage because 46 percent of their yearly subsistence work is directed to procuring animals, compared to only 12 percent of women's work. Their combined subsistence work on average meets the nutritional needs of the population, taken as a whole.

On average, the Wopkaimin appear to have an adequate diet, but there are significant differences in diet and health between adult men and women. The Wopkaimin are stabilized at a very low population density because of the interrelationship of cultural, environmental, disease, and nutritional factors. A detailed analysis of population dynamics will be provided in another paper to illustrate how gender functions both ecologically and socially to enable the Wopkaimin to adjust to their environment.

2. "Land of milk and honey": the changing meaning of food to an Australian Aboriginal community

Janice Reid

Anyone who has lived with Australian Aborigines cannot help but be impressed by the pivotal position that food occupies in daily life and conversation. In Arnhem Land, in northern Australia, the economic significance, social uses, and symbolic value of food are apparent at the family hearth, in community processes, and in religious ritual. Indigenous foods of totemic importance are celebrated in the song cycles and dances of religious ceremonies. Animals and plant foods are represented in the paintings worked in orange ochers, white clay, and charcoal on sheets of bark or on the bodies of participants in major ritual performances. Life crises, such as birth and death, and periods of ritual transition such as male circumcisions or funeral ceremonies, are marked by selective prohibitions against the killing or eating of indigenous game. Bush and sea foods are energetically collected and shared diligently with kin. Reminiscences about trips to traditional lands are invariably couched in terms of the food collected, its variety, freshness, tastiness, and abundance. Food is, in short, not simply something to eat. It is a medium of exchange, a symbol of various relationships, and a means of expressing a range of emotions in concrete form.

This paper elaborates on the symbolic and expressive attributes of food among the Aborigines of northeastern Arnhem Land, Northern Territory. The people among whom this study was carried out live at Yirrkala and its small satellite communities, or outstations. Yirrkala is a predominantly Aboriginal township situated at the northeastern tip of Arnhem Land in the Northern Territory. To the north is the Arafura Sea; to the east, the Gulf of Carpentaria. The 900 or so Aborigines now living in the township and at its affiliated outstations belong to a group of "clans" – that is, exogamous,

This chapter is based on research carried out in Arnhem Land during a 12-month period in 1974–5 and during subsequent field trips in 1978 and 1979. The primary focus of the research was the change in the indigenous medical system of the Yolngu people of Yirrkala, but data were also collected on food practices and beliefs. The research was funded by the National Science Foundation (United States), the National Health and Medical Research Council, and the Australian Institute of Aboriginal Studies.

The author is grateful to Nancy Williams for generous advice and assistance based on her own studies among the Yolngu, and to Nangaypa Dhamarrandji, the Council, and the people of Yirrkala for their valued help and hospitality.

named patrilineal descent groups – designated the "Murngin" by Warner (1937/1958). But the people refer to themselves, and are now commonly referred to by others, as "Yolngu."

Most of the outstations, or as Yolngu prefer to call them, "homeland centres," have been established since the early 1970s. The move by many families and clan groups back to their own lands was a response to the stresses of settlement life, the threats to Yolngu culture of a sedentary and semiurban lifestyle, the growing problem of alcoholism, and the establishment of a bauxite mine and the town of Nhulunbuy near Yirrkala. The outstation movement, though fueled by Aboriginal aspirations, was facilitated here and in other remote areas of Australia by the government policy of self-determination introduced in 1972. By the end of the decade, there were 52 outstations in northeast Arnhem Land alone, relying for basic services on the main settlements and supplementing hunted and gathered foods with packaged foods such as sugar, tea, flour, oats, rice, and canned fruits from community stores.

The homelands of the Yolngu lie in a tropical, monsoonal area of Australia having well-marked wet and dry seasons. The vegetation of the area varies. Inland, especially on higher ground, is open bushland and savanna woodland. Several species of *Eucalyptus* are prominent. Some upland areas consist of wide expanses of grassland. The coastal vegetation is more luxuriant, consisting of pockets of dense monsoonal forest and, in the estuarine environment, expanses of mangrove swamps (Specht 1958a).

The edible resources of the different ecological zones are diverse and plentiful. In the rivers and sea are fish, mollusc, crustacea, turtle, and dugong. The waterholes and swamps team with wildfowl such as goose, duck, tern, and junglefowl. Eggs are plentiful in certain seasons. Meat is provided by kangaroo, emu, crocodile, wallaby, opossum, bandicoot, porcupine, and reptiles. Seasonal foods include wild fruits, berries, nuts, yams, and corms of the waterlily. In the dry season certain foods such as turtle eggs and cycad palm nuts (leached, ground, and baked into a bread called *ngäthu*) can feed large numbers of people. For the Aborigines of the tropical north, life was not, except in rare droughts, "a precarious and arduous struggle for existence." On the contrary, the Yolngu were, in company with other hunter-gatherers "the original affluent society" (Sahlins 1972), the caretakers of a rich and diverse land and the beneficiaries of its bounty.

Each Yolngu clan is territorially based and is corporate with respect to its ownership of defined tracts of land. Ideally each clan owns two major bounded estates, one coastal and one inland, which together furnish all the types of resources available in this part of Arnhem Land (Williams 1982). Each person has the right to exploit the resources belonging to his own and his mother's clan, but rights of use and access may also be granted by the related owners of other estates. The features and resources of the clan territories are held to have been created by the ancestral spirit *Wängarr* (or "dreamtime") beings. In the mythology some of these beings were transformed from humanlike spirit beings into natural species or land forms. Others became the distant human ancestors of people living today.

Prior to the establishment of Yirrkala and its neighboring missions, Milingimbi and Galiwin'ku (Elcho Island), the Yolngu were seminomadic and foraged in small groups of less than 100, often less than 50, people. The groups fluctuated in size according to the availability of food resources, often dispersing in the wet season and congregating for social contact and the performance of ceremonies in the dry season. Camps were optimally located for the hunting and gathering quest. The local group usually consisted of men linked by patridescent, their wives, unmarried daughters, mothers and other relatives, such as sisters' husbands, who joined the group for short periods of time (Warner 1937/1958; Thomson 1949; Peterson 1973; White 1979). Today the Yolngu live either in large communities or in family or clan groups at outstations on their clan lands.

The meanings of food

Studies of the use and role of food in human society suggest that nowhere is food value free. The ways in which it is obtained, prepared, presented, and shared are determined as much by cultural prescriptions and emotional associations as by the physiological need to eat (Richards 1932; Bennett 1943; Simoons 1961; Young 1971; de Garine 1972; Schieffelin 1977). It might be expected that this would be doubly true for any society whose food labors were not mediated by complex technology and for which the productivity of the land and the exigencies of the weather determined whether its members would flourish or starve.

The symbolic and social functions of food in Yolngu society are closely related to the economics of the hunter–gatherer life-style and the social organization of its members. These aspects of the gathering and distribution of goods are described below with reference to contemporary ethnographic observations of Yolngu society and the statements of individuals of the society. Food is discussed as a means of expressing social ties and relationships to land, as a marker of social roles and transitional states, and as an emerging dimension of identity in contemporary society – an idiom for statements about Aboriginal rights and integrity.

Social relationships

The giving and receiving of food is perhaps the most constant and explicit means of expressing social relationships in Aboriginal society. One of the more visible manifestations of this principle is the butchering and distribution of game according to kinship status and seniority. Such formalized rules of sharing have been widely described for hunter–gatherer societies (e.g., Damas, 1972, on three central Eskimo groups). Of the Ngatatjara of the Western Desert, Gould (1967:55) has written

The stated rule for the first phase in the division of meat is that in-laws of the spearman...get the first choice of pieces. Then it is the turn of the spearman's brothers to choose, older brother (*kuta*) first, then younger brothers (*malanypa*)....After relatives belonging to these categories have chosen their portions, the spearman may take whatever remains.

Among the Yolngu, the principles governing sharing are those of seniority (an elderly and respected person may receive a choice portion), and of close attention to one's obligations and the needs of all (generally close kin) who are present when food is divided and have a legitimate claim on the food.[1] The apportioning of a cooked turtle during the groundbreaking trip to a new coastal outstation site south of Yirrkala in 1974 illustrates the protocol governing the division of food. The members of the party consisted of the senior man of the landowning clan, his two wives and children, a widowed cousin (FZD) and her children, his uncle's (FB) son and family, his wives' father and family, and a group of related young, single men (i.e., four family groups and the unmarried men). On the second night there, a turtle was captured while laying her eggs on the beach, and was killed and eviscerated. The carapace (still containing the meat) was filled with hot stones, plugged with grass, and propped upright in the sand to cook. In the morning the three wives (or mothers) of the family groups brought containers and waited as the first wife of the senior man cut and distributed the meat. Preferential attention was given, through his wife, to the elderly father of the woman butchering the meat, but everyone at the camp, including the single men, received a precise and generous share of the meat.

The boundaries of the group that shares food vary according to the situation and the amount available. On outstations a substantial catch of fish or meat will be shared with the whole community (usually a set of closely related families). At Yirrkala where many related people live cheek by jowl

1 At Donydji, an inland outstation associated with Galiwin'ku, certain cuts of large animals may be distributed to specified categories of kin. For instance, when a kangaroo has been butchered, the hunter keeps the head, rump, and lower back muscles and gives one leg to his father-in-law and one to his older brother and others. The tail is said to go to the hunter's father, who shares it with his brother-in-law (the hunter's father-in-law); the kidney, heart, and lungs also go to the father, who shares it with his sons (the hunter's brothers); and the liver and stomach, to the hunter's father-in-law and sister's son(s). Similar rules of distribution pertain to the buffalo, emu, and other large game. The male recipients of the cuts and organs give meat to their wife or wives in descending order of seniority (i.e., the senior wife has priority and may distribute meat to junior wives). Thus there is a strictly recognized passage of meat through the local group (Neville White, personal communication).

I did not observe, or elicit, similar conventions among the Yolngu affiliated with Yirrkala, perhaps because I did not pursue the topic in depth, because the conventions have lapsed, because large game is not often caught (especially by people living at the main settlement of Yirrkala), or because such rules never existed. White has suggested (personal communication) that the relative scarcity of protein inland (compared with its abundance on the coast where fish, shellfish, and marine animals are plentiful) may have necessitated greater care and precision in the distribution of meat than is needed on the coast.

with one another, the limits to the food-sharing group are often less clear. Households are usually large and intermittently swelled by visitors who come and go each day. Often the social security benefits or wages of one or two people provide all of the household's food needs. The dependence on expensive store foods strains the financial resources of families. Sometimes food is dispersed sparingly across a large range of needy kin. More often it is consumed quietly by those present at a hearth when it is cooked. Underlying most presentations of food (Mauss 1969) is an expectation of delayed reciprocity. Although no one is denied access to another's resources, it is generally expected that households will procure their own food. Unreasonable or constant demands on other family groups for food earns the supplicants a poor name and places them in an invidious social position. As Thomson has written:

> The kinship pattern is a system of obligations and counter obligations, and even if he is content merely to discharge these to the extent necessary to maintain his prestige, a man must necessarily work hard. To receive gifts of food and other presents which demand return gifts, and not to reciprocate, places a man under an obligation, which to a normal individual is an unbearable blow to his pride. (1949:35)

However, it is also true that conspicuous generosity builds social (or perhaps nutritional) capital. It attracts praise and goodwill and ensures that the giver will have a legitimate claim in times of need on the fruits of other people's labors. The mental records of the gifts and obligations of others are rarely verbalized, but the time, depth and precision of this social ledger is apparent in the occasional complaints of people about a situational imbalance.

On one occasion, while visiting an outstation I made the mistake of taking a photograph of a boatload of people returning from a day's food collecting without asking permission. Nothing was said at the time, and I was mildly puzzled at being put on a vehicle returning to Yirrkala before a load of native yams had been distributed. An American (N.W.), who had, as is customary, been "adopted" into the landowning clan, stayed, and came back later. Many weeks later at Yirrkala, I was invited by my "sister" (i.e., a woman who had invited me to become a member of her own clan) to participate in the now rare collecting, hulling, leaching, and grinding of cycad palm nuts for the bread, *ngäthu*. She made and cooked three loaves and gave one to me. I unwrapped it, divided it into three portions, and wrapped each in paperbark. My "sister" wanted to know what I was doing. I explained that one loaf was for our friend, a white Australian school teacher, who was her honorary brother. She nodded approvingly. The other was for our friend, N.W. My "sister" was offended and annoyed. "But they (her adoptive clan) didn't give you yams when you were at their outstation!" At the time my Yolngu "sister" had been 50 miles away. Clearly the breach of protocol had been such that she had later heard about it and, saying nothing to me, entered it in her mental record.

The absolute outer limits of reciprocity are, in effect, the outer limits of a reasonable level of trust. Beyond one's clan and the group of clans linked to it by birth and marriage are alliances of clans with whom social contact is rare and food virtually never shared. At the occasional large ceremonial gatherings (such as funerals) when groups of several hundred may gather, an apparently large and homogeneous assembly in fact consists of a number of discrete extended family groups who create hearths, do their own cooking, and share only with close kin. Distant, classificatory kin have neither claims on nor obligations toward an individual. In fact, they may be suspected of being hostile and should not be given access to a person's food lest they "poison" it, or sing a spell over the food and cause his illness or death. One of the major anxieties of the relatives of chronic (usually middle-aged male) drinkers at Yirrkala who have died in recent years (Reid and Munung-gurr 1977) is that "stranger Yolngu" from other settlements who fly in to drink in Nhulunbuy poisoned their drinks. Latter-day sorcery includes, it is said, the use of "battery acid" or "aspro," which is slipped into the beers of unsuspecting victims at the hotel. Such ready access to a person's food or drink by a stranger was unknown in precontact (and prehotel) times.

Finally, certain dyadic relationships in Yolngu society are formalized by the giving and receiving of gifts. These may include utilitarian objects, sacred objects, and food (Thomson 1949). Traditionally a man had a woman bestowed upon him as a mother-in-law. Such contracts remain open to renegotiation. One woman told me that she had been betrothed as a child to a man from Elcho Island, but another man who was living at Yirrkala "was working for my parents and supporting them with turtle meat, other food, and wood, so they decided to give me to him" (see also Thomson 1949:43–5).

In summary an individual at Yirrkala is born into a social universe in which every known person is a close, distant, or classificatory relative. Throughout his or her life, these relationships are expressed and consolidated in secular and religious contexts by exchanges of services, goods, and food. In this way, the rights and duties that inhere in specific kinship relationships are given form, and the bases of future security and support are established. A person who failed to share, to distribute his or her resources to members of his kindred, would become a social isolate. For a Yolngu, social isolation is a denial of existence and an intolerable burden which no one would willingly incur.

Relationships to land

People routinely express and assess the beauties and quality of their traditional land in the idiom of food. More than once when I asked someone about the progress of his or her outstation, I was given a perfunctory description of the buildings and ventures underway, followed by a fond and proud declaration that there were "*darawa* [many] fish!" or that the area was, as one woman said, "*too* [i.e., abundantly] rich *ngäthawu* [in food]." As Williams (1982:136) has observed:

> Any Yolngu person, like Aborigines in other parts of Australia, is likely to begin a conversation about his or her land with an enthusiastic recitation of its natural resources. . . . A young man, for example, who had been attending school for several years in a city in the southern part of Australia, returned to Yirrkala in 1975 and assumed a position of leadership in the mission organization. He began to plan the development of a settlement on his own clan land some eighty miles from Yirrkala, land about which he had been educated but which he knew only recently from his own experience. I asked him, after his initial planning visits to his clan land, what it was like. He answered with great feeling, "It is the land of milk and honey."

The emotional tone of statements about the productivity and diversity of the resources of one's clan land implies far more than a well-stocked larder. Such statements are expressions of pride, of identity, and of ownership of the land.

The intimate association between food and land is manifest in the granting or withholding of rights to hunt and gather. Thus the rights of access to the food of a particular estate are clear markers of a person's membership in a certain clan and the relationships between his clan and other clans. A person has the automatic right to hunt or gather on his or her clan's land. A man will also have a legitimate claim on the food of his mother's clan's land. Other categories of kin may directly, or indirectly (as by announcing an intention to go hunting in the presence of the owners) seek permission to harvest food. One would rarely expect to be refused permission if all the customary courtesies had been observed. Williams (1982:151) has written: "In Yolngu society. . . to control land is not to enjoy it exclusively but rather to exercise the right, which is at the same time an obligation, to allocate rights in its resources to others."

The obligation to share the land and its food can, however, be overridden by other considerations. Owners have the right to veto the harvesting of certain animal species if doing so would contravene certain religious injunctions or existing restrictions on the killing of certain animals. After a death, for instance, a temporary ban may be placed on the killing of an animal, such as a crocodile, of special, totemic significance to the dead person and his clan. Both women and men of the clan have the right to exercise this veto.

Where unlimited rights are given to people to enter and hunt on a territory not their own, they are expected to observe the integrity of the land and not abuse it in any way. Again this principle is more apparent in the breach than the observance. On one occasion I accompanied a group on a visit to some oyster beds (a long platform at high-tide mark, thickly encrusted with large, succulent oysters) on Yirritja moiety land.[2] I was filling my billy-can with gutted flesh when one of the women brought some grass from the cliff top and set it alight on a section of an oyster bed, thus cooking small patches and making it easier to extract the flesh from the open oysters. This was clearly contrary to Yolngu principles of conservation. The senior man present, the leader of a clan of the Dhuwa moiety, turned and admonished me lightheartedly not to tell his wife (who belonged to the clan that owned the land) what we had done when we returned to camp, or she would be angry.

If familiarity with the land enables a person to exploit and conserve its resources effectively and wisely, the land's familiarity with the people who live on it will also influence their success in procuring food. Williams (1982) has described the guardedness, verging on hostility, that emanates from the land and the spirit beings that animate it. The land and its resident spirits are jealous of their resources and will not yield them up to a stranger. When a prominent and senior clan and community leader from Yirrkala visited the southern coast of New South Wales for the first time, he was not disappointed or surprised to have caught no fish on his first day there. He explained that the land did not know him yet and would probably be more generous tomorrow (N. Williams, personal communication). A person not only is an owner and custodian of his land and its resources, he also has a relationship with the land and *Wängarr* spirits in the land, similar to his relationship with other human beings. He must exercise caution and restraint and take care not to offend the spirits by trespassing in sacred areas or by other actions.

When people of the Manggalili clan were first living at their new out-station, the infant grandchild of the clan head became ill. The man later explained that the child's mother had sharpened a digging stick and had scratched her leg with it. The major female *Wängarr* spirit-being of that area "didn't know who she was or why she was doing this. She got angry because in that place you're not allowed to use a digging stick for ordinary purposes, like digging yams, because she used it [in mythical times] when she was mourning, to cut her head [a ritual expression of grief]." As a result the baby became ill. Its life was saved by the clan head, who made a tea of the salty wild Yirritja type of honey (*yikaki*), washed the infant with the solution, and gave him a little to drink. The honey, he explained, is a sort of "sugarbag medicine," which is imbued with the power (*ganydjarr*) inherent in the ground on which grows the grass on which the bees feed. This power derives from creation activities of the *Wängarr* spirit beings.[3]

---

2 All Yolngu clans and the people belonging to them, along with the land and its plants and animals, belong to one of two moieties, Yirritja or Dhuwa.
3 I am grateful to the head of the Manggalili clan, to Howard Morphy, who worked intensively with him, and to his brother's daughter, for this information.

It is unclear to what extent concepts of health and healing were linked traditionally to land and food. The instance cited above suggests that the sacred power of the land can be utilized to cure illness. The head of the Manggalili also attributed a prophylactic effect to certain powerful foods. He said that in order to stay healthy he had drunk sugarbag (honey) tea himself every morning, bathed in the brackish lagoon which also has sacred associations (and was described as having power "like a *marrnggitj*" or traditional healer), and washed in and drank the water in which "special" rock oysters were boiled or steeped each day. He avowed that "when all the family went to Djarrakpi, they were skinny, but when they came back, they had shiny long hair and round faces."

Whether they are based on indigenous concepts of good health, on the teachings of Europeans, or on their own observations, the statements of other Yolngu suggest that they perceive a clear and causal association between outstation life on traditional land, and diet and health. The outstation diet is essentially a syncretic diet, a combination of fresh Yolngu produce and imported staples from the Yirrkala store. In 1974, the leader of an inland outstation in northeastern Arnhem Land listed the foods that are common daily fare: eight species of freshwater fish, the corms of the waterlily, sugarbag (native honey), wild yams, kangaroo, emu, goanna, blue-tongued lizard, blanket lizard, long-necked tortoise, flour, Uncle Toby's Oats, Cornflakes, Weetbix, rice, sugar, tea, syrup, powdered milk, and jam.

Improvements in the health of children and old people – the at-risk groups, in particular – have been noted both by visiting health personnel and by outstation leaders. A Djapu leader remarked in 1977, shortly after his outstation, Wandawuy, had been established, that certain of the young children used to be constantly in and out of hospital when they lived in Yirrkala. At the outstation, however, the honey, fish, shellfish, and other fresh land and seafoods "cure" them. One prominent ritual leader said that

> when the old men living at the outstations come to Yirrkala, they get sickness every time. When they go back to their homeland and taste many different foods, they die at the right time [that is, not prematurely]. The young people always change when they go to the outstations and become strong. But even when people go to the outstations, tobacco, sugar, and tea will follow the people and make them sick in their land. But we get hunted food, bush honey, wild meat, and many other foods. When I go there, I have oysters, crabs, fish, turtle eggs, and stingray, and it makes me happy and strong and opens my life.

To summarize, the getting and the sharing of indigenous foods are intimately bound up with sentiments about land, with a sense of knowledge and competence in utilizing and husbanding its resources, with rights in land, and the duty to grant and control access to it, and with feelings of physical and emotional well-being.

Social roles

Food is also a key dimension of female and male roles in Yolngu society and of a person's self-esteem as a capable individual, a woman or man, a mother or father.

Economic and social roles within the society were (and continue to be) distinct and complementary. Prior to European contact, the women gathered vegetable foods and small animals or seafoods, whereas the men hunted larger game. As has been found for some other hunter–gatherer groups and elsewhere in Australia, the contribution of the women to the daily diet was both more reliable and probably greater than that of the man.

Nonetheless, for both sexes productivity, skill and knowledge of the local ecology are valued and necessary skills. Adults have a prodigious knowledge of their own land and its resources and take pride in exploiting these effectively and providing amply for dependents. White's (1979) research among the Yolngu of the inland outstation, Donydji, reveals the depth and detail of Yolngu understanding of the location and seasonal cycles of vegetable and animal foods, and the highly elaborated vocabulary that describes natural features and ecological zones and for which the English language has no precise counterparts.

The other side of the coin of the possession of knowledge is the transmission of it. Education in seasons, crops, game habits, hunting techniques, and the home range was perhaps the bulk of the knowledge acquired by a young child. The education of daughters by women and sons by men was a continuing affirmation of their mastery of their home territory and the value of their knowledge and life experiences. The memories that one middle-aged woman of Yirrkala retains of her childhood center largely on the food quest and related paraphernalia:

> My mother taught me to make a digging stick when I was young, and dillybags [woven from handmade bark string]. You cut down the tree, get the fiber, roll it, and chew it until it is soft and put it in the sun to dry. When you make the dillybag, you put it in the wet sand to keep it workable. I also learned to make [feather and string, ritual] armbands, headdresses, fishing line, turtle line and harpoon [ceremonial] string, and to use colored parrot and white eagle feathers. My mother taught me all the different foods – yams, fruit, oysters, clams, crabs, all the names of all the fish, how to make *ngäthu*, where to find wild honey and turtle eggs, to collect [corms of the waterlily], how to spear stingray and large fish...I spent a lot of time when I was young, out hunting.

Hamilton (1975) has convincingly argued that the establishment of missions and government settlements in Arnhem Land and the transition from a nomadic, food-gathering economy to a cash-based, European economy stripped women of the status traditionally afforded them as independent, economic producers. If, she writes, "women as food-producers are the means of production, and therefore of intrinsic value to men, the transfer to a cash economy immediately makes them redundant" (p. 173) and "a burden on their menfolk instead of a valuable asset" (p. 177). Further, when Maningrida, where Hamilton worked, was established, efforts were made, in keeping with the European cultural stereotypes of the male role, to employ men, not women. The inappropriate concept of the nuclear family as the consumption unit in which the husband supports the wife and children was used by whites in their administration of jobs and settlement rules. This created a profound imbalance in power and in the distribution of resources and subverted the Aboriginal mother's self-image and economic independence.

At Yirrkala the mission policy was somewhat different. The founding missionary, Wilbur Chaseling (personal communication) established fruit and vegetable gardens and building programs, encouraged people to visit or even remain on their own land, and "made a rule from the very beginning of employing as many women as men." The men worked with picks, shovels, and axes, clearing and digging the ground for future crops. The women engaged in lighter work, planting and weeding the crops and collecting grass, ash, and leaf mold from the bush: "Work was available for anyone who wanted it." Chaseling also attempted to establish a market for women's carvings and men's bark paintings. Nothing except medicine was given away. European staple foods ("three meals a day") and material goods in the early years were exchanged for Yolngu labor and craft.

In the 1950s, the distribution of free rations and free communal feeding for children, common in other remote areas, were instituted. Both ceased in 1971. Income from salaries, pensions, and child endowment are now used to buy food from Yirrkala store and the shopping complex in the newly established mining town of Nhulunbuy, 20 kilometers away by road. Nevertheless, as long as people remain at Yirrkala, critical aspects of adult male and female roles – their ability to provide for their own needs and those of their children by hunting and collecting – are attenuated.

At the same time, the experience and skills of a lifetime, once conscientiously transmitted to the children, have become less relevant. From the 1950s onward, Western schooling has been available, and children have acquired the skills of literacy and numeracy which older people neither possessed nor could transmit. Children learn traditional subsistence skills intermittently, generally at outstations or on the weekends and during irregular trips away from the settlement. Even then it is remarkable how early in their lives children learn skills of survival. In 1976, a mother became separated from her four- and five-year-old children while walking from an outstation to Yirrkala, 160 kilometers away. Police and Yolngu search parties found the two after eight days. They had survived in low-lying coastal country in the dry season, by eating beetles, fruits, and nuts and by digging for water. The police sergeant in charge of the search commented (in a social context in which police are not often given to sympathetic comments about Aborigines): "It's one of the great feats of human endurance...no child of European stock could have done it" (Anonymous 1976).

The outstation movement has, to an extent, countered the more extreme imbalances in experience and knowledge between young and old. In these Aboriginally controlled communities, the leaders actively recognize the value of the education of children if their aspirations for the outstations are to be realized. An independent outstation needs Aboriginal teachers, health workers, radio operators, and store managers. All of these positions require a Western education. On the other hand, daily hunting and gathering trips and the ceremonial revival occurring in northeastern Arnhem Land have enabled adult men and women to reassert traditional roles. In 1974, the leader of Gangan outstation told me:

> Groups are going out [to establish outstations] because of the township...[Nhulunbuy]. They feel some things about it are good and some bad. I feel that it pulls people away so that they lose their culture and mix with European culture. Some parts of it are bad like drinking, stealing and gambling. The school, the hospital, and work are good for people....
>
> I disagree with having people walking [around] and bludging. If men and boys are on the clan land, they should come and work together. This is the Yolngu way of life...Young people will be employed in the office and operating the radio. We're also thinking of running cattle and a sawmill. We also have a [large, vegetable] garden....
>
> Before [traditionally] we didn't work [at cash labor]. There was only hunting by the men to get kangaroo and turtle, and the women collected yams and made dillybags. I say no, no, no to the government, church, and strangers. I don't want people to come and try to tell us what to do. Now we have to practise and learn by ourselves. Not only with the money, but also the living, because before we lived mixed together with a different culture and a different Law. We want to talk and think about it ourselves without the Balanda [Europeans] coming and telling us.

Transitional and dangerous states

Many societies impose food prohibitions during life crises, during rites of passage, and during certain physiological changes. In Yolngu society, food restrictions for women obtained at menarche and during menstruation, pregnancy, and daughter or son's early years. Various rules govern the types of foods that can be eaten by initiates and, in some cases, by their female relatives and by participants in certain major ceremonies. Others specify the categories of kin who may not take food from a person who is in a state of pollution as the result of a serious illness or of handling the body of a dead person during a funeral.

During major initiation ceremonies for men and boys a variety of food taboos are in effect. For instance, while the preparations and ceremonies for the circumcision of young boys are in progress, they may not eat sacred (*maḏayin*) foods. On the day of the circumcision, the novitiates, their sisters, and their mothers can eat and drink together early in the morning but then may not eat or drink until the final "freeing" ceremony at which the restrictions are lifted. Young men are also subject to restrictions on eating key totemic animals during major rites of revelation.

It was suggested to me by several different people that some of the middle-aged men had contracted leprosy as the result of participation in the Gunapipi ceremony between 25 and 30 years ago at Yirrkala. I was told that, as this ceremony is not native to the area (having been imported by clans to the south and west), many of the Yirrkala participants did not know the rules governing behavior and diet connected with it. Although they were told to eat only fish, animals, or reptiles that contained no fat – *makiny, djana'miriuw* ("without fat") – some either did not listen or did not hear, ate fatty animals, and now have leprosy.

Food prohibitions were particularly important during a girl's first menstruation. This important life event was usually marked by a small ceremony conducted by close male kin and a period of isolation during which she was attended by her grandmother (her mother's mother, MM) and other close female relatives. During these few days, according to one middle-aged informant:

> I was not allowed to eat fish, kangaroo meat or turtle [i.e., hunted food]. If I ate it the man who caught it would have got hurt when he went hunting again. I was allowed to eat oysters, yams, *rakay* [the corms of the waterlily], wild fruit, and shellfish. When my period finished, I was painted in ocher from the waist to the neck by my *märi* [MM's brother] and husband. My *märi* [MM] then made a fire, put *girrigirri* [the inner bark of the stringy bark tree] on it and a stone for me to sit on. The smoke came up all around me. I also had to bend down and put my mouth over the smoke and drink hot water in which *girrigirri* had been boiled. After three days the paint had come off and I was allowed to wash. Then I was free to talk to everybody and eat what I wanted.

In the years since the establishment of Yirrkala, the ceremony to mark the onset of puberty in women has been performed less frequently. It has probably not been practiced routinely for 15 years. Similarly, observance of dietary restrictions by young women is much less rigorous now than in past. Several older women lamented their carelessness and attributed various misfortunes to their failure to observe these rules. Traditionally women who were menstruating would not eat food shot or speared by a male relative until their period had ended and they had smeared themselves with red ocher. If they ate part of a man's catch, he would have an accident the next time he went out hunting. It was said of one man whose legs were badly scarred that he had been attacked by a shark because a girl who was menstruating ate part of a kingfish he had speared.

During pregnancy, women were also forbidden to eat certain foods, particularly large game animals with sacred associations. The harelip of a young boy at Yirrkala was attributed to the fact that his mother ate emu during her pregnancy. The complexity of the traditional dietary prescriptions is apparent in one woman's description of the restrictions she observed for her three children:

> When I was pregnant, I couldn't eat sacred animals, such as crocodile [*baru*], emu [*maluwiya*], brolga [*gulurrku*], *madayin* [sacred], porcupine [*djirrmana*], bush turkey [*buwata*], turtle [*malarrka*] and its eggs [*mapu*] – this one is very dangerous and only women with grown children are allowed to eat it – the fish called *wutji*, and *wäpa*. If a mother eats *wutji*, her baby will be blind, and if she eats *wäpa*, its skin will be soft, not strong.
>
> However the expectant mother can eat kangaroo [*garrtjambal*], wallaby [*mulpiya*], eggs of the goose [*gurrumatji*] and duck [*mothali*], *maypal* [shellfish], yams, *rakay* [the corm of the water reed], and other fish. After my baby had been born and was still little, I could eat *djindjalma* [mud crabs], eggs [*mapu*], yams [such as *djithama, gangurri,* and *yukuwa*], but not *katabanga* [buffalo], *dalimbo* [sea clam], *mekawu* [rock oysters], kangaroo, wallaby, fish, or *malarrka*. Once the baby is two months old, it is all right to eat these. We used to do this, but now the woman forget it and that's why their children get sick. At two months of age the mother put red paint all over herself and this freed her to eat all these things, besides *dalimbo* and oysters. If she ate these, they would go into her milk and make the baby sick.
>
> I have only been eating wallaby, *garrtjambal*, and *katabanga* [with other, gathered foods] while the children have been growing up. Until they are grown and married, I won't eat any of the *madayin* [sacred] foods. My brother shot an emu when my sister had a two-week-old baby. She took some meat and gave me the legs, but I refused them. I won't eat these animals because I understand the danger of them even when my children have grown. So I left the leg with her, and she ate it. She also ate *djirrmana*. It's because of this that her little boy has not grown and has stayed sickly all the time.

If a person has been seriously injured or ill, certain relatives may not accept food or cigarettes from him (or her) or use his utensils. Informants' specifications of just which kin, and whether or not restrictions extend to classificatory relatives, vary (and need not be detailed here), but the underlying principle is that the patient and his possessions are in a state of pollution and that his relatives would themselves be polluted by accepting food from him or having physical contact with him or his effects. The men who handle a dead body during a funeral (and whose hands are painted to the wrist with white ocher to mark their state) must observe similar behavioral restrictions. Other relatives may observe specific limitations on their diet after a death, either by fasting (a personal choice as a response to bereavement) or by avoiding totemic meat or fish (such as wallaby, turtle, large fish, etc.). In all cases the restrictions are lifted by a purification ritual called *barng* (or series of *barng*) and/or a *liyalupthun* or washing ceremony in a sand sculpture representing a certain sacred area of land. The word "free" is commonly used to explain the effect of the *barng* and *liyalupthun*. They liberate individuals from the safeguards automatically contingent upon contact with dangerous or polluting aspects of life or death.

A major characteristic of most of the states or stages during which certain foods are proscribed is the socially marginal and physically dangerous condition of a person who has shed blood (the circumcised novitiate, the menstruating or recently confined woman, or the injured or very sick person). Blood is variously regarded as a source of power, of danger, or of strength. When contained or controlled, it gives life and power; when lost or uncontrolled, it constitutes a source of danger. Painting with red ocher, the *liyalupthun*, and the *barng* all mark the end of a stage or state, restore the strength lost when the blood was shed, and "free" kin to interact normally with each other again and share food and possessions in the customary way.

Identity

The 1970s in Australia was a decade of change and of conflict for Aborigines. Land rights, crises over mining on Aboriginal land, self-determination, and the outstation movement all became prominent issues after 1971. In terms of these developments, Yirrkala received a comparatively early education in the realities of Australian business, law, and politics. Alarmed by the plans to mine bauxite on their land, Aboriginal leaders appealed unsuccessfully to the national parliament in the early 1960s for recognition of their ownership of the land. Between 1969 and 1971, leaders of the affected landowning clans were complainants in a suit for land rights (Milirrpum and Others v. Nabalco Pty. Ltd. and the Commonwealth of Australia, 1971). Though they lost the case, the Aboriginal Land Rights (Northern Territory) Act of 1976, which was proclaimed in 1977 and gave the Aboriginal people of Arnhem Land legal title to the Arnhem Land Reserve, was partly a result of the Yirrkala case and the publicity it caused. By the early 1970s, a mine, a processing plant, and a European town of 4,000 people (Nhulunbuy or Gove) had been established on leased lands near the Aboriginal community.

The town and mine, as the Aboriginal leaders expressly feared, have come to dominate much of life at Yirrkala. Within a decade, alcohol consumption by Aborigines in the town and settlement has become a major issue.

Though the Aborigines own the land, they express fears that the mining company, Nabalco, may want to excise greater portions of it, that the Act will be changed to limit their control over access and use, and that Europeans from Nhulunbuy will increasingly encroach on this land, in boats and four-wheel-drive vehicles, using it as their playground. The outstation movement was substantially a response to the social disruption and the threat of the European presence.

Though the Yirrkala community has suffered in some ways, it has prevailed in others. This is in part due to the strength and flexibility of Yolngu culture and to its capacity for integration of new elements and adjustment to social and technological change. The clan leaders are assertive, firm, and astute in their dealings with Europeans. The Yolngu are unshaken in their conviction that their "Law" (body of religious knowledge and prescriptions) and their claims to jurisdiction over their own affairs are legitimate and worthy of recognition. But they also, in their actions and priorities, assert the right to enter selectively the Western economy and adopt those elements of Western culture that they regard as attractive or useful.

In the context of social change, food seems a minor issue – not warranting a place beside land and Law. But there are signs that Yolngu food is, because of this very context, emerging as one of a few distinctively Aboriginal provinces and is being used both as a means of achieving rapprochement with Europeans and of expressing conflict. Morphy (1980) describes the customary presentations of bark paintings to departing or distinguished Europeans by the people of Yirrkala. He attributes to the Yolngu two motives in this practice: to teach Europeans about Aboriginal culture and to assert the value of the things that they give. With the gift comes the unverbalized message that the people have retained their identity and that the things that they value, in particular their land which the paintings represent, are different from the things that Europeans value.

For perhaps similar motives, Yolngu families often take new European staff, particularly interested school teachers and health staff, camping. The major feature of these trips is food collecting, the majority of it by the Yolngu. With the permission of the land owners, European school children from Nhulunbuy and Canberra, accompanied by students from Yirrkala School and the Aboriginal secondary college (Dhupuma) and adult supervisors, have spent holidays at outstations near Yirrkala, camping and learning about and eating the foodstuffs to be procured there. While the ideas of camping and fishing are close to the hearts (if not always the experience) of most Australians, the types of food collected are often quite unfamiliar to them, and they do not know how or where to collect it or how to prepare it. Thus food is used by the Yolngu to establish good relations with Europeans in a context in which their superior knowledge and skills are clearly demonstrated to the newcomers.

Food has also been a focus of conflict between Yolngu and Europeans. Outstation residents worry about European pleasure craft and fishing vessels that enter the coastal waters adjacent to their land, though their protests to the authorities are not very effective. The Yolngu of Milingimbi have applied to the Northern Territory Land Rights Commission for permission to close off the waters within two miles of their community, since fishing boats have been sighted at sea and in the rivers on their land. Much concern has been generated by outbreaks of acute food poisoning among people both at Yirrkala and Nhulunbuy. It has been diagnosed as ciguatera fish poisoning. Although Nabalco Proprietary Ltd. denies responsibility, the poisoning is uniformly attributed by the people of Yirrkala to the polluting effect of the plant's effluent on the seas around the area. They cite in evidence their observation that it was first seen in 1972, the year the plant commenced operations, and had never been known by the Yolngu before that time.

Perhaps the most effective recent use of a food – primarily because of its status as a totemic animal – to exact recognition of Aboriginal rights from Europeans occurred after a crocodile attacked and killed a European skin diver near Yirrkala. The crocodile was hunted down by police, killed near its lair, and then placed for public viewing on the oval in Nhulunbuy to "quieten local residents" who were talking about shooting all crocodiles in the area. This action evoked a well-publicized and critical response from a leader of the Gumatj clan. The crocodile is the major totem of his clan, and a ban on killing crocodiles had been in effect since his father died a month before. Subsequently officers of the Parks and Wildlife Section of the Northern Territory Conservation Commission came to the peninsula to survey the crocodile population. A crocodile was netted and injured in the process. When the clan leader heard that the crocodile was to be destroyed, he protested strongly and Parks and Wildlife flew the crocodile to Darwin at a reported cost of $1,500 where unsuccessful efforts were made to save its life. The body of the crocodile was given to the museum in Darwin, which undertook to stuff the animal and return it to Yirrkala. I was told by members of the family of the deceased that they planned to put the crocodile on his grave. (In 1981 the family was still awaiting its return.) (M. Chalmers, personal communication; Anonymous 1980).

These incidents all suggest that Yolngu food is acquiring a new dimension of meaning as Aborigines attempt to manage and express their relationships with Europeans. As an idiom for rapprochement and conflict, Yolngu food has limitations, but it also has clear advantages: It is visible and well understood by both groups (unlike the "Law"), and because it is unambiguously different from European food, it enables Yolngu to highlight the ethnic boundary that separates Europeans and Aborigines in a positive and sometimes advantageous way.

Conclusion

Contemporary Aborigines are sometimes characterized as nutritional dullards who are content to subsist on a diet of damper, tea, and tinned meat.

Betty Meehan (1982b), working with the Anbarra of Arnhem Land, has amply documented that the Aborigines of this area of Australia are connoisseurs of fresh, tasty, and skillfully cooked food, and have a fine sense of balance of the meat, fish, and vegetable components. In this paper it has been suggested that indigenous foods are dear not only to the palates of the Yolngu; food, particularly the resources of the sea and land, is hedged about with meanings and feelings that highlight its central place in Yolngu life and thought. The social and symbolic uses of food are basic to Yolngu conceptions of self, of the stages of the life cycle, of relationships with others, and of ties to the land.

3. Dietary Change among Cook Islanders in New Zealand

Thomas K. Fitzgerald

Nutritional problems, according to Clements and Rogers (1967:200), arise when people overeat (overnutrition or obesity), do not eat enough (undernutrition), or eat an unbalanced diet deficient in some essential nutrients (malnutrition). The type and extent of nutritional disorders are determined by a combination of factors, not the least of which are the human and social factors. These intrinsic human factors have too often been neglected in traditional nutritional studies.

Borderline nutritional problems and obestity are characteristic of the Pacific (McCarthy 1956). The main causes of these disabilities are most often poor selection and unsatisfactory use of food rather than a consequence of poverty or lack of food per se, as is true in many other parts of the world (Holmes 1956). Ignorance about food selection and food use is intensified in situations of rapid change, for example, with the movement of islanders to New Zealand. As these changes produce both desirable and undesirable effects on health status, it is as well to study such migrant populations and their dietary adaptations.

The intent of this paper is to document and describe some of the dietary patterns of Cook Islanders living in Wellington in the North Island of New Zealand, specifically how their food habits are influenced by economic, social, and cultural conditions. Emphasis is on attitudes and values associated with food use rather than on strictly nutritional (nutrient) considerations. Looking at how a migrant group adjusts to new food habits leads one to challenge some of the well-entrenched stereotypes about "islanders" and how they eat, while providing background data for the interpretation of medical and paramedical problems only tangentially related to nutrition. No claim is made that Cook Islanders are representative of all island groups, but it is hoped that this brief ethnography of their dietary patterns in New Zealand will provide at least in terms of broad theoretical issues some insights into the general mechanics of nutritional adaptation in situations of migration and change.

This chapter first appeared in 1980 in *Social Science Information* 19(4/5):805–32, and is included in this volume with permission.

The communities, the sample, and the research methods

Cook Islanders in Wellington form not one community but several, with distinctive eating habits potentially characteristic of each. Two communities are contrasted here: the inner-city Newtown community with the suburban residential neighborhood in the Hutt.

Newtown, an inner-city core community and the oldest part of Wellington, is essentially a receiving area for new immigrants, a kind of temporary "stop-off" neighborhood for a number of migrants, including islanders. Population is cosmopolitan, racially mixed, and generally of a lower socioeconomic status (Salmond 1975:21).

As migrants become more "integrated" or established in New Zealand society, they tend to move to low-cost housing in the suburban areas outside Wellington (e.g., in the Hutt). These "instant" communities are in many ways like Newtown except that they typically lack a certain sense of "community," family ethos, and are not well endowed with social amenities or services. By contrast with Newtown, the island community in the Hutt is more heavily Catholic, with a higher frequency of multiracial marriages, and a neighborhood more solidly middle-class. Trying to categorize all Cook Islanders as a homogeneous group is surely simplistic. In this study, then, two Cook Island communities in Wellington were examined to see how (if at all) they differ in terms of eating habits.

The sample consisted of 62 households (31 in Newtown, 31 in the Hutt). There was a slightly larger number of female respondents than males; the average age was 41. These two groups, classwise, ranged from lower to middle, with more low-income families in the inner-city community of Newtown. Employment rates fluctuated for both groups. Island men tended to occupy positions mainly in manufacturing, construction, and transport. Island women often worked part-time as office cleaners and the like. Seventy-five percent of these respondents declared that they had received only a primary school education. The average number of years spent in New Zealand was 15 for islanders in Newtown and 18 for those in the Hutt.

In this study, both traditional and modern techniques of anthropological fieldwork were employed (Fitzgerald 1977a, 1977b). This included an orally administered questionnaire as the principal research tool. Questions dealt with consumption patterns, food preferences, the way in which various foods were seen as contributing to health, and so on. This information enabled the correlation of food habit information with sociological data, to see, for example, whether there may be differences in eating patterns between Catholics and Protestants, between persons married within the group or to someone other than a Cook Islander, and between individuals from small islands in the Pacific as opposed to larger ones. Besides these formal approaches, many questions only tangentially related to food habits were asked, for example, about gardening, attitudes toward traditional foods, "taboo foods," sharing practices, and ritual food observances such as feasts. Thus field-work involved both casual conversations and more structured approaches.

Professional stereotypes and health education

In trying to reach a minority group through nutrition education, one of the most persistent problems is first to break through the folklore being presented by health care workers about the local population (Freedman 1958). Stereotypes about the *supposed* cultural habits of minorities can act as barriers to further communication. Preliminary to this research, therefore, I interviewed doctors, nurses, and other health professionals who deal more or less regularly with islanders in Wellington in order to see how they viewed this group and its nutritional needs. There is a lot to be learned from talking with people who have worked closely with a population over a long period of time. Even when some of their perceptions are more in the realm of "folklore," these notions can stimulate the researcher to ask more pertinent questions.

From the responses of health care professionals, I was able to put together some general statements about the health (especially nutritional) status of the island population in Wellington. The three most common medical (possibly nutritionally related) problems observed among these islanders were obesity, childhood anemias, and various infections (sores, eczemas, and so on). Less frequently mentioned conditions included respiratory complications, stomach disorders, poor dietary habits, gout, and drinking. Although nearly all the health care workers thought they *should* reach the islander in his/her own cultural setting, surprisingly few (especially among the doctors) said they accomplished this goal. One physician commented: "This is the biggest problem, and we need trained Polynesians to go amongst the Polynesian families to give help and advice." Special attention to nutrition education was not common among these professionals. When nutrition was part of the health care package, primary emphasis was given to infant care or, broadly, family nutrition.

From these interviews, tentative generalizations about the nutritional status of islanders in Wellington emerged. First, gross malnutrition was not felt to be a problem in New Zealand. When there was a nutritional concern, it seemed to be with overnutrition or obesity. The attitude of health professionals toward the anemias was somewhat more puzzling, explanations ranging from poor maternal reserves of iron or low absorption in the presence of infections, to deficiencies in the diet. Respiratory disorders and infections were tentatively linked to the islanders' intolerance of cow's milk (Tonkin 1974:40). Certainly, there was felt to be a need for more awareness of the migrants' cultural stresses in adapting to new foods and of the overall adjustment problems associated with migration. These health care workers wanted also to see more nutritional counseling and more community outreach, for it was commonly believed that islanders as a group do not make maximum use of the health services available (Salmond 1975:73).

In short, most of these health professionals admitted knowing relatively little about the actual dietary habits of islanders in Wellington. Some of them held a number of misconceptions about islanders and their food habits that could only hinder the stated aims of nutrition education and professional/patient communication. In one way or another, almost all had some food-related stereotypes about Pacific Islanders, adding up to a summary impression of islanders as a migrant group who have little knowledge of how Europeans in New Zealand manage a home; who are clannish and live in crowded quarters; and who cannot generally adapt well to European foods. They are viewed as people who eat at odd times of day, and hence their children may go to school before the breakfast hour and not be provided with a school lunch. Further, a few of these professionals stated categorically that islanders know nothing about gardening, do not eat "vegies" (greens) like other New Zealanders, and instead prefer only root vegetables (starches such as taro or green bananas) or else "takeout" foods like fish and chips (Fitzgerald 1978b). Hence, so the stereotype goes, all islanders are obese or overweight. Furthermore one gains the impression that they alone have a drinking problem. One nurse put it this way: "They [islanders] have caught'en on to our bad habits before they have caught'en on to our good."

It is the purpose of this paper to examine these beliefs in some detail in the context of the 62 household interviews with Cook Island families living in Wellington.

Consumption patterns

Meal times and eating patterns

Many Cook Islanders in Wellington still roughly follow the island habit of light-to-no breakfast, with "snacking" during the day, followed by a large afternoon or evening meal. This focus on one main meal may be reflective of a plantation work schedule in the islands. A family would prepare the earth oven before going off to the plantations so that food was cooking while they worked, and they would have a big *kai* (meal) upon returning home. As the occupational structure changes, food habits are altered accordingly.

The difference between residents of the Hutt and those of Newtown, in this respect, are minimal; both show some changes in their eating patterns. Close to 38 percent of all respondents take meals essentially "European style," that is, three meals a day and, less frequently, morning and afternoon "teas." Some people work in factories where a midday meal is served: This opportunity is often seen as an excuse to skip breakfast. Also children returning home from school may institute a pattern of afternoon "snacking." In the case of mixed marriages, food habits often change in the direction of the

European spouse; the children of such unions tend to have a "Europeanizing" effect.

The majority in this sample, though, clearly had a more mixed dietary schedule, a large number taking only two meals a day. In this case, breakfast was the meal most frequently skipped, often in the belief that this practice helps in weight loss. When breakfast is sacrificed, snacking may become more significant, thereby potentially contributing to weight gain. Another reason given for skipping breakfast was the early hour at which many people began work.

About one-quarter of the persons in this study simply could not describe a typical meal pattern, as there were no regular times for eating. The island dictum is "eat when you are hungry" or when food is available. The perishable nature of island foodstuffs has made accumulation and saving difficult. When food was abundant, one feasted; in times of hurricane or famine, there was necessary restraint. This feast-or-famine mentality is a deeply engrained psychological reaction to food use that has shown remarkable persistence. Though there are obvious changes at the family level, in both form and content, the pattern has remained surprisingly unaltered at the individual level.

Morning meal patterns

The notion of "meal patterns" was usually viewed from a family perspective, but most respondents saw the question about breakfast as largely an individual experience.[1] A typical morning meal, both in the Hutt and in Newtown, was light: a cup of tea/coffee and toast or Weetbix (dry cereal); occasionally an egg, and frequently leftover foods. The use of leftovers is significant in the Cook Island dietary. "Cup of tea and whatever food is left over from last night, that's our way," one island woman explained. Many adult respondents – especially women – skip breakfast altogether. The reasons given are the irregular times for eating and work schedules. Although a majority of these adults have either a very light breakfast or else none at all, it is not true that their children regularly go to school without anything to eat. In a study of the multiethnic school at Newtown, it was found, contrary to stereotype, that not a single island child came to school routinely without something to eat beforehand. Their meal often consisted of different foods (taro, leftover meats, etc.), but such a meal was not necessarily poorly balanced nutritionally (Fitzgerald 1978b:15–16).

In cases of mixed marriage, some traditional eating habits of the island spouse seem to be maintained with surprisingly tenacity, even though there

---

1 Instead of asking about "breakfast" per se, I asked, "What, if any, foods do you eat when you get up in the morning?" Like the word "snack," the word "breakfast" has different meanings for different people.

has been obvious accommodation to new foods. Changes are more evident with the second generation.

Most respondents felt they had made some changes in their eating habits while in New Zealand. Besides the addition of new foods, the biggest adjustment was the idea of fixed meal times. Thus, they say, in New Zealand they eat more meals, hence consume more food than in the islands. Certainly New Zealand food offers more variety, and there is more cash to purchase these new food items: Islanders commented: "We eat more over here from over there. Can afford food. Over there not enough money." A male respondent stated the same sentiment differently: "I put on weight in New Zealand – more meat and beer."

It is as well, however, to refrain from adopting the simplistic view of a "pure" island diet that has automatically changed in the direction of a European pattern upon migration to New Zealand. The reality is more complex. Patterns of migration are often represented on an imaginary folk–urban continuum. Following this same simplistic model, studies that focus on changes in food habits have also implied the notion of a "pure" island diet that is gradually shifting toward a more urbane fare (Fitzgerald 1978a:30). Diet obviously changes from place to place – whether in the islands, between islands, or as a result of a move to New Zealand; but such changes are in response to a complicated set of situational variables rather than merely to the fact of migration itself. The direction of dietary change, when one considers both ends of the migrant chain, is *reciprocal* rather than a simple *lineal* modification of the migrant's diet from an idealized "pure" island base (Fitzgerald 1978a:33). There are islanders in the sample who came from European backgrounds *in the islands* and, except for adding new food items to their dietary, made little or no significant changes in the way they ate.

Studies that focus on changes in food habits unfortunately often follow this simplistic model. Urbanization and migration are only two factors in the breakup of a traditional way of life. Foods in the Pacific have always been both geographically and historically variable. An important consideration, as far as understanding change, is to recognize the fluctuating nature of such food patterns. As stated above, the process is *not* a simple, lineal movement on an imaginary folk–urban continuum. Changes have historical antecedents that ebb and flow with the fluctuations between economic recession and economic prosperity. Edible flowers, wild nuts and fruits, and leaves and seeds are today used almost not at all.

The point is simply this: Changing economic and social conditions, historical accident, as well as cultural habits and beliefs, have an important bearing on the availability and use of food. Changes, like food patterns, do not come about in any predictable way due simply to migration along a supposedly lineal migrant continuum.

Snacking or "picking"

Because much of what is consumed is eaten outside regular meal times, it is important to ask people what they eat between meals. This question puzzled some islanders because eating was often unscheduled. "Never time your meals in Raro (Rarotonga)," one person pointed out matter-of-factly. "You eat over there when you are hungry. I still do." The type of snacks consumed by islanders in Wellington can be nutritionally revealing. They do not, in this case, differ significantly whether in the Hutt or in Newtown. Both groups consume, in rank order, the following snacks: fruit, biscuits (New Zealand cookies), tea/coffee/cordials (soft drinks), homemade bread (often with coconut cream or with orange peel grated into it) with butter, and leftovers of various sorts (tinned meats/fish/taro). Tea times, in the New Zealand tradition of regular morning and afternoon breaks, are not yet popular with islanders; thus they typically consume fewer sweets. But such habits are making their way into the island dietary. Tea time is increasingly a feature in some work situations, and it is considered polite at European-type socials (e.g., Tupperware parties) to serve cakes and other sweets.

Snacking in the islands was literally "picking" (New Zealand slang for snacking) from the trees. There is a nice description of such casual eating in *The Frisbies of the South Seas* (Frisbie 1959/1961:42): "We do not have to carry food on these trips, as the shrimp in the stream, the sprouted coconuts, and the wild fruit provided sufficient snacks." A considerable amount of seafood was eaten raw on the reef, which reminds us of the fact that food consumed in the house is often a poor index of total food intake (McCarthy 1956:16). In the islands, snacks included different foods: more fruit, leftovers from the *umu* (earth oven), and fish eaten raw on the beach. "Picking" (snacking) in the islands was less formal, more casual, and usually out of doors. Morning and afternoon teas were rare, with sweets (lollies) usually unavailable. Instead of soft drinks (cordials), so popular in New Zealand, one would drink the refreshing liquid of the fresh coconut. When Cook Islanders migrate to Wellington, some major changes occur in snacking patterns.

Shopping and spending

In the islands, many people have their own gardens. Foods available through shops are limited in variety and are expensive: Islanders tend to shop on Saturdays and only for staples, such as tinned meats, soap, flour, sugar, kerosene, and cigarettes. In New Zealand again, most shopping is done once a week (75 percent), with a few families buying groceries biweekly and only a fraction shopping daily. Most shop at the large supermarkets, especially those living in the Hutt, where bargains or "specials" are featured. It is common for people to "shop around" from center to center.

In the islands, husbands typically shared cooking responsibilities, laying the *umu* or earth oven being a major task. In New Zealand, such sharing continues. Close to 45 percent of the respondents share grocery shopping with another family member; in 19 percent of these households, husbands alone do the shopping. In New Zealand, shopping can be a somewhat different experience for many islanders because there is more variety in foods and because shopping is based entirely on a cash economy. A female consumer had this reaction: "In the islands, you have all the time to shop. Over here, you are working."

Typically, in the islands the diet was supplemented with nonpurchased food, for example, the weekend catch of fish. This practice has dwindled in New Zealand, even though Wellington is a city by the sea. Only 50 percent of respondents fish regularly. Most felt it was inconvenient, and that it was easier and cheaper to buy fish. In the case of mixed marriages (the rate is high in the Hutt), the European spouse may not be accustomed to fishing as a regular activity, and the habit soon becomes attenuated. A surprisingly large number of people say that they refrain from fishing because of the fear of polluted waters. Environmental pollution is a relatively new concern for New Zealand, but considering the country's small size, a potentially devastating threat.

Both in the Hutt and in Newtown, almost 60 percent of the total household budget goes for food, followed by household expenditures, clothing costs, and alcohol, in that order. It is hard to overestimate the symbolic importance that islanders customarily attach to food and food-related activities. Whereas the average European might feel reticent about spending two dollars a kilo for such and such a food, the average islander might not. It is simply a question of the order of priorities. Under the category of "food," one must include contributions for buying food for religious and social functions (feasts) to feed the many visitors attending such gatherings. Significant social events, such as weddings, funerals, and hair-cutting ceremonies, celebrate the "togetherness" of the extended family.

Alcohol consumption is difficult to gauge accurately except through participant observation. One of the most persistent stereotypes about islanders, however, is that they are problem drinkers. Where this belief is coupled with the unfortunate association of "islanders" with lower-class crimes of violence, mistrust may eventually prevail among Europeans. According to a study of "arrests by ethnic grouping," Duncan (1971:283) claims that there are many more charges against Europeans than any other ethnic group. The rate of alcoholism, too, is highest among Europeans (Rose 1960). Yet, the idea that islanders are uniquely subject to alcohol abuse is widespread in New Zealand. Duncan (1971:284) has suggested that Polynesians and Europeans use alcohol for radically different ends. Islanders supposedly drink for the purpose of getting drunk; Europeans, by contrast, see drinking as an opportunity for companionship and recreation. It would seem naive, however, to assume that Europeans drink only for wholesome recreation. The rate of alcoholism among all New Zealanders would cast serious doubts on such illusions. Alcoholism, like obesity, is surely a New Zealand problem, not just an island or Maori one. Attention is probably focused on islanders because they are culturally exotic and hence relatively conspicuous, and are geographically concentrated (e.g., Newtown), helping to define them as a "problem" group.

Gardening and food exchanges

Associated with food selection are the practices of gardening and the ceremonial exchanges of food. Here one may contrast Newtown with the Hutt. More people in the Hutt have gardens. The weather is better, the soil is good, and fewer families live in flats. The majority in both areas (67 percent) garden seasonally. The notion that islanders do not know how to garden is certainly not true of Cook Islanders. This stereotype is derived, no doubt, from the study of islanders who migrated from harsh atoll environments where gardening is indeed difficult. Even on an atoll, though, islanders have learned ingenious ways to adjust to poor soil conditions (e.g., taro pit gardens).

A wide variety of goods are grown in the gardens, including cabbage, silverbeet (Swiss chard), tomatoes, carrots, onions, lettuce, and potatoes. Many of these vegetables New Zealanders refer to as "greens." Because a number of people apparently believe that islanders eat primarily starchy, root vegetables (taro and potatoes), I asked specifically about the leafy green vegetables. In addition to those mentioned above, I discovered that 66 percent of these island families grow (for their own consumption) a green vegetable which they call *rukau*. This vegetable, rich in vitamins and minerals, is the leafy top of the taro plant, hence a form of "greens." Taro (the root of which will not mature in Wellington's cooler climate) is to the Pacific Islander what roast lamb is to a European New Zealander or hamburger to an American. Taro is, culturally speaking, a highly symbolic food.

Yet, when doctors ask their Polynesian patients what they eat, they are unlikely to hear the words *rukau* or taro. It is considered impolite among islanders to talk about things the other person does not understand. When I first asked a Cook Island woman, "Do you grow *rukau*?" she looked at me with blank surprise: "Do *you* know what *rukau* is!?" If I had not specifically asked, I might well have concluded that islanders in Wellington eat *only* European vegetables.

To digress a moment, this point reminds me of an amusing "field" story that may help to underline the importance of trying to gain an inside view of a people's cultural habits. I went to interview a Cook Island woman, taking along an island interpreter who knew the family in question. As we walked in the door, the lady said abruptly to my interpreter in Cook Island Maori:

"I'll allow the interview, but I'm not going to feed any bloody *Pakeha*,[2] so get that straight!" As I understood some New Zealand Maori (Cook Island Maori is similar), I got the message loud and clear. During the interview session, I casually mentioned several of her relatives that I had already visited, commenting positively on the meal I had taken with one in particular; something like this: "My, she had the best *rukau* I've ever tasted!" From that point on, the tone of the interview changed. She became more relaxed, opened up, finally stopped, and called out to her daughter: "Helen go out and put the corned beef in the *rukau*. We have visitors for lunch."

Islanders do not, of course, purchase all of their food. Some is still received from home (islands); from fishing, as described above; or in the form of gifts from relatives, friends, and neighbors. Exchanging food is common among islanders in Wellington (89 percent of the families interviewed do so fairly regularly), although apparently it is less common than at home in the islands. "Yes," replied one Cook Island woman, "where I come from [Atiu], we are all like brother and sister. If you get some food, you share with all." To quote another: "In the islands, we share everything. Over here, only neighbors do."

There are some suburban contrasts in this practice. In Newtown, where the proportion of island families is higher, sharing is primarily among kinfolk. In the Hutt, where housing is governed by the "pepperpotting" policy (i.e., deliberate interspersing of ethnic groups in housing developments), exchanges are with neighbors as well as with relatives. There is also slightly more food sharing or food exchanges in Newtown.

One of the most characteristic features of the life of Cook Islanders in Wellington is the degree to which these migrants have kept the family together through various linkages (e.g., visits, letters, monies sent home, and gifts) maintained between Wellington and their island home (Curson 1973:24). I was curious about the prevalence of shipping food back and forth from Wellington to the islands or vice versa. Apparently 30–5 years ago, there was a steady flow of goods. Today, such exchanges are cumbersome and expensive. Most respondents said they did so today only "rarely." One person expressed this somewhat doleful sentiment: "A bit, purely now for nostalgia. It's too expensive." Boats run infrequently. By the time fruit arrives, it may be rotten. It is cheaper to buy island food in Wellington. By air, the cost is increasingly prohibitive, and thus, gradually some of the cultural links are disappearing.

Food preferences

What is a "good meal"?

In middle-class communities in industrialized countries, variations in food consumption can often be accounted for by preference alone. Food "likes" and "dislikes" become important indicators of nutritional status.

2 *Pakeha* generally means "any non-Maori," usually a European New Zealander.

Cook Islanders describe "a good meal" as one consisting of "meats" (usually several and most often including fish), vegetables (sometimes island ones, though in the Hutt more typically European), and/or "spuds" or potatoes (which incidentally are usually not included in the category "vegetable"). Coffee or tea (soft drinks or milo for children) are the preferred beverages. Pudding (dessert) is not a regular feature of island meals, but fruits are popular. What people *prefer* to eat is not, of course, what is necessarily consumed. Like many working people, these islanders may regularly consume somewhat inexpensive cuts of meat (more sausages, chops, mince, corned beef). Even so, meat consumption is high among islanders; it is not uncommon to see three to four meats on the table for the large evening meal. Islanders also frequently mention imaginative cultural blends in preparation of foods, such as island chop suey, island mayonnaise, or the all-time favorite "quick tea" of corned beef mixed with a "greens" (*rukau* or silverbeet) and cooked with onions and fresh tomatoes. Such "cultural blends" (culinary syncretisms) were slightly more common in Newtown than in the Hutt, where children of racially mixed parentage sometimes refused to eat "island" foods. One island mother expressed the attitude in this way: "I usually go back to my island food, but my kids go the New Zealand way of food – steak and eggs."

Basically, then, the island diet in New Zealand is mixed: essentially *Pakeha*-type fare with "a touch of the islands about it," such as use of coconut cream for flavoring, more use of fish and root vegetables, and less reliance on sweets. This diet differs from that in the islands proper, where typical foods such as raw fish, coconut products, "pokes" (pudding), taro, or breadfruit in season are readily available. Even here, though, the picture is changing rapidly. It is well to remember that there is no homogeneous dietary pattern found throughout the Cooks. "In the islands, you *used* to get good island food," lamented one respondent. "Now in Raro, people too lazy to plant. Everyone works. Yet the cost of living is so high there."

Migration from the Cooks to New Zealand has resulted in some unforeseen consequences. Because most of those who move to New Zealand are in the "middle range" age group, their departure means that the work force on the islands is depleted, as those left behind are the oldest and the youngest. This results in a demographic imbalance in the islands. The migrants then customarily send money back to their relatives in the islands, thereby helping to create a cash economy and the concomitant desire for more imported goods (including foods). Traditional subsistence activities (e.g., taro farming) dwindle in response to these changing conditions. The reality, then, is less a shift from a supposedly "pure" island diet to the more "modern," urban fare of New Zealand, but more of a complex, reciprocal process of interaction and influence.

We also inquired of these informants whether they served island foods to visitors or relatives. One respondent summed up the practice with this statement: "If relations come, I'll cook a bit of island food, like raw fish, taro, and coconut sauce. Will try to cook what visitors like. Probably European food for Europeans." It is generally felt that Europeans will not like island food, but to serve only European food to islanders would be a cultural affront. Although most adult islanders prefer their island foods, they have managed to make good dietary adjustments. "Would serve island food if got any," one islander said bluntly. "If not, too bad. We eat something else. We get used to the *Pakeha* way now."

Likes and dislikes

Cook Islanders clearly "like" rather than "dislike" most foods. In fact, from both the Hutt and Newtown, few persons were found who actively disliked any food. This seems to be a fairly typical island trait. To the question, "Do you have any food dislikes?" one Cook Island woman replied sarcastically: "Nothing like that in my stomach!" The few foods listed as "disliked" included culturally exotic (unfamiliar) foods such as mushrooms, tripe, sweetbreads, and rhubarb; alcohol (listed as a food and generally feared); and certain specific types of fish (which in the islands would have been considered *tapu* or "forbidden" to eat under certain circumstances).

Food "likes" in New Zealand included a mixture of island favorites (fish and taro heading the list) and European foods (chicken and steak being most popular). The emphasis on meat as a high-status food in New Zealand is no doubt significant. There were only a few discernible differences noted between the two residential areas: In the Hutt, respondents mentioned a wider variety of vegetables; and "tinned corned beef with coconut sauce" was more frequently mentioned in Newtown. In both areas, respondents occasionally referred to "smokes" (cigarettes) as a food.

Taboo foods

In the islands, certain foods may be forbidden (*tapu*) for certain families at certain times of the year or in certain circumstances. Thus, each informant was asked if he/she had any *tapu* notions about food. Only about one third of the sample in each group admitted to having any food *tapus* in New Zealand. Most admitted that the idea was real enough in the islands. One respondent tried to explain this duality: "Back home, yes. Don't think of those things here. Can't eat certain types of fish [eel], coconut crab, crayfish. At home [I] think twice [before eating such food], especially when pregnant. The baby will come out in spots." Respondents made a complete mental compartmentalization; *tapus* were largely confined to the islands. In New Zealand such restrictions either have lost their efficacy or are translated into a modern medical framework. If a doctor in New Zealand advises his island patient not to eat, say pork, the islander may refer to the food restriction as a *tapu*. Folk feelings about food as related to health can be significant factors influencing selection or rejection of certain foods, and deserve more attention from food scientists.

Foods as health symbols

Self-perception, food, and health

Conditions psychologically perceived as being problematic by one group may not be so perceived by another (Reeder 1972:37). The way islanders see "health" or "illness" may be different from the way medical personnel view them. It was instructive, then, to inquire how these migrants perceived their own health and whether they saw nutrition as being in any way related to health. Differences between the Hutt and Newtown were, in these responses, mostly nonsignificant. Individuals in both areas felt they had "largely good" health (73 percent), with little significant change noted since coming to New Zealand. Where changes were acknowledged, most believed there had been improvement in health status in New Zealand, usually attributed to better medical facilities in that country.

Although these respondents complained of a variety of medical problems, they tended to see little relationship between these complaints and diet, obesity being a notable exception. Awareness of body weight is an area where health education apparently has had some real impact, although with some unexpected consequences. Unfortunately, islanders have begun to adopt the European stereotype that they are *all* given to overeating (66 percent said they were "overweight"; only 32 percent felt "about the right weight"). The response of a female Cook Islander sums up this self-perception: "I think I'm *over*weight. I think, we [Cook Islanders] are *all* overweight!" In the islands, plumpness was once considered socially desirable (a sign of high status); in New Zealand, Cook Islanders increasingly view even mild "heaviness" as suspect, although most often inevitable. A portly female respondent pondered these differences in cultural value with this comment: "When you not eat enough in the islands, they say you not eat enough. . . . In New Zealand, when you eat a lot, they say you fat."

Dieting, then, is not very popular among islanders; 78 percent had never been on a doctor's diet. Of those who had tried, most had been unsuccessful: "It is difficult to stay on [diet]," one woman rationalized, "especially if you come from the Cook Islands." Some respondents attributed this failure to the frequent attendance at Cook Island feasts. "When I go to party [feast] and look at food, I forget all about the diet." An even more characteristic remark came from this 50-year-old overweight female: In response to her doctor's chiding her about being overweight, she answered flatly: "If my stomach is full, I am happy. If not, I'm unhappy." How does a health care worker argue with such a priority?

Although clearly some islanders have an obesity problem, it is not so clear that being mildly overweight is necessarily a health hazard (Prior 1976). In cases where obesity is a major health problem, it is likely to be as much a New Zealand problem as a characteristically island one.

Health, intelligence, and mental illness

The question about the association of foods with health, intelligence, and mental illness was revealing. Whereas in a study of suburban Americans (Fitzgerald 1979), it was found that close to 100 percent saw a fairly close connection between food and general health, not more than 88 percent of Cook Islanders associated these ideas at all. Food is viewed as something to enjoy rather than a source of nutrients for the maintenance of good health. Responses were mostly equivocal. Where there was a perceived connection, the relationships were unsophisticated: "If you don't eat, you get sick with empty tummy." Another respondent was even more to the point: "If you don't eat, you die."

Even fewer saw any relationship between food and intelligence (only 33 percent). A few were emphatic in their denials: "No, born with intelligence." Where there was a recognition, it was usually believed that breakfast was the most important meal, especially for children: "Well, I always believe I must give my children a good breakfast before going to school."

To reiterate, Americans tend to make rather strong associations between food and general health; slightly less frequently they see a connection between food and intelligence, and almost never been food and mental illness. By contrast, fewer Cook Islanders in New Zealand see a relationship among any of these ideas, but more see a relationship between food and mental illness (50 percent) than between food and intelligence (33 percent). Why? For one thing, in the island way of viewing the world, less division is made between body and mind. When one is out of order, so is the other. One informant explained the connection thus: "I think, if you are happy in yourself...makes a big difference in the way you live." Also islanders see food as virtually anything taken through the mouth; hence alcohol and "smokes" are seen as examples of food consumption, and most Cook Islanders are aware of the emotional hazards of drinking. "I reckon drink makes people mental," remarked one respondent, summing up this perception.

Attitudes about food

In answer to the question, "What foods do you consider healthful or unhealthful?" close to 50 percent of these respondents rejected any association; this is in line with the fact that a large number saw no relationship between food consumption and general health status. Responses ranged from "Don't know; never think about that," to "All food is the same – all good." Some people did, however, feel that certain foods were *especially* good for one's health; included were fruits, fish (or seafood), "greens" or vegetables (including *rukau*), and meats. There was no significant difference between responses in Newtown or the Hutt. Furthermore, it was felt that food in New Zealand was more healthful than food in the islands. "With food from the islands," one lady pointed out, "get sore stomach; but I still like it." This notion is no doubt due to the association of some traditional island food with so-called "fattening foods." In fact, one respondent divided all food into two categories: "Some are fattening, some are not." She was keen on avoiding what she believed to be the fattening ones. Generally, then, "unhealthful" foods were *considered* "fattening": sweets, too much meat, potatoes, starchy foods such as taro; foods fried in oil (takeout foods); pork; or – in Newtown – *tapu* foods (eel, rats, etc.). Some persons even listed "smokes" as an unhealthful "food." Although certainly not as concerned as Americans over additives in food, a few Cook Islanders mentioned "manmade foods" (soft drinks and ice cream) as suspect.

These informants placed a high value on food per se and were not especially concerned with its health-giving potential. One thoughtful remark reiterated this idea: "Don't really look at food for its nutritional value. If it's edible, it's good." Coupled with this liking for foods in general is the cultural dictum requiring food to be taken as part of the host–guest relationship. If you have visitors, you feed them. If you are a guest, you eat heartily. This is simply good island etiquette. One woman phrased this idea differently: "It's a sin not to take food when you see it. You'll offend your host if you don't eat lots."

The Cook Island feast

The island feast is more than simply a big meal. It is a social ritual marked by singing, dancing, and a recementing of family ties. This extravagant ceremonial emphasis on food creates an impression of great bounty, which enhances the prestige of the host, even though in reality he may be experiencing difficult times. Most islanders feel great embarrassment if unable to provide abundantly. Feasts, then, typically feature a variety of meats (tinned or fresh corned beef, roast chicken, raw fish or shellfish, pork or lamb cooked in an earth oven) and vegetables [ordinarily island chop suey or chow mein, taro, island mayonnaise, various "pokes" (puddings) of pumpkin, banana, taro, or pawpaw in an arrowroot base; rice, potatoes, *kumaras* (sweet potato), noodles, and potato salad], as well as doughnuts and fruits for dessert. Such extravagant displays of foods are tied up with personal *mana*, political power, economic ability, and family obligations:

> Thus we find that all ceremonial feasts in Polynesia are characterized by these features: The quantity of food provided, the ostentatious manner in which it is displayed, the liberality with which it is presented to the guests, the large amount of waste entailed, and the reciprocal nature of the obligation which the guests at such feasts incur. (Bell 1931:120)

Traditionally such events marked transition rites, such as at christenings, weddings, haircuttings for little boys, and funerals. More European-inspired festivities include church openings, twenty-first birthdays, Christmas, Sunday gatherings, and (in New Zealand) welcoming parties for visitors from the home islands.

There was some difference noted between the Hutt and Newtown. More people attend *umukais* (feasts) in Newtown where island food is more readily available. With the mixed couples in the Hutt, often only the island spouse will attend such gatherings.

Informants usually saw little difference between feasts held in Wellington and those at home, except that in the islands there was often more food, though less varied. Some clearly felt that only at home could things be done "properly," that is, according to island etiquette. One island man made this point: "Not much difference today. Long ago, real old style. When we put on a feed, we had a whole pig, coconut shells, taros, and so on, all laid out on the ground." Even in Wellington, though, some families have an *umu* in the backyard or else easy access to one. Feasts in the city may not be the same village enterprise as in the islands; yet most occasions are financed by contributions from attending guests, and island foods are in relative abundance even in Wellington. "People spend a lot of money here for island food," one Cook Islander explained. "There is pressure on people to entertain one another. We follow same way. It is our Maori way. We can't leave these things behind."

Sometimes Europeans are quite critical of what they consider to be the wastefulness of the average *umukai*. Even a Cook Islander will occasionally refer to this aspect: "I like feasts, but they are wasteful. There is never enough food. If you tell them (relations) two potatoes, they bring half dozen." In all fairness, the waste may be exaggerated. Europeans will cater a wedding party to the tune of thousands of dollars, whereas a Cook Island family would put on the same function through donations and food prepared at home and at much less cost. At the end of the party, the food is simply redistributed. Little actually goes to waste. Beyond this, the *umukai* has a larger cultural function. It is one of the few occasions to bring family and friends together, to reassert identity as Cook Islanders, and to express cultural values of generosity and sharing. A Cook Island school teacher captures this idea beautifully: "A feast is not only for 'show' but a reciprocation of kindness, favors, and sharing. In New Zealand, it is almost a necessity to show feelings for family and close friends and to keep ties with the folks back home. Sad about the mammoth feasts costing so much, but it brings the families together – a unity which could so easily disintegrate in a place like Wellington."

Food stereotypes and "the other's meal"

There is need, especially in situations of change, for accurate, reliable interpretations of how each group feels about the other, in this case about "the other's meal." We already have some notion of the stereotypes that European New Zealanders have about islanders and their eating habits, but how do islanders imagine that European eat?

Each informant was asked: "How would you describe a *Papaa* [Cook Island word for European or *Pakeha*] meal?" The responses are revealing. As one might guess, in the Hutt where there is more of a mixture of island and European, there was more awareness of European foods and eating habits in general; otherwise the responses were similar to those of the Newtown residents, who not uncommonly denied any special knowledge: "Don't know; never visted a *Pakeha* home." Hesitation in answering such a question more likely reveals the islanders' need to sound polite and noncritical of the other group. A few genuinely bicultural individuals, however, found the question puzzling because it required a compartmentalization of food experiences that was not totally appropriate for a bicultural identity. Nonetheless, it was possible to gain a composite picture of a *Papaa* meal based on these responses.

Islanders see the European meal as basically "not much to eat." By contrast, they see themselves as eating a lot. "Islanders can eat more than Europeans," one respondent insisted. "It's little bites with them. Islanders have piles of food and lots of waste." Associated with the perception of small helpings, Europeans are also characterized as spending much less money for food, the implication clearly being that they are less "hospitable." In short, Europeans are pictured as a bit stingy with food: "With *Pakehas*, what they give you, that's your lot. You don't ask for a second helping." It is as well to remember that we are dealing with cultural stereotypes.

There were some obvious differences seen in the manner of cooking. Europeans are believed to prefer roasting and frying. The two most frequently mentioned characteristics of the *Papaa* meal were "roasts" (especially beef or lamb, including roasted potatoes and vegetables) and "puddings" (sweets). Other minor features that seem to stand out in the island imagination included the use of stews, casseroles, and soups; the English habit of serving cold "salads" (meats with potato salad or cold slaw); and the ubiquitous thin sandwiches served with a cup of tea, either for lunch or as a snack. The European meal contrasts with island fare in featuring gravy instead of coconut sauce; more diversity in beverages, with a heavy emphasis on milk; silverbeets (Swiss chard) instead of *rukau*. Also, *Papaas* routinely employ a knife and fork as compared to the more "natural" island use of the fingers. Basically, then, islanders view Europeans as "formal" eaters (more regularity of meals, several courses, and formal invitations to meals). Positively, islanders consider European food habits as "less fattening" and "less wasteful."

Some food stereotypes were especially amusing. Europeans, when asked what islanders eat, will often reply "beer, fish and chips." Some islanders have an identical notion about Europeans: "A Kiki-style meal? Bloody fish chips!" Islanders feel that Europeans also are heavy drinkers. If one thing emerges from these data, it is the realization that there is room for more and better intercultural communication. One might well begin with an appreciation of what and how people really eat.

Summary and conclusions

Dietary changes and nutritional implications

Clearly, economic and social conditions associated with migration have had an important bearing on the availability and use of food, hence, ultimately on nutritional/health status; also changes in life-style and diet are related to changes in disease patterns.

In the Cooks, islanders were accustomed to a diet moderate in fat content and low in cholesterol; moderate also in protein, derived mainly from fish and tinned meats; and high in carbohydrates, principally staple root vegetables. This diet contained a significant amount of unsaturated marine oils, from the high intake of fish, which helped to cancel out the cholesterol-raising effect of the fats in coconuts (Davidson 1977:12–13). It was a diet relatively high in fiber content, low in sodium (salt), as well as low in refined carbohydrates (sucrose). Naturally, variations occurred from high to low islands, from rural to urban environments, and among individual consumers.

In New Zealand, dietary changes reflect the social adaptations the migrant has to make to the new environment, including adjustments to an increased income, the availability of new or familiar foods, and shifting work patterns. These changes in diet are similar to those found in other industrialized, urban settings. An increase in monetary income is generally translated into an increase in the proportion of calories provided by fats and a decrease in those provided by starchy foods (root vegetables), accompanied, however, by an increase in sugar consumption and other refined carbohydrates such as cereals, rice, and flour. There is also a tendency toward an increase in the proportion of calories provided by animal proteins (FAO 1969; quoted in de Garine, 1972:156). Certainly protein intake is noticeably high among Cook Islanders in Wellington (a large intake of meats, daily and at feasts). Consumption of fats, too, is higher except perhaps as compared to the dietary on atolls where coconuts are a mainstay of the diet. (Fats in New Zealand come principally from milk, cheese, and meat consumption.) Although an increase in carbohydrates is evident in New Zealand, what may be more significant are the kinds of carbohydrates consumed; the trend has been away from eating staple root vegetables toward a diet based more on refined carbohydrates. This diet characteristically has more sodium and less fiber.

The change in disease patterns is related to changes in diet. Today, in the islands and in New Zealand, there is less typhoid, tuberculosis, leprosy, yaws, and filariasis. The characteristic diseases for these migrants are the familiar diseases of affluence. Coronary artery disease, hypertension, gout, diabetes, and liver disease (perhaps related to alcohol consumption) are on the increase (Hodge 1972:27–9). These diseases may be related to diet.

Food habits and intergroup relations

From the data presented, what generalizations might one make about the diet of Cook Islanders in New Zealand, and how is diet related to intergroup relations?

The Cook Island diet – though clearly mixed – has distinctive elements of its own, different certainly from the typical European (*Pakeha*) diet and not to be confused with that of the average New Zealand Maori. (Cook Islanders, for example, have no particular liking for muttonbird, *puha* [thistle], or mussels.) The Cook Island diet differs somewhat from that of other islanders, and this chapter points out some degree of diversity within the Cook groups in Wellington. Not all Cook Islanders in Wellington share the same eating patterns. In contrasting responses in Newtown with those from the Hutt, at least minor differences were observed that principally revolved around these factors: availability of island foods, marriage to someone other than a Cook Islander, and work schedules. The biggest differences in eating habits were noted among children of interracial couples living in the Hutt. Considerable cultural divisions seem to be developing between migrant parents and their children. In Newtown, there is more evidence that parents still pass on some basic island patterns of eating, even when the food items themselves have changed or been modified.

Another not unrelated conclusion is that New Zealanders have little knowledge of island customs, including food habits, and show relatively little sensitivity to the islanders' need for cultural distinctiveness. The tendency in New Zealand is to lump all islanders into a lower-class category (this despite the fact that in the islands there is a complicated class system) and to assume that all "islanders" eat alike. The research data presented here refute a number of food-related stereotypes about Pacific Islanders. It was *not* found, for example, that islanders as a group have any particular problems adapting to New Zealand foods, that their children routinely go to school without breakfast, that islanders are ignorant of the mechanics of gardening, or that they avoid eating vegetables or "greens." On the other hand, some real differences were observed in the areas of meal scheduling, snacking patterns, food exchanges, food taboos, and attitudes toward food and health.

Stereotypes about island food habits are often blatantly contradictory. Europeans will allude to the "fact" that island children must surely go to school without anything to eat; yet, in the same breath, they will criticize islanders for spending so much money on food (especially expensive cuts of meat), which presumably the island children do not eat in the mornings. Also the generalizations that all islanders are overweight and that all overweightness is a health hazard need some revision (Prior 1976). It is possible that obesity is really a health hazard only under certain conditions: For the Polynesian, obesity could be of some adaptive advantage. One must question, too, the common assertion that islanders get drunk faster than the average European. As yet, we simply do not have reliable figures to make such a judgment (Challis 1970).

Food stereotyping is part and parcel of a whole discriminatory package that groups all "islanders" into a New Zealand lower class. To do so is to invite problems in communication that help create an "eth-class" which is also an urban proletariat group in New Zealand (Macpherson 1977:111). This raises the question of who is responsible for whom in the migration relationship. Clearly in the past the burden of adjustment was more on the migrant. Part of the difficulty is that European New Zealanders prefer not to admit to cultural diversities.

New Zealanders need to become more familiar with island customs. One might start with knowledge of island foods, trying to look for some of the positive contributions that island food habits might make to the larger New Zealand dietary. To provide more good information about food values, both island and European, couched in a good educational format, is the real challenge of health care workers in this area. The island preference for fruits rather than lollies (sweets) should, for example, be emulated rather than discouraged. For a group in which many do not tolerate milk, the island vegetables (*rukau* and taro) are good sources of the B vitamins as well as relatively high in calcium (Murai, Pen, and Miller 1958:94). Europeans could learn something about the nonnutritional, subjective aspects of food consumption at almost any island celebration or feast. Islanders complain that New Zealand educators teach only one type of nutrition. Surely nutrition education is based on the belief that there is some good in every ethnic food pattern and that island food habits – at least potentially – can make as much of a contribution to health as European ones (Abel 1954).

A major conclusion of this research is the sad fact that too few health workers know much about islanders in Wellington – specifically, about how they eat. A consequence of this cultural indifference is that islanders do not use the New Zealand health services to maximum advantage. Doctors and nurses see little of islanders in their own contexts, and even when they do, are often too psychologically far removed from their island patients.

Unfortunately it is necessary, first, to break through the "folklore" presented by health care workers about the *supposed* cultural habits of minorities. In order to do this, health educators need to have more knowledge of the interests, values, and even prejudices of those being educated. In other words, they need to begin to appreciate the *cultural context* of such learning for the particular groups being taught. This emphasis on the cultural as well as on the biological significance of food habits is fundamental.

4. Taro and timber: competing or complementary ways to a food supply

Nancy Pollock

In the 1980s, most Pacific Island nations are facing a crucial decision regarding their food source. The Asian Development Bank (hereafter ADB) report on *South Pacific Agriculture* suggests that there are only two options: "maintenance of a largely subsistence economy...or permanent dependence on aid from outside, given the severe environmental constraints that exist" (ADB 1980:xxxi). This paper will examine these two alternative means of food supply, and present a third option, namely the use of forest resources, which could provide a double-edged alternative in line with traditional practices of shifting cultivation. This option to use forests is available only on high islands, however. Thus the choices of growing one's own food, depending on aid for one's food, or using forested areas both to provide cash and to clear areas for agricultural production confront the people at both the government level and at the level of the kinship group or individual. It will be argued that the third alternative minimizes the high risks of a food source entirely derived from dependence on overseas aid. It also allows some continuity with the recent mode of production, that is, using forested areas for shifting agriculture plots, but also exploiting the commercial market for timber by selective logging, thereby yielding the necessary cash.

The main issue underlying the glaring problem of the source of food supply is that concerning the best use of the land. With all indications pointing strongly to a continued strengthening of the cash economy, the issue that must be resolved by both families and governments is whether the land can produce more subsistence crops, plus the commercial crops necessary to yield the all-purpose cash, or whether existing stands of timber on that land can be sold off to yield cash. The most rational decision must surely be the one that offers minimal risks, and thus is considered likely to provide a continuous food supply.

Self-provisioning versus increasing involvement in the wider market sector is an issue not confined exclusively to the Pacific, but also pertains to many other developing countries. On the Pacific Islands, the smallness of land area and the isolation and limited resource endowments (see Table 4.1) of the central and eastern islands offer little for commercial and/or industrial development, if this is the desired goal. The high islands, particularly

Table 4.1. *Population, land and sea areas*

Country	Estimated population (mid-1979) [1]	Land area (km²) [2]	Sea area (km², ×1000)	Population density (persons/km²) [1]÷[2]	Estimated annual percent growth rate (Past 10 years)	(Past 5 years)	Estimated percentage growth (1969–79)	Latest census year	Total population latest census
American Samoa	31,400	197	390	159	1.7	1.5	18	1980	32,395[a]
Cook Islands	18,500	240	1,830	77	−0.9	−0.7	−9	1976	18,127
Fiji	619,000	18,272	1,290	34	2.0	1.8	22	1976	588,068
French Polynesia	144,600	3,265	5,030	44	2.9	2.2	33	1977	137,382
Guam	100,000	541	–	185	1.8	0.6	19	1980	105,816[a]
Kiribati	57,300	690	3,550	83	1.7	1.6	18	1978	56,213
Nauru	7,300	21	320	348	1.2	0.8	12	1977	6,966
New Caledonia	139,000	19,103	1,740	7	3.1	1.2	36	1976	133,233
New Hebrides	114,500	11,880	680	10	3.4	4.4	40	1979	112,596[a]
Niue	3,600	259	390	14	−3.8	−2.1	−32	1976	3,843
Norfolk Island	1,900	36	400	53	3.1	1.1	36	1971	1,683
Papua New Guinea (PNG)	2,944,000	462,243	3,120	6	2.3	1.9	25	1980	3,006,779[a]
Pitcairn	100	5	800	20	–	–	–	1976	74
Solomon Islands	217,700	28,530	1,340	8	3.3	3.1	38	1976	196,823
Tokelau	1,600	10	290	160	−0.6	0	−6	1976	1,575
Tonga	95,800	699	700	137	1.6	1.7	17	1976	90,085

Trust Territory of the Pacific Islands	132,500	1,832	6,200	72	3.0	2.3	34	1973(80)	115,251
Tuvalu	7,400	26	900	285	2.5	4.6	28	1979	7,349
Wallis and Futuna	10,200	255	300	40	1.8	3.2	20	1976	9,192
Western Samoa	155,000	2,935	120	53	1.1	0.8	12	1976	151,983
South Pacific Region	4,801,400	551,039	29,390	9	2.3	1.9	25.1		
South Pacific Region (excluding PNG)	1,857,400	88,796	26,270	21					

[a] Provisional.

Source: Adapted from South Pacific Commission 1981 (April):5.

the larger more westerly ones such as Fiji, the Solomons, and Papua New Guinea, have a much wider range of resources, botanical, geological, and climatic, and more freshwater streams and montane areas than the eastern islands. This limited resource base is exacerbated by an increasing human population, particularly in urban areas (see UN world growth figures in Schuster 1979). Thus the source of food supply is an immediate urgent problem.

This paper will examine briefly the direct mode of food production for the main Pacific Islands in terms of the shifting agriculture mode of land use; this has provided a long established relationship between agriculture and the forested areas of large islands. By viewing this as one of several alternative uses of the biotically limited ecosystem, we shall provide data to show that one other alternative allows an economy based on both subsistence and cash, whereas a third alternative favors total dependence on cash for food supply. Both direct food production and food purchased with cash, whether wages or lease money, are subject to considerable risks. Several risks will be discussed as they emerge from case studies of timber for cash development projects.

Cash mode of production – agriculture

The need for cash as a multipurpose exchange medium is now firmly established in Pacific Island economies, but it is still in short supply. In the 1980s, using one's land to grow crops that will yield a cash supply has been the most direct form of production; these crops may take the form of either food crops or materials for handicrafts. The main difficulty is finding a regular and worthwhile market. Because all the larger islands produce the same crops, there is little demand among the islands themselves, even to supply the wants of the tourist industry. Those crops, such as tomatoes, bananas, pineapple, and watermelon, meet an off-season demand in New Zealand but are subject to blight, disease, less growing experience on the part of the cultivators, and marketing/shipping problems. Thus they are not a reliable source of cash.

Nevertheless agricultural products constitute more than 91 percent of the domestic exports for Fiji, Tonga, Western Samoa, and the Solomons (ADB 1980, appendix F:495) (Table 4.2). These economies depend heavily for their export earnings on the commercial production from the land, and without those earnings the balance of trade would be even more negative than it is now (Table 4.3). Only Papua New Guinea has a diversified economy that allows it a favorable balance of trade; agricultural products make up only 39 percent of the total domestic exports; copper ore and concentrates make up a further 38 percent. Thus the current dependence rests on three main agricultural crops: copra, cacao, and coffee. As Castle (1980:119) has pointed out:

Table 4.2. *Contribution of agriculture to domestic exports*[a]

		Value of agricultural exports (US$, × 1000)	Percentage of total domestic exports	Average annual rate of change (%)
Cook Islands	1977	1,798	74[b]	1972–7 5.9
Fiji	1973	59,025	91	1970–3 2.5
Kiribati	1977	2,776	13	1974–7 −20.7
Papua New Guinea	1975	195,886	39	1971–5 20.4
Solomon Islands	1977	32,282	98	1970–7 32.1
Tonga	1978	5,098	98	1972–8 2.2
Western Samoa	1977	15,365	99[b]	1972–7 31.1

[a] Includes agricultural, forestry, fishing, and hunting exports.
[b] Share of total exports (includes reexports).
Source: Adapted from Asian Development Bank 1980:495.

Dependence on a narrow range of primary commodities for export has meant that total export earnings are particularly liable to sharp fluctuations from year to year because of movement of world market prices and variations in the volume of domestic output stemming from climatic and biological factors, as well as producers' decisions in response to price changes.

Copra production has provided a cash supply for Pacific Islanders for 120 years. But with fluctuating prices, other tree crops, notably coffee and cacao, have been added to the cash crop possibilities. Copra is still a mainstay but is likely to continue to bring reduced returns to producers as the replacement of old trees is slow; therefore, it is viewed as a last-resort source of cash (see Pollock, 1978, for a discussion of the return to copra making among a Tuamotuan atoll population for whom other sources of cash dried up). Cash cropping has developed to a limited extent, limited to the level of lively exchange in the markets of Honiara, Nuku'alofa, and Apia, but at an unreliable level of supply to overseas markets such as New Zealand. Thus although agricultural products form a major proportion of the export economies of

Table 4.3. *Total and per capita trade, 1979*

	Trade Total (A$'000)			Trade per capita (A$)		
Country	Exports	Imports	Balance of trade	Exports	Imports	Balance of trade
American Samoa	111,804	80,613	+ 31,191	3,561	2,567	+ 994
Cook Islands	3,466	20,604	− 17,138	187	1,114	− 927
Fiji	231,225	422,388	− 191,163	374	682	− 308
French Polynesia	25,454	421,892	− 396,438	176	2,918	− 2,742
Guam	38,084	398,034	− 359,950	381	3,980	− 3,599
Kiribati	21,209	15,545	+ 5,664	370	271	+ 99
Nauru	67,270	10,559	+ 56,711	9,215	1,446	+ 7,769
New Caledonia	319,557	319,438	+ 119	2,299	2,298	+ 1
New Hebrides	37,017	55,530	− 18,513	323	485	− 162
Niue	342	1,915	− 1,573	95	532	− 437
Norfolk Island	1,168	8,987	− 7,819	615	4,730	− 4,115
Papua New Guinea	858,605	701,944	+ 156,661	292	238	+ 54
Solomon Islands	62,692	52,681	+ 10,011	288	242	+ 46
Tokelau	16	288	− 272	10	180	− 170
Tonga	6,854	26,210	− 19,356	72	274	− 202
TTPI[a]	21,937	—	—	161	—	—
Tuvalu	257	1,851	− 1,594	35	250	− 215
Wallis and Futuna	0	6,023	− 6,023	0	590	− 590
Western Samoa	16,463	66,974	− 50,511	106	300	− 237

South Pacific Region total

1975	965,000	1,445,000	− 480,000	217	325	— 108
1976	1,000,000	1,445,000	− 445,000	220	317	— 97
1977	1,274,000	1,805,000	− 531,000	270	383	— 113
1978	1,327,000	2,006,000	− 679,000	277	418	— 141
1979	1,823,000	2,611,000	− 788,000	380	559	— 179

[a]TTPI, Trust Territories of the Pacific Islands.
Source: South Pacific Commission 1981 (April):9.

Table 4.4. *Imports by SITC major commodity groups, 1979*[a]

	Am Sam	Cook Is	Fiji	Fr Pol	Guam	Kiribati
Food	11,915[c]	4,327	66,492	80,171	50,817	4,696
Beverages and tobacco	2,696	1,102	5,181	10,459	16,145	1,505
Crude materials	1,177	351	4,368	9,471	1,430	262
Minerals, fuels, etc.	20,276	1,625	77,875	35,770	196,980	2,258
Animal and vegetable oils and fats	839	70	5,540	2,551	1,036	19
Chemicals	2,411	1,664	29,558	25,492	8,759	862
Manufactured goods	9,366	4,612	80,802	110,862	37,201	1,799
Machinery and transport equip.	20,147	4,447	94,946	89,175	47,099	2,606
Miscellaneous manu- factured goods	3,913	2,334	43,972	56,957	32,278	1,448
Miscellaneous transactions	7,871	73	13,654	983	6,306	91
Total[b]	80,613	20,604	422,388	421,892	398,055	15,545

[a] Imports by Standard International Trade Classification (SITC) groups are not available for all countries.
[b] Totals may not add, owing to rounding and currency conversion.
[c] Numbers represent Australian dollars (×1000).
Source: Adapted from South Pacific Commission 1981 (April):13.

Pacific Island nations, they are not a reliable source of cash on which either governments or individuals can rely. As Castle points out, not only is the share of agricultural output in the gross domestic product falling, but the proportion of the labor force engaged in agriculture is also declining (1980:109). In its place, the government sector is providing an alternative source of employment "strongly supported by external aid in the majority of cases" (ADB 1980:480). This increasing number of people in the employed sector as a means of access to cash is having a significant influence on the kinds of foods consumed, and thus on the sources of food supply.

A major government concern is whether these wage earners use their cash to buy local foods or imported foodstuffs, in the latter case thereby worsening the balance of payments situation. With diminishing numbers of workers in agricultural production and increasing numbers seeking wage employment, an alternative source of cash income is urgently needed. If that source could be closely allied to a natural resource, rather than to industry, government, or aid, then it might be a low-risk alternative, particularly if that resource were renewable, as in the case of forestry replanting schemes.

Another solution to the increasing use of imported foodstuffs, mainly by wage earners, is the possibility of growing more of the kinds of foodstuffs

New Cal	Niue	Norf Is	Solo Is	Tonga	Tuvalu	W Samoa
51,841	570	798	6,627	6,989	746	13,641
13,144	194	709	1,985	1,677	163	1,898
4,236	31	13	231	739	40	1,016
65,121	296	258	6,753	2,635	146	6,327
1,854	4	0	607	20	8	453
21,923	127	516	3,446	1,632	67	2,984
51,376	364	1,163	9,193	4,756	250	12,351
66,861	122	1,612	19,734	5,769	215	24,086
42,530	207	3,333	3,879	1,893	167	3,970
552	0	585	224	100	50	247
319,438	1,915	8,987	52,681	26,210	1,851	66,974

that are being imported at home. Cereals, meat, and sugar are the three main food imports in most of the Pacific Island communities; these together with other food imports amount to 20–5 percent of the total imports of these nations (Table 4.4). Western Samoa imports 28 percent of its total imports in the form of food. Furthermore, this proportion has generally tended to increase during the 1970s (Castle 1980: 120). This factor – i.e., the ever increasing dependence on imported foodstuffs – is of major concern to many Pacific Island governments, and import substitution forms a significant part of island development plans (see Somare's Eight Point Plan, 1973, as an early example of this kind of statement).

Meat imports account for 35–40 percent of the food imports of Papua New Guinea, Tonga, and Western Samoa, but only 15–22 percent of those of Fiji and the Solomons. The reason for the lower proportion of meat consumption in the latter two countries is partly the strong vegetarian emphasis among many of the Fiji Indian population, and the better developed cattle and fishing industries in the Solomons. Castle (1980) is pessimistic about this situation: "In no case is it readily apparent that the replacement of a significant portion of canned meat imports would be economic in the foreseeable future" (1980:121).

He is more optimistic about "import replacement of other food imports, such as dairy products, frozen and canned fish, vegetables and fruits, [because] the technical possibilities are greater and progress has already been made in this direction in several countries during recent years." Nevertheless, he feels that this might be at the expense of labor, land, and other resources that might be part of more highly valued export or import substitution activities (1980:121).

Cash mode of production – forestry

The other resource to which this paper addresses itself is the areas of forested land. As a potential source of cash this has only recently been considered. Total areas range from the minimal on atolls where the coconut tree is the most suitable plantation crop, to the forested areas on high islands. These form only 4 percent of the land area in Tonga, but 45 percent in Fiji, 52 percent in Western Samoa, and 86 and 90 percent, respectively, in Papua New Guinea and the Solomon Islands (ADB 1980:294). This indicates a significant resource which is only partially tapped. The forest cover is not likely to be high yielding, as the quality of timber for commercial purposes is low grade. Nevertheless, given the grim picture painted above regarding sources for the all-elusive cash supply, it may be a partial solution.

Commercial exploitation of timber resources, it will be argued here, is high risk because of the initial dependence on overseas capital for logging and milling operations; it is also high risk because of the foot dragging over replanting in areas already cleared of forest in Fiji and the Solomons. Replanting has not taken place at the estimated rate on which the project was sold to the people of North Georgia, for example. Nevertheless, inasmuch as the forest represents a resource that Pacific Island people have been using since they first arrived in the Pacific, and perhaps even in Southeast Asia before that, these risks can be reduced by planned usage so that continued patterns of shifting cultivation fit in with logging, reserves, large-scale agriculture, and smallholder use as recommended in the establishment of the Gogol Wood Chip Project in the Madang area of New Guinea (*Man and the Biosphere Report* 1976), as discussed below. Thus if this planned development example is successful, it will be a useful demonstration of the possibilities for combining a direct source of food production with a cash-earning use of another resource from the land, namely the forested area.

Direct mode of production

The food supply on many islands of the Pacific is largely derived from root crops and tree crops. The main root crops of taro (*Colocasia esculenta*) and yams are losing importance to cassava and sweet potato, which are more easily grown. Coconuts, bananas, breadfruit, pandanus, and sago are the main tree crops (ADB 1980, table 9:198–202). These staples provide a seasonal variety and steady supply of the basic carbohydrates to which marine foods and chickens, pigs, and dogs are sometimes a relish, or "foods to be eaten with the main foods."

Shifting agriculture is the main means of production for the root crops. A plot is cleared, usually of secondary growth, sufficient root crops planted for the needs of the next 10–12 months, and as these become available, then a new set of plantings is set out in the nearby cleared area. If the plot is of sufficient size, three lots of taro and yams may have been grown in the one cleared area before it is left to rest and regenerate. Then another plot must be cleared and the process recommenced. On Niue a taro plant takes about 10 months to mature from time of planting to harvesting, but a cassava plant takes only five to six months. Also cassava can be replanted in a recently cultivated plot without a reduction in yield:

> Cassava can be grown practically anywhere, and because it yields well even on poor soils, it is frequently last in the cropping sequence. . . . It gives good yields even on heavily-cropped soils and does not require a lengthy fallow, and also yields more per man-hour than the other food crops. (Maude 1973:175)

With the increasing pressure for more production because of population increase, Maude noticed in Tonga that not only are the plots being used longer by this device of replanting cassava in an already used plot, but also that the fallow period is being shortened to one to three or four years, compared to three to five years elsewhere (1973:175). So there has been a subtle change in the root crop staples, and also in their mode of production. This intensification process in Tonga is matched elsewhere by the extensification process that is noted on Savaii in Western Samoa, where some shifting agriculture plots are being cut higher and higher on the hillsides and thus are cutting into primary, not secondary forest growth. Watt has stated that Western Samoa is losing annually approximately 1,000 hectares of forest cover due to swidden agriculture or a changeover to permanent agricultural land use (figures for Western Samoa based on Trotman, n.d.). Again the reasons for this cutting into primary forest are given as the necessity for reduced fallow periods due to increasing population pressure, increased cash crop planting, or other causes (Watt 1980:296–7).

On Niue where this problem of population pressure does not exist (in fact, the reverse is the problem – too rapid loss of population migrating to New Zealand), root crops continue to be the main focus of production, and fallow for bush plots is three to five years (see Pollock 1979). Niue is an interesting example of a society where people combine an avid dependence on root crop foodstuffs, three or four different types being served at the main meal each day, together with a high dependence on imported foodstuffs, particularly tinned meat. Thus to their "subsistence affluence" Niueans are able to add imported luxury foodstuffs. Their island is small enough that they can work an eight-hour day for a salary or wages, and harvest their taros on their way home from work in the afternoon. We can thus argue that either they are at a transitional stage between evaluating "the benefits of commitment to the monetary economy as being higher than those which can be gained from the integral subsistence sector" (Ward and Hau'ofa 1980:60), or that their small island environment allows them to both work their bush gardens and work for wages, thereby continuing their traditional agricultural practices alongside a pattern of wage work (Pollock 1979). This second statement must indicate a state of risk lower than the first, where any transitional state is fraught with uncertainties.

A significant factor in the direction of change in the source of food supply in the Pacific is the general attitude toward one form of food procurement over another. Finney has pointed out that being an excellent farmer no longer carries the prestige of the past, but rather "is considered dull, dirty, and old-fashioned, while wage labour is exciting, clean, and a modern way to earn one's living" (Finney 1975:188). Given this negative view of agricultural work and the declining numbers of persons actively engaged in it (Castle 1980), one wonders if there is some way to "clean up" agricultural labor, to make it attractive enough to that sector of the population that desperately wants a steady cash income, but does not want to give up living on its own land and the self-satisfaction that this provides. Agricultural production is not regarded as particularly arduous, but it is not the level to which people aspire. Rather they would prefer to see their children educated and with a steady wage job. Hau'ofa has summarized this view:

> The aspirations for material goods and for services among the Pacific peoples are already so high, and rising that rural development, as presently conceived and executed is not able to meet them. Pacific Islanders aim not for a rise from poverty, which in general they do not have, but for a shift from one form of relative affluence to another. . . . The indigenous peoples of the Pacific have never been peasants and do not have attitudes to labour and life born of centuries of struggle for survival. (Ward and Hau'ofa 1980:485)

He assessed the alternatives presently available to be (1) moving more toward a Western style of living (presumably this means a heavily import-based way of life), or (2) reducing one's aspirations and deriving other alternatives (Ward and Hau'ofa 1980:487). Capitalism or else? Presumably within an interpretation of Western living, people could continue to produce their root crops and pick their tree crops, and also work for wages, just as they currently do in Niue. But how can so many jobs be created for those 61 and 51 percent of the populations of Western Samoa and Tonga, respectively, that are currently economically active in agriculture? Furthermore, where will the money come from to buy the rice and tinned fish which they will need if they stop producing food crops? The current level of wages in Western Samoa indicates that given an average annual wage of $1600, or a minimum daily wage of $2.50 per eight-hour day will not provide enough Tala to buy many 50-pound bags of rice and cans of corned beef, if there is no taro from the bush to supplement it (*Savali* [weekly newspaper of Western Samoa] 29 March 1981).

Forest resources for cash and subsistence

Forested areas are contiguous and continuous with agricultural areas of subsistence and/or cash crop production on most Pacific Islands. Thus these must be considered as a single, not two separate ecosystems. As a total unit, shifting cultivation areas and forest areas have provided the source of basic foodstuffs since the first human settlement of the Pacific, right up to the present day. The general appearance, best seen from the air, is not of neat, clean, rectangular, cleared, ploughed fields, as a European-based agricultural economist might expect, or hope to find. Rather the areas of native forest, secondary forest, and cleared areas form a patchwork pattern with little regularity, and certainly not clearly defined boundaries.

Thus the use of forest resources fits in closely with the existing modes of production whether for subsistence, or for cash, in terms of its role as a natural resource. Traditionally, high island populations in the Pacific have depended heavily on the presence of forested areas into which they could extend their shifting agriculture plots when necessary, or as a shelter belt, as a regeneration and receding source, and as a source of birds and other animal foods that prefer forest cover. Thus the forest is an integral part of the popular view of the island ecosystem, and it is part of, not distinct from, the agricultural areas.

> Traditionally the natural forest... provided products which met many of a rural community's basic needs of food, shelter and fuel. While this dependency is not as strong today, there are still many communities in rural areas of South Pacific countries which rely on products of the forest for their livelihood and well-being. (Watt 1980:298)

Food products, support for wildlife population (principally pigs and birds), wood products for building, fencing, carving, etc., and not least, firewood, are some of the noncommercial uses of forest resources.

The forest areas are also important areas of conservation necessary in any land use pattern, whether the direct mode of production or the cash mode. Ethical proscriptions surround the uses of forested areas and thereby provide some limitations on the extent to which they can be exploited either for subsistence or commercial purposes. Forested areas are often cited as homes for spirits of ancestors, or have a very stringent tabu existing against anyone entering, as in the case of Niue's Huvalu *tapu* Forest, which covers

Table 4.5. *Estimated rates of depletion of commercially operable forest areas and duration of the commercial forest resource*

	Estimated annual area logged (ha)	Estimated duration of resource at cutting rates (years)
Cook Islands	—	—
Fiji	3,500	60
Kiribati	—	—
Papua New Guinea	19,000	500
Solomon Islands	5,000	20
Tonga	30	15
Western Samoa	2,700	30

Source: ADB 1980:297.

approximately one-fifth of the land surface of the island. No one may enter the forest without permission from the trustees of the forest. [A zoologist who wished to collect dung from the fruit bat (*peka*), which is known to roost in the forest, was finally refused permission to enter the forest in 1975 after making several strong pleas to the trustees.] The guidelines that were established to conserve that forest, which were first outlined by Smith in 1906, are still in operation. Such conservation measures serve first to protect the land from erosion, as well as to provide shelter for species that might otherwise be heavily exploited or exterminated. Niuean crabs grow to become large delicacies within the protective cover of Huvalu Forest, and have to be baited on the edge of the forest if they are to be caught for home or tourist consumption.

Gillison has pleaded for restoration of the tropical forest ecosystem by controlled management of this diminishing resource (Table 4.5). Shifting cultivation and fire are two man-introduced factors that have altered the tropical forest ecosystem; shifting cultivation and fire, he argues, if continued at the relatively small scale on which they have been practiced to date, amount to "a natural" level of disturbances of indigenous subsistence that have persisted as a "management" process for many thousands of years and from which probably much of the tropical forest ecosystem *sensu lato* has been derived. He further has warned against the effects of overintensive shifting cultivation, such as degradation of the soil, erosion from runoff, and slips (Gillison 1976:65). An example of the latter consequence is borne out in the case of Fiji by the bad slips and loss of gardens resulting from the heavy rains associated with Cyclone Wally in April of 1980 (M. Crozier, personal communication).

Table 4.6. *Estimated areas of natural forest*[a]

	Estimated total forest cover	Land area	Forest cover as as a percentage of land area
Cook Islands	n.s.	24	—[b]
Fiji	820	1,827	45
Kiribati	n.s.	68	—[b]
Papua New Guinea	40,000	46,224	86
Solomon Islands	2,570	2,853	90
Tonga	3	69	4
Western Samoa	154	293	52

[a] Expressed in hectares ($\times 1000$).
[b] No statistics available.
Source: ADB 1980:294.

The forested areas of the Pacific Islands are more extensive in the South-west Pacific than in the Northeast, and the species diversity and volume of standing timber per hectare also increase along the same gradient (Table 4.6). "Thus Papua New Guinea and the Solomon Islands have the greatest areas of forest, the largest percentages of land under forest, the greatest species diversity, and the greatest commercial log volumes" (Watt 1980:294). The Hawaiian Islands would be an exception to the northeast rule, though it is hard to judge accurately the extent to which these islands were wooded before the sugar plantations were introduced in the 1860s. Daws (1974) mentions that Cook reported that the islands of Kauai and Maui were heavily wooded, though shortage of firewood at Kealakekua Bay, Hawaii, was one contributing factor that is alleged to have counted against Captain Cook, who is reputed to have drained an already scarce resource.

Human use of these forested areas goes back at least seven thousand years in the Southwest Pacific, with agricultural practices well established in Papua New Guinea by 4000 B.C. (Golson 1976). This process of shifting agriculture allowed for a widely scattered population of low density for the area available. The people converted areas of forest to grassland, and, through hunting and (perhaps for protection from enemies) firing, maintained – or extended – large savanna areas (White 1976:36). Thus use of the forest brought about some alteration of that ecosystem, but, as Clarke has argued, it was in the interests of these shifting cultivators to encourage the regrowth of trees to protect their livelihood:

Two sets of persons prize the tropical forest environment as a site for agriculture and a home for man. One is made up of the nonforest dwelling researchers – such as are at this symposium (MAB) [*Man and the Biosphere*] – who see an association of trees as the way to preserve the fertility potential of tropical soils without external subsidy and who argue that shifting cultivation…is the ideal solution for agriculture in the humid tropics. The other set of persons are the shifting cultivators themselves who give a variety of reasons for favouring forest-fallow cultivation. (Clarke 1976:107)

Furthermore, Clarke has rationalized that cultivating in the forest requires less labor to produce a specific unit of food than cultivating grassland soils or operating a permanent-field system of agriculture.

Lea (1976), in discussing the many uses by human populations of the tropical forest ecosystem, has sounded three warning notes: First, the human capacity for creating large-scale environmental damage is increasing. Second, agricultural systems and the use of fire convert forests to grasslands. Third, the increasing density of populations engaged in shifting cultivation brings about a metamorphism in both the forest and the people. Lea has illustrated all of these with respect to his familiarity with various New Guinea societies in both the Highlands and coastal Lowlands. He has concluded:

It is a truism that man is part of the tropical forest ecosystem but the statement does need emphasis. It is a habitat in which humans live and obtain their sustenance and so any planned modifications of the system in the pursuit of economic growth or even rural development need to be tempered with caution. All too often we forget that the forest is an ecological niche into which some societies fit and obtain cultural enrichment, happiness and sustenance. History unfortunately is full of examples of non-logical forces entering what is essentially a fragile ecosystem and even if they do not destroy the forest, they create cultural disorientation and serious social disruption. (Lea 1976:89)

Use of forests for commercial as contrasted with subsistence purposes began in Papua New Guinea in 1940 when small amounts of cabinet timber (walnut) were exported. During the war years, demands for log timber increased, but as White demonstrated graphically, the dramatic increase in nonconifer logs harvested has continued since 1963. This timber has come mainly from the Lowland rain forest (White 1976:37).

In the Solomons, small-scale export logging was started in 1924 with the kauri stands at Vanikoro Island, but it was not until the 1950s that a forest department came into being and the government decided that its best policy was to acquire substantial areas of good timber land for working by timber companies. By purchasing customary land in three main tracts on Isabel, New Georgia, and Vangunu, and securing some alienated land on Gizo and in the Shortlands, government set in motion the then slow procedure of timber development, which became a marked activity in the 1970s. An important corollary was that the Solomons Forestry Department was to do the replanting work; after some delays and a slow start, a more vigorous replanting scheme is now in action. In the Solomons, production takes the form of logging for export markets and sawn timbers for local use. However, landowners are not totally happy with the existing arrangements, and the latest proposal is for an "agreement signing between the land owners and the timber companies according to Forests and Timber Ordinance following direct negotiation by the timber companies themselves with the land owners" (Kera and Maenu'u 1976:73). But as both Kera and Maenu'u (1976) and Rence (1980) have pointed out, landowners were concerned because of previous cases where "trustees had shared royalties amongst themselves instead of among the whole clan or tribe" (Rence 1980:19). Moreover, the timber companies felt there was insufficient security for their investment. In 1978, a new approach was tried with the setting up of the North New Georgia Timber Corporation which became the owner of nearly all the timber on North New Georgia. Membership of the corporation was to consist of all people living in the area. The chiefs were to nominate the director of the corporation, and they were also to distribute profits from the selling of timber to the members. Agreement with Lever Pacific Timbers, one of the major logging companies in the Southwest Pacific, and part of the Unilever multinational corporation, was to be reached at a meeting in February of 1980, according to Rence (1980:18–19).

This example of the risks in setting up acceptable terms for the logging industry in North New Georgia in the Solomons is only one illustration of the bargaining that is being carried out in various parts of the Pacific for the most recently exploitable commercial resource: timber. The two reports express great concern for the social effects, for the powers of decision makers, and paramountly, it would seem, for who shares in the profits. But no mention is made of the subsistence farming, slash-and-burn garden plots. The expectation appears to be toward a purchased diet:

> If agreement is reached, the isolated area of North New Georgia will one day be crowded by timber workers and job seekers. This will create problems of squatting and other social problems.
>
> People have not yet realized the consequences of destroying our natural environment and polluting our rivers and sea. All they expect is money. The operation of logging in North New Georgia is creating inevitable problems for future generations, though it will make people alive today much richer. (Rence 1980:19)

"The Gogol Wood Chip project is another example of the attempt to maintain the timber land for the indigenous people while a multinational works the timber" (Cavanaugh 1976). John Waiko's account of his village, Binandere, reveals how those people resisted two overseas companies that were attempting to gain timber rights to their land. Sixty thousand hectares of heavily forested land belong to a total Papua New Guinea population of 37,000. These people managed to resist exploitation by outsiders until 1971 when a foreign company assessed the boundaries and bought timber rights. The PNG Minister for Conservation and Environment tried to negotiate timber rights for Kawin Corporation Proprietary of Hong Kong and Parsons & Whitmore, an American/Australian Company. In February of 1974, the village people expressed concern that they must have representatives to negotiate with Kawin. They also expressed resentment at the lack of sufficient notice of meetings; negotiations between the government and the companies were too far advanced before the village people were notified. "The priority lay in allowing the Company [P & W] into the area, not in getting the people a good deal. We refused to abandon the interests of the people in this way" (Waiko 1977:413). The village became divided into one group supporting P & W and the politicians and another group opposed to the intention and approach of the company. Politicians favored P & W instead of Kawin.

P & W wanted to employ 119 locals at most. The people wanted to remain owners of the land and also wanted village development such as stores and roads. Waiko and others represented their own villagers, even though they were called "educated big heads" by their opponents. They spoke in their own language, and pushed for the need to retain subsistence resources; they avoided formal meetings, talked informally to the people, and used local analogies and examples; thus they managed to stay in close contact with the villagers' own wishes. Waiko spoke against the company. He outlined the issues pertaining to the kinship rights to land, separations of generations, the traditional way of life, the self-interest of politicians, and politicians' use of the short-term view, so that villagers felt that the politicians were not working for them. Waiko has summed up: "The wealth of our forefathers was derived primarily from the forest and land. Today the wealth of the bulk of the population stems from those areas of saved forest" (1977:417).

A third case study illustrates the Western Samoan Government's efforts to assert its economic independence by carrying out a 1963 UN study recommendation for development of village agriculture and commercial forestry and fisheries. As Shankman (1979) has reported, the government began forestry negotiations, in the mid-1960s, with Potlatch Corporation, a large American wood products firm; the corporation persuaded the government that only large-scale private foreign investment could develop the islands' hardwoods and proposed to build a multimillion-dollar mill and timber harvesting operation. A very significant feature of the negotiations was the company's request to lease timberland amounting to 14–23 percent of the entire country if the project was to be profitable.

> The company requested changes in Samoan land tenure that would allow it to lease enough timber land – to make the operation profitable. Potlatch also asked the government to fund new harbor and wharf

facilities at Asau and manage timber replanting. In return, the company promised jobs and revenues; as the operation moved toward full production in the early 1970's, Potlatch became the country's largest private employer. Government revenues from the operation, however, proved elusive. The Asau facilities cost the state far more than anticipated, requiring foreign loans, and the imbalance between government costs and corporate benefits led to tension between Potlatch and local officials. At the same time, the last of the islands' primary rain forests was being irrevocably damaged by inadequate forest management.

Then, in 1976, Potlatch declared its Samoan subsidiary unprofitable. The balance sheet now superseded development; the corporation that a decade earlier had persuaded the government of the benefits of foreign investment now offered the state the opportunity to buy its losing venture. Fearing dislocation if the operation closed, the government purchased the subsidiary and is now attempting to make it profitable. Whatever the outcome, Potlatch has left a legacy of distorted development priorities and misplaced spending of government money. (Shankman 1979:1)

This case study reveals the negative side of an attempt to develop this natural resource by using outside capital. Watt (1980) has suggested that development of forestry decisions must be taken on the appropriate scale of operation. Although large-scale operations may contribute greater economic benefits and save the cost of initial road construction in rural areas, the ecological impact may be greater and the life of an increasingly valuable resource reduced. He has suggested that an alternative approach would be by way of smaller-scale operations which would beneficially contribute to skill development, inculcate self-reliance, and have less ecological impact (Watt 1980: 314). The risks would thereby be reduced.

In the case of Western Samoa, the age of the coconut trees is such that they can contribute to the logging industry.

If this material could be disposed of more easily, substantial gains to the coconut industry would follow.... A side benefit from the commercial utilization of coconut stems – for fence posts, building materials or roofing shingles – is that the products manufactured are, in every case, substituting either for imports or locally produced forest products. (ADB 1980:406)

The processing of such coconut stems at sawmills is already in operation in Tonga and Kiribati (Watt 1980:320).

A more successful example of the large-scale operation that Potlatch envisaged for Western Samoa has been incorporated by the Fiji Pine Commission. Using land held under customary land tenure, the forestry department has begun an active replanting scheme on plantation scale. Twenty-eight thousand hectares of grasslands have already been planted mainly with *Pinus caribaea*, though some hardwoods are to be included. This land was previously underutilized, and, given the necessary financial and labor inputs, can also serve as an export contribution (the first shipment of pine to Japan took place in July, 1980); moreover, by providing building materials processed locally, it can provide a means of import substitution. Local processing of this material in the form of saw logs prior to export offers the potential for additional local employment. Thus with the rapid growth rate and this employment factor, Watt reckons that "plantation forestry is, therefore, one of the rurally based activities where South Pacific countries have a physical advantage over nontropical countries. The major challenges are to realize that potential, where land is available, and turn this plantation growth potential into a comparative cost advantage" (Watt 1980:302).

Implications for food consumption patterns and nutritional status

Sale or lease of timberlands is a threat to the continuity of the food supply because of the implications of such a move toward greater cash dependency. Irregularity of payment of sums due, or lump sum payment, may lead to a situation of feast or famine, particularly for those who are unused to budgeting their income for household expenditure. Lack of adequate facilities in which to store sacks of rice or flour, in addition to lack of banking facilities, may lead to periods of low or poor nutrition until the next payment is received. Moreover, with no subsistence crops to fall back on, together with urban health problems, the situation is exacerbated. The familiar food crops, such as taro and yam, have also been subject to cuts in availability because of hurricanes and storm damage, but, over years of learning to cope with such natural disasters, knowledge of substitute foods for those not available has become part of traditional lore. Use of foods from the forest and bush, such as wild yams, Polynesian chestnut, and arrowroot starch, plus the stored fermented breadfruit, enabled them to manage until the main starch crops regenerated. (Malnutrition was not a feature of the health of Pacific peoples, until the urban sector developed.)

Bread and rice, bought from the store, are not considered as filling as taro and yams, nor do they provide the wide spectrum of nutrients. Tinned fish must be watered down to add some flavor for all, or mutton flaps, the cheapest meat, must be stewed to provide a fatty "accompanying dish." Fruits are expensive, even in the market. Thus, not only is a caloric minimum hard to maintain with cash, but the nutritional balance is considered unsatisfactory by nutritional analysts. Purchases of biscuits and sweets to amuse and fill children, particularly, drain the cash supply and don't fill.

A balanced program allowing both taro and timber to coexist would permit a more varied diet. This is an important element in the view of the good life for Pacific populations I have studied (N. J. P. fieldnotes 1975, 1982). Not only is the range of foodstuffs important, but also the ease of preparation and the social status associated with these foods. For these reasons, eggs have become much more widely used in recent times in the Pacific. Departments of Agriculture can assist with development of quickly maturing varieties of taro, yams, and sweet potatoes and with development of food technology to offer these traditional foods in modern form, such as chips; these new practices would ensure that the foods produced are being consumed. Programs such as the FAO Root Crops program and the Eat More Local Foods campaigns in Fiji, Tonga, and Western Samoa indicate the increasing level of consciousness of this issue.

The children are the most vulnerable group in this issue. Not only do they constitute 50 percent of the population, but their dependency on the way their future is being mapped out in terms of uses of island environments makes this a crucial area of concern. Their food preferences are being set now by the foods available, whether traditional starch staples, or purchased foods. What they choose to eat sets the pattern of demands for foods.

Taro and timber are two choices for directions of development of both good food production and food consumption in Pacific nations. It has been argued here that they should not be considered as alternatives to one another, but should be taken together as closely intertwined modes of using the local environment to provide a food supply. Separately they offer unsatisfactory food intake whether socially or nutritionally, but together the purchased foods can be added to the local foods, with less drain on the import bill.

Conclusions

The main concern throughout this paper has been the degree to which Pacific Island nations can provide their food supply using their own environment. The limited resource base, the limited markets for exporting any surplus food crops, together with the likelihood that other Pacific Island nations will have similar surplus crops such as taro means that the strong agricultural base in its present form has only limited potential for meeting balance of payment discrepancies. Selling agricultural produce at the local level is thus a risky form of cash return.

Furthermore it has been argued that the continued practice of shifting agriculture combined with a limited development of forestry would provide both subsistence foodstuffs and the desired cash at the minimum risk. This use of the environment for dual economic ends would both fit with traditional patterns of production and provide alternative means of access to the all-important cash.

Such a land use pattern requires a conceptualization of the total environment such that bush plots, fallow, secondary growth, and exploitable forests be considered part of one unified system. The products of such a system would be both consumables in the form of foodstuffs, some surplus and cash crops for an income, as well as the returns from forestry in both wages and land-lease money from an overseas company, as the people of North New Georgia are trying to negotiate.

This multipurpose use of the environment requires careful monitoring of all stages of its development by the agriculture and forestry departments of the governments concerned, in close consultation with the local people involved. The dangers of exploitation of the forestry resource by agencies with a single purpose, profit, have been demonstrated by the Western Samoan Potlatch case.

Imported foodstuffs exacerbate the major imbalances in trade, while only partially fulfilling the food demand. The need for cash at the local level is well established, and dependence on imported foods is a recognized though undesirable alternative means to direct production of foodstuffs. Careful monitoring of the flow of locally produced foodstuffs both from the production and from the marketing sectors, as well as the consumption sector, will enable the risks to be kept under surveillance.

In this paper, I have argued that the risks to the food supply can be minimized if several options are kept open. Both taro and timber can be obtained by direct production, and thereby assist in providing subsistence foods and cash, while also reducing the trade imbalances. The risks of an uncertain supply of food must be a concern shared by health and welfare sectors of government as well as by the agriculture and forestry sectors. The health and welfare of future generations are particularly vulnerable when their environment is being sold away, and their food supply is thus made more uncertain. A balance of subsistence and cash foods will help to minimize the impact on total calories consumed, but the dangers of malnutrition will arise from consumption of "convenience" purchased foods and from difficulties in budgeting for the household food supply. Taro and the traditional starches are filling foods; their purchased substitutes are not so filling. Similarly the gap between developments in the production sphere and those in the consumption sphere must be narrowed to ensure an adequate diet.

Part II

CULTURAL MEANING AND PERCEPTION

5. "The worst disease": the cultural definition of hunger in Kalauna

Michael W. Young

Of all diseases, hunger is the worst. *Dhammapada* xv. (A.D. ca. 100)

What is hunger?

It is an anthropological truism that "food" is culturally defined, and that "foodways" (to use the folksy idiom) are as diverse as any other set of customs evolved to meet the bodily needs of humans. While often ignorant of the strictly nutritional import of their food, people know what they like and are apt to complain of hunger when they cannot get it. Yet for all that has been written about the wondrous variety of food preferences, little has been said about the "great leveler," hunger. Anthropologists have tended to assume (along with nutritionists, physiologists, psychologists, and neurologists) that hunger is everywhere the same in a way that appetite most emphatically is not. A recent textbook on medical anthropology declares that appetite is "a cultural concept that may vary greatly from one culture to the next," whereas "hunger represents a basic nutritional deprivation and is a physiological concept" (Foster and Anderson 1978:266). This fussy emic-etic distinction does scant justice to the ordinary-language connotations of "hunger" in English: It is a grave and solemn word with an almost spectral presence. By reducing it to a physiological concept, these authors would preclude investigation of its semantic range in other cultures. Could Erasmus have said "Appetite teaches many things"? Would Napoleon Bonaparte's *mot* have been recorded if he had said "Appetite governs the world"? Surely, hunger deserves more considerate treatment by anthropologists and other scholars with a vested interest in the varieties of alimentary experience.

It is a regrettable irony that those most able to study objectively the phenomenon of hunger are those least likely to have experienced it profoundly themselves. [However, we must except some remarkable studies of starvation in situ, such as Holmberg's among the Bolivian Siriono (1950/1969) and

I am grateful to the Australian National University for funding several periods of fieldwork on Goodenough Island, and to Dr. Debbora Battaglia for a critical yet sympathetic reading of my text. It could not have been written without the patient help, over many years, of Manawadi Enowei, Adiyaleyale Iyahalina, and Kawanaba Kaweya.

Turnbull's among the indurated Ik (1972); whereas for sheer tenacity of research under the most harrowing circumstances imaginable, the doomed Jewish physicians who studied hunger diseases in the Warsaw Ghetto deserve the highest accolade (Winick 1979).] Some minimal agreement is necessary, therefore, as to what we mean by hunger.

Like other animals, the human species evolved in an environment in which food was scarce, and it might reasonably be supposed that the sensation of hunger confers some selective advantage; for at the very least, hunger functions as an unmistakable stimulus to procure food necessary for the organism's survival. Much research in the behavioral sciences has been predicated on this view of hunger as a drive, as a sensation (albeit beyond finite definition) that communicates a basic biological need. (We might note that its uses in metaphor acknowledge the insistent, relentless, and aggressive nature of the drive: It is a goad, sharper than the thorn or the sword; it "knows no friend" and "breaks through stone walls." Yet other metaphors postulate hunger's likeness to other felt needs – for love, for spiritual sustenance, or, like Richard III's, for revenge.) Experimental research on the feeding behavior of animals found the need for a concept complementary and opposite to that of hunger. If hunger brings depletion, repletion brings satiety. The most interesting problem then became the regulation of food intake as an organism oscillates between the two states. Lesions made in the hypothalamus of a rat's brain stimulated overeating (hyperphagia) or noneating (aphagia), depending upon whether the medial or lateral locus of the nerve centers was destroyed. A "satiety" center and a "hunger center" were accordingly postulated, the destruction of which led, respectively, to voracious feeding and obesity, or to a disdain for food and death by starvation. There is some doubt, however, as to the reality of these "centers" as localized brain functions and, more pertinently, as to whether the hypothalamic "appestat" plays such a determinant role in the regulation of feeding. The fact that when the brains of crabs and blowflies are removed they will eat until they burst suggests that, in the higher animals too, a far more complex system of neural forces is involved in the stop–go mechanisms of satiety and hunger, one that is not exclusively located in the "hardware" of the nervous system but that also entails the "software" of more elusive psychological processes (Morgane and Jacobs 1969). It should come as no surprise to anthropologists that animals do not "eat for calories" any more than most humans do, and that (as every good restauranteur knows) the sensory properties of food, particularly its taste and odor, are more important to the feeding animal than its nutritive value. Behavioral scientists allow that sensory signals can be learned as well as being innate with respect to the quality and quantity of food ingested, which would indicate that, within yet to be determined limits, hunger is subject to modification by cultural conditioning. Like the sex drive (though doubtless to a lesser extent), hunger can be inhibited or stimulated at the neocortical level. In the last analysis, it is the awareness or consciousness of *being* hungry (or "having" hunger, as many languages express it) that matters; as well as teach – as Erasmus had put it – hunger can, it seems, also learn. A minimal definition of "hunger," then is the awareness of a bodily compulsion to eat, whether or not it can be gratified.

In what follows, I explore the parameters of a particular cultural definition of hunger which, although anchored to the minimal definition given above, encompasses a range of experiences markedly different from our own. It is objectified as a sorcery-inflicted disease, invoked as a spectral threat to the community, and experienced in the belly with the utmost anxiety. In Kalauna, a community of some 500 people on Goodenough Island in southeast Papua, hunger and satiety are invested with an ideological importance which, I suggest, induces acute sensitivity to them. Hunger is felt with keener anguish than is common elsewhere, and satiety relished with greater relief. It is not because Kalauna people feel these states intensely that they elaborate them ideologically, but rather because they have so ritualized satiety, and so politicized hunger, that they are culturally cued to a heightened experience of them. Hunger in particular is a signification of such dramatic import that it possesses the power to influence people's perception of their body states.[1]

Food and diet

Like many other Melanesians of the Southwest Pacific, the people of Goodenough cultivate numerous varieties of yam, taro, banana, and sweet potato as their principal subsistence crops. Cassava (manioc), pumpkin, maize, cucurbits, beans, tomato, pineapple, and other fruits are of fairly recent European introduction, and none of them is regarded as "proper" food. Other native foods include the ubiquitous coconut, breadfruit, Tahitian chestnut, and a variety of green relishes, roots, and small nuts. Pigs are supremely important, and other than the odd chicken they are the only domesticated source of protein. But Kalauna men hunt and fish – as much for the sport as for the catch – and provide the occasional wallaby, pig, cuscus, bird, or lizard; they also catch prawns, eels, fish, shellfish, and bush hen (megapode) eggs. Lest this colorful catalog give an impression of dietary diversity and plentitude, I hasten to add that most people seem content most of the time with a rather narrow range of comestibles. Pork is eaten when social opportunity offers, on a feast-and-famine basis; the other sources of protein are almost negligible in their contribution to the daily diet. Nowadays, cash

---

1 Although I deal exclusively with Kalauna in this account, I take it to be fairly representative of Goodenough as a whole. With a total population of some 14,000, the island is culturally homogeneous though there are several dialect groups and between 30 and 40 multiclan communities. The "hunger syndrome" I describe for Kalauna, however, is not everywhere of equal intensity or importance since the Methodist Mission (among other agents of change) has brought about a pervasive restructuring of values. Kalauna is among the most tradition-oriented villages on Goodenough.

earned from the sale of copra or men's labor abroad is used to purchase tinned meat and fish, rice, flour, biscuits, tea, and sugar. But again, it is the rare Kalauna family that can count on any of these "luxury" European foods as a regular supplement to the diet. The usual appetitive response to these foods is to scoff them all at once; packets of biscuits, flour, or sugar are never kept in the house for later. This contrasts with the attitude to the "proper" foods (au'a), which are so carefully measured, apportioned, counted, and even hoarded.

Boiling is the most common and preferred method of cooking, though tubers and fish (never pork) are sometimes roasted. Most cooking and general food preparation is done by women, nowadays with tradestore utensils; men cook for feasts in large clay pots traded from the Amphlett Islands. The domestic household is the commensal unit, and it usually consists of a man and his wife (or wives), their unmarried children, and sundry dependents such as aged parents, foster children, or unmarried siblings of the householder. The housewife prepares one or two pots of food for the evening meal, though if the gardening regime allows she will also cook at midday. Cold leftovers are eaten for breakfast. When planting, men and women eat nothing at all in the daytime; this is in accordance with the belief that the ancestral spirits will deny their fructifying aid to gardeners with food already inside their bellies. During the planting season, then, men and women do their days' work on empty stomachs, mitigating pangs of hunger by chewing betel nut or smoking home-grown tobacco or black trade twist. When not actually planting, they may roast tubers in a garden fire or eat snacks of sugarcane, coconuts, or sweet bananas. The main meal of the day, served just after dark, usually consists of one or two of the staple foods (according to season) boiled in water with a measure of seawater for salt flavoring. During the season of scarcity from late November to March, only plantain, sweet potato, and cassava may be available, though a meal consisting of cassava alone testifies to real scarcity – or poverty – and no one willingly admits to having fed on such despised food. Other dishes may accompany the staples. If there is chicken, pork or fish, it is usually cooked with greens (tree "cabbage," taro tops, or pumpkin shoots) and coconut cream squeezed from the shredded flesh of the nut. But most families, on most days of the week for most of the year, eat only ungarnished, farinaceous staple foods, washed down with the thin but nutritious soup in which the food has been boiled.

The most relished and prestigious dish in Kalauna, ceremonially prepared for feasts in large clay pots, is *kumakava*, a rich and succulent pudding made from diced taro or plantain (only the hardest and best varieties will do), simmered for hours in thick coconut cream until the pieces are coated with a glutinous oil. This pudding keeps for a day or two and is also delicious served cold. With *kumakava* and pork boiled with greens, the culinary art of Kalauna reaches its apogee. Such feast food is eaten no more than a dozen times a year, however, and the daily fare tends to be bland, bulky, and (by Western standards) deadly monotonous. It is relatively lacking in animal protein and fresh fruits. For all their ingenious uses of food as a symbol, and for all their preoccupation with its political deployment, Kalauna people appear to be indifferent cooks.

Nutrition and scarcity

Few data are available on the nutritional status of Goodenough Islanders, though some sample surveys of young children were conducted in 1979. The most comprehensive finding was that, of 1,852 children weighed and measured, seven percent were below 60 percent of standard weight-for-age – an index of serious malnourishment.[2] This indicates that even in a fairly prosperous year (as 1979 was thought to be), the nutritional needs of Goodenough children left much to be desired when measured against the 1973 WHO standards adopted by the government of Papua New Guinea. It might be expected that in years of genuine scarcity there is widespread malnourishment among children, though a search of the records at the two health centers on the island yielded fewer than a score of cases of marasmus and infant malnutrition among the several thousand entries covering several years. Considering how important the hunger "disease" is thought to be, I had expected to find many more.

What can be said about the incidence of "real" scarcity? Again, in the absence of long-term ecological studies, my information is largely impressionistic. The Massim region as a whole (which is coterminous with the insular and coastal areas of Milne Bay Province) is subject to periodic drought. My own analysis of the records suggests that the D'Entrecastaux Islands experience drought with an average frequency of seven years (the range is two to fourteen). Not all parts of Goodenough are equally susceptible; the mountain districts fare better than the coastal plain and littoral. Kalauna is a mountain village an hour from the sea, though some of its garden lands lie on the coastal flats (see Young 1971: chap. 2 for details). Generally speaking, drought may be local, but the more widespread it is – both within and beyond the island – the more acute are the scarcities because they cannot be relieved by trade. There are other proximate causes of food scarcity, if none so insidious as drought: hurricane winds, excessive rain, and various insect pests.

There is clearly a real ecological basis to Goodenough Islanders' preoccupation with hunger, though I would argue that it is a necessary but not sufficient cause for the extraordinary richness of the "food complex" that dominates Kalauna's ethos. As I have shown elsewhere, all other values and symbolic idioms lock into this overarching concern with food production, food

2 Personal communication from D. Leonard, Nutritionist, Department of Health, Alotau, Milne Bay Province.

preservation, and food giving; evidently, Kalauna culture has gone to inordinate lengths to make food the measure of all things (Young 1971). The ecological nudge provided by periodic drought (experienced as a threat of famine) has produced more than a mere adaptive response; a symbolic, cultural edifice built upon a realistic food-anxiety has seemingly gained a momentum of its own, and become incommensurate with the level of actual threat from the environment. The other D'Entrecasteaux cultures that we know anything about (Dobu, Amphletts, Molima, Duau) do not appear to make of Hunger and Greed such fearsome specters, nor do they erect such elaborate defenses against them. At any rate, Kalauna's institutionalized preparedness for drought and famine appears to be somewhat in excess of its needs – especially nowadays when there are a variety of additional foodcrops and a virtual guarantee from the government to rescue the population from starvation if necessary. It is helpful perhaps to invoke Irving Hallowell's (1954) concept of a "culturally constituted environment" to remind us that it is not the "real" or actual threats that a people respond to, but the ones mediated by their culture's definition of them.[3]

The ethnophysiology of eating and the sociology of shame

Kalauna people readily acknowledge the value of food for bodily strength and growth:

> We chew food and swallow it. It goes down and stays in the belly. The stomach squeezes it. The food becomes excrement, but the juice goes all over the body. It renews our strength and makes us grow.

A slightly different theory stresses the need for "good" food:

> We don't know properly how it works but it appears thus. Our stomach squeezes the food and extracts juice. Bad juice passes out as urine, good juice remains in our body. It goes into our blood and makes our body strong and able to work well. Good food makes good bodies. Bad food passes out as excrement.

---

3 I have refrained from making comparisons with neighboring cultures, though there is scope for a detailed study of local variations on the theme of hunger. Elements of the Kalauna "hunger syndrome" (to be outlined in the remainder of the chapter) appear separately or with different emphases and in different combinations elsewhere in the Massim region. In Duau (Normanby Island), for example, there is appetite-spoiling magic analogous to Kalauna's *sisikwana*; and from the perspective of psychoanalysis Roheim has characterized Duau people as "oral sadistic," obsessed with hoarding or "withholding," and their culture as "a gigantic effort to say 'we are all good mothers'" (1950:240). Again, in the Trobriand Islands, yams are hoarded and allowed to rot, hunger is shameful, and abstention from eating a virtue (Malinowski 1935:220–6). The *vilamalia* ceremonies which "anchor" food in the village and create prosperity are clearly similar to the *manumanua* rites of Kalauna (Malinowski 1935: 226–7). Finally, the people of Wamira on the mainland of Goodenough Bay live in what they regard as "perpetual famine"; yet while bemoaning the scarcity of food, they deliberately underutilize their irrigation system, as if fearful of abundance and the "jealous and gluttonous greed" it would bring (Kahn 1979, 1984). What appears to be missing in these other cultures, however, is the Kalauna notion of a specific, hunger-inducing sorcery.

"Juice" (*huyona*) might be more effectively defined as "essence," because it is held to be the irreducible nutritive component of food. Food that is being digested ("squeezed") in the stomach is called *ba* or *ba'a*, and it is described as being "sweet." (Appropriately, the technical term for stomach contents, chyme, is from the Greek *chymos*, meaning juice.) Because it is the "juice" that remains incorporated after digestion, *huyona* can be grammatically inflected to denote inalienable personal possession: *Huyoku* is "my juice or essence," which figuratively means "my individuality," "my personhood." *Huyoku* can be extrapolated further to mean "my child," though in this sense it is a euphemism for *aku molu*, "my sexual secretion," a more obscene expression.

The importance of "juice" in Kalauna's theory of nutrition is such that the skin of the aged is likened to copra (coconut flesh with the juice extracted), and when the juice of the body dries up, a person withers and finally dies. Parents tell children they must eat food for the juice that will help them to grow; but they also warn them against eating too much food lest it hinder their growth. Besides stomach cramps and sleepiness, an excess of food is said to induce a sluggish disposition, a bad skin, and an unsightly swollen stomach (though "bad" food is also held to be responsible for this last condition). Corpulence is virtually unknown, and a small tight stomach is much admired; it is evidence of "good" food and a restrained appetite. "Good" food can also be described as "clean" or "pure." It is prescribed for pregnant and parturant women, for the sick, and for children during infancy. This class of food consists of "white" or light-textured yams, taro, and bananas. So-called "red" or "yellow" staple foods should be avoided by such people, and in the case of pregnant or parturant women, they are tabooed along with "greasy" foods including all meat and fish.

Another set of evaluative criteria crosscuts the one just described. It is based on the contrast between "hard," "dry" foods (particularly yams and taro) and "soft," "wet," or crumbly foods. The former category (*valaiya*) is especially associated with the practice of *sisikwana*, the magic of hunger suppression, and *lokona*, the disciplined practice of hoarding food until it rots (Young 1971:159–66). After yams have been stored for several months, they become hard and dry, but to Kalauna taste they are excellent eating. The principal reason for preferring hard, dry food, however, is said to be its capacity to fill the belly and satisfy the appetite for long periods.

> *Valaiya* is truly *sisikwana* food. We eat a little, it fills our bellies, and we remain content. We do not eat again until next day! But *lakwada* [soft, pulpy food] is for children and those without teeth. It does not stick to your stomach, and soon you want to eat again.

That there is a contradiction between the two sets of preferences will be obvious: One is based upon the value of clean, pure, juice-laden food for growth and strength; the other is based on the value of hard, dry, and juiceless food for quelling the appetite. The contradiction is easily resolved, however, when it is understood how these evaluations are contextualized. The contexts may pertain to age or sex (children are not encouraged to eat "hard" food, and parturant women can eat only "pure" food), but it is more analytically illuminating to view these contexts as "domestic" or "political" social domains. There is a considerable difference between food valuations appropriate to each of these two domains (Young 1971:195). In brief, the domestic values of food concern its nurturing properties, for it is the substance of kinship and life itself; the political values of food concern its shaming potential, for it is the stuff of status battles and "fighting with food." Hence, clean and juicy staples are redolent of hearth and home, infancy and motherhood; whereas hard and dry *valaiya* has the flavor of the political arena, the whiff of tough and disciplined manhood. By stating a preference for one over the other, one is stating one's social identity, one's alignment with nurture or antinurture – for to give juiceless food is to deny nurture, and to eat it is to pretend that one does not need to eat at all.

Attitudes toward eating in Kalauna are also shaped by the dichotomy between domestic and political domains. Eating is normally confined to the family circle in the privacy of the house. Men are served first, women and young children eat after them. "Feasts" are more properly distributions, when food – usually raw but sometimes cooked – is carried away to be consumed in seclusion at home. Even after some 70 years of Christian missionary influence, rare is the event when a group of unrelated people eat publicly together. This testifies to the shame associated with eating in an exposed, political context. When away from home, people will endure long periods of hunger rather than be seen to eat in public, and even in their own village they are sensitive about who may see them eat. In general, affines and traditional "enemies" (between whom competitive food exchanges are made) should not observe one another eating. This acute sensitivity is explained by the fear that men have of being thought to be gluttonous. Because so much status hangs upon the size of one's gardens, the amplitude of one's tubers, and the amount of surplus stored in one's back room (all of which, in this demonstratively egalitarian society, are indicators of one's political standing in the years to come), then it is expedient to foster the impression that one eats very little. The less a man eats the more he has to give away. On the assumption that they will gossip, visitors are fed royally, for stinginess is a vice almost as despicable as greed.

On a recent visit to Kalauna I read, with admittedly mischievous intent, the following newspaper extract to a group of companions, some of whom had been practicing Catholics for many years. The report concerned the Pope's "strenuous schedule" and "hearty appetite" during his visit to Ireland in September 1979, and it disclosed details of the food he was served by eight nuns in the Papal Nunciature in Dublin. For supper:

> There was smoked salmon to start with, then Polish beetroot soup and Canneloni [*sic*], followed by roast beef, carrots and peas, with roast

and creamed potatoes. This was followed by a choice of six desserts and cakes, all washed down by a light Italian wine. After only a few hours' sleep the Pope was awakened to a hearty Polish breakfast of fruit juice, a selection of fruits and cheese, then bacon, egg, sausages, tomatoes and black and white puddings. (*Canberra Times* 1 October 1979)

Predictably, my Kalauna friends were aghast at evidence of what in their judgment was a cardinal sin – though the more forgiving were prepared to admit that they did not fully understand white man's customs. Less predictable was their astonishment at the gossipy license of the writer who was privy to such scandalous information; he must, they concluded, have been an "enemy" of the Pope.

Magic of prosperity and famine[4]

The ritual leaders of Kalauna, "men who look after the village" or *toitavea-lata*, are men who have succeeded to the most powerful positions in the lineages of Lulauvile, the "food-bringing" clan, which claims (but is not always granted) superior rank. These men are guardians of the Lulauvile myths and magic of prosperity; through their magical skills they can regulate the community's food supply, and their ultimate sanction is the power to inflict mass hunger. In this political ideology the ownership of the magical means of production is crucial – but it is no more important than the ownership of the means of destruction. The one is believed to be the obverse of the other. Hunger is pivotal in this scheme, just as the belly is central to the human body, the source of its keenest pleasures and most calamitous woes. The *toitavealata*, then, of which there may be two or three at any one time, are the most respected and feared men in Kalauna, because they are believed to possess the power for bringing prosperity and abundance (*malia*), or conversely, deprivation and famine (*loka*).

Loka is a concept of doom. It is presaged by numerous omens: falling trees, the cry of rare birds, earth tremors, and other mysterious events. There follows an ineluctable sequence: The wind strips trees of fruit, the sun bakes the earth, the crops and animals die, driving the people to wander desperately with rolling eyes and snatching hands, scouring the forest for wild foods, until finally they are driven to the cannibalism of children (Young 1971:173–4).

Antithetical to the concept of *loka* is the plenty, abundance, and prosperity of *malia*. It is the glut associated with a good yam harvest and the "good times" of feasting when people stay contentedly in the village and celebrate with nightlong dances. The seasons and the legendary history of Kalauna are conceived as oscillating endlessly between periods of *loka* and

4 For an expanded version of this section, see Young 1983:53–60.

malia, smaller cycles within longer ones. Time undulates like the mythical vengeful serpent, Honoyeta. *Loka* scatters the people; *malia* reunites them. The cycle of diastole and systole (the community does indeed expand and contract over time) is conceptually coordinated with the sequence of famine and plenty. Although there is something fatalistic about this picture of relentless oscillation – geared perhaps to the ecological pattern of recurrent drought – it is human agency, with all its contingent and unpredictable characteristics, that is held to be ultimately responsible. Human agency, that is, as influenced by the exemplary and timeless models of motivation provided by the mythical heroes.

The duties of the ritual leaders, the *toitavealata*, are of two broad kinds: to perform the magical rites that accompany the annual gardening cycle, and to enact the special rituals of *manumanua* to counter the threat of famine. This latter ceremony (which means "staying in the house") was traditionally performed during the hungry period of the northwest monsoon; but since European contact it has been performed only contingently and with decreasing frequency – possibly because the diversification of crops obviated it.

The rites of *manumanua* are simple. The only active performers are the *toitavealata*, who build a crude "house" of charmed sticks, vines, and leaves, then sit upon the ground and interminably recite their myths and sing their spells. The rest of the community is enjoined to silence and total inactivity. At dusk, special pots of food are prepared for the ritual leaders to bespell, making the food bitter and repellant to the appetite. All are then invited to sample the food so that they may cure their hunger.

The symbolism of the plants used in the ceremony give some clue to its meaning; they stand for the desirable qualities of size, strength, tenacity, endurance, drought resistance, and bitterness. Even more telling in their imagery are the *sisikwana* spells, of which the following is a sample fragment:

> Stay still, I stay still
> Younger brothers, elder brothers
> You wander weakly, starving
> You will stay
> You search vainly, losing your way
> You wander with curled fingers
> You will stay
> Your hearts trembling
> Stay still, I stay still.

This incantation summons the imagery of desperate and aimless wandering in search of food, but it does so to submit it to the control of the refrain, which conjures the soothing remedy of stillness. Again, the myths that the *toitavealata* recite to one another provide further clues to the symbolic concerns of *manumanua*. One of the heroines is a "grandmother" without orifices, an old woman who sits as inert as a stone with sealed mouth, anus, and vagina. She represents the state of *malia* in its nurturant aspects, albeit a locked-up and self-contained abundance. The hero, her "grandson," showers the world with her abundance when he opens her by placing a snake at her feet. She explodes in fright, her orifices burst, and the secrets of *malia* are revealed. But alas, she is resentful of her transformation into an eating being and abandons mankind forever. As a symbol of *lokona*, the practice of conservation by abstention, she provides magic in the aid of *manumanua*. Such themes recur in all the myths: Stillness, retention, and containment are opposed to wandering, expulsion, and squandering. But the supreme antithesis is that of Satiety on the one hand and Hunger on the other.

For weeks after the ceremony, the *toitavealata* perambulate in the gardens, chanting their spells and spitting magic-impregnated betel juice. Through eyes doctored to make them "undesiring," they inspect the crops. The women who weed them should then, it is said, be induced to follow their example: their eyes nondesiring, their bellies tight and contented, their hands restrained, so that, like model housewives, they will not be tempted to gather more than the minimum needed for the family meal. One of the aims of *manumanua*, then, is to banish famine by making food notionally inedible.

> When *manumanua* is done the people can stay contentedly. They stay, and do not finish more than a morsel of their food. They stay, and their food will ripen and rot. They stay, and its scent will become sickly. Ferment flies will gather and sit upon it. *Manumanua* makes us ashamed to take food from our gardens.

A masochistic solution to the problems of food scarcity, perhaps, but one that is admirably direct. In addressing the consumer, *manumanua* magic teaches the belly to be quiet and to sit still – nostalgically recalling the golden age of mythology when people licked stones and had no need to eat food at all.

The collective benefits of *manumanua* are said to be at least threefold: crop prosperity, favorable weather, and curtailed appetite, with the emphasis on the last as the chief condition of *malia*. ("Without *sisikwana* to control our bellies," Kalauna men argue, "crop magic is pointless.") But it is also within the power of the *toitavealata* to revoke the conditions of *malia* and invert them to produce *loka*. Corresponding to the threefold benefits of *manumanua* are three idioms of collective misfortune. The first and second of these are the sorceries of scourge that bring crop pests and excessive rain, wind, or sun. Magic of the weather is known only to the leaders of Lulauvile clan, though some of the other descent lines in Kalauna know how to ruin the crops by conjuring various avian or insect plagues. The third and most cruel idiom, however, is the reciprocal of *manumanua*'s gentle tutelage of the belly – the dire sorcery of gluttony and insatiable hunger. This magic, called *tufo'a*, is the ultimate weapon in a culture profoundly sensitive to human greed.

The dreadful thump of hunger

Having surveyed Kalauna's theory of dietetics and indicated the political and ritual importance of famine in a "culturally constituted environment," we are now able to round out Kalauna's definition of hunger. To do so, we must return to the body, specifically the belly, "the source of everything" as Berthold Brecht once aptly called it. Two questions immediately suggest themselves: How do Kalauna people describe the symptoms of hunger, and how do they imagine *tufo'a* causes it?

The euphemisms used in Kalauna to indicate the state of hunger are a helpful guide to its symptomatology. *Hala* is the blunt, functional term, but so crude and even obscene is it that it is rarely uttered in conversation. Mere peckishness can be alluded to by the phrase *kalimu yada kau* ("I would chew betel nut") or *dauda yada yu'e* ("I would drink water"). A stronger but still somewhat jocular expression of hunger is *yaku vetawana hi kakawa* ("My inner room is empty"); *vetewana* is the partitioned rearmost section of the house, where the best yams are stored. An even more telling idiom is *mafa hi launa* ("drum it sounds/cries"). This refers to the experience of a hollow stomach beating with hunger. There is a range of similar idioms, the common denominator of which is the "bump" or "thump" of hunger, the sound or sensation (as one might imagine) of the contracted belly knocking against the ribs.

The dread sorcery of *tufo'a* extrapolates the casual bumping of an empty stomach – horrifyingly – to the persistent bumping of an ostensibly full one. The first symptoms of *tufo'a* are these:

> My *ba'a* (chyme) slides about and rumbles. I have just eaten, the food has pushed its way down and filled the empty spaces in my belly. It settles. But soon it bumps again. I try to sleep, but I can hear it. The noise does not stop. Something is wrong. It is *tufo'a*.

Another man declared:

> You can feel *tufo'a* begin as soon as you have eaten. Your belly thumps, shoots, rolls about like stones bouncing downhill and hitting things. It is the sign of *tufo'a*, the sign of spirits eating your chyme.

The "spirits" belong to the general class of ancestor spirits, invoked by the sorcerer who performs *tufo'a* magic. They come invisibly to inhabit the victim's belly and eat the food he ingests, like "guests at the feast." The worst thing, then, is that one feels hungry even though one has just eaten. Satiety is impossible, and one eats, as Kalauna people say, "to no purpose" – like the mythical hero Kawafolafola, who was afflicted with a hole in his throat (Young 1983:228–35).

We might note a curious classical parallel between the supposed effects of *tufo'a* and the fate of the hapless Thessalian king, Erysichthon. According to Ovid, Erysichthon was punished by the goddess Ceres for desecrating her sacred groves. She bid Famine "hide herself in the sinful stomach" of the impious king, creating such a ravenous hunger that he exhausts his fortune in the attempt to appease it. "With loaded tables he complains still of hunger; in the midst of feasts seeks out other feasts." But the more he eats the more he wants, "and even does he become empty by eating," until at last, "the wretched man began to tear his own flesh with his greedy teeth and by consuming his own body, fed himself" (Miller 1921).

Tufo'a heads the dismal catalog of Kalauna diseases which are unrecognized, and therefore incurable, by Western medicine. Close on its heels are three others, also feared for their fatality and ineluctable course. *Daiyaya* is an emaciating disease of the "blood," which causes the belly to swell and the spirit of the victim to wander; *yafuna* is a form of possession by malignant spirits which consume the vital organs; *doke* is a debilitating disease caused by ingesting food cooked by an adulterous wife, whose "skirt" grows within the cuckold's belly. Symptomatically, like *tufo'a*, all are fantastic diseases of the belly, and all save the last are believed to be inflicted by sorcery. *Tufo'a* tops the list, I suspect, because it touches the most sensitive nerve, threatens the most vital nexus of values in the culture. Hunger and greed meet in *tufo'a* – the worst disease implants the worst vice.

As an individual affliction, *tufo'a* can take an acute form.

> We are afraid of it because it can kill you in three days. You eat and eat and finish what is in your house. You are not satisfied. You hurry to your gardens, but on the way your belly bursts. It breaks open and the juice runs out, and you die.

This description recalls the "bursting belly" syndrome, a common motif in Kalauna's repertoire of jokes and obscene stories (Young 1977). It titillates because it inverts the dominant value of oral continence or controlled ingestion: A bursting belly denotes uncontrolled expulsion following oral (sometimes sexual) incontinence.

More plausible indications of *tufo'a*, however, are those of the chronic form.

> Our juice runs out. We suffer diarrhoea. Our bodies become thin, but our stomachs swell. We turn to stealing food from other people's gardens. We eat in vain. Then we do nothing but sit in our houses and pick at mats with our fingers.

One of the *tufo'a* incantations actually urges the victim to steal:

> Go, be gluttonous
> Go, be voracious
> Go, your hand snatching
> Go, your leg sidling
> Your gobbling
> Your gluttony.

Another dwells on peeling tubers, and it is sung over a small, porous volcanic stone which the sorcerer uses to sharpen a shell knife – the idea being that the intended victims will peel, cook, and eat up their entire gardens. But the dominant imagery of the spells lies in the insistent refrain of gluttony.

The fantasy elements of *tufo'a* that spice informants' accounts of individual cases easily take a quantum leap into the mass or epidemic form. This is clearly the most terrible, apocalyptic vision imaginable. It assumes the legendary shape of Famine, with its wandering, searching, stealing, apathy, and conclusive exchange of children for the terminal feast. Kalauna's analogue to the self-cannibalism of Erysichthon is the child-cannibalism of the community.

Tufo'a is a suicidal weapon which strains the outsider's credulity (as my Kalauna friends' credulity is strained by the nuclear bomb). It is said that individual countermagic is effective for those few men who know strong *sisikwana*; it can override the effects of *tufo'a* and restore normal appetite, or rather, normal satiety. But there are no magical defenses for women and children, who are, perforce, ignorant of *sisikwana* because it is held to be inimical to their fecundity or growth. (Conceptually, *sisikwana* is antithetical to the values of nurture.) Kalauna people believe, therefore, that women and children are the first victims of general famine, whether or not it is complicated and intensified by *tufo'a*. For this reason, it is said that the *tufo'a* magician must be hardhearted and intransigent enough to see his own dependents suffer before his eyes. The kickback of any communal antisocial magic is nicely expressed in the phrase *awabuwo hi tonona*, "he swallows his own spittle," which alludes to the spell-contaminated, sorcery-impregnated saliva which the magician spits into his paraphernalia.

But what kind of man could do such a terrible thing as *tufo'a*, knowing that he and his own would suffer along with everybody else? My own credulity was strained too, until I witnessed, between May and June 1980, a sequence of events which transformed a mild, unassertive Christian into a tough-minded, vengeance-seeking pagan. He was a *toitavealata*, a guardian of Lulauvile clan, and in May he had been incapacitated by a mysterious swelling of the legs. While nursing a quiet resentment in the local health center, he heard news of the death, in a car crash on the other side of New Guinea, of his eldest son and heir. In trepidation, Kalauna awaited delivery of the body. The grief-benumbed father presided over a select caucus of clansmen and exchange partners (including myself) to decide who was to bury, what mortuary feasts to plan, and what other "arrangements" were to be made. The discussion focused on these "arrangements," and I listened in growing astonishment as the *toitavealata* and his close followers laid careful and callous plans for inflicting famine on Kalauna the following year. Others opposed them, fearful for their children. Yet by the end of the night the hawks had won, or so it seemed, for there was ambiguity in the evasive discourse. The words for "sun," "famine," "hunger," "blight" were never pronounced; and *tufo'a* – like the word "chess" in the riddle to which it is the answer – could not be spoken yet. Instead there was a wealth of local metaphors, mythical allusions, and even a biblical parable. The seven thin cows who ate the seven fat cows in Pharoah's dream (*Genesis* 41) could only mean the time of *loka* which would – thanks to the hunger sorcery of *tufo'a* – eat up the time of *malia*.

News of this fateful meeting was leaked, and the community feared the worst. Almost overnight, people battened down the roofs of their houses in anticipation of a hurricane. The coffin arrived – several days late – and the funeral commenced. It proved to be a harrowing sequence of ill omens. The first grave the buriers dug had to be abandoned because of large boulders beneath the surface. The second grave collapsed while the side chamber was being dug. The third proved to be too small for the coffin, which had to be taken out again for the chamber to be enlarged. Meanwhile the keening and flailing about which accompanies any burial in Kalauna had developed an hysterical edge. Finally, while erecting the inner wall of posts and old metal sheeting to seal the coffin inside the chamber, the coffin was heard to thump hollowly from the inside. The young man had been dead for more than a week, and in my hand I held the coronor's report (he had died of a ruptured spleen, a "burst belly" as people said) and a document which certified that the coffin was adequately sealed for transportation. The coffin continued to thump as the buriers frantically filled the grave, ignoring the bystander who demanded that the coffin be opened for inspection. Later the buriers described the sound as "like thunder," but their interpretation of it was not – as I had naively imagined – the sound of a "ghost" trying to escape, or of a man dead before his time protesting his fate. All agreed it was the sound, the "sign," of *tufo'a*. *Tufo'a* was thumping in the coffin, echoing in the grave the way the belly thumps in hunger, the way a few nights previously a dead tree had fallen heavily in the village, the way boulders had bounded down the hillside the day before, slightly injuring a youth, and the way the sea hawk, *manubutu*, seen hovering over the ridge, had thudded into its prey. In short, the coffin was a focal symbol for Kalauna's fears for its belly; the unquiet body of a leader's son was the vehicle for his vengeance. All of the omens were adduced retrospectively and pressed into service to presage the imminence of mass *tufo'a*. But I had to admit that the synchronicity of their natural occurrence was impressive and even unnerving.

The day following the burial people began to mention that they felt ominously empty, and clutched their bellies after they had eaten, wondering if they felt the warning bumps of *tufo'a*. The mourning father was carried back to his hospital bed, and within a day or two I was obliged to leave Kalauna and catch a boat for the provincial capital. Letters from the field, however, indicated that people were still waiting for "something to happen" five months after they were convinced that the famine or *tufo'a* had begun.

Conclusion

By discursive means I have examined the contents of the concept of hunger in Kalauna. It is a semantic category of extraordinary depth and scope – a truly voracious notion, one that incorporates an ethnophysiology and a theory of dietetics, nourishes a magicoreligious system and sustains a political ideology. It is reality-tested by seasonal food scarcity and periodic drought, though I have judged these to be of less intrinsic importance in the last analysis than the phantasmagoric elements, which, seemingly, have been cultivated to embellish hunger as a master-symbol for all that is deficient, entropic, and anxiety-provoking in the culture. In short, I suggest that hunger stands for all the negative aspects – the dark underbelly, one might say – of the ideological configuration of social values. Considering that these are grounded in the cultural definition of "food," it is perhaps not surprising that a dearth of "food" is signified by an overblown concept of hunger, a hunger that is incompatible with the moral bases of society and that logically predicates the demise of that society. *Tufo'a*-inspired hunger is the means of self-destruction: The insatiable belly of the community is driven finally to consume itself.

With this example from a Papuan culture, I hope to have demonstrated my point that "hunger," no less than "food," can be ideologically exploited, politically and ritually, as a potent symbolic idiom. If so, the formulation of a universal, cross-cultural definition of hunger becomes a precarious if not fruitless exercise. What makes people declare they are hungry is not necessarily a matter of how much food they have in their stomachs, stores, or gardens. The perception of hunger is subject to pervasive cultural doctrines mediated by the social environment in which food is cultivated, exchanged, eaten – or eschewed. A diffuse sensation after all (a common sixteenth-century idiom had it "drooping out of the nose"), hunger is as susceptible as other bodily states to interpretation deriving from the cultural, symbolic order. Paradoxically, although they define hunger as the "worst disease," Kalauna people intellectually thrive on it.

6. Food classification and restriction in Peninsular Malaysia: nature, culture, hot and cold?

Lenore Manderson

People everywhere commonly conceptualize and celebrate the natural environment, social and symbolic order, moral and spiritual qualities, physical experience, and psychological states in terms of dichotomies. These may include oppositions such as male/female, good/evil, clean/dirty, sacred/profane, outside/inside, up/down, light/dark, right/left, dry/wet, and hot/cold. This ideational differentiation does not preclude the perception of qualities or states also as continua; neither need it be sophisticated and elaborate, nor involve the total division of all phenomena into two mutually exclusive spheres (Needham 1973:xxvii). Still, certain basic distinctions may be made and shared by peoples of diverse cultures: Thus the natural world, plants and animals, physiological changes and illness, food and medicines, are distinguished widely in terms of hot and cold, these being used to describe the purported nature of the objects or states rather than objectively identifiable characteristics such as temperature or origin.

In the Malayo-Indonesian region, Aboriginal peoples have used a system of hot and cold both metaphorically and to diagnose and respond to physiological changes, particularly in relation to childbirth and the puerperium (Skeat and Blagden 1906, vol. II:10; Jensen 1966). In addition, ideas of hot and cold were introduced with trade and colonization in the region. In particular, Moslem traders and missionaries visited the Malay Peninsula from around the seventh century A.D., and Arabic medical texts which elaborated Islamic humoral pathology and thus concepts of hot and cold were translated into Malay. However, Hindu priests and merchants, Buddhist missionaries, and Chinese envoys and traders even earlier traded to and lived in the region, introducing both Indian and Chinese concepts of hot and cold. Further, monasteries were established in India for Southeast Asians, suggesting that cultural transmission was not a one-way process (Manderson 1981a). Today, the hot–cold classification of physical states and foods remains a living tradition among all major groups in Peninsular Malaysia (Malays, Chinese, and Indians).

The classification of food as hot and cold relates not to the temperature at which the food is served, nor usually to its raw or cooked state, nor necessarily to its origin. Rather, food tends to be classified according to its reputed effect on the body. A hot food is so classified because it is said, in Malaysian English terminology, to be "heaty"; a cold food has a "cooling" effect (Tongue 1974:77–8). Health is maintained through equilibrium (Laderman 1981). Illness and other physiological disruptions such as pregnancy and childbirth affect the hot–cold balance of the body, and treatment involves adjustment to the diet to redress the imbalance. Overindulgence of foods classified as manifestly hot or cold adversely affect this balance and may lead to illness.

In addition to the classification of hot and cold, foods may also be classified as itchy, windy, sharp, or poisonous, again because of their assumed effects on the body. As with hot and cold foods, these foods may be eaten in sensible quantity by healthy adults, but some caution needs to be exercised for those considered vulnerable, including the very young and very old, the sick, menstruating, pregnant, and puerperal women, and newly circumcized males.

The following discussion of traditional food beliefs and associated restrictions is based on fieldwork undertaken in Peninsular Malaysia in 1978 and 1979. The data presented below are drawn from personal observations, interviews with key informants, and an extensive questionnaire administered to and completed by 278 women in five states: Negri Sembilan and Melaka in the southwest, Kedah and Penang in the northwest, and Trengganu on the east coast.[1] There was no significant difference by ethnicity in the classification of foods, the diagnosis of illness or physiological states, or the application of dietary precautions, and hence in the description below I have not isolated response by ethnicity. The terms provided in the text are Malay.

Hot and cold

The classification of foods as hot or cold, or as itchy, windy, sharp, or poisonous, is neither exhaustive nor rigid. As Laderman has noted (1981), the system is dynamic rather than taxonomic. But in very general terms, animal products, oily and spicy foods, alcohol, and herbal preparations are hot; fruit and vegetables are cold (see Table 6.1). Salty and bitter foods are also often hot; astringent and sour foods and those that exude viscous matter, such as okra and certain plantains, are cold (Laderman 1981). Although groups of food can be classed loosely within particular categories, Malaysians may classify separately certain subspecies or varieties of foods. Thus

1 Fieldwork was undertaken while I was a postdoctoral research fellow with the Department of Indonesian and Malayan Studies, the University of Sydney, and was conducted in association with the Department of Malay Studies, the University of Malaya. The research was funded by the Australian Research Grants Committee and the University of Sydney. I am grateful to officers of the federal and state medical and health departments of the Government of Malaysia for their cooperation and assistance, and to the women who participated in the study. A profile of the respondents who participated in the state surveys is provided in Manderson (1981b).

Table 6.1. *Traditional food classifications, effects, and prescriptions*

Major foods classified	Percent of cases	General effects	Percent of cases	Specific restrictions	Percent of cases	Specific prescriptions	Percent of cases
1. *Hot foods*							
Durian	42.6	warms body	52.2	sickness	43.5	rainy season	39.9
(Durio zibethinus)		fever	10.5	dry season	37.1	postpartum	39.3
Beef	30.2	sore or dry throat	10.0	pregnancy	12.1	feeling cold	9.5
Rambutan	20.9	sweaty, flushed	7.2	feeling hot	9.1	healthy	8.3
(Nephelium lappaceum)		diarrhea	5.7	midday	6.9	night	6.5
Chili	17.4	thirst	4.8	early morning or late evening	4.0	midday	5.4
Black pepper	11.1			other	3.9	certain "cold" illnesses	4.2
Curry	10.6						
Herbs and spices	10.2						
Mutton	9.8						
	(N=235)		(N=209)		(N=175)		(N=168)
2. *Cold foods*							
Cucumber	42.6	cools body	40.7	postpartum	38.5	warm weather	50.0
Papaya	28.6	stomach ache	11.1	sickness	28.5	midday	18.6
Kankong	25.0	weakness	10.6	rainy season	26.6	healthy	13.8
(Ipomoea aquatica)		generally unhealthy	7.9	nights	9.2	feeling hot	8.5
Spinach	16.3	flatulence	6.9	feeling cold	6.0	pregnancy	7.4
Banana	15.5	aching or swollen veins	6.0	early mornings	5.5	fever	5.3
Mangosteen	11.5	generally healthy	6.0	other	5.4	other	8.6
(Garcinia mangostena)							
Mustard greens	11.1						
Bean sprouts	8.7						
	(N=252)		(N=216)		(N=218)		(N=188)

Table 6.1 (cont.)

Major foods classified	Percent of cases	General effects	Percent of cases	Specific restrictions	Percent of cases	Specific prescriptions	Percent of cases
3. Itchy foods							
Prawns	53.2	general itchiness	66.8	blisters or sores	63.7	healthy	62.5
Yam	31.5	rashes, spots	14.7	postpartum	16.3	no skin problems	10.6
Mackerel	27.7	sores fester	8.3	sickness	12.7	after measles	6.7
Cuttlefish	21.3	cough	7.4	already itchy	8.8	preferably never	5.8
Cockles	15.7	skin coarsens,		other	15.4	dry season	1.9
Crab	15.3	deteriorates	6.0				
Tuna	12.3						
Sardines	9.4						
(N=235)		(N=104)		(N=204)		(N=104)	
4. Windy foods							
Gourds	41.6	flatulence	42.7	sickness	47.5	healthy	66.7
Jackfruit	26.2	unhealthy,		postpartum	29.5	midday	7.9
(Artocarpus integra)		rundown	12.5	stomach upset	10.7	warm weather	7.9
Cassava	18.3	stomach ache	11.0	cold weather	8.2	to expel wind	7.2
Brinjal (eggplant)	13.7	bloating, edema	9.6	before meals	4.1	to settle stomach	6.3
Petai, jering	13.1	weakness	8.8	night	3.3	as laxative	6.3
(Pithecellobium ssp.)		breathlessness	6.6			other	9.6
Tubers generally	9.8	headache	5.9				
Ginger	9.2	heartburn	5.9				
Cempedak (Artocarpus champeden)	5.9						
(N=153)		(N=63)		(N=122)		(N=63)	

5. Sharp foods

Food	%	Reason	%	Reason	%	Reason	%
Pineapple	87.4	stomach ache	46.1	postpartum	26.1	to induce abortion, as an emmenagogue	15.5
Mango family	11.2	unhealthy, rundown	12.0	menstruation	21.8	healthy	13.4
Vinegar	10.6	diarrhea	9.0	sickness	15.8	midday	13.4
Lemons, limes	8.2	itchy or sour mouth or tongue	6.6	upset stomach	12.7	aid digestion	12.4
Tapai (fermented sour dough)	6.8			pregnancy	10.3	menstruation	11.3
				night	5.5	warm weather	8.2
				early morning	4.8	constipation	7.2
				rainy weather	4.8	other	9.3
				before eating	4.8		
				other	12.6		
(N = 207)		(N = 167)		(N = 97)		(N = 165)	

6. Poison foods

Food	%	Reason	%				
Trevally	21.8	relapse or worsening of illness	17.3	—		—	
Catfish eel	17.3	stomach ache	14.5				
Catfish	16.5	unhealthy	12.7				
Prawns	14.3	itching	10.9				
Mackerel	12.0	sores worsen	6.4				
Mango family	10.2						
Cockles	7.5						
Chicken	7.5						
(N = 198)		(N = 119)					

some bananas are considered cold, others windy, and still others are not classified or are considered safe or neutral. Similarly red beans and black beans are classified as hot and are considered to be good for the blood; groundnuts may also be regarded as hot but are considered unhealthy, causing sore throats; green grams and french beans are cooling and may cause giddiness; soy beans are also cooling, but soy bean curd and bean sprouts are especially cold and should be eaten with discretion. Different attributes, including color, taste, texture, spiciness, whether the food is raw or cooked, method of cooking, and the origin of the food all provide a general guide to classification and in part explain inconsistencies. Thus most informants classified watermelon as cold because it was "watery" and cooled the body, but occasionally the fruit was classified as hot because the plant grows in full sun. Again, whereas most foods retain their ascribed quality regardless of method of preparation, other foods may change with temperature or cooking ingredients. Spinach and watercress remain cold whether they are stir-fried with oil and chili or steamed; however, whereas rice steamed is either neutral or unclassified, fried rice is hot and steamed rice left standing overnight becomes cold and must be reheated to neutralize that quality. Malays regard plain water at any temperature as cold; Indian women classify ice as hot, cold water as cooling, warm water also as cooling, and boiled water as hot because it has been cooked. Left overnight, boiled water reverts to a cold state (cf. Wellin 1955a). In Western nutritional terms, hot foods have a higher calorific value, a lower water content, and are richer in oils, protein, and carbohydrate, but these are not properties considered relevant in Malaysian classification.

Ultimately the classification depends on the effect of the food on the body, and there is some evidence that this has empirical validity (Ramanamurthy 1969). This is reflected in the use of terms in Malay for hot and cold: *panas* for "hot," which Malays understand to be a contraction of *yang memanaskan badan*, "that which heats the body"; *sejuk* for "cold," from *yang menejukkan badan*, "that which cools the body" (Zainal Abidin 1947). The terms for "itchy" (*gatal*), "windy" (*angin*), "sharp" (*tajam*), and "poisonous" (*bisa*) as applied to foods likewise refer to the reputed effects of the food on the body. Certain foods are classified consistently. Durian (*Durio zibethinus*) is always classified as hot because it makes the consumer feel "heaty" (and see Wilson, this volume, Chapter 12); it may also be classified as *bisa*, depending on the health status of the person implicated. Cucumbers are almost always classed as cold and often also as windy; pineapple is always classified as sharp. But because foods affect individuals differently, there is considerable inconsistency and variation over a wider number of foods. This personal basis for classification with its inevitable variability is common in other cultures where a hot–cold system prevails (e.g., among Mexicans, see Currier 1966). But the variations and inconsistencies simply underscore the dynamic nature of the system and are not problematic for members of the society. As Beck has noted for South Indians, "Disagreements do not greatly trouble people. The important thing is the underlying assumption that foods can be classified into two categories, not the assignment of a particular food in a particular instance" (1969:561).

In addition to the variability that exists and defies the establishment of a definitive classification for more than a few foods, people may classify quite different foods when asked which they consider to be hot or cold, itchy, windy, sharp, or poison. Some 100 foods were classified by respondents as hot, 105 as cold; but no two people provided the same list of foods, and the number of foods categorized at all varied widely. Logan and Morrill (1979) have argued that poorer, less literate, more traditional people in Guatemala more readily incorporate foods, medicines, and illnesses into a binary system of hot and cold, whereas persons of a higher "acculturation status" tend more often to use a neutral category and to classify only food, medicines, and illnesses which are scarce, expensive and/or poorly understood as hot or cold. This implies a hierarchy of cognitive models (traditional:modern :: binary:Western). In Malaysia this is not the case. Respondents from Melaka, drawn from a maternal and child health clinic six miles from the state capital, were highly articulate and provided extensive food lists; the women from the inland Kedah clinic, arguably the most traditional women, the most isolated from the impact of economic development, and the least familiar with Western-style medical services and concepts, were the least able to provide food lists, although they were no less familiar with the classification system and its general principles. Here, saliency seems the appropriate explanation. Women classified the foods with which they were most familiar; urban women had access to and ate a wider variety of foods, and accordingly their food lists were the more extensive.

Not all foods were classified as hot or cold, but this should not suggest that the excluded foods were considered to be positively neutral, in balance, or bland. In Burma a range of foods are so categorized, and a true "ternary" classification system appears to operate: Burmese in fact distinguish three degrees of hot, three of cold, one bland, and two neutral categories of food, with other foods still excluded from the system (Nash 1965:196). In Malaysia some people classified certain foods as neutral (*sederhana*, "the mean"): These foods tended to be seasonal, irregularly available, and/or expensive (cf. Logan and Morrill 1979). More often, a neutral category of foods appeared to be residual and artificial, and as McArthur has noted (1962:133); "to describe the absence of the properties as a neutral property is perhaps to attribute to them a property which the Malays do not." Foods that fall outside the hot–cold classification, and are not itchy, windy, sharp, or poison, nor explicitly *sederhana*, tend to be foods that constitute the staple diet. Rice and freshwater fish, considered essential to the daily diet, are usually not classified and are incorporated into the diet even when otherwise severe taboos operate, as during the puerperium (cf. Laderman 1981).

Finally, whereas in classical humoral theory the differentiation of hot and cold occurs by degree to the fourth degree and Malays used this fine means of distinction certainly early in the twentieth century (Gimlette 1913/1971), in contemporary Malay society foods are not ranked by degree. However, respondents recognized variation in intensity between certain foods classified as hot or cold, and would stress that durian, for instance, was very hot but chicken only mildly so; cucumber was very cold, papaya moderately so. In addition to the apparent disappearance of classical ranking by degree, there is little evidence also of the continuation of the parallel classical differentiation of wet and dry. This seems to be general in all cultures where some sort of humoral medical theory has existed and where the hot–cold dichotomy has persisted (see Anderson 1980). Malaysian Indian informants used only the hot–cold classification; a few Chinese were familiar with wet and dry and listed a number of foods as hot–wet, cold–wet, hot–dry, or cold–dry on the basis of the physical effects of the food on the body (for example, dry foods were considered to cause a sore throat and harsh dry cough; wet foods caused a "wet" cough with loose phlegm). A number of Malay women were also able to identify wet and dry foods, but in many cases the classification of a food as wet or dry appeared to be based on the physical characteristics of the food – thus jelly was wet, milk powder dry – rather than on the innate qualities of the food or its effects on the body (Manderson 1981a:952).

Physical effects of classified foods

As summarized in Table 6.1 classified foods have specific identifiable effects on the body which reinforce or provide the key to their classification. Thus hot foods make the consumer feel warm, and are normally regarded as healthy, providing energy and "increasing the blood." An excess of hot food, though, can cause fever, a rise in temperature, sweating, sore throat, thirst, hoarseness, or stomach pains, diarrhea, and vomiting. Cold food cools the body, but may cause "weak knees," aching or swollen veins, numbness, rheumatism or arthritis, stomach ache, convulsions, breathlessness, or flatulence. Zainal Abidin (1947:41–4) in fact has distinguished two types of "cold" (*sejuk*): cold food that leads to anemia, such as spinach, and cold food that is refreshing and invigorating, such as langsat (*Lansium domesticum*). Windy foods, such as gourds and jackfruit (*Artocarpus integra*), cause flatulence, bloating, edema, and general debility; several foods classified as windy are also classified as cold. Itchy foods include seafood and tubers, and their overindulgence may result in rashes, pimples, festering sores, and general itching. Sharp foods, such as pineapple and other astringent foods, sometimes also classified as hot (as in the case of *tapai*, a fermented sour dough), may cause sharp pains in the body, stomach cramps, and diarrhea, and may cause dysmenhorrea for the menstruating woman and induce abortion. The classification of foods as *bisa* or "poisonous" is perhaps the most variable: As a general rule, any food that is believed to exacerbate a preexistent ailment is poisonous. Thus a hot food is poisonous during a hot illness; an itchy food is poisonous when the individual already has skin lesions or a rash, for the consumption of itchy foods at this time will exacerbate the condition or retard recovery. In many instances, as Laderman again has pointed out (1981:54–5), foods classified as poisonous are indeed poisonous: A number of fish classified as itchy or poisonous are implicated in toxic reactions; hence the classification, although predominantly symbolic, is also often based on empirical observation.

Time of the day and the season of the year both are believed to affect body temperature, thus influencing the consumption of classified foods. Early morning, the evening, and night are colder periods; so is the rainy season (*musim hujan*). Midday and the hot dry season (*musim panas*) are hot. When body temperature is assumed to be hígh, because of the time of day or season, or because the person has been working hard in the hot sun, then hot foods should be avoided; at the start or end of the day, or in cold or wet weather, the body temperature is presumed to be lower and the individual is presumed to be more vulnerable to cold, and thus cold foods should be avoided. Itchy, windy, sharp, and poison foods may also be prescribed according to time of day or year, although in part because the secondary classification of these foods is hot or cold. In general, cold foods tend to be most readily available during the hot season, but unavailable during the season of proscription (Laderman 1981:8).

Bodily imbalance through the overindulgence of classified foods or through their consumption at an inappropriate time, or as a result of illness or changed physical state, may be corrected by the treatment of opposites. Thus a cold illness is treated by the avoidance of cold foods and the consumption of hot foods. However, in a few cases, the imbalance might be rectified by treating "like with like": Thus an excess of wind in the body may be treated by the consumption of windy foods to push the expulsion of wind (through farting and belching, for example).

Illnesses themselves may be classified as hot or cold; at such times the patient is vulnerable to the respective foods hot or cold, itchy, windy, sharp, or poisonous. In accordance with the diagnosis, classified foods should be avoided. For example, measles, smallpox, and chicken pox are regarded as hot, as evidenced by the fever and rash, and hot (and itchy) foods should be avoided until the patient has recovered. One informant maintained that even the preparation of hot foods should be avoided in the house of a patient during the initial stages of infection. Arthritic, rheumatic, and neuralgic ailments, and complaints regarded also in the West as colds or chills, are cold illnesses which can be relieved if not cured by strictly avoiding cold foods and taking hot foods. In addition, as I have discussed at length elsewhere (Manderson 1981b, 1981c), pregnancy is diagnosed as a hot state and the postpartum as cold, and food taboos again operate accordingly. Menstruation is not classified along these lines, but sharp foods may be proscribed to avoid dysmenhorrea; alternatively some women prescribe sharp foods to shorten the duration of the flow. Circumcision, performed on young Malay males, is treated in a manner akin to the puerperium, with both cold and itchy foods proscribed until the wound has healed (Manderson 1981b).

Age, sex, and diet

In addition to diet, illness, time of day, and season, age and sex influence the hot–cold balance of the body. The very young and the very old are considered to be colder than healthy adults and are vulnerable to cold complaints such as stomach aches and diarrhea in infancy, rheumatism and arthritis in the elderly. Manifestly cold foods should be avoided to control this imbalance. Similarly, women are considered to be cooler than men, although the difference is marginal, and neither adult men nor women assiduously avoid hot or cold foods. However, certain classified foods are considered to be either dangerous or good for men or women, the young or the old.

Traditionally, infants and toddlers are considered to be vulnerable to cold foods which might cause stomach aches and diarrhea, wind and weak bones; in addition certain foods such as particular fish (and according to a number of my informants, chocolate) are believed to cause worms and are proscribed or restricted. Evidence from as recently as the early 1970s suggests that rural Malay mothers widely observed the taboos on cold food for infants and small children. Chen (1972:234), for example, has reported that Trengganu villagers associated xerophthalmia, nyctalopia, and Bitot's spots with worms, which were attracted to children's eyes from the stomach when cold foods were consumed; cold foods such as fruit and vegetables – the very foods rich in vitamin A which might alleviate such eye disorders[3] were therefore excluded from the diets of affected children. McPherson (1965:126) has similarly associated the susceptibility of young Malay children to eye disorders with the exclusion of cold foods from the diet; McKay (1971) has reported that parents failed to give their young children cold or sour food for fear of malaria (see also Chen 1970; McKay et al. 1971; Chong 1969). In the 1978–9 survey on which this paper is based, however, women's responses regarding the diets of infants and toddlers tended to be determined by Western ideas transmitted by clinic and other health personnel, and hence even when asked what foods traditionally were suitable or unsuitable for the young, in response women referred to recently available food items and provided Western nutritional reasons in justification. In general, responses indicated a broader range of permitted foods than suggested in earlier studies, although women unanimously excluded excessively cold foods such as spinach and gourds, overtly hot foods such as chili and durian, sharp foods such as pineapple, and sour and salty foods. Additionally, adult food generally was proscribed for infants because of the risk of the infant choking or suffering diarrhea. Women tended to exclude rice from the diets of both infants and toddlers, and instead to advocate a well-cooked rice porridge; they advocated milk, including powdered milk and Nestum (a milk- and cereal-based infant food). The diets of toddlers tended to incorporate a greater number of foods, including hen's eggs, beef, vegetables (because of their vitamin content) and some fruits; again overtly hot food was considered unsuitable because of the danger of stomach upset, cold food because of stomach upset and wind, and itchy and poison foods because of the dangers of infection and disease.

Because the elderly, like the very young, are considered to be vulnerable to cold, cold foods should be limited if not avoided in old age. Cold foods might cause a general decline in health, weakness, aching veins and joints, and wind. Gourds, papaya, ice, and rice left overnight were identified as especially cold foods to be avoided by the elderly. On the other hand, hot foods would provide strength and forestall physical deterioration. By contrast, cold foods were considered to be healthy for younger adults, because they would cool the bodies inherently polarized toward hot and thus provide a balance; additionally cold foods taken by younger people were considered to provide resistance to infection. However, older children and adults were usually free of proscriptions.

Likewise, men and women in healthy, "normal" states are free of dietary proscriptions. Cold foods were considered to be good for men who by nature, choice of food (e.g., rich restaurant meals), and habit (e.g., smoking) are hotter than women. Few respondents indicated any restrictions that applied to men, these restrictions relating to a limited number of excessively cold or hot foods only. On the other hand, a wide range of food taboos were invoked for women during critical periods of humoral imbalance, in particular after childbirth when women are considered to have lost heat and to be vulnerable to cold and wind. Dietary and other precautions, such as "mother roasting," are taken to replace the lost heat and thereby to restore the hot–cold balance of the mother's body, and to protect her from catching cold either atmospherically (e.g., from a draught) or as the result of diet. Thus whereas pregnant women, polarized in the direction of hot, should limit the amount of hot foods but may freely eat cold foods, postpartum women should avoid all cold foods including, according to tradition, virtually all fruit and vegetables (Wilson 1973b; Manderson 1981b, 1981c). Failure to observe these restrictions might result in serious illness at the time or at a later date: According to one informant, "you might be all right at first, but when you're forty plus, you'll have aching veins."

Notwithstanding the general liberty granted adult men and women, certain foods are considered potent and may be either taken or avoided because of the special effects they might have. Whereas the energy provided by hot foods is perceived in general terms, extremely hot foods may also be regarded as providing sexual energy and are treated as aphrodisiacs: for example, durian. Chinese informants also regarded brandy, the meat of a black dog, and bull's testes as hot foods that aided male virility. Cold foods, on the other hand, might negatively affect sexual potency. Water from the immature coconut, for example, was commonly considered to be especially cold, causing impotence and sterility in men and infertility in women; one informant claimed that 50 percent of Malay men on an island off the west coast of the peninsula were impotent because they regularly drank coconut water rather than rainwater (a report not verified by the author). Coconut water was also frequently blamed for "weak knees" or "soft knees"; one 40-year-old respondent claimed that she had had weak knees and had been unable to walk for two days after drinking coconut water. Other cold foods, such as "overnight" eggs (i.e., eggs cooked the previous day), would enlarge the testes if eaten and should be avoided by men. A number of women claimed that manifestly cold foods like soybean curd would cause a heavy vaginal discharge; certain fruits such as *mengkudu besar* (*Morinda citrifolia*) were also believed to cause a heavy discharge. [Burkill (1966, vol. II:1493) also has associated this fruit with vaginal discharge or leukorrhea and has noted its use as an amenagogue.]

Contemporary dietary practices and precautions

In line with the belief that healthy adults may eat freely, few respondents reported regular food restrictions. Excluding obvious religious taboos (the prohibition of pork for Malays, beef for Indians), the avoidances were as often the result of Western medical advice as the result of traditional food beliefs. Thus a few women avoided salty food because of hypertension, sweets because of diabetes; others regularly avoided excessively hot or cold, sharp or poisonous foods. Mostly though, food avoidances came into effect only in the event of illness. On the other hand, there was little variety in food eaten in the home. Typically, breakfast, eaten from 5 to 9 a.m., would consist of traditional cakes made of rice flour, coconut milk, and palm sugar, or from steamed glutinous rice and grated coconut. Less often bread, biscuits, fried rice, noodles, and eggs were eaten; tea or coffee was the main beverage. The midday and evening meals, taken from 11 to 2 and from 6 to 10, respectively, both consisted of steamed rice with side dishes of fish and vegetables. Some beef and chicken were consumed, but irregularly. In Malay and Indian households, the side dishes would often be cooked with coconut milk, chili, garlic, and spices, or served as a soup. Chinese would use soy sauce with ginger, garlic, and onion as major condiments. Afternoon tea and other snacks usually consisted of cakes, traditional or Western style, and biscuits, occasionally a porridge made from mung beans or deep-fried banana or sweet potato, taken with tea, coffee, or milo. Few households reported eating fruit regularly as part of a major meal or as a snack, although observation of

Table 6.2. *Contemporary food avoidances*

Circumstance/ age	Some traditional taboos observed	No traditional restrictions	No response
Infants	73	16	11
Toddlers	36	54	10
Older children	4	90	6
Children's sickness	69	27	4
Respondent's sickness	42	50	8

daily diets suggests that this reflects people's attitude to fruit rather than to their actual behavior.

During critical periods, diets were more likely to be restricted, although, with the exception of postpartum confinement, not as rigidly as prescribed by tradition.

In general, respondents applied traditional prescriptions in feeding their infants and toddlers, eliminating excessively hot and cold food from the diet, avoiding "hard" adult foods which might be indigestible (including rice unless prepared in the form of porridge), and certain other foods which women individually associated with infantile ailments and allergic reaction. By the time the infant was six months old, it had been introduced to some fruit, vegetables, and animal products; by two years, most children were eating a diet not dissimilar to that of older members of the household with the exception only of certain extreme items: pineapple, because of the risk of diarrhea; chili, because of stomach aches; chocolate and sweets, because of the fear of worms and tooth decay (clearly the latter reason reflects health clinic advice). Older children were not affected by food prescriptions, although respondents nevertheless mentioned the dangers of sharp, itchy, and highly spiced foods (see Table 6.2).

No food avoidances were commonly observed by men. Women, although familiar with traditional precautions during pregnancy, avoided few foods, and stressed that fruit and vegetables, and high-protein and vitamin-rich foods should all be taken for energy and nutrition (Manderson 1981b). By contrast, women followed traditional procedure during their own confinements, following both the behavioral prescriptions and dietary taboos at least in part and usually for the full 44-day-period (or 30 days for Chinese and Indian women) (Manderson 1981b, 1981c).

Again, during episodes of illness respondents tended to implement dietary restrictions in accordance with humoral therapeutic principles, but particularly in the event of sickness of their children rather than for themselves. Food avoidances during illness varied with the diagnosis of illness, although respondents also stressed the importance of avoiding any extremely classified foods. Milk, hen's eggs, rice porridge, and thin soups and broths were regarded as most appropriate for sick children and adults; highly spiced foods were excluded, as were other foods believed to cause nausea, such as rice, or which the patient did not especially like in any case (for the response rate, see Table 6.2).

Conclusion

In introducing this discussion of traditional food beliefs in Peninsular Malaysia, I referred to the near-universality of binary opposition or association by contrariety. Lévi-Strauss has argued that elements classified within a dichotomous system "do not mean anything *in themselves*. It is only as members of pairs of significant oppositions that they take on meaning" (Poole 1973:54, emphasis in the original; and see Lévi-Strauss 1966:65–5). The hot–cold classification of food and illness, then, assumes importance not by virtue of the inclusion of particular items within the classification system, but by the very nature of the system as a symbolic expression of cosmology. Even so, for adherents of the system, the classification has a practical application, which may coincide with empirical reality or observation. McCullough (1973), for example, has analyzed the hot–cold syndrome in Yucatan as a biocultural adaptation to the ecology, providing behavioral guidelines which operate as prophylactic measures against heat cramps and heatstrokes. Among Malays, Laderman (1981) has argued that the classification system serves often to control the consumption of foods which may be toxic, even though at other times the food restrictions which derive from their classification may be dysfunctional rather than prophylactic or therapeutic.

Although I am sympathetic with these empirical arguments, I tend toward a structural explanation of the system, particularly with respect to the use of the classifications in providing a response to and the management of seasonal changes and more especially illness and physiological changes. Here, I am less concerned with the opposition of hot and cold in itself, but rather with the use of food classifications which at critical periods provide the guidelines for dietary regulation which, according to Malaysians, ensure return to normalcy or health. What I wish to suggest, as a conclusion to the above description of Malaysian food beliefs, is that the associated restrictions – and food taboos generally – are a means of articulating the ascendance, or allowing for the control, of culture over nature.

In this final section, I argue for the predominance of nature, as opposed to culture, during life cycle events and episodes of ill health when food precautions are invoked. At the outset, I should stress that whereas the categorization of physiological states as hot and cold comes from my informants, the distinction between nature and culture does not. It is, however, as I shall illustrate, an attractive way of explaining the periodic observation of food restrictions.

I have noted above that the restrictions operate particularly in extreme youth and old age, and during circumcision, illness, menstruation, and child-birth. Although a state of healthiness is no less "natural" than that of ill health, at times of illness the vulnerability of individuals to nature becomes especially apparent. Onset of illness typically cannot be predicted and hence cannot be prevented. Subsequently, diagnosis is made, the illness labeled and described, including often description in hot or cold terms. This is a cultural process. Following diagnosis, steps are taken to control the illness. For the period of physical debilitation, various precautions – cultural procedures – may be observed to avoid further decline and to facilitate recovery. Response may include the employment of medical and/or magical practitioners, but treatment also involves the regulation of the patient's behavior and diet, including, if appropriate, manipulation of either hot or cold elements. Early and full recovery demands faithful observance of the prescriptions.

During menstruation, women are again the victims of biology and thus linked to nature rather than culture. The onset of menarche and the recurrent menstrual cycle are beyond control without radical intervention (e.g., by the use of drugs) or as a result of other factors also outside immediate cultural control (e.g., as a consequence of acute malnutrition, with conception, or with aging). Not only may menstruation be uncomfortable or painful, accompanied by mood changes, or disrupt a woman's usual everyday activities as well as often her religious observances, but also menstruation, with the regular recurrence of blood, suggests an obvious natural link: Hence women's "animality is more manifest" (de Beauvoir, cited by Ortner 1974: 74). Malaysian women consider menstruation to be a natural event, and refer to it colloquially either as a "monthly sickness" or "dirty sickness." Because menstruation is a natural/biological process, it is beyond direct social and cultural control. But menstruating women can be controlled socially and culturally by restricting their behavior, (e.g., not entering a place of worship, not washing their hair) and their diet. I would suggest that natural bodily functions no less than illness symbolize the vulnerability of culture and society in general to nature. The body as a complex structure, Douglas has argued (1966:115), is a source of symbols for other structures, including social structure. Thus taboos invoked during menstruation as well as during illness reestablish cultural order and ensure the health not only of the individual but of society as a whole.

The passages of childbirth – pregnancy, parturition, and the puerperium – similarly are natural events which, although they may be avoided, prevented, or terminated, as processes are beyond human control. The relationship between the woman and the fetus, the duration of pregnancy, and the physiology of lactation cannot be manipulated through human intervention. These are biological and natural functions. Again, however, control – or the illusion of control – over nature by culture is effected through a range of behavioral and dietary precautions, derived from the classification of the biological state first as hot or cold. The precautions are believed to care for the mother and the fetus/neonate, to protect them both magically and medically, and during the puerperium, to protect also others who by their association with the woman are in ritual danger. Like pregnancy and birth, lactation is natural; hence the maintenance of food taboos, at least in theory, for the duration of breast feeding including beyond the puerperium.

Infancy and early childhood provide less dramatic but still clear links with nature. Ortner (1974:77–8) argues:

> Infants are barely human and utterly unsocialized; like animals they are unable to walk upright, they excrete without control, they do not speak. Even slightly older children are clearly not yet fully under the sway of culture. They do not yet understand social duties, responsibilities, and morals; their vocabulary and their range of learned skills are small. One finds implicit recognition of an association between children and nature in many cultural practices.

In Java, children to the age of five or six are considered to be *durung djawa*, "not yet Javanese" (Geertz 1961:109). Child rearing provides for the socialization and enculturation of the child, turning the natural into the cultural. Again, then, I would suggest that food taboos, although related to the physical and alimentary vulnerability of children and their early inability to eat (chew) adult foods, at the same time operate to establish cultural order and predominance.

Circumcision provides a means by which boys break their association with nature. Food taboos are invoked not simply because the young male is physically vulnerable until the circumcision wound has healed. Ortner (1974:78, 80) has argued that initiation rites – in the Malay context, the *khatam Koran* and circumcision – provide rituals to enculturate the child, transforming him from a natural to a fully human, cultured being. Further, during the period of initiation into adulthood, the child is in a state of danger and marginality. This danger is controlled or managed by a complex of rituals, of which food taboos are a part. Again, both by the manipulation of flesh (the circumcision operation) and by the imposition of behavioral and dietary restrictions, the domination of culture over nature is articulated.

Old age, like infancy and early childhood, is classified in vernacular terms as cold. Aging brings people closer to death, and as a result the aged may be seen to be closer to nature than culture. Death represents the final triumph of nature. Although death itself is inevitable, the passage toward death may be manipulated symbolically if not in actuality. Food restrictions provide a means for the management of aging. Hence dietary regulations become increasingly important as people move from the relatively invulnerable stages of adulthood toward their death.

The classification of hot and cold can perhaps also be linked with the opposition of nature to culture. Lévi-Strauss (1969) has provided us with insight here in his analysis of the raw and the cooked. Although in Table 6.1 above, I have listed only the most frequently classified hot and cold foods, in the most general terms raw food is usually classified as cold, and food that may be eaten raw, even if cooked, may still be classified as cold. Excepting durian and a few other fruits, hot food is eaten in prepared form; it includes meats, alcohol, coffee, and condiments. Cold food then is generally raw and is closer to nature; hot foods, through cooking, are incorporated into culture.

Hence early life and old age, death, femaleness, and raw foods are closer to nature and are cold; relatively, adulthood, life, maleness, and cooked foods are hot and are closer to or represent culture. Pregnancy is hot because it represents life, both biologically and symbolically; confinement following childbirth is cold because the woman is no longer "with life" and because the lochia flow is reminiscent of menstruation and suggests both ritual danger and ill health. Circumcision again involves blood loss and hence is nearer to nature and vulnerable to cold. Food taboos are most often and most rigidly observed when the diagnosis and consequent restrictions are cold, not hot: Those of pregnancy are minimal compared to those of the puerperium. In sum, the following oppositions emerge: culture:nature :: hot:cold :: life:death :: male:female :: order:disorder. Thus restrictions on cold rather than hot foods retain their importance as a means of controlling nature, maintaining life, and establishing cultural order.

Finally, notwithstanding the above linked oppositions, why *food* taboos? The need to eat is natural, but eating, like cooking, is a social and cultural activity. Food is necessary biologically to sustain life, but humans learn how to eat, what to eat, and when and with whom they eat. Established, ordered food habits represent social order. Control of food availability and choice, then, provides a means of controlling and transcending nature.

7. Classification of food from a Groote Eylandt Aboriginal point of view

Julie Waddy

For nomadic hunters and gatherers such as the Australian Aborigines, the daily quest for food was a dominant aspect of life. In general food was not preserved, though seeds and other fruits were dried in the arid areas of Central Australia. So, as there was virtually no form of cultivation, Aborigines depended on their daily collecting of food to satisfy their hunger. Their diet varied with the success – or otherwise – of their efforts, and with the seasonal availability of food.

The dependence on their environment for food meant that Aborigines had an intimate knowledge of plants and animals that were potential food sources. Many early workers have recorded Aboriginal names of plants in particular, noting their food value and other uses, e.g., Maiden (1889), Roth (1901–10), and more recently Cleland and Johnston (e.g., 1937/8). The current interest in Australian native food plants is reflected in the popularity of books such as Cribb's *Wild Food in Australia* (1975), in which he and his wife have collected together plants referred to by many different authors. The most recent contribution is Levitt's *Plants and People: Aboriginal Uses of Plants on Groote Eylandt* (1981), the most comprehensive work to date of Aboriginal uses of plants for any one Australian tribe.

Folk classification

Most references in which the names of plants and animals are listed and their uses noted contain little, if any, indication of the relationships which Aborigines perceived between the various species. It was generally assumed in the past that there was a more or less one-to-one agreement between a scientific species and its Aboriginal name. Thus obtaining the name and noting the uses of a plant were frequently considered to be sufficient.

It is only in recent years that research workers have come to realize that the study of the biological relationships between species, as perceived by folk in a given culture, can be a valuable field of inquiry in its own right. The major contributions to folk classification studies, based on exhaustive studies of either the plant or the animal kingdom, have been by Conklin (1954) for the Hanunoo of the Philippines; Bulmer and his colleagues (1968,

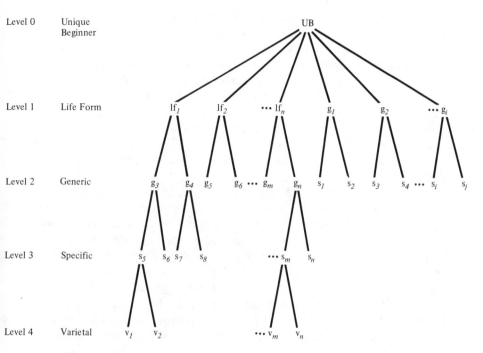

Figure 7.1. An example of a classificatory hierarchy. (From Berlin, Breedlove, and Raven 1974:26.)

1972, 1973, 1975; Majnep and Bulmer 1977) for the Kalam of Papua New Guinea; Berlin, Breedlove, and Raven (1974) and Hunn (1977) for the Tzeltal of Mexico; and Hays (1979) for the Ndumba of Papua New Guinea. Each of these researchers has described the folk classification system of the area studied as hierarchically organized.

An example of a classificatory hierarchy is shown in Figure 7.1, taken from Berlin, Breedlove, and Raven (1974). Relating this hierarchy to English folk classification, we can talk about animals as the unique beginner in the animal kingdom. Our life-form taxa include fish, birds, snakes, insects, and animals in the sense of mammals. Generic taxa include kangaroos, finches, tree snakes, and so on. Specific taxa include gray kangaroos, red kangaroos, and so on. (For a summary of the main issues of folk biological classification, see Waddy 1982; for further details, see Waddy 1984).

To the best of my knowledge, little attention has previously been given to the possibility of a hierarchical classification of food as a system distinct from biological classification. In English we talk about food as a unique beginner, and then subdivide into fruit, vegetables, cereals, meat, milk, and so on. Taking the category vegetables, we can distinguish between green vegetables and root vegetables. Green vegetables include such groups as peas and beans, cabbages, and Brussels sprouts. There are snake beans, lima beans, soya beans, and so we could go on. It may be noted that terms such as peas and beans are identical to the folk generic taxa of the biological classification system, and terms such as snake beans and lima beans are identical to the folk specific taxa. However, the superordinate terms of the food classification system differ from those of the biological classification system, at least in English and, as I will show, in Anindilyakwa. Thus I believe the distinction between the two systems is real and should not be ignored.

Rudder (1978/9:354) has reported what he called "use classes" for the Djambarrpuyngu-speaking Aborigines of northeastern Arnhem Land. Within the major class "food," he has reported a division into vegetable and meat foods. Each of these may be further subdivided. Although he has not considered these classes within the framework of the principles of folk classification suggested by Berlin and others, his data would appear to fit easily within such a framework. Others have noted the same division into flesh and vegetable foods, with or without additional subdivision into named categories (e.g., Gould 1969:260; Heath 1978:44–5). However, there has been insufficient detail to interpret the data in terms of a hierarchical classification.

Meehan (1982a) has made a detailed analysis of the classification of shellfish by the Anbarra Aborigines of northern Arnhem Land. She has reported that there is a root word referring to all edible flesh, both plant and animal, and another term for all vegetable foods. The four animal flesh categories parallel the biological classification of the animal kingdom. Two of these categories include shellfish. As far as I am aware, this is the only detailed study of Aboriginal biological classification that has been published.

The Groote Eylandt setting

Location

My own work has been with the Aborigines on Groote Eylandt. This island, which is roughly 40 by 60 kilometers, is situated in the Gulf of Carpentaria, approximately 45 kilometers from the nearest mainland (see Figure 7.2). The land is part of the former Arnhem Land Aboriginal Reserve but is now Aboriginal owned.

Language

The Aboriginal language of Groote Eylandt and the surrounding islands is Anindilyakwa. This language is characterized by multiple noun classes, extensive prefixing and suffixing systems, and very long words. Stokes (1981) has described its phonology. It is still the first language of children and the only language spoken by some of the oldest Aborigines on the island.

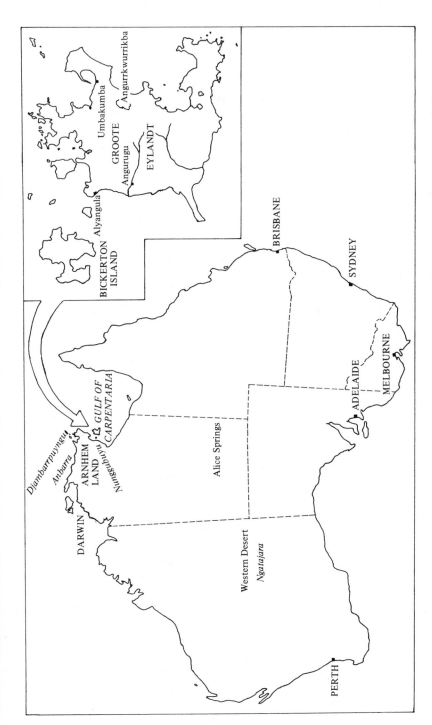

Figure 7.2. Map showing Groote Eylandt and surrounding islands in relation to the mainland of Australia.

Habitats

The island has a wide range of habitats. The most extensive is the tall open forest formation typical of much of Arnhem Land. There are many dense pockets of monsoon forest, often behind the coastal sand dunes. These dunes are very variable in extent and in vegetative cover. Quartzitic sandstone outcrops are common, although the highest point on the island is only about 200 meters. There are seasonal swamps and billabongs and several rivers which have never been known to run dry. Mangrove forests are found at intervals around much of the coast. (For further information, see Specht 1958a; Levitt 1981.)

Sea habitats are also important, as they are the source of much food. Coral reefs are still very popular as fishing places. There are many places where laterite and sandstone have provided suitable habitats for rock oysters and other shellfish in the intertidal zone. Extensive sand/mud flats occur, including much of the area of Angurrkwurrikba, a saltwater lake in the center of the island.

Seasonal availability of foods

Food is sought in a particular habitat, depending on the season. There are two main seasons, the wet and the dry, controlled by the northwest monsoon winds and the southeast trade winds, respectively. However, it is possible to break up the year further according to various aspects of the weather or according to the availability of food. Thus, for example, the beginning of the dry season can be referred to literally as "the time for yams."

Late in November or early in December, as the buildup of heat and humidity intensifies just before the wet, the bush fruits begin to ripen. For the next couple of months there is an abundance of bush fruits. The most popular of these today is the wild plum *Buchanania obovata*. Bush fruits are found particularly in the open forest and along the coastal dunes, but some are also found in the monsoon forest.

By the beginning of the dry season, the only available fruit of any consequence is the custard finger, *Uvaria* sp. This fruit and the long yam (*Dioscorea transversa*) are both found in monsoon forests and are still sought after today. Root vegetables have always been a particularly important food source in the dry season. The round yam (*Dioscorea bulbifera*) is no longer dug because it requires processing to remove a poisonous substance (Levitt 1981: 41). Other root vegetables are found in the open forest, on the coastal dunes, and in seasonal swamps and billabongs. Those found in wetter areas, such as the rushes *Eleocharis dulcis* and *E.* sp. aff. *fistulosa*, can still be collected later in the year during the buildup to the wet season.

As the yam season gets under way, the various wattles begin to flower. The flowering of *Acacia aulacocarpa* reminds people that it is time to collect the eggs of various tern species that nest on some of the offshore islands. The flowering of other wattles is a reminder that certain fish species have plenty of fat and are good to eat. These examples illustrate not only the importance of different habitats but also the interrelatedness of Aboriginal observations.

As the dry season progresses, much of the open forest is burned off to remove the tall grasses of the wet season. This simplifies hunting for wildlife such as bandicoots, native cats, various goannas or monitor lizards, and the blue-tongued lizard, not to mention "sugar bag," the honey found in the wild bees' nest. The tiny wild bees (*Trigona hockingsi*) nest in trees hollowed out by termites. The trees must be chopped down to extract the honey. Burning off also encourages the growth of fresh grass shoots to attract wallabies, the largest land mammals on the island. As far as I can tell, the pattern of burning off is random, spreading out from population centers and accessible roads and beaches.

Later in the dry season, when the flowers of the stringybark (*Eucalyptus tetrodonta*) are falling, the fruit of the tamarind tree (*Tamarindus indica*) is ripe. This tree was introduced by the Macassans on their annual voyages to collect trepang or sea cucumbers for trade with the Chinese. At about the same time, the burrawang (*Cycas angulata*) is ready to be collected in certain coastal dune and open forest areas. The nuts from this cycad contain the poison, macrozamin (Riggs 1954), which can be removed by soaking the fresh nuts in a cage of burrawang fronds in running water for from three to five nights. These nuts are then crushed and roasted in hot sand and ash before being eaten, but the details of preparation vary depending on their state (see Levitt 1981:48–51). Sometimes nuts used to be buried in a hole at the edge of the river and left for several months before being roasted and eaten. This was the only form of food preservation known to the Groote Eylandt people.

When the cocky apple (*Planchonia careya*) starts flowering about September, it is time to go and get turtles – and their eggs – from many of the beaches around the island. Turtles – like dugong, or sea cows – are still highly prized for their meat. Stingrays and shovel-nosed rays are also sought after about this time of the year, as they are considered to have plenty of fat and are therefore to be good eating. Aborigines on Groote Eylandt look for animals at a particular time of year because "that's when they're fat!" As Worsley commented (1961:170), "In recounting a hunting-success, one is always asked 'Was it fat?'"

Historical context

The first non-Aboriginal outsiders known to have settled on the island did not do so until 1921, and their contact with the Aborigines of the island was very limited in the early years.

Included in the first small party of non-Aborigines to settle on the island was Norman B. Tindale, whose interest at that time was particularly in entomology. However, he made very valuable records of many aspects of the life of the Aborigines on the island at that time (Tindale 1925, 1926). His records included comments on a number of the plant and animal sources utilized by the Aborigines and their method of collecting or hunting them. He noted a few Anindilyakwa names of plants and animals.

In 1948, members of the American–Australian Scientific Expedition to Arnhem Land recorded many of the scientific species present on the island and in the seas nearby. Only Specht (1958b), recording plants, and Taylor (1964), recording fish, included Anindilyakwa as well as scientific names. Specht found 53 scientific species with Anindilyakwa names that were potential food sources.

Other members of the same expedition collected data on the diet and nutritional status of Aborigines in Arnhem Land. McCarthy and McArthur (1960:180–9) observed food collecting for two weeks among several families on Groote Eylandt. McArthur (1960:98–110) grouped the various plant foods according to "the type of country in which they are found," but made no mention of the way in which Aborigines classify their food. Little detail is given for animal foods.

In the course of his work on the changing social structure of the Groote Eylandt people in 1952–3, the anthropologist Peter Worsley recorded as many Anindilyakwa names of plants and animals as he could obtain, noting in particular those utilized as food sources (Worsley 1961:181–9). He also provided scientific names where possible but often could give only a rough English translation. However, he did arrange his data according to the major categories perceived by Anindilyakwa speakers. These categories are given in Table 7.1, together with the name of each category in the current practical orthography.

Worsley commented on the apparent "paucity of terms for the internal organs" (1961:159). He succeeded in obtaining three terms, *awa* (liver), *mulugwa* (*mulkwa ~ mulukwa*; stomach, womb, intestines, etc.), and *andonda* (*arndirnda*; heart or kidneys). In fact the last of these refers only to the "heart," as "kidneys" are *andira*, but *mulkwa* is a general term, referring to "all abdominal organs." I have recorded another ten words for the internal organs of a turtle, not to mention twelve terms for specific parts of the flesh of a turtle, and another seven terms in reference to turtle eggs and their various states. It is difficult to find suitable English equivalents.

In 1968–9, Turner studied aspects of kinship, totemism, marriage, death, and the means of existence among the people of Groote Eylandt and Bickerton Island. In his book he briefly referred to a number of food sources (1974: 162–6).

In 1972–5, Miss Dulcie Levitt, who had been a missionary on Groote Eylandt with the Church Missionary Society since 1951, recorded the Anindilyakwa names and uses of 400 scientific species of plants (Levitt 1981). She was particularly interested in food and medicinal uses. Miss Levitt's book includes approximately 250 Anindilyakwa plant names.[1]

Current work

I have been at Angurugu on Groote Eylandt since 1975. My task has been to collect and classify plants and animals and to obtain their Anindilyakwa names and uses, associated stories, anatomical terms, and anything else that could conceivably come under the heading of biology from an Aboriginal viewpoint. I have continued the work of Levitt on the plants and have obtained over 500 animal names in Anindilyakwa, building on the initial lists of linguist Judith Stokes.

More recently I have been studying how all these plant and animal names can be fitted together to give classification heirarchies of the whole animal and plant kingdoms, akin, at least in structure, to scientific classification hierarchies (Waddy 1984). Such a hierarchy, as perceived by Groote Eylandt Aborigines, is illustrated in Figure 7.3. It may be noted that the term *akwalya*, "all animal life," may also be translated as "animals in the sea" and "fish." Its meaning would depend on the context. This multiple use of the one word is like the use of the English word "animal," which can be used to refer to all animal life, as in the animal kingdom, or to animals meaning mammals, as in the common phrase "animals and plants."

The numbers of taxa indicated in Figure 7.3 refer to those designated generic taxa by Berlin et al. (1974:26–7). These are the taxa that would be equivalent in English to kangaroo, honeyeater, python, or parrotfish. It should be noted that the majority of named Anindilyakwa plant and animal taxa are of a similar cognitive status to these generic taxa. Whereas in English we commonly subdivide generic taxa, giving, for example, red kangaroo and gray kangaroo, in Anindilyakwa there are very few named taxa of this nature. This does not mean that distinctions cannot be recognized, but rather that they are not significant within the culture. Further, in a folk system there are many instances of one-to-one correspondence between a folk generic taxon and a scientific species.

Having established this hierarchical classification of the animal kingdom, I then realized the necessity to explore the classification of food because the term *akwalya* can also mean "flesh food."

Groote Eylandt food classification

Tindale (1925:76) thought that "the general name for food [in Anindilyakwa] is 'anunga' or 'unina'." In fact, the term *aninga* is used only for "nonflesh foods." Worsley (1961:162) found "no general word for 'food'" in Anindil-

---

1 Detailed lists of species obtained by earlier workers, updated to accord with current scientific names and practical orthography in Anindilyakwa, are included in Waddy (1984, vol 2:1–199).

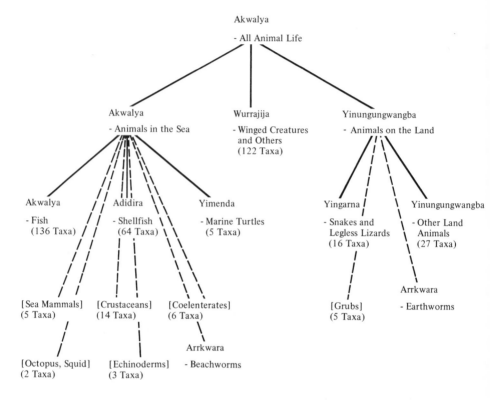

Figure 7.3. Biological classification relationships in the animal kingdom from an Anindilyakwa speaker's point of view. Numbers of taxa are those designated generic by Berlin et al. (1974:26–7). (From Waddy 1982:72.)

yakwa, but a "fundamental distinction" of "animal" or "flesh food" (*akwalya*), and "vegetable" or, more strictly, "nonflesh food" (*aninga*). Turner (1974:167) also found this. However, Worsley considered this use of the term *akwalya* to be colloquial because he believed the true meaning of the word to be "fish" or "animals in the sea." I would interpret the use of the same word, *akwalya*, to indicate overlap between two areas of classification, the one referring to the biological world as a whole and the other to that part of the biological world that is considered edible. Because Aboriginal interest in the animal world was so related to food, it is not surprising that there is some overlap of terms.

Although a distinction between plant and animal foods was reported by previous workers, no further categorizing of food was noted. I have found, however, that *akwalya* (flesh food) and *aninga* (nonflesh food) can be subdivided.

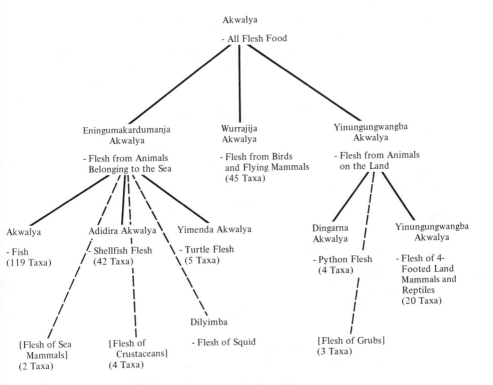

Figure 7.4. Classification of *akwalya* (flesh food), indicating the numbers of Anindilyakwa taxa considered to be edible.

Flesh food (akwalya)

Figure 7.4 shows the basic subdivisions of animals as food within the animal kingdom. (For further details, see Waddy 1984, vol 2:369–89.) Comparison with Figure 7.3 shows that the distinction, at least on paper, is largely a linguistic exercise of adding the term *akwalya* after the biological term. Thus *adidira akwalya* is "shellfish," i.e., edible flesh that comes from shells.

Figure 7.4 also shows the number of taxa that are potentially edible, including those that are no longer eaten today and those that were only eaten by old people or children. For comparison, these same numbers are given in Table 7.1, alongside Worsley's summary of food sources (1961:158). Although Worsley indicated that his data were highly likely to be incomplete, he apparently did not bargain on so many synonyms being available for the one Anindilyakwa taxon. A revised figure has been given beside his data, calculated by comparing his lists of species with current lists where identifications are now available. A few very small species of fish, the small bait-

Table 7.1. *Number of "edible kinds" of animals and plants recorded by Worsley (1961:158)*[a]

	Anindilyakwa names		No. of "edible kinds" i.e., Anindilyakwa taxa		
	Worsley, 1961:181–9	Current orthography	Worsley	Corrected[b]	Waddy
Land animals (including reptiles)	*jinuŋwaŋba*	*yinungungwangba*	19[c]	15	24
Birds (sea and land)	*wuradjidja*	*wurrajija*	76	63	44
Marine animals (fish, dugong, stingrays, dolphins, etc.)	*augwalja*	*akwalya*	98	87	126
Plants and trees	*ega* (trees)	*eka*	83	69	93
Crabs and shellfish			39	35	44

[a] The Anindilyakwa names obtained by him for the categories into which these "edible kinds" were grouped are also shown.
[b] See text for explanation.
[c] Worsley's original figure was 79, but this appears to be a typographical error.

crabs, and mammals found only on the mainland have also been deleted from Worsley's "edible kinds." It should be noted that Worsley has grouped marine mammals, turtles, and squid with fish, thus using *akwalya* in the sense of all marine animals, although crabs and shellfish have been grouped separately.

Worsley apparently did not obtain the term *adidira* for shellfish. This category actually includes hermit crabs, but all other crustaceans are seen as an unnamed category separate from shellfish. Only the bait crabs are grouped as a named subcategory within the crustaceans.

In Worsley's lists, he indicated one "generic" term, i.e., *mangiyuwanga* (shark) (1961:183). In fact, *akwalya* (fish) may be further subdivided into several levels, as indicated in Figure 7.5, which shows the divisions within the food classification system. The first division is essentially into cartilaginous and bony fish, as in the biological classification system. The cartilaginous fish (*aranjarra*) are normally cooked on a blazing hot fire, the flesh chewed and formed into balls, covered with fat from the fish, and then kneaded into flat cakes and baked in the ashes (Tindale 1925:84). Flesh prepared in this way is called *amadukwarra*. On the other hand, bony fish, again *akwalya*, are normally baked in the hot sand and ashes and eaten without further preparation, although, if a large number of fish are caught at one time, they may be cooked with the aid of hot stones in a simple form of earth oven. The term *amadangkwa*, used for the flesh of bony fish, is the same word that is used for the flesh of other animals and of humans.

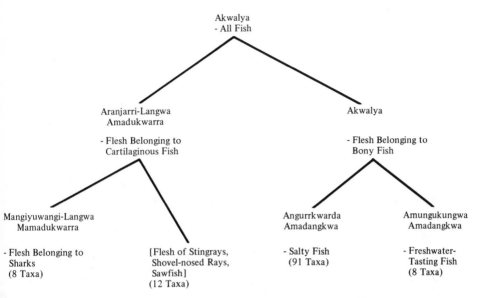

Figure 7.5. Labeled food categories within *akwalya* (fish), indicating the numbers of Anindilyakwa taxa considered to be edible.

Within the biological category of cartilaginous fish are sharks (*mangiyu-wanga*) and an unnamed category comprising all the stingrays, shovel-nosed rays, and sawfish. In considering this latter group as food, a distinction is made between young stingrays and older rays. The latter are said to have black *amalya* (fat) and are not generally eaten. Young stingrays have white or "clean" *amalya* and are collectively termed *yukwulyenja*. They are still eaten today. Shovel-nosed rays and sawfish are not included within this term, but again it is younger ones which are favored.

The bony fish may be differentiated on the basis of taste according to whether they belong to saltwater or freshwater. The flesh of saltwater fish is referred as *angurrkwarda amadangkwa* (salty flesh) and that of freshwater fish as *amungukungwa amadangkwa* (freshwater-tasting flesh). For the salt-water fish, further grouping is possible on the basis of form, but the resultant groups are unnamed.

The same applies to shellfish. It is more natural to group shellfish on the basis of habitat, such that each group is literally named "shells belonging to habitat X." I have not found any food-related criteria for grouping shells.

As well as the named higher-level taxa which include flesh obtained from the sea, there are two small covert taxa, namely, flesh of sea mammals and flesh of crustaceans. Because of the distinctive nature of the members of these covert taxa, the named taxa cannot simply be considered as unaffiliated generics. The smaller bait-crabs are not considered edible, at least by some. It is possible that children may still catch and eat the smaller species.

The category *wurrajija akwalya* applies to the "flesh of winged creatures," including birds, flying mammals, and one or two insects. The birds can be grouped initially in a somewhat similar fashion as in English where we distinguish seabirds from land birds. Further subdivisions can be made on the basis of form and habitat but not on food-related criteria. The number of edible taxa shown in Table 7.1 includes those birds whose eggs are eaten but not necessarily the flesh. There is a major discrepancy between Worsley's and my data, which I have been unable to resolve completely. One of the older men, who remembers Worsley's visit, cannot recall some 24 of the birds marked edible by Worsley as ever being eaten, neither their flesh nor their eggs. It may be that some of these birds or their eggs were eaten occasionally by some people in the past. Perhaps chidren may have eaten some of the smallest ones.

Within the land animals, the snakes (*yingarna*; see Figure 7.3) may be subdivided into *dingarna* (pythons and tree snakes) and *yingarna*, which includes the remainder but especially the poisonous snakes. Only the pythons are considered edible, although they are not normally eaten today.

Within the category *yinungungwangba akwalya* (flesh of four-footed land animals), wallabies and other small mammals are eaten, though they have never constituted a major portion of the diet. Small mammals, goannas, and freshwater turtles are most frequently caught by the women. Lizards are caught and eaten by children. The crocodile is only occasionally eaten. Four taxa of grubs have been considered edible, though they are not generally eaten today.

Eggs, including bird, lizard, and turtle eggs, are somewhat of an anomaly within the food classification system. Some people have considered that they must belong with *akwalya* (flesh food), knowing full well what hatches from the eggs. But one older man recalls one of the older people telling him when he was young that eggs belong with *aninga* (nonflesh food). The word for "egg," *yinumamuwa*, and the term for "fruit," *amamamuwa aninga*, are both derived from the same word, *amamuwa*, which means "small round thing." It is of interest that birds' eggs are considered to be nonflesh food by the Ngatatjara (Gould 1969:261) and by Nunggubuyu speakers (Heath 1978:44), but as flesh food by Djambarrpuyngu speakers (Rudder 1978/9: 355) and in the Western Desert (Douglas 1976:59). Generally, if the eggs are eaten, so is the flesh. For six bird taxa, only the eggs are eaten, and these were included in the total number of edible birds.

Nonflesh food (aninga)

Figure 7.6 shows the categories of nonflesh food as perceived by Groote Eylandt Aborigines. (For further details, see Waddy 1984, vol 2:390-3.) The

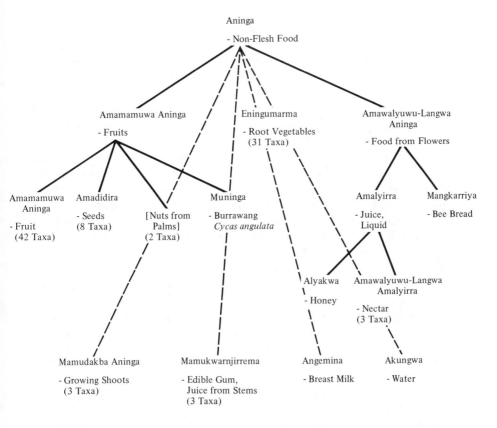

Figure 7.6. Classification of *aninga* (nonflesh food), indicating the numbers of Anindilyakwa taxa considered to be edible.

numbers of taxa shown in each category can be compared with Worsley's total of 83 shown in Table 7.1. The great majority of edible plants have a one-to-one correspondence with scientific species. However, the list of edible plants have a one-to-one correspondence with scientific species. However, the list of edible species recorded by Worsley includes five Anindilyakwa synonyms, three names that refer to specific parts of a plant, three plants the flowers of which provided a source of nectar or pollen for bees rather than people, and several other anomalies. The number of taxa shown in Figure 7.6 includes three of which both fruit and root may be eaten. Some of the edible roots were eaten only when no other food was available.

The major category is fruit. This category is basically divided into fleshy fruits and edible seeds. The latter can be subdivided into woody nuts containing seeds and dry pods containing seeds, though these groups are unnamed. The flesh of seeds may be referred to as *amadangkwa*, the same word as is used for the flesh of animals and humans. The large woody nuts of the pandanus palm and the coconut are considered to be a separate subcategory because "you throw away the skin and find the food inside," as one person explained to me. The cycad nuts form another subcategory, because there are no flowers before the nuts. The latter are also the only fruits that must be processed before eating.

All fruits are considered to belong to dry land, that is, to monsoon and open forest, sandstone outcrops, and coastal sand dunes. In the opinion of one knowledgeable man, the blue waterlily, *Nymphaea gigantea*, is anomalous because it produces edible seeds and yet it grows in billabongs. The habitat data that Miss Levitt and I have gathered suggest that three taxa – *alung-kwalyalyirra* (*Eugenia armstrongii* and *Melastoma polyanthum*), *alungkwa-marda* (*Carallia brachiata*), and *marrangkwurra* (*Dillenia alata*) – always grow beside rivers or billabongs, indicating that the Anindilyakwa habitats *adalyuma* (river) and *awurukwa* (billabong) are interpreted in a much narrower sense than one might expect from an ecological viewpoint. Another six trees are sometimes found beside rivers or in areas subject to seasonal swamping but are more often found in drier areas. All other edible fruits, including seeds, are found growing in drier habitats.

Most fleshy fruits and all edible seeds apart from the waterlily are found growing on woody plants. Nine fleshy fruits are found growing on nonwoody plants, all of which are vines or creepers.

Root vegetables can be grouped on the basis of habitat into those found in freshwater swamps and billabongs (12 taxa) and those found on dry land, the same division as is made for the nonwoody plants in the biological classification system. Only three trees are considered to have edible roots. Root vegetables do not appear to be grouped on the basis of food-related criteria. Growing shoots of young palm trees are also eaten.

Apart from fruit, the only other category that is generally subdivided is food derived directly from flowers. The initial distinction is between firm, yellow bee-bread, derived from pollen, and juice or liquids. Liquid foods include nectar and the highly prized wild honey. The nectar from flowers such as *Grevillea pteridiifolia* can be shaken on to the open hand or into a container in the early morning and drunk.

The gum of several taxa, including the wild peach (*Terminalia carpentariae*) and one of the wattles, may be eaten. Grouped with these taxa is the giant spear grass *Heteropogon triticeus*, the stems of which may be sucked like sugarcane. It should be noted that the stem of the blue waterlily was also eaten occasionally, although it did not seem to fit in this category. This is the only record of any green vegetable matter being eaten in the days before other vegetables were introduced.

Milk is also considered as a nonflesh food. In discussing the various categories of food one day with one of the older men, I asked, "What about water? Where does it fit in?" "*Aninga*," he said and proceeded to elaborate. In the old days, fish of one kind or another were obtainable year round. But after eating fish, you could still ask, *"Eba aninga* [Is there any nonflesh food]?" Something was needed as a contrast to the fish. If there was no other bush food available, "you could always get water." Water was something that could satisfy the need. And so water is classified as *aninga* with other non-flesh foods.

Introduced foods

The adaptability of the Aborigines on Groote Eylandt is seen in their ability to incorporate introduced things into their classification systems. Fruits such as apples, oranges, bananas, and mangoes are easily fitted in with bush fruits. Peanuts and other seeds can be grouped with seeds from bush fruits. Carrots and potatoes can readily be incorporated with other root vegetables.

In English, we recognize peas and beans as vegetables. However, to an Anindilyakwa speaker they are *amamamuwa aninga*, which is food developed from flowers.

Cereals provide an interesting case. Rice still has its grains, and so it fits with seeds. In fact, any cereal food having small, more or less round particles can be fitted with seeds. But what about flour and damper, today's staple item of diet? One of the older men suggested that it should still be grouped with seeds because he had seen on television how wheat was processed into flour, but another said he felt flour would have to be put into a class on its own because it no longer had round particles.

Sugar can be fitted into the category that includes edible gum because sugar is recognized as coming from the stem of a plant. Milk products can easily be grouped with milk. Cordial and other soft drinks can be included with water, although orange juice was considered to belong with fruit by one of the men because it came from oranges.

What about tea? Again the men have become aware through television or other films of the origin of tea leaves. But there is a problem here because, as can be noted from Figure 7.6, there is no category for the leaves of plants. Grass is wallaby food! No leafy green vegetables were eaten on the island, the only possible exception being the stem of the waterlily. In fact, in the past there has been disinterest in the introduction of leafy green vegetables, such as cabbage and spinach, apparently for this very reason: Leaves are not a category for human consumption! The term *aninga* can still be used to apply to nonflesh food eaten by animals. To return to the question of tea, it seems that it should be grouped with other foods derived from the leaves of plants, thus forming a new category.

Introduced types of meat do not present any great difficulty because the categories are already there. Beef, lamb, and pork fit with other land mammals, and chicken fits with birds. Fish and other flesh foods from the sea are in fact more highly categorized in Anindilyakwa than they are in English.

Food restrictions

Groote Eylandt food classification is not affected by whether the animal or plant has any totemic significance, with one exception, namely the scrubfowl (*Megapodius freycinet*). The eggs and flesh of this bird are not now eaten, though they were eaten in earlier days. It seems likely that the restriction has been introduced through increased contact with neighboring tribes from the mainland.

There are a few restrictions on certain mammal flesh during one of the ceremonies, and on certain turtle flesh and possibly some other flesh for pregnant women and young children. The flesh of the hawksbill turtle (*Eretmochelys imbricata*) is not eaten by pregnant women and young children. McArthur (1960:124–5) found that there was considerable variation among informants as to what foods were tabooed following circumcision and in association with pregnancy.

The only other restriction of which I am aware is that placed on the eating of certain fish. Several fish such as red bass (*Lutjanus bohar*) and Chinaman fish (*Symphorus nematophorus*) may be eaten only by old men. If young men eat them, they are said to go prematurely gray. One wonders if it is more than coincidence that several of these fish are considered by scientific experts to be poisonous and/or to be carriers of ciguatera poisoning, though there is no apparent awareness by the Aborigines that these fish will make one sick.

Conclusion

Food classification is related to our attitudes to food. For example, the English food category "vegetable" is defined by the *Oxford English Dictionary* as an edible herb or root which is commonly eaten with meat. This definition carries considerable weight, so that to most people tomatoes would be considered a vegetable along with cabbages and potatoes. Education has led to a general emphasis on the value of foods within English food classification, such that meat is a source of protein, cereals a source of carbohydrates, and so on. English-speaking people generally expect a meal to consist of a variety of foods, with at least one item from each of the food categories, taking the value of the food into consideration.

Groote Eylandt Aborigines look for the contrasting satisfaction of foods from their two basic categories, flesh and nonflesh foods. If there is plenty of fish, they may be "hungry" for "sugar bag." If there are plenty of yams, they may be "hungry" for shellfish. They do not look for variety of foods at any one time but rather for flesh food and nonflesh food. Similar observations have been made by Meehan (1982b:115) for the Anbarra of northern Arnhem Land.

On Groote Eylandt in the past, the choice of food was generally limited by the success of the hunters and gatherers in finding what was seasonally available. They were not as concerned about whether the food was raw or cooked, hot or cold, or sweet or sour, as about what food was available. They did not appear to be concerned about the relative value of foods nor about eating at a specific time of day, nor about the order in which different foods should be eaten. They ate when they were hungry – and as the food became available!

Worsley (1961:178) has stated that the Aborigines of Groote Eylandt "have an objective classification – land-animals, flying things, etc. – and a subjective one dictated by their primary concern with these species – division into food and non-food." To the extent that personal preference will always dictate what is considered to be food, I can agree with Worsley that Groote Eylandt food classification is subjective, whereas biological classification is, at least relatively speaking, objective. However, I cannot agree with Worsley that either food classification or biological classification is in any sense "rough-and-ready" (Worsley 1961:159, 178). In point of fact, it is the initial classification into edible/inedible that is subjective. The classification of foods per se is quite objective.

The Aborigines of Groote Eylandt have developed a sophisticated system of food classification based initially on the distinction between flesh and nonflesh foods. The classification of flesh foods (*akwalya*) closely parallels that of animals within the animal kingdom and is based largely on distinctions in form. The classification of nonflesh foods (*aninga*) focuses more on the nature of the food source. Thus nonflesh foods are subdivided into those developed from flowers, i.e., fruits; those from the ground, i.e., root vegetables; those derived from pollen and nectar; those derived from growing shoots; those derived from stems; and, in addition, milk and water. Two of these categories are further subdivided. Additional categories such as food derived from leaves are being accepted today. Each can be expanded to include appropriate introduced foods in addition to traditional food sources.

Plants had a much wider variety of functions than did animals within Aboriginal culture. They were identified largely on the basis of vegetative characteristics rather than on the form of their edible fruit, which was available only for a short time each year. Plants were thus classified biologically on the basis of form into those with woody stems (*eka*) and those with non-woody stems (*amarda*) (Waddy 1982:70). If an animal is edible, almost every part is eaten. But different parts of plants are edible. Thus in the classification of plant foods, the focus is on the part that is edible, e.g., fruit or root. A similar situation is found in Djambarrpuyngu, where there is overlap between biological and food classification within the animal kingdom; however, within the plant kingdom *biological* classification is based largely on form, whereas *food* classification is based on the part that is eaten (Rudder

1978/9:354). In Nunggubuyu, there is again overlap between biological and food classification within the animal kingdom, but Heath (1978:44) has given insufficient detail to establish the basis of food classification within the plant kingdom.

This study on the classification of foods is directly applicable to the teaching of nutrition, particularly the need for a balanced diet. Home science teachers in the local school and nurses in the local community health center have been encouraged to utilize the Anindilyakwa food categories as a basis for nutrition education rather than using European categories alone. It is the introduced food such as flour, sugar, and other processed foods that have contributed so much to poor dietary standards in many Aboriginal communities today. The dietary balance has changed from that of earlier years, and this needs to be understood in the terms of the food classification system in use in the community, not in the terms of an introduced system of classification. To ignore the folk classification system is to reinforce the idea held by many Aborigines – that there is something intrinsically superior about anything that is introduced from European culture. In fact, bush foods, being basically unprocessed, are naturally fresher and contribute to a healthy diet when eaten in the right balance from the perspective of the folk classification system.

Food classification from a Groote Eylandt Aborigine's viewpoint, like biological classification, is basically an objective process. The resultant systems of classification may be different from English or scientific systems, but they must nevertheless be accepted as valid alternatives, as interpretations of the plant and animal world from an Aboriginal perspective.

Part III

INFANT FEEDING PRACTICE

8. Infant feeding practice in Malaysia: the variables of choice

Marianne Spiegel

Breast feeding, like bottle feeding, is for humans a learned behavioral response; a social activity sensitive to social influences. Hence, a discussion of which infant feeding strategy is best or most appropriate, must first specify *for whom*. Many social actors are legitimately concerned with what infant and child feeding practices are to be considered normative. Limiting this set, however, is no easy matter. Children, women, families, households, even societies qua societies all press reasonable claims. Sorting them is an ideological, not a scientific, act.

Ideology also informs our judgment about the legitimacy of change in long-standing social custom and about the practices that may be held accountable. Although in the 1970s multinational manufacturers of powdered milk formulas undoubtedly positioned themselves to profit from social change, they were not, simply, villains; nor did they, in spite of contributions, create or determine change. The issues are more complex.

This chapter, then, is a preliminary attempt to investigate for certain Malaysian groups the social, cultural, economic, and political impingements on infant feeding practice. Recognition that social change is contingent on historical circumstance, and that personal adaptation generally occurs in the context of family and household units, is central to the argument. I take two positions, (1) that "breast is best" is best treated as a testable hypothesis (Thomson and Black 1975:163), whose variables have not been sufficiently isolated; and (2) that biological explanations for social relationships are reductionist. As Winikoff (1978:895) has said, intervening social, economic, and behavioral relationships may be more powerful in determining the outcome of changes in a biological system than the intrinsic biological relationships themselves.

The "breast is best" controversy

Related issues require disaggregation: What, historically, was common infant feeding practice, and has its incidence declined? Who decides the feeding method, and what variables affect choice? Under what conditions is bottle feeding dangerous to the health and well-being of infants and young children?

How may supplementation be appropriately used? Which is more economically rational, breast or bottle feeding? What should be the focus of remediation, feeding practice or the amelioration of poverty? There has been consensus on only one issue: When the sole consideration is a newborn's health, breast feeding, in traditional and modern societies, in rural and urban sectors, and in all socioeconomic groups, is best for babies at birth and for some months afterward.

Coalitions such as INFACT (Infant Formula Action Coalition) (*INFACT Notes* 1978) and the Interfaith Center on Corporate Responsibility (ICCR), a "sponsor related movement" of the World Council of Churches (Margulies 1975, 1977, 1978; Baer 1978)[1] and individual specialists including Derrick and Patrice Jelliffe (1978), Michael Latham (1977), Ted Greiner (1975, 1977), and Alan Berg (1973a, 1973b) represent one pole of a continuum of opinion. They have argued that a worldwide trend toward increased incidence and earlier onset of bottle feeding has been in response to a worldwide conspiracy by multinational corporations to promote artificial feeds.[2] Not only, they have continued, is bottle feeding dangerously expensive, but given the inadequacies of public health practice in many Third World countries, the incidence of infant mortality and morbidity is directly attributable to a decline in breast feeding. Resources have been targeted to mobilize world public opinion and to pressure formula manufacturers to moderate their marketing tactics.

The converse, that their products are responses to felt consumer needs for more adequate artificial feeds, has been argued by Nestle S.A. (1978, 1979a, 1979b),[3] representing infant formula and baby food manufacturers, and by Dana Raphael's Human Lactation Center (Raphael 1973; *Lactation Review* 1977, 1978). Evidence has been assembled documenting the incidence of mixed feeding in traditional populations, the impact of development on traditional culture, and the benefits of formula feeding when measured against other nonbreast feeds. It has further been contended that the issue of costs is not so straightforward as had been presented and, most importantly, that focus on Nestle's role has been diverting resources from the war against the real enemy – poverty, both individual and national.

1 In 1979, the coalition went international. The new consumer federation, IBFAN (International Baby Food Action Network), actively supported the 1977 Nestle boycott, directed from 1979 until 1984 when it was rescinded by INBCC (International Nestle Boycott Committee). INBCC now operates under a new name, International Negotiators for Babyfood Code Compliance. Its concern is with issues of labeling, literature, gifts to medical personnel, and issues of supplies and samples. This last, hinging on an agreeable definition of "have to be fed on breast-milk substitutes" (WHO 1981:17), is in active negotiation. INFACT, IBAN, and ICCR still maintain interest in the breast/bottle controversy. They monitor international compliance, pressure independent nation-states for strengthened codes, and, in general, keep the issue before the public.
2 Probreast advocates have recently modified their position. An ICCR Brief (3A) in the January 1980 *Corporate Examiner* states "While the promotion of infant formula is not the only cause for the widespread decline of breastfeeding in developing countries, it has been identified as a significant factor..." (see also Chetley 1985:10).
3 See also the report prepared for Nestle in 1982 and updated in 1985 (McComas et al. 1982/ 1985:3), which continues to stress the need for breast milk substitutes.

At the same time, though there is agreement that some 85 percent of women are physiologically capable of breast feeding sufficiently to sustain adequate infant growth (Berg 1973a:30), there is controversy as to optimum duration of exclusive breast feeding. Some have argued that unsupplemented breast milk provides sufficient nutrients during the first four to six months of an infant's life even if the mother's diet has been inadequate during pregnancy and continues so during lactation (Ledogar 1975:127; Thomson and Black 1975:169). Others have suggested, under such conditions, an optimum three-month period (*Lactation Review* 1978:3). Although additional studies on relationships among long- and short-term maternal nutrition and health, the quantity and quality of breast milk, duration of lactation, and infant growth and development are necessary to understand the role and timing of supplementation (Thomson and Black 1975:165; Winikoff 1978:897),[4] it should be noted that implicit in the argument are contending views as to whose claims to health and well-being – mothers' or children's – are most valid. That others, as participants in social networks, have legitimate claims, also requires attention.

The two following sections review the above issues in detail.

The pro-breast position

Human milk is advantageous for human infants, first, because mammalian milks are species specific. Each milk differs from others in amino acid pattern; protein and fat composition; sodium, vitamin, and mineral content; pH value; etc. Because the elements interact to produce a particular biological system, the attempt to humanize cow's milk or to reproduce human milk is, at best, difficult (Jelliffe and Jelliffe 1977:912–3). Furthermore, evolution has enhanced optimal meshing of the growth needs of a particular species with the chemistry of its milk (Berg 1973a:30). For example, human milk, compared to cow's milk, has a low protein content. Newborn calves grow at much faster rates than human infants, and therefore need more protein. For humans, the most immediate postgestation task involves growth of the central nervous system including the brain, for which composition of human milk appears optimal.

Second, current data provide evidence that, in addition to systemic immunological protection acquired transplacentally and through colostrum, breast milk, when given without supplementation, provides antibodies which actively protect babies from bacterial and viral gastrointestinal infections; from diseases, such as polio, which have intestinal ports of entry; and possibly, from respiratory ailments (Gerrard 1974:757–61). At about six months of age, the infant's own immunological system is mature enough to handle its own defense, though immunological effects may continue after weaning (Winikoff 1978:897).

4 See also Whitehead et al. 1978; Waterlow and Thomson 1979; Jelliffe and Jelliffe 1979; Waterlow 1979; Scrimshaw and Underwood 1980.

Third, breast feeding protects infants from the dangers of infection transmitted by unsterile water; contaminated bottles, nipples, and utensils; and lack of refrigeration (Jelliffe 1968:42). Fourth, because unsupplemented breast feeding is, ideally, a finely tuned food and fluid supply and demand system (Jelliffe and Jelliffe 1978:19), its use should guard against the twin dangers of obesity among the affluent and infant malnutrition and starvation due to formula overdilution among the poor (Jelliffe and Jelliffe 1978:272). Further, the psychological well-being of the developing infant may be enhanced by hormones released by lactation, which initiate and sustain appropriate maternal behaviors (Winikoff 1978:898). Significant research substantiating this last claim is particularly sketchy.

In order that babies continue to maintain the overall advantage conferred by unsupplemented breast feeding from birth, experts have agreed (Jelliffe and Jelliffe 1975:557; Thomson and Black 1975:169) that between four and six months of age, a baby's all-milk diet should be supplemented. The recommendation is that locally grown, semisolid, cereal-based weaning mixtures be supplemented for an extended period of time with decreasing quantities of breast milk. Such milk supplies essential, high-quality protein in sufficiently concentrated form for babies to receive, within the limited quantity of food they are able to ingest, enough proteins and calories to meet increased growth demands. Use of home-grown weaning foods is recommended to avoid the need for a second transitional stage, from commercial preparations to the traditional foods that finally replace all others.

Further, because passively acquired immunity is fading, if adequate infant nutrition fails, malnutrition and infection will interact synergistically, particularly in the form of rampant diarrhea, to increase dramatically the incidence of morbidity and mortality. Historically, a most critical transition for toddlers occurred in their second year of life, when they were expected to relinquish special diets and practices, such as the number and timing of feedings compatible with their age-dictated needs, and to accommodate their schedules and tastes to adult practice (Jelliffe and Jelliffe 1978:117). At weaning there is often a failure of nutrition; when it occurs early, the age at which malnutrition occurs is correspondingly reduced (Thomson and Black 1975:167; Winikoff 1978:899). The possibility of irreversible brain damage is heightened in such circumstances (e.g., see Jelliffe and Jelliffe 1978:284). Bottle feeding, it has been charged, by contributing to early onset of protein–energy malnutrition (PEM), increases the risks (Gordon, Wyon, and Ascoli 1967:372; Jelliffe and Jelliffe 1978:173).[5]

Thomson and Black (1975:167) have suggested, moreover, that there is no reason to believe that prolonged breast feeding, without attention to hygiene, reduces infection and consequent malnutrition in older infants. Further, they have suggested that breast feeding for long periods may actually

5 The more significant social problem in Malaysia is, as Chong has suggested (1976:249), moderate malnutrition and correspondingly less severe physical disability.

be harmful because the assumption made, that the child is being well fed, is inaccurate. (See also Rowland, Paul, and Whitehead 1981.) And, they continue, breast feeding may have always functioned simply as a lifesaver, a stopgap, rather than as a preferred practice, for the obvious reason that society lacked the ability, as it now lacks the will, to provide more appropriate substitutes. The correlations between poverty and its concomitant conditions, poor sanitation, inadequate nutrition for mother and child, and bottle-related deaths, need more careful study (Labouisse 1978). The presumption that increased PEM is caused by increased bottle feeding per se, is a simplistic one.

Arguments for breast feeding also focus on economic and contraceptive benefits to domestic groups and nation states. As regards domestic income, the argument is sketchy. It usually runs thus: Breast milk, even if the cost of supplementing lactating mothers' diets is included, is much less expensive than formula or cow's milk. No cash outlay is required. Nor, in subsistence economies, is cash necessary for adult food purchases. Dugdale (1971: 249) extended the argument, weighing cash income from Malaysian women's work against cash outlays for baby food. In a more promising analysis, Popkin and Solon (1976) reviewed the issue of income versus time. Only in the poorer households in their study was increased cash income insufficient to offset time lost from breast feeding. Malnutrition among this group had, therefore, increased with increased work in the marketplace. Jelliffe and Jelliffe (1978:51) have agreed that under conditions of poverty, the child whose mother stays at home is better off. That the incidence of bottle feeding rises with increased income may then be explained in one of three ways: (1) Women can now afford to bottle feed and this is their preference; (2) work away from home logistically precludes breast feeding; and (3) women's time is now so valuable that it can be considered misused when employed to breastfeed. The issue needs resolution.

Cumulatively, the protein loss from unrealized breast milk, the natural resource, is enormous (Zeidenstein 1977:5–7). For countries with limited supplies of complete protein, the large percentage of foreign exchange required to meet the deficit assumes importance. Comparative benefits to a nation state when its women breast-feed versus when they are employed in the marketplace are a related issue.

Family planning may be affected by decreased incidence and shortened periods of unsupplemented breast feeding. The maintenance of amenorrhea and, possibly, the reduction of fecundity after renewed menstruation appear to be related to the secretion of the hormone prolactin (e.g., see Petros-Barvazian and Carballo 1979:17; Simpson-Hebert and Huffman 1981) which, in turn, is related to round-the-clock frequency and intensity of suckling. Supplementation decreases suckling through decreased hunger. According to Sai (1979:7), breast feeding, particularly in developing countries, is the most widely and effectively used contraceptive. Its merit, however, may relate to cultural taboos against intercourse during lactation, which in turn relate to marriage patterns and sexual norms and not to physiological effects per se (Winikoff 1978:890). For countries intent on limiting reproduction, the risks and cost may increase with increased bottle feeding, particularly where newer methods of contraception are little used (Berg 1973a:31). Knodel (1977:1115) has suggested that bottle-related increased death rates may even reduce contraceptive use as families plan to assure the survival of an optimal number of children. On an individual basis, though certainly better than nothing, lactation as contraception is not highly reliable.

Many writers particularly emphasize the convenience of breast feeding, but neglect to mention or minimize the nursing mother's insufficiency of relief, chronic fatigue, reduced mobility (Kent 1981:11), nursing problems (WHO 1979:30–4), and repeated infections. As Thomson and Black have pointed out (1975:170), the satisfaction and convenience of breast feeding may be highly overrated.

In sum, early unsupplemented breast feeding has for babies nutritive, physiological, immunological, and possibly psychological advantages. However, without sufficient analysis, probreast groups have argued its convenience, role in fertility reduction, and cost benefits to mothers, families, and to nation states. Without examining changes in social and economic landscapes which I shall stress, they have emphasized the minimal need for artificial feeds of any kind and have implicated manufacturers' promotional activities as the root cause of increased usage. Women's own voices have rarely been heard; their points of view rarely elicited; their health and well-being rarely taken into account. Instead multinational coalitions have engaged multinational corporations in acrimonious debate.

The Nestle position

Ostensibly the same, "breast is best" (Nestle 1978:1), Nestle's position in the 1970s differed from its opponents' in its emphasis on the need for early supplementation and its active promotion of mixed feeding (Ledogar 1975:134; *PAG Bulletin* 1977a:68; Nestle 1979b:23–4).[6] Its advertising copy (Greiner 1975:57) implied that large numbers of women lactate inadequately. Though research contributed by the Human Lactation Center was by Nestle's (1979a: 3) own admission inadequate, they remained committed to the position that supplements were necessary, on average, after the first three months of a "Third World" infant's life (Nestle 1979a:3). The timing of the controversy was important. At six months, decreased breast milk and appropriate local weaning foods will sustain adequate growth. The assumption Nestle had made, or at least had wanted the layman to make, was that such a mixture

---

6 In fact, throughout the boycott and as negotiations proceeded, as public relations pressure mounted, Nestle consistently modified its position (Grant 1984:1).

would, at three months, be harmful to an infant's relatively less developed digestive tract. Only supplementation by formula, they implied, would adequately sustain life. However, liquids or semisolid supplementation actually diminish breast milk supply. A less hungry baby suckles less. Quantity, related to amount and intensity of nursing, is reduced. Thus supplementation becomes imperative. The more you supplement, the more you must, and Nestle may have been counting on just that physiological fact to sell formula.

Nestle has also claimed that the relationship between infant mortality and morbidity and bottle-fed formula is spurious [Nestle 1979a: Memorandum of Facts (enclosure):6], as indeed it may be. Two arguments were cited. First, the need for replacement, supplementation, and follow-up has always existed. Mixed feeding, starting at an early age, has been the norm over time in most societies (Nestle 1979a:2). Prior to the introduction of quality baby products, various nonnutritive gruels, bush teas, barley water, cornstarch, and arrowroot mixtures and, later on, sweetened condensed milk were used as infant foods. Management points to the nearly 50 percent decrease in infant mortality in Third World countries between 1939 and 1947 and to increased incidence of formula feeding, and expresses amazement at outrage over its policies. Nestle's studied neglect of parallel socioeconomic changes does not release its critics from their need to examine relations between infant mortality and nonbreast feeds. Such study is requisite for establishing linkages among socioeconomic status, bottle content, and infant and toddler malnutrition and mortality (*PAG Bulletin* 1977b:42).

Furthermore, Nestle's claim to historical precedent to justify the promotion of artificial feeds, while not wholly unwarranted, is damaged by imprecision as are the rebuttals of its critics. Because patterns of change cannot be ascertained without accurate baselines, and because there is significant difference between partial and complete breast feeding, precise definitions of terms such as "breast feeding," "bottle feeding," "mixed feeding" (Sai 1979:8), and the catchall term "weaning," are requisite.[7]

Second, Nestle also dismissed the charge that, because formula may necessitate the use of water and implements under unhygienic conditions and without adequate refrigeration, the company contributed dramatically to the incidence of infant infection. Babies fed the aforementioned bush teas, or even water alone were, they said, subject to the same hazard. They may have been right, but they were ignoring the more important and more deadly issue. The cost of milk substitutes in relation to income is, for much of the developing world, extraordinarily high. Supplementation once commenced can be discontinued but only at the risk of malnutrition, starvation, and death. Therefore, low-income women who cannot sustain the cash outlays

7 All parties to the controversy are still paying the price for imprecise definitions. Whether or not change in practice has occurred since passage of new restrictive national and international codes and whether such change is attributable to those restrictions is not now known.

but also cannot now adequately nurse, have no choice but to dilute formulas, effectively decreasing nutrients. Weakened babies, exposed to increased environmental infections introduced by feeding paraphernalia, more readily sicken and die. Although evidence has accumulated that socioeconomic correlates and the initial health status of the child are more telling than simply bottle-feeding practice, formula promotion in such situations was obviously unconscienable. All evidence did sustain the relationship between bottle feeding and mortality rates, never mind what was in the bottle (Knodel 1977:1112; Petros-Barvazian and Carballo 1979:20).

Nestle also discounted their responsibility for bottle feeding among low-income groups, because, they said, 85–90 percent of its infant formula products were sold to city families with adequate incomes [Nestle 1979a: Memorandum of Facts (enclosure):16]. That no statistics confirmed the statement's accuracy was directly attributable to the milk companies' refusal to release the relevant data (Baer 1978, part I:1).[8]

Manufacturers, in sum, highlighted their contributions to healthy infant development. In particular, they denied they had acted as social-change agents or as promoters of artificial feeds to low-income households. Instead they stressed their role as developers of nutritious supplements for inadequately nursed infants. By their refusal to recognize the complexity of social change and the role they, as manufacturers, might play by providing choice to families in transition, they positioned themselves for the confrontation that culminated in passage by the World Health Assembly of the 1981 International Code of Marketing of Breast-milk Substitutes.

Social groups

If infant feeding practices are indeed socially determined, then it is necessary to sketch the social frame: first, to define by occupation, residence, ethnicity, religious practice, and, particularly, socioeconomic status and nature of the cooperating unit, the social groups that make feeding decisions in Malaysia; second, to substantiate social, cultural, economic, and political influences affecting choice. This latter task is best accomplished through consideration of seven broad, interrelated variable sets:

1. The differential ability of households to provide basic subsistence. I refer here to domestic group composition, wage and labor patterns, cash availability and necessary work-related cash outlays, degree of economic risk associated with particular occupations, and economic support systems.
2. The nature and flexibility of women's work roles.

---

8 In 1978, Nestle rescinded the use of mass media advertising, contending that formula was reaching families for whom it was never intended. Such admission calls into question the nature of the social groups who were originally targeted by Nestle as potential consumers.

3. Urban/rural development; the commercialization of agriculture and its effect on the size and shape of cooperating domestic units.
4. Cultural food practices; who eats what, when, with whom, and in what order.
5. Priorities and public policies for economic growth, including a country's current and projected ties to the world economy.
6. Aggressive advertisement and promotion of commercial infant foods.
7. Beliefs and practices of indigenous medical and health-related professionals.

These factors will be discussed after I propose ways to discriminate among distinct Malaysian social groups.

There are three major population groups in western or peninsular Malaysia: Malays, Chinese, and Indians. The former, some 54 percent of the total population, is the focus herein. Although approximately 30 percent of the total Malaysian population resides in urban areas (those with populations of at least 10,000), the Malays themselves reside overwhelmingly in the countryside (Chong 1976:241). Most are engaged in subsistence and commercial agricultural pursuits, including rice and coconut harvesting, farm laboring, rubber tapping, as well as shore fishing and petty trading. Underemployment in the countryside is considerable. In the cities, new migrants find that unemployment runs high.

Malays, overall, are poor. They have high infant and toddler mortality rates (Goto et al. 1974:425; Yusof and Yusof 1974:14) and maternal mortality rates higher than those for Malaysian Chinese or Indians (Chen 1977: 122). In 1973, mean, including in-kind, household income was $269 a month. The top 10 percent of the population accounted for about 40 percent of total income; the bottom two-fifths, for 12 percent. Of households with incomes below $100, 90 percent were in rural areas, and 34 percent of rural households, versus 9.4 percent in the urban sector, had such incomes (Government of Malaysia 1973:2–3). Although there has been improvement since 1973, Malays still lag behind other ethnic groups in economic performance (Government of Malaysia 1979:44).

As mentioned, Malays are an overwhelmingly rural population. However, it has been documented (Kent 1981:39) that the incidence of bottle feeding in Malaysia is 35.7 percent higher in urban areas than in rural locations. Furthermore, Thomson and Black (1975:164) and Hofvander, Sjolin, and Vahlquist (1979:111) have argued that breast feeding is sustained longest in those communities with fewest economic and educational advantages.[9] In one rural area in northern Malaysia, such practice also correlated with individual household income. Most poor and lower-middle-income mothers breast-

---

9 For the relationship between breast feeding and educational level in Asia and Latin America, see Kent (1981:30–1). For Malaysian women, there is a 23.5 percent difference between those with no education and those with at least secondary education.

fed their infants. In the higher income groups, their number was substantially reduced (Teoh 1975:178). Thus it may be that bottle usage relates to rising incomes, to place of residence, and, possibly, to cash availability, modern transport, sanitation waste disposal, etc. If so, and if, as pro-breast advocates have argued, morbidity and mortality increase with bottle feeding, then it is necessary to explain the following: Is the apparent relationship between greater incidence of disease and relative affluence verifiable? It is not.

To begin with, in Malyasia, the relationship between urbanization and infant mortality rate is complex. Between 1957 and 1974, the urban population increased 51.82 percent, 27 percent more than population growth as a whole (Yusof and Yusof 1974:29). Overall, infant and toddler mortality rates dropped. For instance, in Sarawak the infant mortality rate went from 84.8 in the 1940s to 33.9 in 1969. However, the share of urban infant deaths sharply increased for all ethnic groups, though Malays, a high percentage of whose households are in the low-income category, accounted for a disproportionate share. The above does not apply to those areas characterized as metropolitan towns (population 75,000 and above) which feature a disproportionate share of hospitals, health-related facilities, and medical personnel. States that recorded falls in urban infant mortality, though the urban rate remained higher than the rural, did not report rapid urban growth. Where urban infant mortality grew, population grew quickly. This suggests that in the earlier stages of industrialization, low-income residents experience socioeconomic and health conditions such as inadequate housing, congestion, poor sanitation, a contaminated water supply, changes in diet, unemployment or employment in lower categories of the occupational structure, and/or changes in patterns of social relationships that are productive of social pathology (Yusof and Yusof 1974:17–25). The hypothesis that it is among this group that bottle-feeding rates increase and infant mortality remains high, and that the two are in some measure related, is, for Malaysia, in need of verification.

Although some studies have attempted to do just this, most are insufficiently rigorous. They present synchronic data; employ extremely small samples, frequently self-selected; and/or use ill-defined and aggregated variables.

Dugdale (1970) discussed breast feeding in Kuala Lumpur, Malaysia's capital city, using as a self-selected sample the 50 percent of newborns who, in the study year, attended clinics. Malays were poorly represented, accounting for only 22 percent of live births. Dugdale found that as income rose, the frequency of breast feeding and the duration of the practice over time decreased. In fact, between 1960 and 1966, breast feeding for low-income Malays with one child actually increased. For all family sizes and all income groups, Malays breast-fed more and longer. Furthermore, Malay women with children went out to work less than their Chinese counterparts. Here trends that link feeding practices with income, ethnicity, religion, and work patterns begin to emerge, but they are more speculative than sure.

Infant nutrition is another matter. Goto et al. (1974), admitting less than rigorous data, found no correlations between feeding practice and mortality rate. On the other hand, infant malnutrition does more clearly correlate with family size, including number of living and dead siblings; birth order; closeness of spacing; and low birth weights (Winikoff 1978:896), in turn related to the status of mothers' nutrition. Malnutrition, in fact, seems clearly a class phenomenon (Jelliffe and Jelliffe 1978:270). Chen (1975) found that in 1971, of 174 children admitted for pneumonia and diarrhea to University Hospital in Kuala Lumpur, 34 percent suffered from PEM. Those so suffering tended to come from poorer homes and to have a larger number of siblings born in rapid succession. Of those with no clinical malnutrition, 60 percent were breast-fed for 3.9 months, as against 68 percent for 3.9 months for the malnourished group. No significant difference emerges. There is, however, an association between the type of milk given to the non-breast-fed group and malnutrition. Of the malnourished babies, 29 percent (versus 15 percent of the normals) received sweetened condensed milk. The rest received powdered milks.

Rampal (1977) studied 5,360 school-aged children in rural and urban settings. However, the urbanites were from upper-middle-class families, whereas rural children came from lower- and middle-income homes. Irrespective of race and sex, rural children had significantly higher rates of protein–calorie malnutrition than their urban counterparts.

Chen (1976) found that when household income was taken into account, irrespective of ethnicity, for higher-income school children growth achievement was greater than for poorer ones. In fact, growth achievement for high-income Indian children, who are a component of the slightest and poorest of the three main ethnic groups, was similar to that of high-income Chinese, the tallest, heaviest, and richest of all groups.

Dugdale (1971) reported that in Kuala Lumpur, babies from large families grew more slowly than babies from small families; that low income and size of family related to incidence of alimentary ills; and that there was no relationship between type of feeding and frequency of respiratory or alimentary illness. Further, from birth through 40 weeks of age, breast-fed babies never gained more rapidly than those on bottles. Chen and Dugdale (1972) reported for Petaling Jaya, a satellite city west of Kuala Lumpur, findings similar to those for rural Malays. Poorer families experienced more pathology. Chong (1976) reported major deficiency diseases, nutritional anemia, low birth weights for age, protein–calorie malnutrition, among low-socioeconomic-status preschool children in both rural and urban areas.

In sum, although studies are inadequate, they provide evidence for the suggestion that infant malnutrition, its causes and solutions, are embedded in a broad, changing socioeconomic frame (Berg 1973b:7). That frame, too complex to admit simple cause-and-effect relationships, is too often ignored by coalitions eager to score political points. The fact of poverty, in particular, is brushed aside. Further analysis of the relationships between location and incidence of infant and child morbidity and mortality on the one hand, and income levels, family size, and mothers' own nutritional status on the other, requires research designs that illuminate rather than oversimplify causality.

Domestic groups: traditional patterns

A second section of the frame deals, as mentioned, with changes in the cultural patterns and social structures of domestic groups. The earlier Malaysian model appears well documented (Rosemary Firth 1943/1966; Raymond Firth 1946/1966; McArthur 1962; Djamour 1965; Colson 1971). Newer models are appearing that pertain to both the countryside and the city (Laderman 1983). The consensus among ethnographers makes clear that the typical Malay, who lived traditionally in rural, uncongested, small, primarily conjugal households of something under five persons, was surrounded from birth to death by an intimate and economically, socially, and psychologically supportive network of real and fictive kin. Even women living without men were entitled to such support, and ties between maternal relatives appear to have been particularly strong (Djamour 1965:22). Further, the official community frame itself was supportive. Dignitaries considered it their duty to mediate between the newer, larger social structures and individual villagers.[10]

The aforementioned all-female network, mutually obligated to support, was particularly important during pregnancy, childbirth, and the early postnatal period. However, for young girls, preparation for child rearing was begun at a much earlier age. Such youngsters, who together with all females remained formally in the background, observed, and from the age of five or so on, participated in child rearing. They did not attend school and, in fact, as adolescents retreated even more completely into their respective homes. At this time mother–daughter links intensified, such that even after the latter's marriage, they remained both physically and psychologically close. As has been said, breast feeding is not simply an instinctive behavior, but a dyadic process, socially and culturally taught and conditioned. Learning such a process becomes easier when supported by long-standing emotional ties. Besides subconscious, psychological preparation for breast feeding through its assimilation as a nonevent, young Malay women were also actively taught the traditional skills and information necessary for successful breast feeding.

After childbirth, cultural beliefs sustained other planned supportive practices. That first-time mothers were expected to be still living in their natal households (Djamour 1965:80), is but one example. Such an arrangement

---

10 Whether the social structure and transmittal process among Malay females actually operated as summarized is difficult to assess. How much poor and inimical practice was institutionalized through information networks is difficult to judge, as is the extent to which network breakup and reconstitution permitted sounder practices and reduced sanctions on deviance.

encouraged the worry-free atmosphere physiologically necessary to the un-
inhibited letdown reflex (milk ejection reflex) requisite to unrestrained milk
flow. It enabled supportive personnel to immediately ease mothers' worries
over milk quantity and quality. It was also expected that not-so-new mothers
would have established residence close to their own mothers, or, if this were
not possible, they were expected to return "home" in the last stages of pregnancy (Djamour 1965:80). Thus, they, too, could enjoy the support, advice,
and reassurance of women, grandmothers, sisters, paid midwives they had
known and trusted since childhood (Colson 1971:76).

Practical support was also forthcoming. Malay women did not immediately return to normal domestic and extradomestic tasks after a baby's birth.
For some seven days (McArthur 1962:24), they rested with their babies,
making the necessary adjustments to their new status, and working toward
the establishment of successful feeding practice. For 44 days, women were
confined in their tasks to light work around the house, while the network,
including a woman's older children, supplied all other necessary labor. In
fact, all members of a household, together with neighbors and friends, collectively spent several hours a day relieving a child's mother of the physical
and emotional care which her young offspring required (see Djamour 1965:
92–101). Nor, later on, were mother and child alone and isolated. Productive and domestic work were not necessarily physically separate nor was
productive labor necessarily rigidly scheduled.

Though McArthur (1962:41) reported women to have complained that
nursing from about 18 months on is stressful, weaning typically did not occur until around two years of age, usually at the time of subsequent pregnancy or when a child was well established on a rice diet. According to
Rosemary Firth (1943/1966:110), the process was conducted haphazardly.
However, no studies substantiate the particular reasons for weaning, the
relationship of timing to earlier breast- or bottle-feeding practice, the methods used, the mix of foods at different stages of the process, and/or the nutritional effect of particular weaning behaviors on infant health. R. Firth did
report (1943/1966:109) that breast milk was never regarded as a sufficient
food by Malaysian women and that, therefore, supplementation commenced
at birth. Corn flour, rice paste, and mashed bananas served as favored semisolid supplements. Unfortunately, this evidence is too anecdotal to be useful in establishing normative and actual feeding practice and its change over
time.

We do know that, traditionally, children received no milk after they were
weaned. Domestic animals were rarely milked, and tinned milk, though locally available since about 1885, was very expensive (Manderson 1982). It is
further reported that toddlers were denied vegetables and fish (Whyte 1974:
122); that they rarely ate fruit (Rosemary Firth 1943/1966:23); that food
intake was limited by side dishes that were too tough and too highly spiced
for them to digest (Chen 1974:87); and that, therefore, toddlers' nutritional

intake was poorly balanced (Chong 1976:249–50). In less developed countries, deaths in the second year frequently exceed half the number of deaths in the first year of life (this latter figure heavily influenced by the excessive number of deaths in the seven days following birth), and also exceed the combined death total in the third, fourth, and fifth years (Gordon et al. 1967:358). Because the toddler mortality rate in industrialized countries is only 15 percent of the infant mortality rate, the second-year death rate can be considered a practical index of community malnutrition. Even with the advent of bottle feeding, this rate has declined in Malaysia, though, as with the infant mortality rate, urban rates have risen in relation to rural ones (Yusof and Yusof 1974:140).

To what the general decline and changed ratio is attributable is still speculative. We know that mean duration of breast feeding has declined markedly in Malaysia (Kent 1981:17), that urban areas have sustained the dramatic rise in bottle feeding. We do not know whether there is a significant difference in duration of breast feeding between urban and rural areas; whether weaning methods differ by place of residence, or whether they have changed significantly in either place and if so for whom. Once again, available evidence points toward the need for further investigation of the relationships among poverty, nutritional practice, and mortality rates.

Domestic groups: structural change and new child-rearing patterns

Individuals make short-term decisions which accumulate. At some point, nonparticipants, looking back, feel that aggregate, incremental changes constitute a new synthesis. For Malaysia as a whole and for certain groups in particular, household structure and practice is not now as it had been. However, at this juncture, the differences can be discussed only as apparent trends. Statistical corroboration is lacking.

Even in the countryside, women in increasing numbers have gone, formally, to work. As land shortages have developed; as capital and productivity requirements have changed with modern technology; as market structures and meaningful universes have enlarged (Raymond Firth 1946/1966:7–8), subsistence and small-scale, kin-organized, commercial agriculture and accompanying handicrafts and sideline activities, easily pursued at home, have become less feasible ways to earn a living. Women are away from their homes more often and for longer periods of time (Laderman 1983:87). In rubber tapping, for instance, women in season are away from their children for six to seven hours a day (McArthur 1962:21). Should they, after childbirth, delay for long their return to the fields, all would go hungry. Furthermore, such women might be subjecting themselves to familial and community reproof (*PAG Bulletin* 1977b:43). We do not know what concerns take domestic precedence, or under what circumstances.

Whether or not the incidence of working women and the kind of work performed significantly correlate with feeding practice is also unknown. Nor do we know how much what kind of work may interfere, in terms of energy requirements, physical availability, and time constraints, with optimal feeding practice (*PAG Bulletin* 1977b:42). We do not, for example, know the conditions under which babies may accompany their mothers to the work site. McArthur (1962:45) has stated that the most common reason mothers advanced for supplementation was that they might work. However, supplements were used by only half the working mothers in her rural sample. Such evidence conflicts with that of R. Firth (1943/1966:109–10) who stated that supplementation traditionally commenced at birth. It also conflicts with that of Baer (1978, part II:3) who without adequate documentation cites Chen's (1978) mimeographed paper as evidence that the duration of breast feeding is not significantly different for working mothers and housewives. Kent (1981: 14) also notes with interest the lack of relationship between aggregate labor force participation and feeding practice.

Vavra (1972:101) has stated that female labor force participation rates in rural and urban western Malaysia are among the highest in the world. However, he has made it amply clear that industrialization per se does not mean an automatic increase in female labor force participation. In Malaysia, the female rate of employment had been higher in the countryside than in the cities. (Work here does not necessarily mean paid, steady, or structured employment.) However, new technology in agriculture has changed the picture in complex ways. For families who move to the cities, the limited size of the modern sector, un- and underemployment among men, and biases against women's participation, may mean that the latter have a difficult time finding employment (Vavra 1972:107). The picture may be even more grim for married women, because in certain industries, employers appear to favor young, docile, unmarried females (Grossman 1978:3). For families remaining in the countryside, technologically created unemployment produces the same situation. Married women remain at home, or, increasingly, find work opportunities more structured than those to which they had been accustomed. Vavra (1972:114) has pointed out, however, that between 1957 and 1967 the rate of employment among 20- to 34-year-old women, many married and with children, did rise, although the female employment rate still peaked at ages 20 and 50, whereas, overall, the curve for Malaysia showed a continuous rise till age 60. Of course, none of the above speaks to the issue of correlations between female employment – its kind, duration, and continuity – and feeding practice. Detailed observational and longitudinal data are here requisite.

If indeed women are increasingly working outside the domestic frame, that frame itself must have undergone extreme change. For analytic purposes one would need to know what individuals share a common budget;

who contributes to that budget, as for example, the extent of adolescent participation (Djamour 1965:43) in the face of a high unemployment rate among youth;[11] what economic unit is responsible for feeding the child (*PAG Bulletin* 1977b:43); as well as who lives with whom and under what circumstances; and finally the incidence of female-headed households and their source of support. Formerly, the budget-sharing group tended to be the conjugal household residing at one location (Djamour 1965:53; Rosemary Firth 1943/1966:82). In cases of divorce or where the occupational structure necessitated separation, women and children tended to stay together, sometimes shifting for themselves and sometimes assisted by ex-husbands or maternal kin. However, the extent of complementary responsibility on the part of husband and wife differed by case. In the past, isolated individuals might attach to the conjugal group but, though frequently sharing certain tasks, usually had separate budgets. What units, and what individuals within them, have responsibility for reproductive costs has certainly not, for modern Malaysia, been adequately investigated (Rapp 1978:287–94); nor has the relationship between the responsible unit and the method of feeding. In fact, as yet, there is no way of knowing the composition of the social group that actually makes a feeding decision.

The extent of labor force participation by women might also bear on the strength of their personal support networks. If such networks are collapsing, to be replaced by governmentally allocated and purchased services, then relevant governmental policies require consideration (see below). First, however, it is necessary to establish, as Stack (1974) did for one Midwestern black population in the United States, or as Parish and Whyte (1978:235–47) have broadly sketched for rural Chinese women, the existence of women's support systems, their relative strengths, methods of operation, changed or unchanging priorities, the extent of their services including ability to supply the necessary social supplements to child care and other domestic tasks considered women's work. Stack's example suggests that women find ways to compensate effectively for conditions imposed by larger social structures. By implication the question becomes the degree to which women themselves are committed to continuance of breast feeding. Are they relieved that alternatives exist that, at least, sustain infant life and that also afford women themselves respite from recurring illness and malaise? It is instructive that authors (Greiner 1979:64) have suggested that working women should shift a newborn's daily pattern such that the infant sleeps most of the day and has most of its feeds at night without mentioning the concomitant drain on the mother who works all day and nurses when she needs to sleep.

To assess women's collective ability to form self-support networks requires recognition of domestic and extradomestic conditions. For Malaysia, the

11 The rate has run as high as 17.3 percent among urban youths (Government of Malaysia 1979:5). Mehmet (1983:37) has stated that it often takes young men two to three years to find work.

existence, extent, and significance of the following factors need documentation and assessment:

1. A social structure such that two incomes are necessary to sustain life and health
2. Separation of home and workplace
3. Isolation of mother and child within the household while others go "out" to work (Jelliffe and Jelliffe 1978:192; Rapp 1978:283)
4. Rigid work schedules and rapid return after parturition to full work responsibility (Wong 1975:17)
5. Physical distance between older kin in the countryside and young people in the cities, which effectively removes the teachers of traditional practice from the environment in which they are needed (Jelliffe and Jelliffe 1978:223)
6. Participation in the labor force by older women, which also effectively accomplishes the above result described in (5)
7. School and, later, paid work, which infringes on the time young females can devote to participation in child rearing, with the result that the practice of child care must be more directly taught within a shortened time frame
8. Excessive workloads for women (*PAG Bulletin* 1977b:43; Jelliffe and Jelliffe, 1978:184), abetted by decreased help from school-aged children (Djamour 1965:44) and by institutional disinclination to adjust work in the marketplace to domestic
9. The breakup of communities that sustained midwife practice. In rural areas a young woman would grow up knowing who her midwife would be. Today a government-registered midwife is unlikely to be a member of the community in which she practices.
10. Decreased economic security due to a new all-cash market economy and newly created needs
11. The need for men to follow the job market and for women either to follow their husbands or remain behind and assume heavier responsibilities. Such mobility abets the breakup of existing networks of cross-cutting ties and precludes the formation of new ones (Djamour 1965: 59; Jelliffe and Jelliffe 1978:20).

Women, attempting to juggle the requirements of home and work, become increasingly tense and distracted and more frequently experience lactation failure (Berg 1973b:99). Because emotional response plays a key role in milk production and availability (Jelliffe and Jelliffe 1978:20), competing demands, overwork, and diminished social support begin a cycle in which incomplete feeding leads to hungry, irritable babies, thence to increasing anxiety, culminating in feeding failure. Young females becoming socialized to child care practice absorb this scenario rather than the more relaxed traditional one. It is instructive that institutional and consumer publications as well as individuals advocating breast feeding, focus on training health care workers to replace or extend outmoded support systems with, if necessary, purchased or institutionalized services (see WHO 1979:37; WHO 1981: 11; Young 1985; Chetley 1985).

Modernization, a market economy, and new employment structures may mean that more Malaysian families are in social situations where the incidence and duration of breast feeding has always been low. Thus women's ability to vivify kin-oriented support networks sufficiently to halt the documented slide (Kent 1981:21) may be limited. The probability of network reconstitution or replacement by nonkin structures depends in part on women's willingness to obligate themselves to increased workloads. That it is also dependent on governmental policy is the subject of the following section.

Government policy

Domestic groups operate in larger contexts. National policy, affecting women's roles and infant feeding practices, is by and large made by men. I suggest their basic concern is whether women are more economically useful in the marketplace or as conservators of the natural resource, human milk. Important considerations then are:

1. Is there room for both men and women in that marketplace?
2. If opportunities are limited, should they be reserved for men?
3. If limited space is available for women, which category of women should work outside the home? If mothers, how much can they be imposed on to both conserve milk and produce goods? Because women have worked when pregnant, and when bleeding, why not when lactating (Helsing 1979:72)?
4. If it is not possible, without crèches and nurseries at the workplace, to motivate women sufficiently for them to want to nurse, is it economically worthwhile to build and staff facilities, which are at most second best, neither providing for optimal demand schedules nor for appropriate developmental stimulation?

In Malaysia, with a dearth of jobs in the urban marketplace, the push to breast-feed may serve to keep married women from competing for scarce employment.

In the 1970s, the Malaysian Government curtailed milk company activities and began new programs to promote breast feeding (Baer 1978, part II: 1–18). There has not been follow-through. Several circumstances invite skepticism. The government's reliance on a weak, industry-based national code in place of WHO recommendations (*IBFAN News* 1985:4) is one. That continued investment by multinationals in the Malaysian economy is encouraged by government policy, to the extent that Nestle has been permitted to restructure without giving a majority shareholding to local investors, is another (Pura 1984:13). Government can bally-ho its commitment to infant health without alienating the multinationals whose assistance it needs. The third concerns reliance on manufactures for export. It is to management's advantage to create a secondary labor force of young, unmarried, relatively temporarily employed women, thus eliminating the need for career ladders and salary increments, maternity benefits, flexible schedules, and nursing breaks. If government emphasis is on gross domestic product at the expense of equitable distribution of resources, as has been charged (Mehmet 1983; Sundaram 1983), then management policy befits government goals.

The Malaysian Government has stated clearly national economic goals and implementation methodology. However, it is important to understand not only de facto policies, but what, by implication, is considered neither appropriate goal nor tool. In the *Mid Term Review* (Government of Malaysia 1973:lv–lx), the government unequivocally declared its intent to eradicate poverty and restructure society in the context of an expanding economy, such that no person should, in the future, be less well-off than he now is. Such intent precluded the redistribution of income or assets as a means for increasing the socioeconomic status of the Malays, the largest, most marginal group and potentially, as individuals, chief beneficiaries of policy design. The extent of inequality of asset distribution and concomitant inequality of opportunity for growth and modernization is severe. In 1970, 61 percent of total share capital of all limited companies was in foreign hands. The Malaysian Chinese owned 22.5 percent; the Malays, merely 1.9 percent (Government of Malaysia 1973:10). Foreign ownership of fixed assets was 57.2 percent; the Chinese owned 26.2 percent; the Malays and Indians combined, 1 percent. Progress in individual Malay control of corporate assets has been only incremental. In agriculture, 70.8 percent of acreage planted in the modern corporate sector was foreign owned. Even in the noncorporate, individual sector, where the overall value of assets is extremely small, the Malays planted only 47.1 percent of total acreage. The top 10 percent of households which, in 1957, accounted for 34 percent of the wealth, controlled 40 percent in 1970. The share of the bottom 20 percent fell, in the same period, from 5.8 percent to 4 percent (Mann 1977:11).

The Malaysian Government's policy has been to restrict resources for bolstering small-scale, labor-intensive farming. Instead, emphasis has been on increasing the size of individual holdings, developing new land, and modernizing agricultural techniques. Those removed from traditional agriculture will continue to be resettled either in underdeveloped areas or in the modern urban sector. Job creation will continue to center on manufactured goods for export (Government of Malaysia 1979:154), in particular textiles, clothing, and electronic components (Mehmet 1983:41). Although commercial food crops will continue to play an export role, the value of primary products alone cannot, on export, produce the revenue necessary to bolster national growth. Several problems have resulted. One is obviously the dislocation and gross changes in household structure, deployment of labor, and organization of domestic activities previously described. The other concerns exacerbation of family and social dislocation resulting from difficulties of policy implementation. Industrialization has been, and, as policy indicates, will continue to be, capital intensive (Government of Malaysia 1979:74). Whereas employment in the manufacturing center almost doubled between 1957 and 1970 and has continued to grow, agricultural employment grew at less than half the work force growth rate. Thus with half the labor force in 1970 engaged in agricultural work and only a tenth in manufacturing, unemployment rose (Mann 1977:7). Though government figures for 1978 indicate that the employment picture has brightened in the urban area, emphasis on informal sector employment and the exacerbation of urban poverty by migration (Government of Malaysia 1979:35/38) invite skepticism as to the manufacturing sector's ability to absorb surplus agricultural labor. A second implementation difficulty has concerned itself with less than projected growth rates in Malaysia's trade-dependent economy resulting from recurring worldwide recessions (Peng 1983:32-3).

Nestle, too, in spite of their contention [1979a Memorandum of Facts (enclosure):13-14] that their presence has created jobs; trained personnel; raised living standards; improved agricultural practice; stimulated local growth by the purchase of local agricultural products; and improved nutrition, health education, and sanitation, is one of many multinationals whose participation in national economic ventures has contributed to inequity (Mann 1977; Lappe 1977:385). Wasserstrom's demonstration (1979:5) of the effects of milk company activity on cropping patterns and thence on lower-class livelihoods, although set in rural Mexico, is a vivid example of the differential effects of a uniform policy. In Malaysia, too, income gaps have widened (Sundaram 1983:3).

I suggest, in answer to questions posed at the beginning of this section, that the Malaysian Government's infant feeding policy serves to restrict married women's entrance to the workplace. How babies fare, although a related matter, has lower priority. Unemployment is high; unmarried as opposed to married women's labor, more sought after by employers, creates greater resources for the state; women's traditional tasks are conceived to be home-centered; and the development of measures to ease nursing mother's work force participation are too costly to employers and to the government. A state policy that insists on social services for employees is not in a competitive position in the world market. How infant feeding practice is affected is speculative. Women at home may choose to breast-feed. Or their economically necessary but sporadic participation in the labor market may make formula more convenient, as might their social isolation in new urban settings. Poverty may limit lactation's contribution to infant health. There are no simple answers.

Medical personnel and practice

The following two sections will summarize medical personnel and milk company practices that may have contributed to past growth in formula feeding in Malaysia.

Both Latham (1977:201) and Jelliffe and Jelliffe (1978:187–8) have insisted that Western medicine is a curative, rather than a preventative system; that Western medical education is pathologically oriented and makes no attempt to teach an understanding of the social and psychological aspects of "normally successful physiological events" (Jelliffe and Jelliffe 1978:188) such as breast feeding. Because Malaysian doctors have, for years, been trained in the Western tradition (Van Esterik 1977:150), it should be expected that they, too, have little understanding or concern with alternate systems for dealing with pregnancy, childbirth, and neonatal care. Nor should they be expected to understand concomitants of poverty (Margulies 1978:46) or life-styles dissimilar from their own elite path.

McArthur (1962:101–7) has suggested that the typical Malaysian woman using new medical facilities could be expected to respond in the same ways she always has when dealing with members of the upper classes. She responds, not as a consumer expecting to take part in decision making, but as one who owes deference to the highborn or well-placed educated professional whom, she assumes, knows best. Because the public health movement, with which she is urged to align herself, has incorporated into its practice middle-class Western values, attitudes, and expectations, one could speculate that Malaysian women might experience contemporary pregnancy, childbirth, and infant rearing as alien and frightening, instead of as events congruent with early socialization experience, and, therefore, predictable. For example, in place of the midwife whom she has known all her life, the typical Malaysian woman giving birth in a hospital is exposed to strangers, nurses, and doctors concerned to devise routines that ease staff work at the expense, sometimes, of consumers who are treated as patients, sick people. McArthur (1962:101–7) has also suggested that the situation is exacerbated for adult Malaysian women, who tend to be shy and reserved. Criticism affects them such that they become loath to ask questions, expose their lack of understanding, or disagree with suggested practice. Their reserve is interpreted by staff as patient ignorance or as acquiescence. Either conclusion serves to validate the preferred practice of the professional.

Particular routines are particularly disadvantageous for women attempting to establish good breast-feeding practice. For example, a newborn's suckling reflex is normally strongest 20–30 minutes after birth, the strength of this reflex contributing to the letdown reflex and to the avoidance of mammary congestion (Jelliffe and Jelliffe 1978:351), both of which contribute to the uneventful establishment of good breast-feeding practice. However, when a newborn is sedated, suckling is diminished. Separation of mother and child at birth, which inhibits an initial demand schedule, also contributes to feeding difficulties, as does maintenance of scheduled feeds, convenient for staff, during a newborn's hospital stay (Haire 1973:175; Helsing 1978:3–4). Staff, again for its own convenience, may frequently introduce bottle feeding before lactation is fully established (Ledogar 1975:142; *PAG Bulletin* 1977a:67), thus increasing lactation difficulties including those attendant on insufficient milk supply. Baer (1978, part I:17) has suggested an additional impairment in practice. He has indicated that, in spite of stated policy, nurses have been trained away from breast feeding and can do little to actively support mothers attempting to establish sufficient lactation and unsupplemented breast feeding. Such a situation, compounded by overall hospital routine, tends to increase anxiety. Because, as mentioned, tension easily inhibits the letdown reflex, the odds against hospital-born babies being successfully breast-fed are long.

Once out of the hospital, changing mores appear to affect a baby's ready access to breast milk. A woman on a bus is more likely to quiet her infant with a pacifier than to breast-feed on the spot (Jelliffe and Jelliffe 1978:188). Explanations for such behavioral substitution theorize about desire to imitate elite behavior, about recognition of the breast as a sexual object and about breast feeding as less sophisticated, more "animal-like" than bottle feeding. Such interpretations beg the question. Changing attitudes toward the breast are, I suggest, responses rather than causal explanations. As such, they are in need of explanation and, thus, in need of rigorous investigation.

Multinational promotion

The wrath of INFACT (1978), ICCR (Margulies 1975, 1977, 1978), and assorted individuals (Ledogar 1975; Greiner 1975) has been directed, almost exclusively, at multinational milk corporations. Although these companies, as mentioned, positioning themselves to profit from social change, had frequently resorted to inappropriate innuendo and half-truths, had appealed to fear and superstition and had encouraged harmful bottle feeding, a simplistic counterattack has contributed more to continued distortion and misunderstanding than to resolution. Though credit is due those who expose corporate practice, to suggest, as Latham has (Greiner 1975:10), that advertising and marketing practices are "possibly the single most important reason(s) for the rapid decline of breast feeding in developing countries," is irresponsible. The purported decline, though valid for Malaysia, is less well established for other countries. Furthermore, the timing of the decline in Malaysia is speculative and may well have antedated the increase in formula promotion (Kent 1981:21–2).

As Ledogar (1975:127–9) has reminded us, in the 1960s and 1970s the birth rate in the United States and other industrialized countries had slowed.

Formula manufacturers were experiencing the lowest annual rate of domestic sales growth of any industry; thus the expansion overseas. Bristol Meyers provides an example (Greiner 1975:63). By 1971, 40 percent of Enfamil sales were outside the United States, and international sales, up 20 percent from 1973 to 1974, grew most quickly. Enfamil spent on advertising three times what it spent on research.

To what particular markets have milk companies appealed? Nestle [1979a, Memorandum of Facts (enclosure):16] has suggested that it is an urban population of relatively affluent working mothers who already practice supplementation. Greiner (1975:18; 1977:4) emphatically disagrees. He has alluded particularly to the concentration of advertising, in the language of the poor, in mass media outlets such as radio, television, billboard, point-of-purchase displays, and movie theaters. Because the multinationals have consistently refused to release consumer statistics, Greiner has been careful to say that he could only speculate as to target population.

For Malaysia, the picture is clearer. In an article (*Malaysian Business* 1977: 45–6) directed to Malaysian businessmen and devoted primarily to methods for capturing the infant food market in Malaysia, emphasis was on capture of the vast rural market where, according to Baer (1978, part I:2; part II:6) breast feeding is still the norm. The article, published in spite of the Malaysian Government's aim of reversing the bottle feeding trend, noted that government interference was a problem, but expressed confidence that changing values would, nevertheless, contribute to growth in sales. Given elite control of both government and industry and elite-fostered change in economic organization, there is no reason to dispute the claim.

Television, radio, newspaper, billboard advertising, and covert sponsorship of "prettiest baby" contests had relied on several mechanisms to induce mothers to bottle-feed.[12] One depicted an obviously healthy baby accompanied by slogans such as "when mother's milk is not enough," "when breast milk fails," or "for a healthy baby" (Greiner 1975:48–50). It was considered a thinly veiled attack on the efficacy of breast feeding, because doubt and anxiety induced by advertising also inhibit milk flow (Jelliffe and Jelliffe 1978:228–9). A second method had been to feature white babies on milk cans and in advertisements, thus subliminally suggesting that if whites, who, after all, have captured most of a given country's assets, use such and such a product, it must be good. A third had been to use hypnotic jingles, which Greiner has suggested (1975:21) were not just commercials but had the force of scriptural authority. Such speculation does not address the issue of whether such methods make converts to infant formula out of those originally inclined

12 Many of the practices described herein have been expressly forbidden by the WHO code and eschewed by the infant formula industry: for example, mass media advertising, point-of-sale displays, "milk nurses," mass distribution of samples, and personal gifts of high value. In addition, labels and literature must carry a "breast is best" statement and a warning of the hazards of improper use. All this is not to suggest that there is not a considerable incidence of abuse nor that pressure on health-related personnel has eased.

to breast-feed, influences those who had been experiencing ambivalence, or speaks only to the converted. Further, the implication that women exercise no considered judgment, discernment, or restraint is fallacious and mischievous.

In fact, milk companies did not rely solely on such methods. They leaned heavily on directed personal contact with both the consumer and the medical practitioner. Their monetary contributions to developing industries such as television, where they may have contributed the bulk of a new station's advertising income (Jelliffe and Jelliffe 1978:341), and to the health and hospitals industry were necessary expenses. Until such practices were banned in Malaysia (Baer 1978, part II:15) in 1976, milk companies hired "milk nurses," whose duties included penetration of hospital wards for the purpose of introducing new mothers to the advantages of bottle feeding. These nurses, often working on a commission basis, followed up initial contact, either before or after parturition, with free samples, home visits, and home delivery (Ledogar 1975:137–8; Margulies 1977:78). Milk companies, recognizing that brand loyalty was considerable, paid their "nurses" well and extended them benefits and incentives, such as shorter work weeks and use of cars (Baer 1978, part I:1). Because wages were more than competitive with those paid by hospitals and public health stations, milk companies found themselves in the enviable position of being able to hire away medical personnel who had been trained at great expense by the state. However, when such personnel were unavailable, they also hired poorly trained and poorly educated women to serve as their representatives. After the wards were closed to "milk nurses," their activity slowed but hardly ceased. They still managed to obtain lists of newborns and mingle, out of uniform, with ward visitors. Although the uniform had given them a certain prestige, they managed well without it (Baer 1978, part II:9–10).

Milk companies also supplied posters and calendars for clinic and hospital waiting rooms and for doctors' offices. The Malaysian Government ordered these removed or covered because their presence in a medical facility implied medical endorsement (Margulies 1977:76). Compliance has been slow, particularly in private facilities (Baer 1978, part II:8).

Direct promotion to health professionals was a widely used technique. What companies aimed toward was a doctor's recommendation to new mothers of their particular product. They frequently singled out practitioners known for their exceptional influence on patients. Not only were constant reminders of their product in the form of calendars, pens, free samples, presciption pads, printed formula slips, innoculation cards, note paper, and plastic cups supplied, but also companies equipped hospital nurseries with name tags, information booklets, and discharge packs (Greiner 1975:14; Ledogar 1975:141; Margulies 1977:79), sponsored conferences, supplied travel and living expenses to attending doctors, furnished free formula to hospital nurseries and well-baby clinics, and funded research. In developing countries, such funding is sorely needed. The expectation was that doctors and other health professionals would repay the favors in kind.

Infant food companies advertise their products extensively in medical journals, thereby supplying revenue to needy publications and providing much needed information to doctors and nurses (Jelliffe and Jelliffe 1978:228). In many countries, once medical training has formally ended, what little additional information a doctor acquires is from just such journals or from company salesmen (Nestle 1979a:4) and company-sponsored pediatric conferences (Baer 1978, part II:12). Because, as mentioned, most doctors belong to elite groups, an initial proclivity for bottle feeding probably exists. It receives constant reinforcement of a quasi-scientific nature. Nor were midwives forgotten. Because they, particularly, are in constant contact with mothers about to give birth, they received their share of free milk samples.

The telling argument for many has hinged on the rate of growth of bottle-feeding practice in capitalist countries, as compared to the rate in the socialist countries of, for example, the People's Republic of China, the USSR, Hungary, and Bulgaria (Greiner 1977:22). Their logic has dictated that because it was the capitalist countries that allowed uncontrolled advertising of infant foods for the benefit of multinationals and because the rate of usage supposedly grew so rapidly in those countries, the blame for the increase could be laid at the feet of the companies. It is not necessarily so. Countries that encourage breast feeding do so for many of the reasons that support bottle feeding in other countries. Certainly there are economic priorities and questions of values that need addressing, as well as foreign policy issues and national policy in regard to the organization of production. If one is attempting to make a case for breast feeding as a normative as well as actual socialist behavior, to do less than thorough comparative research is, to say the least, unreasonable.

Conclusion

Out of the international spotlight, the breast–bottle controversy still simmers. On what basis feeding decisions are made and by whom remains a valid question, answerable only in the context of particular countries, social groups, and categories of people. That a decided shift has occurred everywhere in the world, such that the incidence and duration of unsupplemented breast feeding has declined widely and rapidly, although still a questionable assertion (Popkin, Bilsborrow, and Atkin 1982:1092), is in the Malaysian context, certain. When it occurred and to what it is attributable, in spite of information about educational standards, residence, mother's age, religious preference, ethnicity, and economic status, are questions that can only be answered speculatively. Well-researched survey data does not substitute for on-site, long-term participant-observation, focused on families and households. I would, in disaggregating socioeconomic variables, stress three issues: domestic unit labor profiles and budgetary units in relation to market conditions; household income; and role conflict and time constraints among women who must produce goods, prepare food, stay healthy, and feed babies

(*PAG Bulletin* 1977b:43). In short, it will be from contextual domestic group research that testable hypotheses will be formulated.

I am not so naive that I view multinationals as deliberate agents of individual socioeconomic enhancement; nor so naive that I view IBFAN, INFACT, ICCR, and others as interested only in the welfare of individuals. In fact, I find it particularly telling that (1) women's rights, roles, feelings, privileges, obligations, are so little considered by all parties; (2) current Western ideology and cultural categories are facilely used to examine conditions in other cultures; and (3) the passage of the WHO recommendation adopted by some 10 percent of sponsoring countries, and movement by Nestle to moderate its practices was deemed sufficient to reduce the publicity surrounding the issue. Whereas milk industry motives are relatively transparent, those of pro-breast coalitions are puzzling.

Is it more certain that, however one feels about the relative merits of breast and bottle feeding, the causes and directions of change might be more surely known and influenced with more complete and more precise information? I would answer, the first step is that it be meticulously gathered.

9. The children of Kyaka Enga: culture, diet, environment, and health in a Papua New Guinea Highland society, 1950–1960

Barry Shaw

The central highlands of Papua New Guinea was first explored by foreigners in the 1930s but not effectively colonized until after the 1939–45 war. The life-style, isolation, and "primitiveness" of the people attracted great interest: Many university, mission, and colonial government researchers worked with varied motives to "understand" or "help" the people. Of particular interest (and concern) to nutritionists was the almost wholly vegetable diet, of which 80–90 percent by weight was from the sweet potato (*Ipomoea batatas*).

A nutrition survey expedition of 1947 (Hipsley and Clements 1950) which surveyed in detail the diet, food production, social organization, and health of four areas of the country concluded that the adult population, although small in stature, was reasonably healthy, but that dietary protein intakes, especially for children, were too low as compared with the adjusted standards which they adopted for Papua New Guineans.

Subsequent nutrition research concentrated on dietary and epidemiological surveys, whereas policy prescriptions focused on dietary intervention and especially the need to feed highlanders more and higher-quality protein (e.g., Bailey 1963). In 1963, a symposium at the Australian and New Zealand Association for the Advancement of Science conference was devoted to means of encouraging Papua New Guinean Highlanders to eat peanuts (not an indigenous food).

A number of anthropologists and other social scientists studied food consumption as part of ethnographic and other studies but generally suffered from a lack of current nutritional knowledge (e.g., Rappaport 1968, and comment by McArthur 1977). Human biologists such as Sinnett (1975) and Malcolm (1970) took a holistic approach, but were unable to consider adequately, social and economic variables. Group interdisciplinary research is fortunately becoming more common – for example, the group of geographers, along with a physician, an agronomist, and a nutritionist, who studied

I am indebted to Michael Lipton, Emmanuel de Kadt, Ralph Bulmer, Lenore Manderson, and others at the Institute of Development Studies, Sussex and the Australian National University, for helpful comments.

child nutrition in the Membi Plateau (Allen et al. 1980) and current work being done at the Institutes of Medical Research and of Applied Social and Economic Research. At the same time, there has been a post-Independence surge of enthusiasm by some foreigners and Papua New Guineans for a "Melanesian way" partly fueled by the popularization of the idea of "subsistence affluence" in a conceptualization now distant from that propounded by Fisk (1962) and Sahlins (1972). Although this is a healthy reaction to the heavy-handed paternalism of an Australian colonial administration, its romanticism needs to be tempered by an accurate knowledge of "traditional" life and conditions.

Knowledge of living environments, nutrition and health, and their cultural referents in the precolonial and early colonial period is also important as a bench mark to assess the impact of the rapid social and economic changes brought about by the transition from tribal to peasant societies and their growing dependence on and linkages with the domestic and international economy. Lambert (n.d.) has justly been attacked by Hide (1980) for asserting, on a weak empirical base, a direct link between cash cropping and malnutrition. The impact of the changes of the past 30 years on child nutrition is complex, and some points were set out in Shaw (1980), but rather as a plea for further research than an assertion of causal links.

In several nutritional studies (e.g., Venkatachalam 1962; Oomen and Malcolm 1965; Bailey 1965), estimates were made of the volume and quantity of human milk consumed by infants and children. However, in general, dietary studies of children did not include human milk consumption. The prevailing medical view in the 1950s was that although suckling could go on for several years, its dietary significance was limited to around 1½ to 2 years. Thelma Becroft, medical officer at the Baiyer River hospital just after the first pervasive colonial contact with the Kyaka Enga of the Western Province of the Papua New Guinea Highlands, not only carried out a longitudinal study of human milk consumption and composition, but also documented child-feeding norms and their cultural supports, including child spacing. About the same time, Ralph Bulmer studied the economy and society of the Kyaka as an anthropologist. A number of other medical workers also chose to research the Kyaka because of the hospital facilities. Other relevant work was also done on nearby groups such as the Raiapu Enga, the Mae Enga, and the Yandapu Enga.

This paper is an attempt to synthesize these results in the light of current knowledge, and to piece together in some detail the health, diet, and environment of children under five years of age between 1950 and 1960 and to relate this to Kyaka life and economy. It highlights the importance of human milk in an otherwise bulky diet as well as the rigid child spacing, which made possible human milk consumption until the child was four years old or more, and which was central to the woman's role as mother, child rearer, and food provider.

Table 9.1 lists the main sources on which this synthesis is based. The detail in this paper may often be frustratingly slight, but it is clearly impossible to present all the relevant material within a single chapter. The interested reader should therefore consult the original works.

Throughout, the following convention is used:

1. Infant: child from birth to less than one year old.
2. Toddler: child from one year old to less than five years old.
3. Child: child from birth to less than five years old.

The Kyaka

The Kyaka (or Kyaka Enga) live in the Western Highlands Province of Papua New Guinea (Figure 9.1) and in 1955 numbered about 10,000 extending over 400 square-kilometers of which 220 square-kilometers is regularly inhabited. Their domain covers a wide range of altitude, from the peak of Mt. Hagen (4,100 meters) to the confluence of the Baiyer and Lai rivers only 30 kilometers distant at 600 meters; however, the greatest population density (300–500 per square-kilometer) is in the 1,200- to 1,700-meter range.

The climate is fairly uniform throughout the year, with shade temperatures at 1,500 meters rarely reaching 27°C in daytime or falling below 15°C at night: The frost line is around 2,100 meters beyond the gardening zone. Rain falls on two-thirds of the days of the year (2,500 millimeters annually) with some concentration in the October–April period.

The climate and soils of the inhabited areas are among the most favorable in the Papua New Guinea Highlands for the production of traditional (and many exotic) food crops. Food production is dominated by the sweet potato (*Ipomoea batatas*), which accounts for 80–90 percent of the food intake, plus a wide variety of other foods according to season. The Appendix sets out the major foods noted by Bulmer. Pigs are of immense social importance as an indicator of wealth and status, but their dietary contribution is small because they are killed only on festive occasions, the most important being the *moka* (or *te*) when hundreds may be killed, cooked, and distributed. Although pig meat is relished, its giving/receiving is vastly more important than its consumption: "Much of the meat travels for days and through many hands, being recooked several times, before it is finally eaten" (Bulmer 1960a:369), often causing gastric complaints; when unbearably putrid, it may be discarded. Apart from the *moka*, a family may consume pig meat, and then in small quantities, perhaps once in four to six weeks (Bulmer, personal communication). Except for small amounts of pork, some hunted animals, and fish from streams, the diet is essentially derived from vegetative sources, dominated by tubers. The pig is also important as an integral member of the household, sleeping in the house and eating cultivated food. Pig husbandry is set out in considerable detail in Bulmer (1960a:89ff).

Table 9.1. *Summary of sources*

Researcher and reference	Group	General description
Becroft 1967a	Kyaka	Longitudinal study of human milk consumption
Becroft 1967b	Kyaka	Child spacing, child feeding, and child rearing
Becroft and Bailey 1965	Kyaka	Supplementary feeding trial
Becroft, Stanhope, and Burchett 1969	Kyaka	Mortality, causes of death, life tables
Bulmer 1960a	Kyaka	*Moka (te)* ceremonial exchange system
Bulmer 1960a, 1960b	Kyaka	Social and economic life of Kyaka in detail
Bulmer 1965	Kyaka	Brief Kyaka ethnography, Kyaka religion
McKay 1960	Kyaka	Child growth
Burchett 1966	Kyaka	Amebiasis
Cleary and Blackburn 1968	Kyaka	Air pollution in houses
Beral and Read 1971	Kyaka	Response to carbon dioxide
Blackburn and Woolcock 1971	Kyaka (and others)	Chronic liver and lung disease
Blackburn, Green, and Mitchell 1970	Kyaka (and others)	Prevalence of *Haemophilus influenzae*
Woolcock et al. 1970	Kyaka	Nature of chronic non-tuberculous lung disease
Blackburn and Green 1966	Kyaka	Thatched roofs and lung disease
Woolcock and Blackburn 1967	Kyaka (and others)	Epidemiology of chronic lung disease
Woolcock, Colman, and Blackburn 1972	Kyaka (and others)	Ventilatory lung function
Hipsley 1969	Kyaka	Oxygen uptake and carbon dioxide excretion
Oomen and Corden 1970	Kyaka	Nitrogen balance, fluid balance
Feachem 1977	Raiapu Enga	Environmental health
Feachem 1973	Raiapu Enga	Environmental health
Sinnett 1975	Yandapu Enga	Health, nutrition
Sinnett 1977	Yandapu Enga	Nutritional adaptation
Waddell 1972	Raiapu Enga	Ethnology, diet, agriculture
Meggitt 1958	Mae Enga	Ethnology, diet

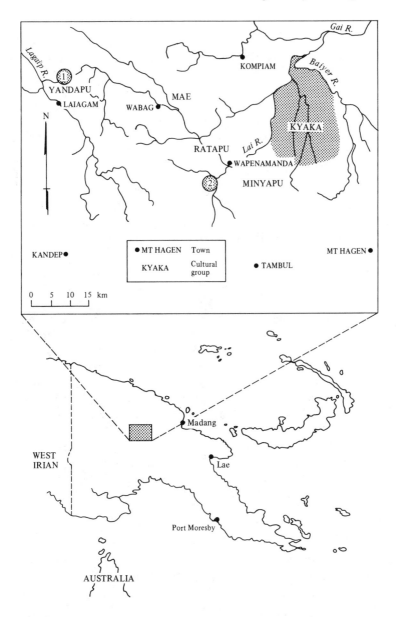

Figure 9.1. Sketch map of Papua New Guinea and Kyaka territory. Other field locations mentioned in the text include, in the shadowed areas, (1) Yandapu (Sinnett 1975) and (2) Raiapu (Feachem 1973, 1977). For a more detailed map of the study area, see Waddell (1972:15).

By Papua New Guinea standards, the Kyaka resource base was a favorable one:

> It does not seem that any section of the community, rich or poor, young or old need enjoy a different standard of nutrition from any other. . . . *The occasional cases of very obvious malnutrition among children cannot, I think, simply be explained in economic terms.* Furthermore, this high standard of subsistence is achieved without, it seems, excessive expenditure in terms of horticultural labour. (Bulmer 1960a:86; my emphasis)

Recent history

The first foreign contact with the Kyaka was probably a 1933 expedition which even then only skirted Kyaka territory (Bulmer 1969a:19). Steel axes were traded in soon after, and although (Australian) government and mission stations were established soon after, these were 15–25 kilometers to the south and had minimal contact with the Kyaka. It is unlikely that there were further patrols into the area until after the 1939–45 war, when the administration acted to control intergroup fighting. In 1958, a government livestock station was established on one border of Kyaka territory, and the Baptist mission began work in 1949. A police post was set up in 1951, and although the indigenous police stationed there exerted considerable power, the most pervasive influence was that of the mission, with ten to twenty or more foreign staff. Mission influence is set out in more detail in Bulmer (1960a:450ff).

The medical staff were particularly concerned with infant welfare, and by 1955, had enrolled over 1,000 children under five years of age at the Kombares Clinic. The published work of Dr. Thelma Becroft, medical officer at the Baiyer River hospital from 1952 to 1964, reflected this concern and largely forms the basis of this study. Bulmer, an anthropologist, studied the Kyaka during two field visits totaling 17 months between 1955 and 1960.

Social organization and the routine of everyday life

Kyaka do not have hereditary chiefs, but rather a meritocracy based on the power and influence of *numi*: men, who through their abilities, actions, natal status, and marriage allegiances are successful in the competition for power and respect.

Bulmer (1960a, 1960b, 1965) defined the basic domestic unit as a "hearth group" or eating group, centered on the growing, harvesting, preparation, and eating of food. In a single house, women and children slept, food was prepared and eaten, and pigs were kept. Men slept in a separate compartment or in a separate house. Houses were dispersed in ones and twos rather than "villages," with siting decided more on the strategic considerations dictated by intergroup fighting than proximity to gardens or water (Bulmer 1960a:123, 1960b:2).

The hearth group was centered on the woman's economic role as gardener, cook, mother, and pig keeper. Of 101 married men, Bulmer (1960a: 478) reported 80 with one wife, 15 with two, 4 with three, and 1 with six wives. Polygynists' wives did not necessarily live in the same hearth group. The majority of hearth groups had three, four, or five members plus up to ten pigs: Pig numbers were variable according to the status of the husband and the stage of the *moka* cycle.

Seasons were not pronounced and gardens produced food the year round, with an annual work cycle of a "steady though not too arduous grind...at any time from perhaps one-fifth to one-twentieth of local land being under cultivation, the remainder lying fallow...." (Bulmer 1960a:47). People stirred at sunrise, the women stoking fires, heating food from the previous night, releasing pigs, and feeding pigs and family members. Women then walked to gardens carrying digging sticks, spades, and net bags. Children under five years normally accompanied the mother, infants carried at the back in net bags, older children on the mother's head or shoulders or walking. Favored pigs might also have been taken to gardens, which could have been up to 1.5 kilometers distant.

At the garden, women cultivated the crops and harvested food for that day's meal. The daily journey home was particularly arduous, contributed to by the terrain, the load of food for family and pigs, children, pigs, and tools. By mid-afternoon they were preparing the belly-distending late-afternoon meal, which accounted for perhaps 70 percent of daily food consumption for adults. Pigs were called home and fed on sweet potato and food scraps. Rain is common in the late afternoon, and cooking and socializing often took place in the house. After dark, the household, including pigs, slept by the warmth of the fire.

"Men's work" was more flexible and less regular, and (unlike that of women) had benefited greatly from the introduction of steel and from the decline in group fighting, even by the early 1950s. Men cleared ground, made and maintained fences, collected firewood, built houses, cultivated some crops, and hunted. Bulmer (1960a:189) suggested that one man could maintain three hearth groups "but this would not allow him the opportunity to be present at courts and other public occasions, visit exchange partners and do all the other things an ambitious man needs to do." Polygynous men frequently maintained bachelors to assist their work.

A typical Kyaka hearth group with two or three adults, two children, and four pigs might have consumed 15 kilograms of sweet potato a day and 2 kilograms of other vegetable. Together with a 5- to 10-kilogram child, this implies a daily woman's load of 22–27 kilograms, not including tools

Table 9.2. *Spacing of Kyaka children surviving infancy, 1940–1965*

Period	1st–2nd years (no. cases)	2nd–3rd years (no. cases)	3rd–4th years (no. cases)	4th–5th years (no. cases)	5th–6th years (no. cases)
1940–50[a]	4.8 (64)	5.3 (209)	5.3 (202)	5.1 (70)	4.1 (14)
1951–55	5.1 (115)	5.1 (252)	4.2 (25)	–	–
1956–60	5.1 (175)	4.8 (32)	–	–	–
1961–65	5.0 (27)	–	–	–	–
Mean	5.0	4.0	5.2	5.1	4.1
Range	3–10	3–10	3–10	3–7.6	3–6.9

[a]Accurate birthdates from 1948.
Source: Becroft 1967b.

(Bulmer 1960a:86). Bulmer recorded loads of up to 32 kilograms of food alone (1960a:96).

Child spacing

Becroft (1967b) noted five years as the "normal" spacing of Kyaka children. In a study of 1,185 children surviving infancy, mean child intervals were five years for children born from 1940 to 1965, with no interval less than three years: Even a three-year interval met with strong social disapproval in 1966 (Becroft 1967b:811). The results of her study are summarized in Table 9.2.

Bulmer (1960a:134ff) reported similar findings and strongly suggested that a small maternal family with this age difference between surviving children was essential to the Kyaka economy:

> It is an observable fact that a woman with one infant to care for can manage well with her other household and garden duties. One child, carried in a string bag for the first year, and later clinging pick-a-back to its mother's shoulders or toddling by her side, is manageable. I think it is safe to assume that two infants would not be so, and that a general reorganisation of domestic life would be a necessary consequence of briefer intervals between births. Further, the spacing of children facilitates the use of older siblings to care for younger ones. By the time an infant is two years old its older sibling will be about six and already old enough to be left in temporary charge of it. Again, a woman with four children is of necessity working larger garden plots to feed them than a newly wedded wife does, but by this stage the eldest child is already old enough to be materially useful in the garden and the

home. *Thus the autonomy of the one-woman hearth-group as an economic unit is related to the spacing of children.* (Bulmer 1960a:140; my emphasis)

This spacing was achieved through a number of interventions:

1. Intercourse was forbidden from the time conception was known to the complete weaning of the child and was supported by the belief that semen poisoned mothers' milk. Intercourse was not resumed until another child was desired (Becroft 1967a, 1967b; Bulmer 1960a:134).

2. Unwanted pregnancies were terminated by skillful abdominal pumeling. This included pregnancies of unmarried mothers, and pregnancies claimed not to have resulted from intercourse. It was usual for a woman becoming pregnant at a time when intercourse was proscribed to insist she had a nonhuman "weed" in her uterus and to seek an abortion (Becroft 1967b; Bulmer 1960a:135, personal communication).

3. Infanticide was normal for one twin, very young motherless children, and possibly not unusual for firstborn children when the mother wished to keep open the possibility of divorce (Bulmer 1960a:138ff).

4. Contraceptive herbs and abortifacients were said to exist, but neither Becroft nor Bulmer found direct evidence (Becroft 1967b; Bulmer, personal communication).

5. Adoption in infancy was rare, especially because it required induced lactation and the cessation of intercourse and could conflict with property rights of other children. Before 1950, many orphans died (Bulmer 1960a:143,324).

6. Intercourse resumed after the death of a breast-fed child: A child dying under age five was normally replaced.

The feeding of Kyaka children

In general no foods (except human milk) were seen as especially suitable for infants and children, and the adult diet was gradually introduced. The dominance of the sweet potato in the adult diet can be seen from a dietary study of 16 adult Kyaka in 1967 (Oomen and Corden 1970:15) in which average daily food consumption (edible portion) was 1.6 kilograms, of which 1.4 kilograms, or 81 percent, was sweet potato. Similar findings were reported for the Mae Enga (Meggitt 1958) and Yandapu Enga (Sinnett 1975). When other tubers such as potato and taro are added, the total tuber proportion by weight for the Yandapu was over 90 percent (Table 9.3).

Such a large proportion of sweet potato created considerable problems for children because of its bulk in relation to protein content (Binns 1976), especially in a basically vegetable diet. Sinnett (1975:33) found a variation from 1.0 to 2.0 grams of protein per 100 grams (mean 1.4 grams) of crude

Table 9.3. *Food intake at morning and evening meals of Yandapu Enga,
1966-1967*

	Males, age group:						
	0-4	5-9	10-14	15-19	20-29	30-39	40+
Tubers (%)	93.7[a]	97.5	96.0	98.5	94.7	97.7	98.0
Other vegetables (%)	4.1	2.3	2.2	1.3	5.3	1.4	1.8
Pig (%)	2.1	0.2	1.7	2.3	0.0	0.9	1.1
Total (g/day)	513[b]	956	1163	1415	1848	1701	1652

[a] Percentages by weight.
[b] Total intakes underestimated by amount of human milk consumed (Sinnett 1975)
and food eaten at other times, especially in bush and gardens (Sinnett, personal communication).
Source: Sinnett 1975:31.

protein in 14 varieties grown among the Yandapu Enga and 470 to 651 kilojoules per 100 grams (mean 575 kilojoules). The essential amino acid profile showed it to be deficient in sulfur-containing amino acids (methionine
and cystine) (Peters 1958:41; Oomen et al. 1961; World Health Organization
1966:35), which would accentuate the bulk problem unless other foods with
complementary essential amino acid profiles were also eaten (such as the
dark-green leafy vegetables common in the Papua New Guinea Highlands).
But even with other foods, the bulk of the traditional diet was a problem,
especially if food intakes were at a few large meals instead of frequently
throughout the day.

The child spacing among the Kyaka, which allowed children to be with
the mother at the garden each day, not only had the advantage of frequent
human milk feeding, but also allowed frequent feeding with food from the
garden cooked on an open fire – of particular importance in a society where
food is not stored at the house. Beyond five or six years old, children might
have left their mothers to join groups of youngsters foraging in the bush for
food from animals, eggs, and plants.

Weaning was not normal until the decision to have another child at around
4½ years although 10 percent of a group of 125 children were still not weaned
at 5½ years (Becroft 1967b:811, 1967a:601).

> Weaning is a matter for mutual decision between mother, child and
> father. It is customary for the father to care for the child of either
> sex during weaning. If he can quieten the cries, especially at night,
> by offering sweet potato or bananas, then weaning has been completed
> to the satisfaction of all concerned.... should the child protest too

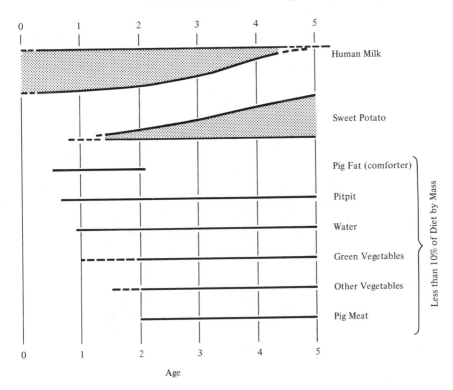

Figure 9.2. Feeding patterns of Kyaka children. Pitpit: *Saccharum Edule* (edible inflorescence of a variety of perennial grass). Each food was not necessarily eaten at each meal. Patterns were indicative only; there was some variation. (From Becroft 1967a, 1967b; Bulmer 1960a; together with Meggitt 1958; Sinnett 1975.)

much, the father may give in and allow breast feeding to continue a little longer. Emotionally, this arrangement could not be improved on, for the child's attachment is shifted from mother to father before the arrival of the next baby. Jealousy of siblings is very rare. (Becroft 1967b:811)

The pattern and timing of food introduction is summarized in Figure 9.2. Solids were not introduced until at least two teeth erupted, and often later, and water was rarely given, so that the volume of human milk consumed was crucial to the health and development of Kyaka children, especially because other compact nutritive sources such as eggs, milk, meat, fish, or fats were extremely rare in the child diet. A number of food taboos were important for adults, but rarely applied or did not apply to children (Bulmer, personal communication).

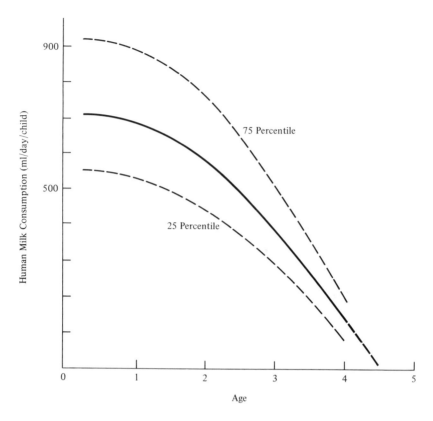

Figure 9.3. Consumption of human milk by 157 Kyaka children, 1962–1965. Smoothed data are derived from Becroft (1967a). Percentiles were estimated from a study of 29 children aged two to six months. (From Becroft 1967a.)

Between 1962 and 1965, Dr. Thelma Becroft carried out a remarkable longitudinal study of 24-hour human milk consumption of 157 Kyaka children, who were weighed before and after each feed (Becroft 1967a). More recent studies by the Papua New Guinea Institute of Medical Research suggest that her figures were underestimated because of the evaporation of urine between weighs from the diapers used (Heywood, personal communication) and some "furtive feeding." The results are summarized in Figure 9.3 and show that even at two years children consumed an average of 600 milliliters of human milk daily, and that consumption by three- and four-year olds was still of considerable dietary significance.

Variation was considerable: The highest consumption was 1,193 milliliters for a 1¾ year old, whereas the mother of twins produced 1,335 milliliters. Failed lactation was unknown (Becroft 1967a). The child slept with the mother, and night feeds were normal for the first two years or so.

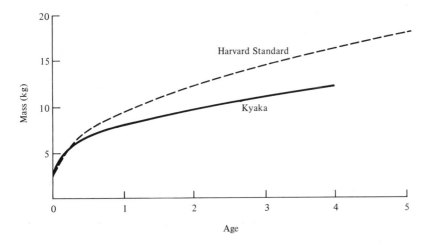

Figure 9.4. Mass-for-age of 902 Kyaka children. (From McKay 1960.)

Growth, health, and mortality

McKay (1960) analyzed the growth of 902 apparently healthy Kyaka children in 1958. Birth mass averaged 2,840 grams, and growth was above Harvard mass-for-age "standards" for the first six months of life whereas after one year, mean mass closely followed 80 percent of Harvard standards (Figure 9.4). Becroft and Bailey (1965:28) referred to this growth pattern as "serious growth retardation from 6 to 24 months." Yet the protein-feeding supplementation trial they carried out on 120 infants 6–12 months old produced no significant change in mass gain over a control group. McKay believed that malnutrition was a major problem among Kyaka children, but based this on cases presenting at the hospital and his view that the diet was poor.

Mass-for-age data were commonly used at that time as a direct indicator of malnutrition, and indeed, formed the basis of the 1978 National Nutrition Survey (Lambert 1978), which used the proportion of children under 80 percent mass-for-age (Harvard scale) as the "malnutrition rate."

> There is little doubt that these figures are useful in dramatising the problem of malnutrition. . . . Beyond this, however, one wonders what the value of these figures really is. In some cases it is likely that their effect is positively damaging. (Heywood 1979:12)

Heywood showed that for a population of under-fives at Tari, in the Papua New Guinea Highlands, their low mean mass-for-age was the result of a slowing in height increases ("stunting") rather than lower body mass in relation to that height ("wasting"). Mass-for-height data showed only a mild

Table 9.4. *Child mortality per thousand live births*

| | Kyaka, 1963– 1966 | Bundi | | Asai, 1962– 1966 |
		Before 1958	After 1962	
Stillbirths	34	n.a.	n.a.	n.a.
0 to 1 month	55	52	44	80
1 month to 1 year	14	36	24	22
1 year to 5 years	19	62	17	170
Child mortality	88	151[a]	84[a]	272
Sample size (live births)	731	688	298	323

[a] Child mortality totals do not agree because of rounding.
Sources: For Kyaka: Becroft et al. 1969; for Bundi: Malcolm 1969; for Asai, Malcolm 1970.

deviation from standards in children from seven months to three years of age, reaching standard ratios at four years. It is therefore almost certain that Kyaka children, who had a similar mass-for-age relationship, were not as malnourished as workers at that time believed. This is consistent with the visual impression of a number of researchers that Kyaka children did not appear malnourished (Bulmer 1960a:86; Woolcock and Blackburn 1967:12).

The slow growth in height of the Kyaka child may well reflect successful adaptations to the diet and environment. Malcolm, who has done much work on child growth in Papua New Guinea has suggested that it is inappropriate to place a value judgment on the outcome of this adaptive process: "While the price of adaptation may be a high early childhood mortality, such adaptation is to some extent a successful one in that the older child...shows few signs of physical disability or illness" (Malcolm 1979: 370). Of the Yandapu Enga, Sinnett (1975:73) said that in terms of Darwinian fitness, nutritional status is adequate: Birth rates are high, adults fit and healthy, and growth of the population satisfactory. For women, heavier children would reduce their ability to carry food for family and pigs.

Many Kyaka children died in childhood. Bulmer (1960a:476) questioned 23 Kyaka women past child-bearing age in 1955. Of the 78 live births, 26 percent had died before adulthood, 9 percent as adults, and 58 percent were still alive; these deaths are possibly underestimates because of unreported deaths (Bulmer 1960a:466). For the Yandapu Enga, Sinnett (1975:42) reported 48 percent of the children of 40- to 49-year-old women as dead before marriageable age.

A mortality survey conducted among the Kyaka between 1963 and 1966 (Becroft, Stanhope, and Burchett 1969) is summarized in Table 9.4 and is

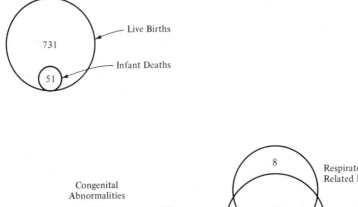

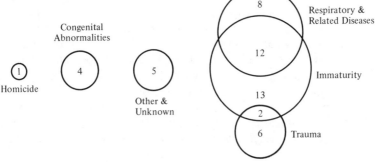

Figure 9.5. Causes of death in Kyaka infants (aged 0–1). Immaturity includes low mass-for-gestational-age and prematurity. (From mortality survey of 731 live births by Becroft, Stanhope, and Burchett 1969.)

compared with child mortality data from the Bundi for two periods and from the Asai, a remote, poorly endowed area with very high child mortality rates. (Causes of infant death are set out in Figure 9.5.)

Child mortality rates from six months to five years of age are generally responsive to improvements in health services, whereas neonatal mortality is more related to the overall changes in adult health and living conditions (United Nations 1962; Scragg 1969; Malcolm 1970:24). This, and Bulmer's recall data, suggest that Kyaka toddler mortality rates in the 1950s were closer to those of pre-1958 Bundi, and, before 1950, higher. Because, according to Becroft (1967b), the spacing of surviving children was being maintained even in 1966, this lower mortality rate would have had only a slight impact on completed family size.

Causes of death of the 12 toddlers dying during the mortality survey were gastroenteritis and dysentery (5), meningitis and encephalitis (3), malnutrition (1), and other causes (3) (Becroft et al. 1969). This sample is very small but indicates the predominance of dysentery and gastroenteritis.

In spite of marriage and trading relationships with nearby groups, the "precontact" highland clans were protected by their relative isolation and low mobility. Some diseases important elsewhere in the tropics, such as cholera and tuberculosis, were unknown. Excursions to lower altitudes by the Kyaka were seen as inviting illness (Bulmer 1960a).

It may be no coincidence that the Kyaka population was concentrated above the 1,200-meter altitude above which Vines (1970:141) found malarial incidence (as measured by spleen rates) to decline rapidly. Nevertheless, malaria was endemic, with *falciparium* predominating (McKay 1960:452; Vines 1970:4). By 1960, regular oral prophylaxis of under-fives made the disease rare in Kyaka infants (McKay 1960:452). Previously, malaria would have been a very significant factor in child morbidity and mortality, both directly and indirectly. Children become highly susceptible in areas where malaria is endemic because maternally conferred passive immunity ceases around six months and the child may be five years old when active immunity is established. The smaller blood volume of children increases the severity of the disease (Wilcocks and Manson-Bahr 1972:54), and natural immunity may be reduced by the absence of the sickle-cell gene in Papua New Guinea (Peters 1960). Chronic malaria not only causes anemia in those surviving the disease, but may also reduce the immune response to other infections.

Chronic nontuberculous lung diseases were common, and Woolcock et al. (1970), who studied the Kyaka in 1969, concluded that the problem began in infancy; Vines (1970:317) found rates of upper respiratory disease of 17, 4, and 1 percent for highlands children under five. Diarrheal diseases were very common: For the nearby Raiapu Enga, Feacham (1977:160) reported over 40 percent of all ages suffering from diarrhea in a five-month period, and 6 percent from dysentery (bloody stools).

Skin diseases were probably similar in incidence to those reported by Vines (1970:369) for the highlands region: Of children one to four years of age, 4 percent had abscesses; 19 percent, scabies; 10 percent, molluscum contagiosum (a viral skin disease); and 31 percent, other skin diseases. Ascaris, hookworm, and trichuris (whipworm) ova were detected in 43 percent, 48 percent, and 26 percent of feces from one to four year olds (Vines 1970:210), but helminth loads and their impact on nutrition and health are not known.

Nutrition

Mean sweet potato intakes for children were estimated from a composite of data from Becroft (1967b), Bulmer (1960a), and Sinnett (1975), and the energy content is plotted in Figure 9.6 on the basis of the mean energy content of varieties collected among the Yandapu Enga by Sinnett (1975:33). This has been added to the energy content of mean human milk consumption and compared with recommended energy intakes of WHO (1973) and Waterlow and Thomson (1979) for infants under six months. These recommendations have then been adjusted for the Kyaka child's mean body mass reported by McKay (1960).

Figure 9.6 and those that follow must be interpreted with caution: They are essentially energy and protein balance-sheets and are indicative only.

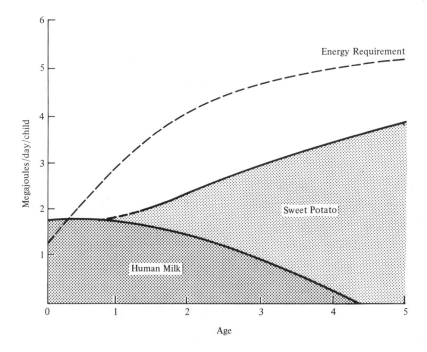

Figure 9.6. Estimated mean energy content of human milk and sweet potato consumed by Kyaka children. The energy requirement is based on data from WHO (1973) and Waterlow and Thomson (1979), adjusted for mass-for-age of Kyaka children (McKay 1960). It is indicative only, because actual energy requirements vary with individuals and environment: See, for example, Burman (1976:48ff) and discussion in WHO (1973:22ff). The data on the energy content of human milk is taken from Bailey (1965); that of the sweet potato, from Sinnett (1975). See comments in text.

These means hide considerable variability: The variability of human milk consumption can be seen from Figure 9.3. Sinnett (1975) reported a 36 percent variability in energy content of various sweet potato varieties; there is wide variation in the consumption of sweet potato, with Becroft (1967b) reporting a range from 40 to 300 grams in 17 children aged 17–24 months. There is also wide variation in fat (and therefore energy content) of human milk, 65 Kyaka samples falling within 1.5–4.2 grams per 100 milliliters (Becroft 1967a:599). Furthermore, energy requirements are variable between individuals and environments (WHO 1973:48). No account was taken of other foods, which, although making up a small proportion of the dietary mass, might have been of considerable nutritive significance.

Figure 9.7 estimates the mean crude protein intakes and compares these with WHO (1973) recommendations. Similar caveats apply as for Figure 9.6, but the magnitudes are different because protein variability in sweet

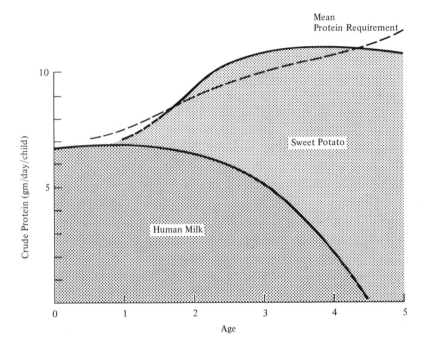

Figure 9.7. Estimated mean crude protein content of the mean quantities of milk and sweet potato consumed by Kyaka children. See text for basis of mean protein requirement. The protein content of Kyaka human milk is based on Becroft (1967a).

potato is very high (1.0–2.0 grams per 100 grams; 1.4 grams per 100 grams; Sinnett 1975:32), much more than energy variability. Further, the utilization of the protein from sweet potato depends on the levels of sulfur-containing essential amino acids in other foods eaten, especially as the ratio of human milk to sweet potato declines.

The question of an appropriate recommendation for protein is a difficult one. WHO recommendations for infants under one year are rather confused (WHO 1973:50ff) and may suffer from the committee approach which produced them (Scrimshaw 1976). The mean nitrogen requirement on which the WHO "safe" recommendations were based (WHO 1973:70) is used here because means are used for other variables. "The safe level of intake is the amount shown to have been necessary to meet the physiological needs and maintain the health of nearly all individuals in the group and is therefore higher than the average protein requirements" (Passmore, Nichol, and Rao 1974:17).

Figures 9.6 and 9.7 are not intended as an assessment of dietary adequacy or levels of nutrition of Kyaka children, but a number of important conclusions emerge:

1. Because food intake tends to be irregular and of high bulk, human milk intakes are extremely important to lower dietary bulk and to increase feeding frequency.
2. Human milk makes a substantial and crucial nutritive contribution in terms of energy and protein up to at least the fourth year.
3. Energy deficits appear likely in the 6- to 18-month age group, depending on the timing of solid food introduction and the amount ingested. (This corresponds to the deviation of growth from the Harvard "standard" in Figure 9.4.)
4. Human milk, which is assumed to have an ideal essential amino acid profile, might also have improved the utilization of protein from sweet potato, which is deficient in methionine and cystine.
5. Because foods other than sweet potato and human milk accounted for only a small portion of the dietary intake, any lessening in the period of human milk feeding, or decline in its amount, could have had severe negative effects unless other foods that match it in terms of nutrition, compactness, and water content were increased in the diet, or introduced.
6. From these data it appears that Kyaka children's nutrition was not severely deficient in protein or energy, but, on the other hand, it was not adequate to maintain higher rates of growth. It is best described as precarious.

A commonly ignored nutrient in human milk is its 87 percent water content (Jelliffe and Jelliffe 1978:28). Very low adult water intakes have been reported for other parts of the highlands (Hipsley and Kirk 1965; Oomen 1967) and among Kyaka adults (Oomen and Corden 1970); however, Feachem (1977:155) reported for the Raiapu Enga a mean volume of water drunk per person of 190 milliliters per day as compared with a volume for Kyaka adults of 232 milliliters per day (Figure 9.8).

Kyaka children were rarely given water until they could handle a utensil, and even then water intakes were low (Becroft 1967a). Most Papua New Guinea Highlanders might have been in a state of chronic dehydration; the same could have been said of the children if they did not get sufficient water from human milk. Human milk may therefore have been of very considerable importance for maintaining fluid balance as well as for its prophylactic impact on many diseases, especially the highly prevalent gastroenteritis and dysentery.

Environment and disease

An infant spent perhaps 14 hours daily in a Kyaka house in close proximity to the mother, other persons, pigs, a fire, and the floor. As the child got older and mobile, he or she would spend more time with other children and experience a wider range of environments.

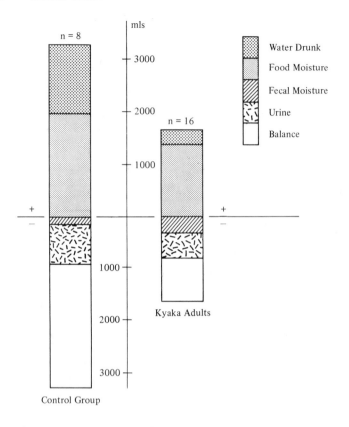

Figure 9.8. Water balance in Kyaka adults. No corrections are made for solids in urine or for metabolic water. The control group consisted of students from Papua Medical College, Port Moresby. (From Oomen and Corden 1970.)

The most common house (*endanda* or "woman-house") in which women and children slept was oblong, 2–3 meters wide, 7–14 meters long, 2 meters high, with a thatched roof of kunai (*imperata* spp.) rising from walls of split timber and bark about 1 meter high. The house, together with typical sleeping patterns, was described and illustrated by Cleary and Blackburn (1968):

> It is divided into three compartments, the first a living room where food is prepared and eaten, the next pig stalls where pigs spend the night, and the third a small stuffy sleeping compartment for humans. There is generally a large hearth in the centre of the living compartment, and another small one in the sleeping compartment or at the end of the pig stalls. (Bulmer 1960a:115)

A fire was alight whenever anyone was in the house – for cooking, for warmth, and as a social focus. Burns, often serious, were very common in young children. One or two very small doors were the only opening, and ventilation at night was by air seepage through the roof and walls. Three to six people of various ages, plus five to ten pigs, would typically sleep in such a house, although there was wide variation.

Raiapu Enga houses were virtually identical:

> The floors are of beaten earth covered with a layer of masticated sugar cane pith, which provides an ideal habitat for many members of the phylum Arthropoda. Of special public health significance are. . .cockroaches, fleas, beetles, bed bugs and lice. Houses are also infested with mites and ticks (order Acarina) and particularly with *Sarcoptes scabiei* which give rise to the high prevalence of scabies in the area. (Feachem 1977:169)

Children, dogs, and pigs often excreted on the floor. Feachem collected eight floor samples and identified considerable mite populations, especially from older houses. Mites are strongly implicated in the etiology of dermatosis, by far the most common disorder in the highland region (Vines 1970), from which 99.5 percent of Raiapu suffered during a five-month period (Feachem 1977:172ff). Minor skin disorders frequently became serious through secondary infections.

Cleary and Blackburn (1968) found very high concentrations of smoke, aldehydes, and carbon monoxide immediately after the fire was lit or stoked, with levels at other times through the night high in the upper areas of the houses. Levels were lower near the ground where people slept, but high enough to be an initiatory or severely aggravating factor in the high levels of respiratory disease found among the Kepena clan of the Kyaka: Twenty-six percent under 40 years and 53 percent over 40 years had chronic lung disease (Blackburn, Green, and Mitchell 1970:570), and this was likely to have its genesis in infancy (Woolcock, Colman, and Blackburn 1970:588). Blackburn and Green (1966) also suspected that vegetable protein dust and/or fungus dust from the thatched roofs might have been implicated in chronic lung disease.

Concentrations of carbon dioxide and water vapor would rise during the night because of the burning fire and the respiration and transpiration of animals and humans. Beral and Read (1971) found an unusually low ventilatory response to levels of carbon dioxide in Kyaka subjects which, although advantageous to a healthy active person, could be a major liability in disease. High humidity in a crowded house would assist cross-infection of the droplet-carried upper respiratory tract infections common in children and adults. Feachem found the degree of crowding in houses to be positively correlated with the prevalence of coughing among newborns to four-year olds and the incidence of skin disease at all ages (1977:173ff).

Table 9.5. *Important waterborne diseases and diseases transmitted fecally–orally in the Papua New Guinea Highlands*

Disease	Pathogenic agent	
Amebic dysentery	Protozoa	(Intermediate agents also may be
Ascariasis	Helminth	involved such as flies, pigs,
Bacillary dysentery (shigellosis)	Bacteria	dogs, lice, mites, rats, fleas,
Balantidiasis	Protozoa	etc.)
Diarrheal disease	Various	
Enterobiasis	Helminth	
Enteroviruses (some)	Virus	
Gastroenteritis	Various	
Giardiasis	Protozoa	
Hepatitis, infectious	Virus	
Leptospirosis	Spirochete	
Paratyphoid	Bacteria	
Trichuriasis	Helminth	
Typhoid	Bacteria	
Hookworm	Helminth	
Strongyloidiasis	Helminth	
Larva migrans	Various larval nematodes	

Source: Feachem 1977: tables IV and IX.

The highly prevalent skin and eye infections were closely followed by diseases related to poor excreta disposal. High population densities of people and pigs could result in fecal contamination of rivers and streams, but poor personal hygiene and excreta disposal were probably more significant factors (Feachem 1977).

Children frequently defecated and urinated in the house and surrounds and adults would only go a short distance to seek privacy. Latrines were encouraged by the administration but rarely used. Pigs or dogs usually ate human feces close to the village, and their proximity to humans facilitated the rapid closure of fecal–oral infection cycles. Although this was limited by the cleansing effect of the persistent rainfall, it might have been accentuated in infants and children by their closer association with the ground in crawling and tottering.

Feachem (1977:155) also reported no bodily washing in houses and only occasional washing in streams and rivers. This not only increased the likelihood of fecal–oral infection but also of those infections responsive to frequent washing such as skin and eye infections. My observation in other parts of the highlands suggests that very young children are washed less than adults, but this is not necessarily true of the Kyaka.

Pigs came into close and frequent contact with the women who tended them, and therefore their children. Talbot (1972) found indigenous pigs in

Papua New Guinea carrying high loads of a variety of helminth and arthropod parasites, some of which have significance for humans. Willis and Wannan (1966) found leptospiral antibodies in 32 percent of children three to six years old and in 63 percent of adults, and considered pigs the most common source. The gut of the pig harbors many of the pathogens of diseases listed in Table 9.5, including *Clostridium welchii* (type C), which can cause *pikbel* (enteritis necroticans) in populations subsisting on high levels of a staple containing a trypsin inhibitor such as sweet potato (Murrell and Walker 1978). Using partially cooked pig meat for continued prestation, often for many days, also contributed to the prevalence of salmonellosis (bacterial enteritis or food poisoning). Rats were common in houses (Willis and Wannan 1966) and might have transmitted disease directly or through parasites such as ticks, lice, fleas, and mites.

The interaction of feeding patterns and environment is well illustrated by the unresolved question of the effect of earlier introduction of foods other than human milk. It is obvious from Figure 9.6 that infants would have benefitted from increased energy intakes in the latter part of the first year, but this could have introduced pathogens at an earlier age, to a child with less active immunity (Heywood 1979).

The complexity of these environmental influences on disease are best summarized by Figure 9.9 from Feachem (1977:175), for the Raiapu Enga, although this figure omits malaria and *pikbel*.

Immunological aspects of nutrition and health

This catalog of diseases and disease vectors is not inconsistent with the general robustness of the population noted previously. Many of the diseases were mild, whereas the severity of others was related to the individual's nutritive and immunological status. Kyaka children would have been under almost constant exposure to disease pathogens, the outcome of which would have depended on their immunological status and general health. The synergism between nutrition and infection is strong, but complex. The classic study by Scrimshaw, Taylor, and Gordon (1968) discussed it in detail, whereas Poston (1979) has given a less technical introduction.

The infant acquires some passive immunity from the mother, which is then supported by the immunological contribution of her milk. This immunological support is patterned on the mother's own immunological status, so that it is environmentally appropriate, and further, there is evidence that the mother–child dyad remains a dynamic immunological system, with the mother also responding to pathogens in the child (Jelliffe and Jelliffe 1978: 84ff; Pitt 1979; Poston 1979:81). A further antiinfective contribution of human milk is that it increases the proportion of food intake from a relatively pathogen-free source, very important in an environment such as that of the Kyaka. If human milk feeding were of shorter duration, correspondingly

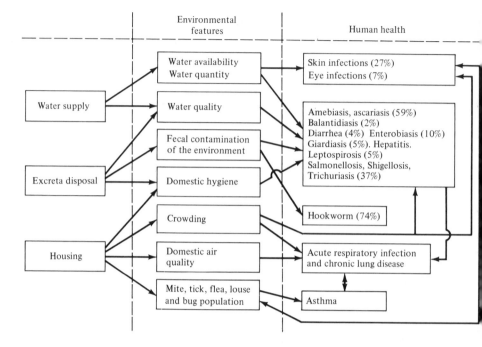

Figure 9.9. A simplified model of the interactions between the environment and human health in the Highlands of Papua New Guinea. Percentages in brackets refer to the prevalence of these conditions in the Highlands (Feachem 1973; Vines 1970). (From Feachem 1977.)

more of other food would have been necessary, increasing exposure to disease organisms.

Nutritional status also affects the immune response (Scrimshaw et al. 1968; Suskind 1977; Poston 1979:190), whereas severe immunological challenge (or disease) may interfere in nutrition, such as by increasing excretory nitrogen loss. Even mild diseases may also cause loss of appetite, or interfere physically through mouth soreness (as in measles and upper respiratory disease) or diarrheal nutrient loss. However, continued breast feeding maintains a feeding option that is not only comforting to the sick child, but is simpler to ingest than solids and is immunologically active, has a high water content, and is pathogen free: For the Kyaka child, this powerful prophylactic remained available to the child until the age of around five years.

Because maternal milk production can rapidly respond to increasing demand, the mean milk intake volumes of Figure 9.3 are no indication of the nutrients available to the sick child who "goes off" solids. Continued human milk feeding, therefore, reduces the probability or severity of the synergic infection–malnutrition cycle which can rapidly prove fatal.

Conclusion

The cultural aspects of food and feeding are multifaceted and complex. For the Kyaka, food was central in the prestations of the *moka*; foods had varying status; many were only cultivated by men; food taboos proscribed some foods for certain people and times; food production largely determined a woman's worth; and food gifts were an outward sign of most interpersonal and intergroup relationships.

Yet I have barely mentioned these in this discussion; rather have I focused on the established patterns of Kyaka child feeding, made some estimates of its adequacy in the face of a bulky adult diet and a difficult and pathogenically hostile environment. In doing so, I have highlighted a number of crucial cultural supports to child feeding patterns and female productivity as well as ways in which cultural aspects of housing, pig husbandry, and hygiene combined to create a relatively hostile pathogenic environment.

The high-bulk adult diet, together with the concentration of food intakes in one evening meal, is quite unsuitable for young children, who require a more compact food source and frequent feeding. By the time the child is five or six years of age, the bulk problem declines and children become sufficiently mobile and experienced to get some food for themselves. Until then, the Kyaka child not only received human milk in nutritionally significant quantities, but also was with the mother almost continually, ensuring a frequent supply of human milk as well as other food prepared through the day. This was further necessary because the Kyaka did not store food for any time in their houses, and accompanying the mother to the garden provided frequent and varied foods. But this would not have been possible if another child was born too soon: Not only would the mother's productivity have been impaired through having to carry two children, and look after them during the day, but the health and nutrition of one or other child (or the mother) would have suffered. At the same time, the long period of suckling substantially assisted child health and survival through its immunological contribution and protection of the child (although to a decreasing extent with age) from its environment. Polygyny, infanticide, abortion, concepts of female pollution, and beliefs about the effect of intercourse during pregnancy also supported this feeding pattern via their impact on child spacing.

It is very tempting to claim that there is therefore an implicit rationale in these cultural supports aimed directly at child feeding and health. But societies and their actions are more complex than such a trivial conclusion allows.

The importance of these "positive" cultural factors in child feeding is even more important when viewed against the "negative" cultural factors which contributed to high morbidity and child mortality through poor hygiene. Whereas the cultural supports to Kyaka children's feeding patterns were obvious and beneficial, these "negative" cultural factors operated in a more diffuse and indirect manner.

Crowded houses, the pattern of pig husbandry, infrequent washing, and ineffective excreta disposal combined together in diverse ways to interfere with established feeding patterns through disease.

The data presented suggest a view similar to that depicted by Sinnett (1975) for the Yandapu Enga: a group of people demonstrating their nutritional adaptation to their environment by slower growth rates and short adult stature, but paying the price of the precarious balance between barely adequate nutrition and disease in the form of high neonatal and infant mortality and moderate-to-high toddler mortality, yet displaying healthy and fit survivors.

In the period immediately after colonial intrusion, Kyaka toddler mortality declined as medical intervention became available for those infective diseases highly responsive to early treatment, thus interrupting some downward spirals of infection and malnutrition. But neonatal mortality, which is more sensitive to maternal nutrition and environmental quality, remained high.

We have been conditioned by some members of the medical profession to believe that declines in child mortality and increases in life expectancy are the direct result of better and more frequent intervention by highly qualified medical professionals. But improvements in nutrition and environment have probably been a greater determinant (McKeown 1979). For the Kyaka, and millions like them, dietary and especially environmental improvement offer the best hope for increasing life expectancy at birth. Experience suggests that this will be a long process and dependent on education (of males *and* females), the expansion of the resource base, improvements in housing and hygiene, *as well as* the maintenance of effective child spacing whether by their traditional means or by other means.

A more general lesson highlighted by the Kyaka data is the dietary and cultural importance of human milk. It is clear that it was a vital vehicle for nutrients for Kyaka children for a long period, and it was also central to the postpartum intercourse taboo. One must not, without sufficient evidence, assume that intakes of human milk are low enough to ignore in older children, as is so often done in dietary surveys. Further, it should be studied as one part of a mixed diet in the case of the child on human milk and other foods: Most of the literature on child diets in Third World countries assumes the weaning transition to be abrupt enough to ignore as a phase in itself. For Kyaka children, it lasted three to four years, and formed a critical part of the buffer against a poor environment.

Postscript

The reader will ask, "What has happened since 1960?" A good question. The answers appear to depend on the valuations one puts on the benefits and costs of the various events of the past years of rapid socioeconomic change in the Papua New Guinea Highlands. Cash is now widely used, coffee and other cash crops are common, and a wide variety of new foods are grown and purchased, including alcohol. Polygyny is declining at church insistence, and abortion and infanticide are illegal. Schooling is becoming available. A dependency on the rest of the country, and the world, has been created, as highlanders move from tribespeople to peasants. At this stage, we can only speculate on the net effect of this period of stress and adjustment, and its impact on the children of the Kyaka Enga.

Appendix. *List of cultivated food of Kyaka Enga in approximate order of dietary significance, 1955*

Sweet potato (18 pre-European and 3 post-European).
Sugar cane (23 varieties, all pre-European).
Bananas and plantains (37 pre-European and 2 post-European).
Maize (8 varieties, all post-European).
Yams (29 varietes, all pre-European).
Taro (19 pre-European varieties, all *Collocasia,* and 1 post-European, *Xanthosoma* – "Kongkong taro").
Green vegetables (12 pre-European species). Only one introduced green vegetable, the cabbage, has so far become popular as a native item of diet, though others are grown sporadically to sell to Europeans.
Cane inflorescences *(Saccharum edule)* (10 pre-European varieties).
Goa beans *(?Psophocarpus tetranglobus)* (15 varieties, all pre-European). Green shoots, seeds insides of pods, and corms are eaten.
Asparagus grass (9 varieties, all pre-European).
Cucumbers (6 pre-European and 3 post-European varieties).
Ground nuts (introduced). Foliage as well as nuts are eaten.
Marita *(Pandanus concoideus)* (20 varieties, all pre-European). This tree is not grown above about 5,500 feet.
Karoka *(Pandanus ?jullianetii)* (11 varieties, all pre-European). Few grow below 6,000 feet. These trees, therefore, though planted, tended, and owned individually, are all found in the mountain forest.
Manioc (cassava) (2 post-European varieties). This is classed by Kyaka with wild yam, which must also be specially treated to extract poison before eating.
Pea beans *(?Dolichos lablab)* (6 varieties, all pre-European).
Breadfruit *(Artocarpus)* (pre-European). Only one variety is recognized by natives. It does not grow above 5,000 feet.
Tomatoes, french beans, pawpaws, pineapples, and passion fruit are now all grown in some quantity and are relished as food, but when possible are sold to Europeans.
Irish potatoes, pumpkins, carrots, shallots, and many other European vegetables are now grown in small quantities, for sale to Europeans, but are not normally eaten.

Source: Bulmer 1960a:62.

10. "Australia's got the milk, we've got the problems": The Australian Dairy Corporation in Southeast Asia

Kathy Robinson

The incorporation of the Third World into the markets of international capital has had far-reaching consequences for the diets of the populations of the capitalist periphery. Increasingly world markets in food reach out into the isolated corners of the globe, on the one hand determining the prices and the ultimate fate of locally produced goods, and on the other hand incorporating the people as consumers for the markets of the big food producing corporations, which are increasingly coming to dominate world food production (George 1979). One of the most notorious instances of this process is the activities of the multinational milk producers, who have been engaging in marketing practices in Third World countries which draw women away from the customary practice of breast-feeding infants, to take up artificial feeding. As family sizes shrink in the developed world and women in industrialized countries return to the practice of breast-feeding their babies, the markets of the baby formula manufacturers shrink in their home territories. They attempt to make up these losses in the home markets and ensure expanding future markets by vigorous marketing of their products in the Third World. Advertising is an important part of this marketing strategy; this is a powerful force which creates new wants and sets new standards of status and propriety (Wilson 1981:21). Promotional activities derive support from the ideology that underpins the capitalist penetration of the Third World. The economic imbalance deriving from the economic exploitation of the Third World comes to be imbued with a moral force, giving differential status to people of the first and third worlds, and this forms the basis of the ideological hegemony that allows exploitation. Governments and development planners of the noncommunist world avow values of progress and modernity, which are identified largely with the life-style of the West. The social and cultural changes that accompany the economic transformation of the capitalist periphery shore up the new economic order and ensure the locking in of the populace to the markets of expanding monopoly capital. For example, the hand-produced textiles, the foods of a self-sufficient rural economy all give way to mass-produced goods from the factories of monopoly capital or the products of agribusiness. The natural human activity of breast-feeding children, most suited to the sustenance of the infant, comes to be identified with the old order which has been left behind. Vigorous advertising on radio, television, billboards, and even in health clinics tells people that the modern mother feeds her child powerful infant formula out of a bottle. This is proclaimed as the custom of the Westerners who hold power, who have the know-how to acquire fabulous wealth, to invent wonderous machinery, and to combat many of the illnesses that have plagued their lives. Much advertising of milk products and infant formulas in the Third World uses white mothers and children to underscore this message. Not surprisingly, bottle-feeding babies becomes part of the quest for modernity. Perhaps by bottle-feeding babies, they will become big and strong and clever, like the babies of the affluent West. (The fact that artificially fed babies are fatter than those who are breast-fed is not lost on the mothers of the Third World, nor the milk-producers who promote "fattest baby" competitions as part of their promotions.)

Most of the marketing of infant foods in the Third World has been carried out by multinational corporations, and it is corporate capital that has been singled out for criticism of morally questionable promotional activities. However, a statutory authority of the Australian Government has been involved in the promotion of artificial feeding of infants in Southeast Asia, through the activities of its subsidiary companies. I am referring to the activities of Asia Dairy Industries (Hong Kong) Ltd., a wholly owned subsidiary of the Australian Dairy Corporation and a number of joint-venture operating companies in Southeast Asia which were partly owned subsidiaries of the corporation.

The activities of Asia Dairy Industries and the operating companies have come under scrutiny in a report recently brought down by the Senate Committee on Finance and Government Operations (Government of Australia 1981). The report was concerned with the irregular financial and management practices of the Asian subsidiaries of the Australian Dairy Corporation, and with the problem of the government's control of these companies. It did not concern itself with what seems to be a more serious problem, with far more deleterious human consequences – the marketing practices of the subsidiary companies in Southeast Asia, in particular the promotion of sweetened condensed milk as food for human infants as a suitable substitute for breast milk. In this paper, I outline the history of Asia Dairy Industries and one of the Asian operating companies, and argue against the promotion of sweetened condensed milk in the Third World.

The Australian Dairy Corporation moves into the Asian market

The story of Asia Dairy Industries and the Asian operating companies is tied up with the story of the troubled Australian dairy industry in the 1960s and 1970s. At the beginning of this period, the industry was in crisis with many farmers on small, uneconomic farms, but overall characterized by overproduction. The industry was heavily subsidized, to ensure minimum standards of living, but these "handouts" were contentious political issues. At the time, there was discussion of production controls, a scheme to help dairy farmers leave the land, and so on. The crisis was exacerbated by the impending loss of Australia's largest single dairy export market – the United Kingdom – with its decision to join the European Economic Community. The Australian dairy industry had a period of grace to adjust to the situation until February 1973, when import levies were introduced. On the domestic market, the (successful) campaign by margarine producers to have margarine quotas eliminated, threatened the future of butter sales. (The 1970s did see a decline in overall domestic consumption of dairy produce – see Australia, Bureau of Agricultural Economics 1978.)

The Australian Dairy Produce Board (forerunner to the ADC as the body responsible for the marketing of Australian dairy produce) began searching for export markets to replace the United Kingdom. It turned its attention to Asia. Since that time, Japan has become Australia's largest single dairy export market (Australia, Bureau of Agricultural Economics 1978:7). The Board also focused attention on Southeast Asia, where Australia had only a very small place in the small market for (mainly) sweetened condensed milk. In 1962, it purchased 50 percent of shares in a Malaysian company, Asia Dairy Industries, which was incorporated in Hong Kong in 1964. The other shareholder was bought out in 1971 (Government of Australia 1981: 36–7), leaving the company a wholly owned subsidiary of the Australian Dairy Produce Board. When the Board's responsibilities were transferred to the newly created Australian Dairy Corporation (ADC) in 1975, the ownership of Asia Dairy Industries was passed on as well.

Asia Dairy Industries' task was to establish milk reconstitution plants in Southeast Asia, through joint-venture companies in association with indigenous businessmen. It was to "provide technical and management expertise and dairy produce raw materials to the joint venture operating companies and to oversight the Corporation's overseas investments" (ADC Annual Report 1979:20). The mass product line of the recombination plants was to be sweetened condensed milk, the milk product already favored on the Southeast Asian market, presumably because of the ease of storage after opening in a hot climate where few people own refrigerators. This product was to be manufactured from skim milk powder, the surplus product from Australian butter production, and from butter oil.

Finance for the Australian portion of the investment in the recombination plants and for the share in Asia Dairy Industries came from the Dairy Industry Stabilisation Fund. This fund had been created by the federal government in September 1948 from "surplus moneys obtained from the sale of butter and cheese to the United Kingdom at prices over and above the Federal Government guaranteed returns to dairy produce manufacturers" (Government of Australia 1981:13). Surplus payments were obtained for three seasons: 1948–51. Until 1977, the only payments from the fund were to finance the Southeast Asian operations. Dividends on profits from Asia Dairy Industries and the joint-venture companies were to be paid back into the fund.

By 1970, the Australian Dairy Produce Board was talking about a "sales boom" in Southeast Asia. Japan was still the largest single market, but Southeast Asian sales had been "considerably enhanced" by the operation of the recombination plants established in the Philippines, Thailand, Indonesia, and Singapore (*Australian Financial Review*, 30 July 1970; hereafter *AFR*).

The chairman of the Board, Mr. A. G. Roberts, reacted angrily to a comment in the *AFR* (21 May 1970) which referred to the "fortuitous development" of the Asian markets, saying this was the result of "commercial courage backed by the dairy industry's own funds."

> Not only do they form an assured market at slightly higher prices for Australian milk powder and anhydrous fats, they also return dividends on the dairy industry money invested. These dividends are now being used to expand operations so further Australian dairy produce can be sold. (Letter to the Editor, *AFR* 26 May 1970)

He further commented that during the decade, the plants had sold milk products worth more than A$25 million.

At the quarterly meeting of the board in July 1970, Mr. Roberts discussed the Asian investments at greater lengths, and outlined the reasons for the choice of Southeast Asia as a new market.

> South East Asian countries had large populations which were beginning to enjoy greater prosperity and greater appreciation of the importance of nutrition, especially for young children. (Quoted in *AFR* 30 July 1970)

He went on to say that these countries had hitherto imported sweetened condensed milk. Australia had a low share of this market as compared with Europe, and, given the closeness of the region, it made sense for Australia to enter into the market. The interest of the national governments in the region for joint-venture investment paved the way for the establishment of the recombination plants (quoted in *AFR*, 30 July 1970).

He spoke of the advantages that accrued to the host countries. Apart from the investment opportunities for local businessmen, the plants provided employment and specialized training in food technology and marketing for local people. The plants used local materials wherever possible – for instance, sugar, tinplate, printed labels, and packing cases; this stimulated local industry. The manufacture of sweetened condensed milk in the home country was an instance of an import substitution for local industry which helped keep down the consumer price of goods otherwise imported, and saved foreign exchange otherwise spent on imported food items (quoted in *AFR* 30 July 1970).

All the plants were operating successfully and playing an important role in the development of food technology in the region, besides helping to provide nutritious dairy products for babies and children. (Quoted in *AFR* 30 July 1970)

In 1972, the plants failed to trade at a profit, and this led to some questioning of the Asian investments. It was suggested that the declines in profits could be costing the dairy farmer money, and that producers who were compelled to sell skimmed milk powder to Asia Dairy Industries could have sold it on other markets at a better price (*Sun* 25 September 1972). In response to this criticism, the Australian Dairy Produce Board replied that Southeast Asia was the only area that offered an expanding market.

Indeed the plants were providing an important tied market for Australian dairy produce. In the 1970s, the annual growth rate in their operations had been 19 percent, reflecting the small base from which they had started, but also the considerable inroads they had made into Asian markets (Simson 1977a). In the three years to 1977, Southeast Asia accounted for a third by value of total exports of Australian dairy products (Australia, Bureau of Agricultural Economics 1977:2). Between 1965 and 1976, the plants had taken 21 percent powder production, and in 1976, this accounted for 6 percent of total dairy production. As exports accounted for 25–30 percent of annual dairy production in the 1970s (Australia, Bureau of Agricultural Economics 1977:2), this was not insubstantial.

The volatile nature of the world dairy market meant sudden shifts in the fortunes of Asia Dairy Industries and operating companies. In 1975 and 1976, there was a world glut of skimmed milk powder, and so prices were low: The year 1976 showed a doubling of the profits of the joint operating companies (Simson 1977a). In this climate, they were planning to double capacity of the plants in Thailand and Indonesia and buy into two more plants (Simson 1977a).

However, at the time as the reconstitution plants were expanding the market for sweetened condensed milk in Southeast Asia, changes in Australian dairy production were threatening the supplies of raw materials on which they depended. The continuing decline in butter production, reflecting the increasing inroads of margarine into that market, meant also a decline in skimmed milk powder. The dairy manufacturing industry began diversifying in an attempt to accommodate to the changing world market. An increase in casein production further reduced the amount of skimmed-milk powder available. Murry-Goulbourn Co-Operative, Australia's largest single manufacturer of dairy produce which had formerly supplied the bulk of Asia Dairy Industries' needs, undertook a contract to supply whole-milk powder to Venezuela. By 1977, the Australian Dairy Corporation was in the anomalous position of not being able to supply the raw materials the plants needed, and Asia Dairy Industries was purchasing skimmed-milk powder from other milk-producing countries for the Asian plants. The annual review *Situation and Outlook: Dairy Products*, published by the Bureau of Agricultural Economics, made much of the importance of the development of the Southeast Asian markets in the early 1970s. By 1977 and 1978, it was no longer given prominence.

Until 1976, the plants had been seen by the Australian dairy industry as an outlet for a product in oversupply, but the change in that situation led to a reassessment of their role. In 1977, Asia Dairy Industries put it to the Australian Government that the operating companies should be able to diversify. In particular, the Thai operating company was pursuing plans for the manufacture of biscuits, and the Indonesian company was keen to expand into ultrahigh-temperature (UHT) orange juice. The then Minister for Primary Industry, Mr. Sinclair, stated that such operations would be outside the charter of the ADC. The Attorney-General was cited as having given advice that

> provisions . . . of the Dairy Produce Act enable ADC to acquire an interest in a corporation incorporated in Australia or elsewhere *only* for the purpose of expansion of existing markets or the securing of new markets for Australian dairy produce. (Cited in Davidson 1980)

Mr. Sinclair expressed the opinion that if ADI wanted to expand into activities unrelated to the dairy industry, the shares would have to be sold off on a commercial basis. The Australian Dairy Farmers Federation countered by saying no buyer except the Australian Dairy Industry would be acceptable to the Asian partners. At this time the federation also suggested that the Dairy Industry Stabilisation Fund be transferred to Asia Dairy Industries to provide working capital for its expanded operations, but Mr. Sinclair also refused this request, saying that the fund should be kept for the industry. This was the first round in a dispute about ownership of the fund, which was part of the inquiry by the Senate Committee on Finance and Government Operations. The dairy farmers tried to argue that it was "their" money and so Asia Dairy Industries and the operating companies were "their" investment. The committee found no basis for this claim, saying the manufacturers and the government (who had paid out subsidies to the industry worth many times the value of the fund) also had an interest in the fund (Government of Australia 1981).

Asia Dairy Industries and the Australian Dairy Corporation were keen to see ADI's future role as an international trader, not dependent on Australian supplies, and the Australian Dairy Farmers Federation concurred in this. The ministerial decision denying such a change was not accepted by the dairy industry, which kept up its campaign to have the plants diversify, and to have the stabilization fund taken out of ministerial control.

In July 1979, the Federation issued a press release calling for a campaign to "save one of Australia's largest most successful and most profitable overseas trading companies" (Australian Dairy Farmers Federation, ADFF 1979).

They bemoaned the fact that because the shares in Asia Dairy Industries and the operating companies were held by the Australian Dairy Corporation as custodians for the stabilization fund, the activities of ADI were severely circumscribed by the limitations on the corporation as a statutory marketing authority.

The farmers argued that Australia could no longer supply the skimmed-milk powder for the Asian plants, and the company wanted to diversify into nondairy products, because it would maintain an outlet for Australian dairy produce which could be valuable in the future, and it would earn a profit for the benefit of the dairy industry. They claimed that the Asian ventures had been financed with the dairy industry's own funds, through the stabilization fund, and they did not want their investment broken up or lost. They proposed that profits made through the diversified activities could be used to help the dairy industry by financing research, developing new markets, and so forth. The Asian plants ought to be retained because of their value to the region, through providing outlets for milk from Asian farmers, and through helping to improve nutrition (ADFF 1979).

The Australian dairy industry had already benefited from the revenues generated by the Asian plants; they had tended to operate profitably and had paid dividends into the stabilization fund (Government of Australia 1981:300). Since 1977, the Minister has authorized a number of payments from the fund, the main expenditure being contributions to the Dairy Produce Sales Promotion Fund for a campaign to promote dairy products in Australia. In 1978–9, the Dairy Industry Stabilisation Fund provided 20 percent of the funds for the promotion campaign. The fund has also been used to finance the development of a new butter/margarine blend for the Australian market (ADC Annual Report 1980). A payment of $1.5 million to the Australian Dairy Farmers Federation to provide secretariat facilities, along with a provision of funds for dairy farmers tours to New Zealand and attendance at management college, has also been made from the fund. The legality of some of these payments was questioned by the auditor-general (Government of Australia 1981:223). Its current balance is over four million dollars (Government of Australia 1981:225). Apparently it is this sort of expenditure which the federation wishes to safeguard.

By April 1980, the government had agreed to the diversification of Asia Dairy Industries activities, and did not pursue the demand that shares in the company be sold off as a precondition for such diversification. The report of the Senate committee expressed doubts about these activities, but did not go into the question of why the government apparently changed its mind on this matter.

Through the 1960s and 1970s, the Asian markets were used in an attempt to stabilize markets for the ailing Australian dairy industry. In the 1980s, this exploitative relation continued, but in a different form, with the Asian ventures no longer providing a tied market for Australian dairy produce, but providing funds through the stabilization fund to aid the dairy industry back home, through payment for domestic advertising and so forth.

P.T. Indomilk: the Indonesian venture

Let us now turn to the history of the operations of one of the joint-venture plants, that in Indonesia, and examine the question of the benefits to the host country of the recombination plants.

Sweetened condensed milk was known in Indonesia before World War II (*Tempo* 1976b), and it was probably introduced at about the turn of the century, at the same time as in Singapore and Malaysia (see Manderson 1982). The market was small, sweetened condensed milk being a luxury item whose use probably did not extend far beyond the colonial rulers and their closest urban associates.

The market has greatly expanded in the past decade. The favorable conditions for foreign investment established under the foreign investment law of 1967 attracted a number of foreign companies into the milk recombining business, including Nestle and Foremost, and Vriesche Vlag, a name known in association with imported milk before World War II. However, the first to enter the market was Indomilk, a joint venture operation between ADI and the Indonesian partner, P.D. & I. Marison NV. The company's factory near Jakarta began commercial production of recombined sweetened condensed milk in 1969. The Indonesian partner began with 10 percent equity, but by 1977 this had reached 50 percent, as they exercised an option to buy an extra 40 percent over a ten-year period. This was Asia Dairy Industries' fourth joint venture, factories previously having been established in Singapore, Manila, and Bangkok. However, it is one of the ventures with the largest Australian equity, the same as Kowloon, the Australian Dairy Corporation having at the moment 31 percent equity in Thai Dairy Industries, 13 percent in HOMPI, the Philippines operating company.

The Australian Dairy Corporation joined a flood of Australian investors into Indonesia after 1967. Most were private capital, but the corporation and the Wheat Marketing Board were two notable exceptions. Both of these investors were seeking to create markets for Australian primary produce in countries where neither food had customarily been eaten, and both products were to be introduced in a luxury food form (McLean 1972).

At the opening of the Indomilk factory in 1969, the Hon. D. Anthony, the Deputy Prime Minister and Leader of the Country Party, made a speech which repeated the claims of the advantages of the factory to the people of Indonesia. The plant would bring employment and technical expertise and would "bring to the Indonesian people nutritious dairy products at a reasonable price and in a form most suited to local climatic conditions" (*Current Notes on International Affairs* 1969:390). Using the ideological formulation the Indonesian Government uses to talk about mutual aid (*go-*

tong royong), he stressed the mutual benefits that would flow to the two countries.

In a nation where the increasing number of rural unemployed is the crucial development problem, the Indomilk plant is capital-intensive, high technology. The cost of establishing the plant was two million dollars, creating jobs for just 300 people (McLean 1972). McLean pointed out that this was a much higher cost than that needed to establish a comparable plant in Australia. This kind of investment reflected the aim of securing markets rather than pursuing investment which takes advantage of cheap labor to enhance profitability (McLean 1972). McLean said that most of the Australian investments in Indonesia at the time were small-scale, high-cost investments with a quick return on profits (McLean 1972).

There is no doubt that the factory has been profitable. Indomilk is the largest producer of sweetened condensed milk in Indonesia, and in 1976 had a 50 percent share of the market, the rest being shared by four main contenders (*Tempo* 1977a).

The annual reports of the Australian Dairy Corporation recorded consistent, profitable trading, and *Tempo* reported that until 1976, profits totaled almost US$25 million. An Australian Dairy Corporation official who had been instrumental in establishing the plant proudly told me that it had made a profit in its first year of operation, whereas a new factory trading in Australia would take several years to reach profitable performance (personal communication 1970).

McLean further commented that the industries established by Australian capital in Indonesia were a waste of Indonesian joint-venture capital and expertise: They were not in areas that would generate sustained growth in other areas, they did not use local materials, and "the Indonesian planners find themselves committed to the protection of plants which are small and inefficient by world standards but large in relation to the domestic market" (1972:62–3). Indeed the only spin-off investment from Indomilk was the establishment of an ice cream factory, by a partnership of P.T. Indomilk and Petersville (ADC 1979:21; Government of Australia 1981:180). Since 1971, the government has closed the doors to further investment in milk processing, thus affording protection to existing investors (McLean 1972:63).

By 1977, there were complaints in the Indonesian press about foreign domination of the milk industry. Local producers complained that the foreign-owned factories would not take local milk and expressed fear that a new milk production industry would be stifled. The government and local businessmen were expressing concern about foreign domination of milk processing, and the government blocked a proposed takeover of Foremost and Vriesche Vlag, in response to complaints from local businessmen that they were not given a chance to make a bid (*Tempo* 1977b). The milk processing plant does not seem to have done much for the Indonesian economy.

However, the most serious criticism of ADC's activities in Indonesia derive not from the nature of the investment, but from the nature of the product itself, and the consequence of its extensive use. In discussing this aspect I will refer to data that I collected in a period of fieldwork in an Indonesian mining community, from 1977 to 1979.

The benefits to the people of Indonesia

We have seen the repeated claims of the nutritional benefits of the sweetened condensed milk produced in the recombination plants for the people of Southeast Asia. In Indonesia, the major nutritional problem is that many people are short of food, and in Java many do not get to eat every day. It has been estimated that in Java,

> about 25 per cent of the child population is so severely undernourished that life is threatened.... Another 25 per cent were moderately undernourished and would reach adult physical size less than their genetic potentials;... Another 25 per cent would have minor malnutrition that would cause some dimunition of body size. (McDonald 1980:186)

Milk has traditionally not been part of the Indonesian diet; indeed one of the incentives for promoting sweetened condensed milk for babies and children may be that many Indonesian adults are sickened by the unaccustomed taste of cow's milk and never drink it. Nor is milk a substitute for any item in the customary diet. It is a luxury item, and although Indomilk is cheaper than imported milk of the same type, it is not cheap in the context of the earning powers of most Indonesians. In 1977–9, the cost of one tin was Rp.250 (about 50 cents Australian) in the village where I was studying – where a casual laborer for the mining company would earn Rp.1000 per day, a high wage in Indonesia. At the same time, a day's pay for a female road worker in the island of Bali was Rp.350. Unfortunately, it is not only those people that can comfortably afford the milk who buy it. A survey that I conducted of households with children under five years of age, showed all but one household purchased sweetened condensed milk regularly. The number of cans bought ranged from two to twelve cans per month, the average being a little over two. It was clear that this was an item, like sugar, the consumption of which increased dramatically with an increase in income. The milk was mainly used in tea, to which sugar was also added. This was so for children as well as adults. It seems that for those children, the milk was little more than an added source of sugar, and an expensive one at that. The amount of protein that could be purchased for the cost of the milk far outstripped the amount of protein they would get from the milk. In this relatively affluent community, the average family would spend the cost of a can of milk for one week's supply of fish, the staple source of protein.

Initially, Indomilk was marketed with instructions for reconstituting the milk as an infant food, from the time of a baby's birth. Almost all brands of sweetened condensed milk marketed in Southeast Asia have such instructions, or carry an exhortation that it is "good for babies" and/or pictures of small babies bottle-feeding (see Fook n.d.). These labels were printed in English, presumably to convey the impression that the milk was a foreign and therefore exotic and desirable food.

The marketing practices of the milk companies began to cause alarm in Indonesia, and on 16 December 1975, the minister for health issued a decree forbidding the use of sweetened condensed milk as a baby food. Each tin had to be labeled, in Indonesian, as "Not Suitable for Babies." The minister stated that sweetened condensed milk could be dangerous for babies under one year of age. However, the nature of the potential danger was not made clear in the directive. It is not altogether clear why he acted at this time, but I have been told that it was because of expressions of concern by Indonesian pediatricians about the danger of feeding babies on sweetened condensed milk.

The directive was relayed to producers only in February 1976, and at this time the director-general for the supervision of drugs and health gave clarification. He said there had been reports from several areas that parents were mixing sweetened condensed milk with too much water, with the consequence that the nutritional value was lessened, and this had deleterious consequences for babies' health. He gave a confused answer to a question about the potential danger of blindness from vitamin A deficiency for babies fed on sweetened condensed milk, and said this was related to the problem of wrongly diluting the milk (*Tempo* 1976c).

An earlier issue of *Tempo* carried a statement from a pediatrician who pointed out that whereas before World War II it was forbidden to manufacture sweetened condensed milk from skimmed milk powder, this was now common practice. (This is the case with Indomilk.) The removal of the fat from milk reduces the vitamin A content, and such a deficiency can lead to vitamin A blindness (*Tempo* 1976b).

In March, *Tempo* further reported that the enactment of the new regulations was proceeding sluggishly: The producers had not recalled any of the old cans from sale, and they complained that the warning on the labels – "Attention: Not Suitable for Children Under One Year of Age" (in Indonesian) – was too small to be readily visible. However, they reported that the instructions for use, with directions for preparation as an infant food, had been removed in accord with the government's instructions. At this time, the director-general threatened to take action against any producers who failed to comply, and also threatened counter advertising on television, warning people that sweetened condensed milk was not suitable for babies (*Tempo* 1976c).

It is a pity such a course of action was not taken; an Australian doctor has reported that Indonesian women were still using sweetened condensed milk as an infant food in 1978. He pointed out that many of the women in Java are illiterate and cannot read the warning. The damage that was done, in implanting the idea in their minds (through advertising, etc.) that sweetened condensed milk was good for their babies has not been undone (*Choice* February 1980).

The advertising of humanized milks as baby food has not been banned (though nonhumanized powdered milks are now covered by the ban; see *Tempo* 1976a). People are subjected to a barrage of advertising of milk for babies and children. Milk advertisements often use white mothers and children, to reinforce the message that this practice is associated with the modern and powerful developed countries, with the goals they are being exhorted to aspire to. Indeed, when discussing these matters people would often express surprise that Westerners were capable of breast feeding. The identification of bottle feeding with the West is so strong, it is assumed to be our custom because we have no choice. I found that the people had already been imbued with notions of the powers of milk as a food that is good for you. Some women who otherwise breast-fed would feed children tinned milk as a medicine when they were sick. Unfortunately, advertising of milk products does not just ensure brand loyalty; it also serves to imbue a general notion that artificial feeding is good for children. In the absence of any specific attempt to educate them otherwise, the majority of Indonesian mothers are not likely to make distinctions between the properties of the various milk products available on the market: Milk is milk.

The case against the advisability for mothers in the Third World to bottle-feed their children has been well documented. It was succinctly put by Dr. S. J. Fomon, when vice president of the Twelfth International Congress on Nutrition.

> In developing countries, babies who are not breast fed die. Contaminated water, poor hygiene, lack of refrigeration, and poverty, causing formulas to be 'stretched' to nutritional impotency, make safe preparation virtually impossible. It is hard enough for these babies to survive under the best circumstances; exploitative marketing and merchandising is tantamount to mass infanticide. (Cited in *INFACT Newsletter* 1980, vol 2:8)

Apart from the problems encountered in bottle-feeding babies humanized formulas – hygiene under poor conditions, lack of money, and lack of understanding of instructions – the use of sweetened condensed milk creates additional problems. As a professor of pediatrics at the University of Indonesia explained:

> SCM contains 40 percent sugar. If a milk solution contains more than 5 percent sugar, the baby can get diarrhoea. For this reason, it must be reconstituted in a four-to-one solution. . . . Consequently, the solution contains less protein than cow's milk. If one feeds the baby a

solution which is adequate in protein content, the sugar content will be too high and the result is a possibility of diarrhoea. If it is diluted further so the sugar concentration is 5 percent, then the protein is too little. Usually mothers don't understand this and they dilute the milk till it tastes sweet enough, consequently their babies are deficient in protein and slow to develop. (*Tempo* 1976b, my translation)

It has further been pointed out that the labels of most of the sweetened condensed milk sold in Southeast Asia have instructions for reconstitution that are so imprecise that no mother could properly reconstitute the milk (*Choice* February 1980:43).

Further problems that arise when sweetened condensed milk is used as a baby food are:

1.   If protein levels are too high, it can cause stress on a baby's kidneys, as can high mineral levels.
2.   The high sugar content increases the risk of dental caries.
3.   Because the milk is made from nonfat milk powders, the baby's diet can be deficient in fatty acids.
4.   Skim milk powders are also lacking in vitamin A; hence there is the danger of vitamin A blindness (*Tempo* 28 February 1976b). However, the sweetened condensed milk sold by Asia Dairy Industries and the joint-venture companies, as with most sweetened condensed milk sold in Southeast Asia, have added vitamin A.

These properties of sweetened condensed milk make it an unsafe food even under optimal conditions that make humanized formulas adequate for babies' needs. The problems that Third World women face in using artificial feeds exacerbate the negative consequences for infants:

Defective home hygiene, lack of parental education and inadequate finance lead to the use of overdiluted, contaminated baby foods which result in episodes of diarrhoea leading to marasmus-balanced starvation, or what is commonly referred to as malnutrition. (*Choice* 1980:42)

When babies are artificially fed, they are more likely to get infective diarrhoea. As a consequence, they may develop an intolerance of sugar of milk (lactose) and the added sugar in the sweetened condensed milk (sucrose) resulting in secondary osmotic diarrhoea. This further exacerbates the calorie and protein deficiencies in the babies' diet, especially if their mothers are overdiluting the milk. They become more and more susceptible to infection and diarrhoea until, over nine months to a year they have malnutrition. (Dr. M. Dibley, cited in *Choice* 1980:42)

The conditions that operated against safe bottle feeding were very much in evidence in the village where I did fieldwork (see Robinson 1985). Clean water was a problem, and, though people understood the need to boil drinking water, they did not really know the reason for this, so could not be guaranteed to use sterile procedures when preparing bottles. A rinse-out with boiled water was generally regarded as adequate cleaning. The indigenous women of the village were very committed to breast-feeding their babies, and the only bottle-fed babies were those whose mothers had died, or who could not provide enough milk. However, bottle feeding was common among the elite Indonesian women in the nearby company town, and, as these women provided the model of urban life-style to which the village women aspired (and they were already emulating them in dress, decor, and so on), one can only wonder how long it will be before they begin to bottle-feed.

Indeed, this community, which was undergoing rapid social change of the type generally regarded as "modernization" because of the transition from subsistence agriculture to wage labor, is exactly the sort of community where one could expect such changes to occur. It is often assumed that women turn to bottle feeding because of structural changes in their productive roles, as they enter into wage labor. However, I feel it is more associated with women's new role as *consumers* of goods in the capitalist marketplace, rather than with their role as *producers* in a capitalist economy. Bottle feeding is identified with the power of the West, the greater physical size of Westerners, and the desirable modern life-style. (During my fieldwork, a woman whose milk had dried up while her baby was hospitalized turned to infant formula to feed him. His enormous physical size, as compared with breast-fed babies, was favorably commented on by the village women and attributed to the Westerner's infant formula, which I had helped her obtain.) Advertising is important in creating these wants and behaviors, but it is not the only important factor. In the village I was studying, ideas about the power of milk had taken hold in the absence of much advertising: Few people read newspapers, and radiocassette players were used more to play cassettes than to listen to the radio. In this situation, the emulation of the elite, who had already adapted to an urban life-style was more significant.

This view, that the decline in breast feeding is more to do with women's role as consumers, rather than producers, is given some support in the findings of the World Fertility Survey (Jain and Bongaarts 1981). This showed that women with higher education, and those who lived in urban areas breast-fed their children for a shorter period than those who had lower education and lived in rural areas. The husband's occupation was also significantly correlated with duration of breast feeding; presumably this is related to whether or not there was enough money to buy milk. The survey found that whether or not women had worked since marriage did not seem to have an important and consistent effect on breast feeding (Jain and Bongaarts 1981:90). A significant factor in the transition to bottle feeding in urban areas is the change in family structures with rural–urban migration. Women in the cities often do not have the supports they had in the home village, which make breast feeding easier. I noticed, during my fieldwork, that the traditional midwife would move in with the new mother for several days after the birth, as would many female relatives. They took over the running of the household and washed the baby's clothes. The new mother was free to focus on the child, and to establish feeding. In the case of first mothers, the midwife and the other women gave instruction and encouragement. After the initial weeks, when the household settled down to normal, a woman with no young daughters of her own would generally get help from female relatives, leaving her free to care for the newborn baby (see Robinson 1983). Many of these supports (especially important in the early days of the baby's life because they would leave the woman relaxed and free to establish breast feeding) are lacking in an urban situation, where women are less likely to have extensive numbers of kin to call on. Indeed, in the village, the few mothers I knew who bottle-fed were young migrant women whose husbands had regular paid employment.

The World Fertility Survey showed a decline in breast feeding, a trend that is likely to continue over time. This represents a growing market for the milk products of industrial capitalism. As with many products of the factories of capitalism, it is not the products in themselves that are deleterious, but the way in which these products are promoted, to serve the need of capital for expanding markets, overriding any concern for the human needs of the populations involved. Humanized baby formulas are very important to mothers who cannot breast-feed, or in cases where mothers have died. The scandal is that milk companies have used unscrupulous marketing practices to sell milk products to women who do not need them, cannot afford them, and do not have the facilities to prepare bottles with proper hygiene.

The problems associated with the introduction of artificial feeding of babies in the Third World are exacerbated by the use of sweetened condensed milk rather than humanized formulas. Sweetened condensed milk has the lowest nutritional value of all infant feeds, but it is also the cheapest and so more within people's reach. In Indonesia, the cost of a can of humanized infant formula is over four times the cost of a can of sweetened condensed milk. The advertising which has exhorted women to feed artificially has not only had the effect of capturing brand loyalty, it has also promoted the idea among women that bottle feeding is desirable and that women who cannot afford the humanized formula may substitute the cheaper alternative.

Throughout Southeast Asia, sweetened condensed milk has been promoted as an infant food. A survey conducted in 1979 showed that in all countries except Indonesia, where the directive referred to above was in force, it was almost universally sold with instructions for reconstituting it as an infant food, or with exhortations that it is good for babies. The products surveyed included four manufactured by joint-venture operatives of Asia Dairy Industries (Fook n.d.). So the Australian Dairy Corporation was in the anomalous and morally questionable situation of selling a product labeled unsuitable for babies in one country, and marketing it, an identical product, as an infant food in four other countries. *Choice*, the magazine of the Australian Consumers Association, took this question up with the Department of Primary Industry and the Australian Dairy Corporation.

The Department of Primary Industry denied any responsibility in the matter, saying that the labeling was the problem of the manufacturing companies. As these were all partly owned subsidiaries of Asia Dairy Industries which is a wholly owned subsidiary of a statutory authority under the Department's control, *Choice* has rightly asked, "Who is in control?" (*Choice* 1980:43). (The question of the apparent lack of control which the Parliament had over the subsidiaries of the Australian Dairy Corporation was one that also vexed the Senate committee; see Government of Australia 1981).

When journalists put a similar question to Mr. Norwood, general manager of the Australian Dairy Corporation, he "defended the Corporation, saying that the sales were within the laws of the country concerned, and it was hardly up to the Corporation to tell other governments what their health laws should be" (Hodgkinson 25 June 1980).

This statement has a hollow ring in the light of the claims by the corporation and other representatives of the dairy industry, of the nutritional benefits of the product, for children and babies.

Following the publication of the *Choice* article, a question was asked in the Senate, of the minister representing the minister for primary industry (Senator Scott) as to whether the government was aware of the article, and whether steps had been taken to stop the practice of promoting sweetened condensed milk as an infant food in Southeast Asia. The questioner asked the minister to investigate "whether perhaps through inadvertance or for some other reason, the ADC, through ADI (HK) Ltd., is undertaking a marketing exercise now thought on medical grounds to be inadvisable" (Parliament of Australia 1980).

I think we can be sure that there was nothing inadvertent in the practice: We have seen the many statements made by the industry and its representatives concerning the nutritional benefits of the product for babies, and nothing was done to change marketing practices in other countries after the Indonesian banning. In his reply to the question, Senator Scott said that Australian Dairy Corporation and the dairy industry have been advised to see that this sort of advertising of sweetened condensed milk as a baby food will not be permitted. In response to a suggestion from the questioner, he replied that he thought there was "an opportunity for the marketing of such an Australian product in the area of food for older children and teenagers, and no doubt it will be suitably promoted along these lines" (Parliament of Australia 1980). None of these issues was taken up by the Senate inquiry into the Asian operations.

It is a sad comment on the values of a government that appears to be more concerned with administrative improprieties than marketing practices of a subsidiary company of a statutory authority of that government, that pursues the expansion of markets to prop up a declining and uneconomic industry at the expense of the health – even the lives – of Southeast Asian babies.

Part IV

RESEARCH METHOD AND DIRECTION

11. Dietary taboos in Java: Myths, mysteries, and methodology

Valerie J. Hull

Detailed descriptions of the diverse and often colorful food taboos found in Java abound in the literature: We are told of *kepel*, the fruit with horizontal seeds that the pregnant woman must avoid lest the fetus present in a transverse position; of bananas grown together, prohibited lest she give birth to Siamese twins. Fish can spoil mother's milk and cause worms if eaten by young children; women should not consume "cooling" fruits and vegetables which will cause impoverished blood. A number of studies – general nutrition surveys (Tan et al. 1970; Sri Kardjati, Kusin, and de With 1977) as well as research on customs relating to pregnancy, lactation, and child rearing (Blankhart, Tarwotjo, and Soetadi 1960; Geertz 1961), and in other works in the fields of food and health (Poorwo 1962; Edmundson 1976) – have produced an extensive catalog of taboo food items and the consequences believed to be associated with their consumption by particular groups in the population. The Appendix to this chapter presents a brief inventory of reported dietary taboos from major sources. Unfortunately, the information we have so far is in fact *only* a catalog or inventory. We have no factual information on the relative strengths of various beliefs; on actual dietary changes during vulnerable periods such as pregnancy; or on regional, generational, or socioeconomic class differences in the society.

Despite the lack of quantitative data, beliefs and taboos associated with food are almost invariably implicated in discussions of inadequate nutrition, and are sometimes assigned a predominant role. Yet many factors are responsible for the nutritional problems that exist today in Java: ecological constraints; transport and storage limitations; food preparation; and, of course, poverty and, for lack of a better term, ignorance. We need better information on these underlying causes, not merely as an academic exercise in how to assign the blame for poor nutrition, but as baseline information for the design of effective programs in nutrition improvement. Although dietary prohibitions are of potentially great impact, nutrition education and other programs will need to be based on more than a catalog of interesting beliefs.

In the following pages we will present several approaches that have been used in collecting data on dietary taboos, and suggest some of the limitations of such research. We will show a few of the common assumptions, some of them myths, that underlie past research. Some basic inconsistencies and gaps in the data remain as mysteries for future research to clarify, and some suggestions are made for methodological strategies most likely to obtain successfully this much-needed information on the role of dietary taboos in Javanese nutrition.

The normative approach

Perhaps the most complete survey of the sociocultural aspects of dietary patterns in Indonesia was carried out by Tan et al. in 1969–70. It covered a sample of 45 families from each of two villages in the provinces of West, Central, and East Java, Bali, and South Sumatra. The specific question relating to dietary taboos was phrased as follows:

Are there any kinds of food that are taboo for:

	Kind of food	Reason
1. Infants 0–1 year		
2. Children 1–5 years		
3. Children 6 years and over		
4. Young girls		
5. Pregnant women		
6. Nursing mothers		
7. Males		
8. In general		

Presentation of results is in the form of examples of responses given in each of the provinces represented, for example:

In West Java, pregnant women are not allowed to eat pineapple or *salak*, a fruit which if eaten in large quantities may cause constipation.... In Central Java the same prohibition against eating pineapple exists. Other foods mentioned are fresh fish, *ikan wader, labu* (a kind of squash) and *kepel*.... (Tan et al. 1970:70-1)

This is what may be called a "normative" approach, that is, eliciting responses which refer to items thought to be prohibited in the society.[1] Treatment of dietary taboos in the ethnographic literature is also based largely on this approach. Geertz (1961), in the most complete ethnography focusing on the Javanese family, discussed taboos during pregnancy in the following passage:

1 It is important to note that the primary respondent for this survey was the male head of the household, except for a section on infant and child feeding. Although in practice other family members probably contributed answers to questions, the source of answers to these questions is not clear.

The mother should not eat certain things: sugar cane – because, if she does, at birth the baby will start to come out, stop, start again, stop, etc.; a fruit called *kepel*, which has seeds with lines running horizontally – because then the baby will be born sideways; eel – because the eel gives birth to young, they say, as humans do. (Geertz 1961:86)

She went on to describe several behavioral taboos, also introduced with the normative phrase "she should not...," and all probably representing a collection of normative statements from a few informants.

These accounts tell us little about the actual behavior of women in complying with the "taboos." Also, and just as important in terms of policy implications, they do not tell us whether the food items mentioned are in fact common in the normal diet, that is, the extent to which a taboo represents a significant deprivation. The relative prominence of a particular prohibition might be indicated by the frequency with which it is mentioned by different informants, and perhaps also by the clarity of response concerning reasons for the taboo. However, this information is not provided by past studies, and we are left with an interesting but basically descriptive account of some taboos which may or may not be relevant to the nutritional status of the population.

The hypothetical approach

A more recent, large-scale nutrition study in East Java collected anthropometric, clinical and dietary data from over 2,000 mothers and 5,000 children 0–15 years of age (Sri Kardjati, Kusin, and de With 1977). Information on dietary taboos for pregnant and lactating women was gathered by asking all women:

1. Are there foods you would avoid when pregnant?
2. Are there foods you would avoid when lactating?

Although this approach is somewhat more direct than one asking about societal norms, it is still a step removed from actual behavior, and might be termed a "hypothetical" approach. The discussion of results is brief, and phrased as though the question were factual rather than hypothetical:

About 10–15%[2] of the mothers observed food restrictions when pregnant or lactating.... Most frequently avoided were fresh fish, *kluwih...capar* or *taoge* (bean sprouts), *lombok* (chilis) and pineapple.

Once again, we are given little more than a catalog of food items thought to be taboo. Yet the survey could have provided more direct, quantitative data by analyzing dietary patterns of women currently pregnant or lactating at the time of the survey. Various clinical and nutritional indicators are presented

2 The range represents varying results from the five areas included in the study.

for these women separately, yet information of dietary patterns (frequency of types of food consumed) were analyzed for the total sample only, with no comparison among subgroups of interest. Response to the survey question above is also not analyzed separately for pregnant or lactating women for whom the question had direct rather than hypothetical application, so we do not know whether variations in response were associated with women's status at the time of the survey.

Direct questions on current dietary changes

A recent study by the author (Hull 1978; hereafter referred to as the Ngaglik study, from the subdistrict of Yogyakarta in which the research was located) interviewed pregnant and postpartum women monthly over a two-year period as part of research into the factors influencing birth spacing.[3] Although nutrition was not a primary focus of the study, basic dietary and anthropometric data were collected in order to investigate the possible role of nutrition as an intermediate variable in the relation between lactation and postpartum infecundity. The study design also provided an opportunity to add a component on infant nutrition and development, an important subject for which longitudinal data are lacking in Indonesia. Survey data were supplemented by periodic, single-round surveys on selected topics such as "morning sickness" during pregnancy, breast-feeding problems, and others; by case studies, direct observation, and field notes; and, for one segment of the study, by taped interviews.

The basic questionnaire on types of food consumed by both women and infants was administered monthly. At this time, several direct questions were also asked on dietary changes related to lactation, pregnancy, and those specifically for infants. In posing these questions, we were specifically interested in beliefs that actually led to a *change* in the type of food that would otherwise have been eaten. These questions thus used a basic format illustrated by the following example for breast-feeding mothers: In the past month is there anything which you normally would eat but this month did not eat, because you are currently breast-feeding? Information was collected on specific types of food and their presumed effect/reasons for avoidance. In addition, women were asked about:

---

3 Over 500 women who experienced a confinement during 1976 were interviewed monthly over a two-year period; data were collected on pregnancy, conditions of delivery, and postpartum variables such as breast feeding, amenorrhea, abstinence, and use of birth control. In addition, weighing and measurement sessions were held every *selapan*, a 35-day period in the cycle of the five-day Javanese week and seven-day Gregorian week. This interval was selected so that women could more easily remember when sessions were held. For the purposes of this discussion the *selapan* interval will be referred to as a "month." At these sessions a basic anthropometric examination was carried out on both mother and infant, and information gathered on illnesses and on diet (according to food groups) during the preceding month (*selapan*).

Table 11.1. *Proportions reporting food avoidance in month preceding the interview, and main types of foods avoided (Ngaglik, 1976–1978)*

Group/status		Percent reporting avoidance	Types of food avoided[a]
Pregnant women			
Trimester I		10	Ice (3%)
II		10	
III		6	
Lactating women			
Months post partum	1–6	38	Fresh fish (7%), salt fish (6%),
	7–12	29	other animal protein (3%),
	13–18	18	ice (3%)
	19–24	14	
	25–30	15	
Breast-fed infants			
Age in months	1–6	2	Fish, fresh and salted (3%)
	7–12	5	
	13–18	9	
	19–24	11	
	25–30	13	
Weaned infants			
Age in months	1–6	—[a]	Fresh fish (4%), salt fish (6%)
	7–12	11	
	13–18	13	
	19–24	13	
	25–30	10	

[a] Only types of food recorded in 3% or more of observations are reported. Food items were coded in 10 categories (e.g., fruits, vegetable protein) with up to 99 codes for individual items (e.g., specific fruits, common sources of vegetable protein). Types of food reported above represent those that reached frequencies of 3% or more by either category or individual codes.

1. Foods they ate in decreased quantity that month
2. Foods they normally did not consume but did eat that month
3. Foods they ate in added quantity that month related to their breast-feeding/current pregnancy status

The results of the direct question on foods avoided are summarized in Table 11.1, which shows the very small percentage of women responding positively to the questions as phrased above. The exception is among lactating women, but even here the percentage declines rapidly as the lactation period progresses. The number of food items mentioned in frequencies of three percent of observations or more is also very small, even though the variations of responses ranged up to over 40 specific foods avoided by lactating mothers. Many, however, were mentioned in only one or two observations out of a total of over 4,500 interviews. We did not receive responses such as *kepel* fruit or twin bananas, as found in the ethnographic literature, primarily because we restricted questions to items normally eaten. Even presumably more common foods such as pineapple, widely reported as taboo during pregnancy because of its abortifacient qualities, were seldom recorded in this context, because this expensive fruit would not normally be consumed except by the wealthier villagers. These results then focus specifically on deviation from normal diet due to food beliefs, and indicate quite minimal impact.

Reasons given for avoiding food items were almost as varied as the types of food items themselves. Fish, the most frequently mentioned taboo item, was avoided out of fear of its causing worms in young children, a common claim in the literature. However, it was also linked to diarrhea, various respiratory symptoms, skin disease, and eye trouble. Breast-feeding mothers who avoided fish were doing so in order to prevent contaminated breast milk, causing these complaints in infants. It must be recalled, however, that some 80–90 percent of mothers of all statuses did not report even this common "taboo" as an avoided food.

This is not to say that these mothers and infants in fact consumed fresh or salt fish on a regular basis. As the next section illustrates, in the majority of monthly observations of young infants, no animal protein at all was consumed. This is also the case for anywhere from one-fifth to one-third of women, regardless of pregnancy or lactation status. An important consideration in that section will be a preliminary investigation of the extent to which this is due to specific taboos rather than general food habits and other underlying causes.

The results of direct questioning on taboos were also analyzed according to background variables, including age and several indicators of socioeconomic status. Although older women of lower education or income tended to report slightly more food prohibitions, well over 80 percent of even these women claimed not to have avoided a food normally eaten.

The direct approach in obtaining data on dietary taboos may have serious limitations if people are embarrassed by their beliefs or behavior, or otherwise feel they should conceal them. Sri Kardjati and colleagues (1977) commented on the low proportion reporting taboos, with the hypothetical approach as suspect for this reason; they claimed that mothers "seem reluctant to admit their food prejudices." Although there may have been some underreporting, it seems unwarranted to make the assumption that low frequencies necessarily mean invalid data. The fact that the patterns in Ngaglik (Table 11.1) vary according to women's lactation or pregnancy status and according to the age of the child, indicates that the responses did reflect to some degree conscious behavior of mothers in certain foods at certain times, even though this occurred in a low percentage of observations.[4]

General data on dietary patterns

Both of the studies cited earlier (Tan et al. 1970 and Sri Kardjati et al. 1977) also collected general data on dietary patterns by asking which of certain basic types of food are consumed and with what frequency (more than once a day, once a day, at least three times a week, less than three times a week, seldom, or never). Data refer to overall household consumption not based on a fixed time reference period (i.e., they refer to what is generally eaten in the household). The main conclusions reached in both studies are that the basic daily diet consists of rice and a chili relish, usually with the addition of a vegetable dish, soybean preparation, or salted or fresh fish. The predominant side dish tends to vary with the area studied. Both studies found not only regional differences but intraregional differences based on more prosperous versus poorer areas. Although Tan and associates (1970:58) claimed that dietary patterns were relatively homogeneous among individual households regardless of socioeconomic status, in fact the data for many provinces do show contrasts in consumption among landholding groups and education categories. In Central Java, for example, large landowners are two times more likely to consume vegetable protein daily than are small landowners.[5]

Similar information was collected in the Ngaglik study; however, data are based on dietary patterns in the month preceding the interview, and refer to consumption by the mother and by the child rather than by the household unit. The weaknesses of data of this nature on dietary intake are obvious and have been documented in other studies: Information is lacking on the actual quantity of food consumed[6]; there are often difficulties in determining standard food groups for comparison and in assigning local foods to appropriate groups; there are problems of recall in general and perhaps also differentially according to specific food categories; and there may be overstatement of prestigious foods and understatement of low-status foods. Nevertheless, such data might give some important supplementary information

4 It must be remembered that percentages reported in the Ngaglik analysis refer to monthly observations; that is, women appear more than once in the distributions, as they are followed longitudinally. In the current analysis, data are examined cross-sectionally; however, future work will be able to trace changes in individual behavior over the two years of the study.

5 Some of the lack of clear-cut findings in the analysis were due to small cell sizes once the data were divided into categories, and to the fact that only column percentages were calculated, representing the percentage in each frequency of consumption group which fell into the various categories of socioeconomic status, rather than vice versa.

6 Chassy, van Veen, and Young (1967:56–7), however, did review several studies which showed that food frequency scores on surveys correlate highly with actual amounts or weights of foods consumed.

in a study of food avoidances through a comparison of patterns among various groups in the population. In the case where avoidances refer to an item of general significance in the diet, we might expect to see an impact on the patterns of consumption among groups for which the item is considered taboo. If, on the other hand, only a single type of food not significant to the normal diet were taboo, we would not expect an effect on the pattern by food types. Such an exercise would thus accord with our objective of assessing the impact of food beliefs on nutritional adequacy.

The average reported frequencies of consumption of food items according to basic nutritional categories will be reported in subsequent discussions. As the main focus of the present analysis, however, we will concentrate on the patterns of avoided foods, or foods reported as not consumed during the month prior to the interview. Table 11.2 shows few markedly different patterns among women of various statuses, the major exception being higher proportions of women avoiding items in the animal protein group during late pregnancy and the first year post partum, but regardless of lactation status. Fruit is also apparently avoided to a greater extent by early postpartum women, and particularly by those lactating. For all food types, there is a slight increase in nonconsumption over the course of pregnancy to the early postpartum period, with a subsequent decline in the late postpartum period.

The figures for children illustrate the gradual addition of new types of food as infants grow older, but by two years of age and older they are still not receiving an adult diet: High proportions did not receive any item from either the vegetable or animal protein group during the entire month preceding the interview, and proportions not receiving green vegetables were nearly as high. The diet of weaned infants appears to be much better, a pattern also reported in an early study by Blankhart et al. (1960). In the case of Ngaglik data, this is due in part to the fact that weaned infants are selected mainly from the upper economic groups, who tend to wean infants earlier and who can afford better diets for their children.

Can these very general patterns provide clues as to the impact of dietary taboos on nutritional adequacy? If taboos were largely responsible for, say, the lack of adequate animal or vegetable protein among nursing mothers, we would expect to see a more divergent pattern for lactating versus nonlactating women than is apparent in the table. Although there are some differences, the changing pattern according to months post partum (1–12 and 13–30) is more striking than that between lactators and nonlactators, indicating that perhaps more attention should be given to dietary changes in the puerperium for all women. We must not lose sight of the fact, however, that even among nonlactating, nonpregnant women more than a year post partum, fairly high proportions are still not consuming foods from desirable nutrition categories. Furthermore, an investigation of income differentials

Table 11.2. *Percentage not consuming a given type of nonstaple food during the month preceding the interview, Ngaglik, 1976-1978*

Group/status	Type of food						
	Green vegetables	Banana	Other fruit	Vegetable protein	Meat/Fish	Eggs	Milk
Pregnant women							
Trimester I	0	40	26	2	22	36	86
II	1	34	25	2	26	43	89
III	3	43	30	3	34	43	90
Lactating women							
Months post partum 1–12	1	43	49	2	31	43	87
13–30	1	38	42	1	18	39	90
Nonpregnant, nonlactating women							
Months post partum 1–12	2	45	41	2	27	41	89
13–30	1	34	30	2	14	34	84
Breast-fed infants							
Age in months							
1–6	99.5	69	98	98	100	98	86
7–12	90	70	91	75	97	84	88
13–18	65	62	72	40	79	63	88
19–24	42	51	53	23	52	47	90
25–30	26	42	48	20	47	43	91
Weaned infants							
Age in months							
1–6	—[a]	—[a]	—[a]	—[a]	—[a]	—[a]	—[a]
7–12	84	44	81	61	91	52	7
13–18	48	41	53	23	65	31	29
19–24	21	35	36	10	43	25	63
25–30	13	33	31	6	19	20	68

[a] N < 30.

in the frequency scores[7] of food items consumed indicates that these contrasts are often greater than those among women of different lactation or pregnancy statuses. Table 11.3 shows patterns according to income for nonpregnant, nonlactating women. Contrasts are particularly striking for the more expensive items in the diet: vegetable protein, fruit, and the various sources of animal protein.[8] Although food beliefs may play a role in women's diets, the significance of economic constraints should not be overlooked.

The inadequate diet of young children is a more complex problem, related to general food habits and notions of appropriate foods at certain ages. In the broad sense of food avoidances, this is significant, and has been addressed briefly by some researchers in other contexts. It has been reported in Malaya, for example, that mothers do not give vegetables to children until their molars appear; otherwise they might choke (McArthur 1962:57). This might not be recorded as a "taboo" per se, yet if widespread, it is obviously a potentially important determinant of infant nutrition.

In the direct questioning on taboos, the proportion of Ngaglik mothers who avoided giving a child food because it was taboo or *pantang* was very low, and increased rather than decreased with age. Logically food thought of as "taboo" would be mentioned only after a child had reached an age when it was actually conceivable that the food could form a part of his or her diet: Fish is not "taboo" for the six-month-old infant, for it is not yet an appropriate food. The result in terms of the child's dietary intake would be the same, but it is important to distinguish the underlying reasons in order to formulate effective nutrition education programs.

7 Dietary data were collected by asking how frequently during the past *selapan* (35 days) women ate foods from various food groups, for example, vegetable protein (pulses and beans and nuts), meat/fish/poultry, green leafy vegetables, and so on. In the field, responses were recorded as in the following example for the category of vegetable protein:

Tempe (fermented soybean cake)	one time every day	= 35 times
Tahu (soybean curd)	one time every two days	= 17 times
Burjo (drink made from mung beans)	three times	= 3 times

This example yields a total frequency "score" of 55, which was the information coded. The scoring system was intended only as a rough approximation of diet patterns, because the final coded item did not distinguish between specific types of food, quantity consumed, or spacing over the 35-day period, and because recall errors would necessarily result in estimates rather than precise information on frequencies. The scores do show interesting variations by season, socioeconomic status, and other variables, however, and are a convenient way of summarizing broad patterns.

8 The more frequent rice consumption of upper-income women may indicate that more of these women eat three times a day rather than twice a day, an aspect discussed later in the section, Decreased consumption of food items during pregnancy. One might then argue that all the frequency figures in Table 11.3 reflect this difference in meal habits and that lower-income women, though eating less frequently, may still consume quantities equal to or greater than upper-income women. Although this is a possibility, the fact that inexpensive food items (cassava, green vegetables) do not show great differences in frequency according to income lends support instead to the conclusion that the frequency scores do reflect quantities consumed, and that there are real differences, in protein consumption especially, according to income.

Table 11.3. *Average reported frequency[a] of consumption of food items in specified categories by nonlactating, nonpregnant women according to income group*

	Income group		
Food category	Lower	Middle	Upper
Rice/maize	79	83	94
Cassava/yam	19	18	19
Vegetable protein	35	43	63
Green vegetables	21	22	26
Fruit (incl. banana)	7	8	17
Meat/fish	8	10	15
Eggs	2	3	9
Milk	2	1	7

[a] The number of times items from each food category were consumed during the month preceding the interview. See footnote 7 for an explanation of frequency scores and coding procedures.

The influence of economic constraints is also apparent in the infant diet. Striking differences in the supplementary feeding of breast-fed infants become apparent as they approach a more adult diet. After age 18 months, we find vegetable protein consumed in the vast majority (about 85 percent) of observations in the upper-income group, but for nearly a third of lower-income infants no vegetable protein was recorded as consumed in the month preceding the interview (data not shown). Differences for the even more expensive items of animal protein were also considerable.

Although these contrasts should not be surprising, it is important to note that reports of economic class differences do not appear prominently in the literature, which has instead stressed that families of all strata eat the same basic diet. Although it may be true that even the diet of the better-off Ngaglik women and children is far from adequate, for the poor it is measurably worse.

Income-group contrasts were supported by anthropometric data, which showed that women in the upper-income category had higher weights, heights, upper-arm circumference, and triceps skinfold measurements at given points in time over pregnancy and the postpartum period. Their infants showed the same pattern; for example, by age 24–30 months, nearly a third of the lower-income children versus 17 percent of upper-income children were below 70 percent of the Harvard weight-for-age standard. Growth patterns for infants from the two income groups, with comparative data from the very poor Gunung Kidul region of Yogyakarta (Bailey 1962a), are shown in Figure 11.1.

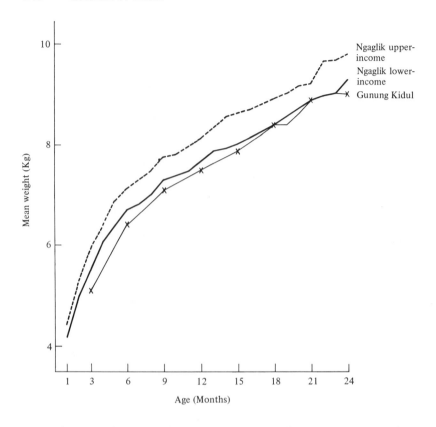

Figure 11.1. Mean body weight by age, Ngaglik 1976–1978, comparing upper- and lower-income groups and data from Gunung Kidul.

Future research: myths and mysteries

Our knowledge of dietary taboos in Java is still rudimentary, and a great deal of research remains to be done in clarifying the role of traditional beliefs on dietary adequacy. In formulating future research priorities and plans, there are a number of points that may profitably act as guidelines. First are a number of assumptions that to varying degrees[9] underlie much of the research on dietary – and other – taboos. They are often detectable implicitly, and sometimes explicitly, in discussions by Indonesian health personnel and policy makers.

9 These "myths" are expressed as extremes for the present argument. Few researchers actually see things in quite this simplified way; however, many do tend toward this end of the continuum. Indonesian elites are often more conservative than researchers in their knowledge of and attitudes toward rural life. These "myths," then, are not merely straw men advanced to construct an argument.

Mean body weight by age, Ngaglik 1976–1978, comparing data for upper- and lower-income groups and data from Gunung Kidul

Age (months)	Mean body weight (kg)			Age (months)	Mean body weight (kg)		
	Ngaglik upper income	Ngaglik lower income	Gunung Kidul		Ngaglik upper income	Ngaglik lower income	Gunung Kidul
0	3.436	3.216		13	8.335	7.897	
1	4.407	4.174		14	8.565	7.922	
2	5.290	4.959		15	8.624	8.007	7.88
3	5.929	5.527	5.09	16	8.705	8.148	
4	6.384	6.052		17	8.810	8.239	
5	6.871	6.410		18	8.936	8.421	8.40
6	7.120	6.716	6.40	19	9.026	8.419	
7	7.333	6.808		20	9.178	8.637	
8	7.490	7.032		21	9.219	8.867	8.87
9	7.714	7.308	7.10	22	9.664	8.978	
10	7.802	7.386		23	9.698	9.021	
11	7.967	7.469		24	9.805	9.291	9.04
12	8.140	7.665	7.53				

Following this section, we record a few "mysteries," including some of the many omissions, conflicting findings, and unresolved issues that have emerged from the information published so far, and that should have high priority for future research.

Some myths

The myth of the superstitious peasant. Descriptions of dietary and behavioral taboos in Java often convey an image of fear-ridden, superstitious villagers. In discussing the period of pregnancy, for example, writers have tended to portray a very cautious period in which women must consciously, and seemingly constantly, avoid a host of foods, gestures, and behavior out of fear of harming the fetus. This picture contrasts sharply with the more matter-of-fact attitude toward pregnancy which we observed in Ngaglik. As we have indicated, many of the food taboos actually refer mainly to unusual food or food not normally consumed for economic reasons. Some of the behavioral taboos are similarly quite trivial prohibitions that would not greatly interfere with normal routine, and some supposed "taboos" were in fact regularly transgressed for the sake of convenience. A good example is the taboo described by Whyte (1974:64):

> In Indonesia and Malaya, the father should not kill or wound any animal during his wife's pregnancy, or the child may be wounded in the same way. This affects the protein intake of the entire family.

Virtually every informant will speak of this taboo; however, this statement gives the impression that it has a marked impact on the family diet, an impression faulty for two reasons: First, as we have shown, normal dietary patterns rarely include animal protein, and when meat is consumed, it is normally purchased in small quantities from the market rather than obtained by slaughtering household animals. Second, the pragmatic Javanese can in any case get around this taboo through an "escape clause": The phrase "*Ojo kaget, jabang bayi*" (or a variation), meaning "Don't be alarmed, baby in the womb," if uttered at the time the act is committed, is believed to prevent the undesired consequences.

Beliefs serve a useful function as an ex post facto explanation if something does actually go wrong with the birth, or with the development of the child. A woman giving birth to a child with a purple birthmark seeks an explanation of why this misfortune should befall her – a remembered purple fruit consumed during pregnancy may provide the explanation and, in some ways, consolation. This kind of belief is, however, conceptually very different from a taboo which affects normal behavior.

Villagers of course have their superstitions; so do urban educated Indonesians, and so do we in the West. Serious research on the effect of dietary taboos must not be misled by overemphasis on the role of superstition in the lives of Javanese villagers.

The myth of the homogeneous village. Research in many disciplines in Indonesia has tended to treat village society as a whole rather than recognizing the diversity based on generations, socioeconomic class, gender, and other characteristics. The Ngaglik study showed that even though dietary patterns were similar, in a very general sense, measurable differences were related to income and other factors. The fact that anthropometric data showed similar variation reinforced these findings.

Other studies have recorded minimal variation in diets. It may well be that in some regions differences are not important, or that differences have increased since the time previous research was conducted. This must be a matter to be investigated, however, rather than assumed.

The myth of the conservative peasant. The ethnographic present is a useful tool for anthropologists but can be misinterpreted by researchers or others who accept a single cross-sectional account as representative of a society's customs and beliefs. In diet as in other aspects of culture, additions, deletions, and other forms of change occur over the years, sometimes with observable impact and sometimes with more subtlety. Changes in diet are accompanied by changes in food beliefs. One of the more frequently mentioned taboos for pregnant women in Ngaglik was ice. Flavored-ice vendors regularly come to the village, which is located some 10 kilometers from the nearest electricity supply, and sell this delicacy to those who can afford it.

Obviously this was not an item in the "traditional" diet, yet it is known in sufficient frequency today to be associated with undesired consequences during pregnancy.[10]

A belief in the addition of green leafy vegetables to the diet during lactation[11] is another example of an introduced belief, a fact attested to by the reason almost invariably given for this dietary change: "*Supaya tambah vitamin*" ("to add vitamins").

Another recent change, one with potentially significant negative impact, has been the flood of sweet biscuits and manufactured candy in Java, to some extent replacing rice, corn, and cassava-based snacks. At a major urban hospital's well-baby clinic, a sweet tea biscuit (*roti Mari*) is listed as one of the recommended weaning foods for infants three months of age. Sweets were not mentioned as foods "bad for children" in either of the large surveys cited above, nor as prohibited foods in the Ngaglik study. It is an important phenomenon for future policy-oriented research.

The myth of tradition as harmful. The notion of "glorious traditions" aside, in many developing countries today tradition is seen as a body of harmful beliefs and practices which form an obstacle to economic and social development. Although, on one level, Indonesia's elite recognize that some aspects of tradition are worth preserving, development programs in villages are too often aimed at eliminating the "old" ways and substituting the "new" in a wholesale manner. I have argued elsewhere (Hull 1979) in the context of traditional birth practices that training courses for *dukun bayi* (traditional midwives) might be better received if they showed respect for the positive practices being performed and tolerance for harmless practices such as recitation of *mantras*, rather than denigrating all traditional ways in their teaching of "correct" modern medical procedures.

In diet as in other spheres of behavior, many beliefs are harmless, helpful at least in a psychological sense, or intrinsically beneficial. For example, the prohibition on eating "Siamese twin" bananas obviously has little nutritional impact and, although interesting, should not receive a disproportionate amount of attention in either the research literature or in nutrition education programs. It is a harmless belief. The prohibition on, or decrease in the consumption of, chilis for the breast-feeding mother is probably a beneficial custom, because it has been shown that some substances pass into the milk

---

10 Virtually all who mentioned ice as a taboo claimed that it would enlarge the baby in the womb, causing a difficult birth. The association of ice with fatness is an elusive one which direct questioning did not resolve; perhaps there is a direct association with added fluid, or perhaps an association of ices with the better-off (and hence fatter) segments of the population who consume it.

11 This addition was reported in the direct questioning on dietary changes, during breast feeding, where as high as 47 percent of women reported adding to the quantity of green leafy vegetables consumed. This was further supported by frequency scores for this category on the actual dietary pattern survey.

and the oils may have an irritating effect on the infant's digestive tract. The near-universal consumption of herbal mixtures by lactating women may also be beneficial, either through increased fluid intake, a psychological effect, or directly through a possible galactagoguic effect.

There are, obviously, traditions that are harmful. Research should aim at identifying and classifying beliefs according to their potential effect, so that policy makers can directly incorporate these findings into their programs.

Some mysteries

The fish taboo for children. Fish is mentioned as taboo in virtually all studies, and is one of the few consistently reported items even among the small proportions reporting dietary taboos in Ngaglik. It has been reported for Malaysia (Whyte 1974:65) and China (Blankhart et al. 1960:23-4). Yet Mely Tan et al. have noted (1970:97) that in one of their study areas where such a taboo was reported, children were observed eating fish cakes, and Tarwotjo and Suhadi Hardjo (1964) found fish to be widely consumed in their study areas of West Java where adequate rainfall allowed fish to be raised. Blankhart et al. (1960:23-4) reported that very young babies in West Java were not given fish for fear of worms, but that their older siblings apparently ate it. Bailey (1962b:244) said that in contrast to Freedman's (1955) emphasis on taboos as an important determinant in preventing children from eating fish, it was in fact poverty that prevented its consumption in his study area of Gunung Kidul.

There are apparently a number of possible explanatory factors, including regional variation based on ecological or other conditions, age patterns, and economic constraints. An elucidation of the form and pattern of this now classic taboo would be an excellent example of research into a reportedly widespread prohibition with significant policy implications.

Decreased consumption of food items during pregnancy. Data from Ngaglik show that during pregnancy increasing proportions of women report no consumption of animal protein; other food items display this same tendency but in a less pronounced fashion. It is not known whether this behavior is the result of specific food avoidances – direct questioning did not elicit such reports – or overall decreased consumption during pregnancy, which has been reported in connection with fears of enlarging the fetus (Whyte 1974: 63), and which was also mentioned by some women in informal discussions in Ngaglik. Discomfort in late pregnancy could also bring about reduced food intake.

The main quantitative data from Ngaglik which support the notion of decreasing food consumption is found in the frequency scores of rice consumption, particularly among upper-income women. The majority of women reported frequency of rice consumption equivalent to three times a day when nonpregnant and during early pregnancy; however, the proportion decreases over the gestation period, so that by the third trimester, in about half the observations the frequency was equivalent to twice a day. The pattern for lower-income women tends to remain constant throughout pregnancy at levels lower than those for the upper-income women, with only about one-fourth reporting frequencies of three times a day or more. Even without data on food quantity, the changing patterns of meal frequency are indicative of dietary behavior requiring further research.[12]

Fruit consumption in Java. To the Western observer, Java fulfills dreams of exotic tropical fruits of infinite variety, changing seasonally but ever in abundance. Yet virtually all nutrition surveys report low frequencies of fruit consumption; in Ngaglik, no fruit at all was consumed for the entire month in anywhere from a third to nearly half of recorded observations. For infants under 18 months of age, the large majority did not eat any fruit. Different patterns by income group tell at least part of the story, for frequency of consumption by upper-income women is, on average, twice as high as for lower-income women.

Over all income categories, fruit consumption is somewhat higher among pregnant women and lower among lactating women. To some extent the former is due to *nyidam*, or "craving," for fruits during early pregnancy. Avoidance of fruit during lactation may be part of a prohibition on fruits for infants, because many mothers fear an effect through breast milk. There may also be some underreporting of fruit where it is consumed in a spontaneous way, from family-owned trees, rather than purchased. But overall we need further investigation of who is, and is not, consuming Java's fruit resources.

Dietary deprivation of children. A common notion in the literature on nutrition is that children eat last and least in many societies, and Edmundson (1976:65) reported this pattern for his study areas in East Java. The research by Tan and colleagues (1970) and by Bailey (1967a), however, has claimed that children either eat first, or that choice bits are reserved for them. Statements made by informants in Ngaglik agree more closely with this latter conception, though clearly this practice refers mainly to older children. The inadequacy of the diet of one- and two-year olds is clear from the figures in Table 11.2.

12 It is also interesting to note that during the lactation period, both income groups showed higher rice consumption frequency scores than at any other time. Upper-arm nutritional indicators for women during the puerperium showed very low values immediately after parturition, a rise during the first six months post partum, and then a gradual decline. In addition, average body weight for lactators was generally higher than for nonlactators at given points in the postpartum period (Hull 1983). Further analysis will focus on the possible relation between dietary patterns and these anthropometric results.

The diet of newborns and maternal attitudes toward colostrum. One of the more interesting topics covered at some length during the Ngaglik study was breast feeding – from initiation of lactation through problems experienced in and attitudes toward breast feeding and its alternatives. Though bottles were not unknown, there was almost universal support and encouragement of breast feeding in the society. In the immediate postpartum period, however, many women delayed initiation of suckling until "true milk" came in, preventing the infant from receiving the early milk or colostrum. Just over half the women reported that they denied this excellent source of nutrition and immunological agents to their infants; colostrum was expressed and, according to some informants, buried lest it be eaten by insects or animals and cause indirect harm to the infant. Infants were either left without food for up to five days, or fed small amounts of, most commonly, coconut water, lime juice, or honey. But an important point to note is that a significant number of women did not share these attitudes; some did not distinguish between breast milk and colostrum, whereas others made the distinction but still fed colostrum to the infant. And among those who avoided colostrum, there was no clear consensus on the reasons for doing so, with as many as 20 percent of women claiming it was a "custom" but that reasons or consequences were not known. There do not appear to be any references to beliefs about colostrum in the major existing nutritional studies in Indonesia.

These and many other "mysteries" attest to the very limited knowledge of dietary patterns in Java at a time when there is increasing emphasis on programs to improve nutrition. Further research focusing on these topics could benefit from a consideration of several important methodological issues that have emerged from results of available research to date.

Methodological issues: some proposals

Main focus, definitions

The term "dietary taboo" is used somewhat loosely in the literature, and various reports refer to prohibitions, avoidances, and folk beliefs about food without any clear definition or reasons for choice of terms. An anthropological study focusing on societal ideology, norms, and sanctions would necessarily have to make a distinction; however, we have argued in this paper that there is a pressing need for more applied research directly geared to policy formulation. For this approach, a broader definition of dietary change – all changes in the diet associated with a particular group or a particular time in the life cycle – is more appropriate. This information would then be supplemented with an evaluation of the relative strength – in quantitative and qualitative terms – and potential impact of these changes on the society. Dietary change would include omissions in the diet, foods eaten in decreased amount, new foods added, and foods eaten in increased amounts.

A classification or framework could be devised as a guide to data collection and interpretation. De Garine (1970) has suggested a classification for dietary change[13] based on:

1. Length (temporary or permanent)
2. Size of human group involved (kin group, socioprofessional group, social class, masculine/feminine, etc.)
3. Periods of the life cycle affected (infancy, pregnancy, lactation, etc.)

However, there is a case for further classifying other aspects, including:

4. The category of food items involved in the dietary change. Taboos or changes can involve whole food groups such as animal protein; a particular food such as bananas; or foods that share certain properties, such as fried foods or watery foods. These may be based on readily identifiable characteristics, or on local conceptions such as the "hot" and "cold" food dichotomy.
5. The reasons underlying the change. Foods may be avoided or added because of a directly observed effect on health (e.g., chilis consumed by the mother, causing flatulence or stomach upset in the breast-fed infant); an assumed effect on health which has been taught either traditionally (e.g., fish cause worms) or in the modern context (green leafy vegetables add vitamins); or because of homeopathic properties (eating bananas grown together could result in the birth of Siamese twins). The type of reason can often imply the degree of accuracy of the belief, a premise that has been a useful conceptualization in traditional medicine: The more the cure resembles the illness, the less likely it is to be intrinsically effective.
6. The impact on the nutrition of the population under study. Dietary changes can be of minimal nutritional impact, as in avoidance of the rather rare *kepel* fruit, or potentially very significant, as in avoidance of dried fish, an important source of inexpensive animal protein.

Such a framework should be useful not merely to aid the construction of a typology, but more importantly to direct data collection and analysis toward useful policy implications. It is not enough to describe food beliefs; we must be prepared to evaluate, interpret and utilize research results to their full potential.

Toward research and policy objectives

Although it is not our objective here to review suitable strategies for nutrition research in Java, a suggestion for the organization of future research

13 The article actually focuses on food taboos only, but would apply in principle to our broader definition of dietary change.

efforts can be offered, based on our assessment of past research and current needs.

There is significant local variation in dietary patterns in Indonesia and even within Java. Large-scale centrally directed surveys collecting statements about food beliefs will have little direct relevance to most conditions. In contrast, small, focused surveys organized at the community level and administered by local personnel could have great potential for meaningful input into programs of nutrition improvement.

At present in Indonesia, attempts are being made to train cadres of community-based nutrition workers who will provide nutrition education, including cooking demonstrations and instruction in food production. Their own training is fairly basic, and the facilities provided them are minimal. But there is scope for accomplishing a great deal under this scheme: One of their most useful activities could be the carrying out of simple surveys of dietary patterns, food beliefs, and other topics related to the community's nutrition needs. With basic training, they could conduct dietary intake surveys supplemented by sensitive attitudinal questions and by informal conversation and observation.[14] These data collection methods could be designed to be free of the "myths" which have limited the results of past research and policy formulation, and would aim at studying nutrition in its social context. Education, under such an approach, would be a two-way process between the nutrition worker and the people, and policy could be continually responsive to ideas expressed by the community.

Despite the emphasis now being placed on nutrition in Indonesia, we know remarkably little about people's food beliefs and habits. Resources are already being used to recruit and train village-level workers, and a research component built into this effort would be a first step in providing the information so clearly needed as the basis for effective intervention programs.[15]

14 Problems of recall, nonreporting of food consumed outside the home, conscious under- and overreporting of certain foods would occur as they do in any nutrition survey, but the results would represent a considerable advance over our present limited knowledge. Probing questions on why certain foods were not consumed during, for example, a one-week study period would determine the extent to which responses centered around beliefs, economic reasons, seasonal availability, individual taste, or other variables. Observation and informal interviews are essential when workers attempt to assess actual behavior in terms of reported behavior and stated norms.

15 Several important sources were unfortunately not available to the writer. These include the series of nutrition surveys carried out by the Indonesian government's UPGK (Nutrition Improvement Programme), and two WHO reports (McArthur 1962 and Freedman 1955) which were quoted in other sources.

Appendix. *Inventory of Javanese dietary taboos*[a]

Source	Group affected	Taboo food

Tan et al. 1970: 66–72 (West Java, Central Java, East Java)	Infants	Generally:
		  Sour foods
		  Hot foods (chilis)
		  "Fishy" foods
		Specifically:
		  Fish (fresh and salted)
		  Beef
		  Eggs
		  Fruit
		  Dried cassava

	Children (1–6 years)	Dried cassava Sour foods Chilis Fish Meat Eggs Coconut cream and grated coconut
	Young unmarried girls	*Ikan leleh* (a kind of catfish) *Pisang ambon* (large banana) Papaya Pineapple *Pisang mas* (small banana) Beaten egg Meat of birds Leaves of sweet potato plant Bean sprouts Chicken wings Chicken tails
	Pregnant women	Pineapple *Salak* fruit Fresh fish *Ikan wader* *Ikan labu* (kinds of squash) *Kepel* fruit Banana fruit if grown together Bud of the banana flower *Pace* fruit
	Nursing mothers	Animal food (meat) Fish or "fishy" tasting food Chilis Pineapple Papaya Young coconut meat and coconut water

Appendix *(cont.)*

Source	Group affected	Taboo food
Tan et al. 1970 (cont.)	Nursing mothers (cont.)	Fried *tempe* Soybean Fried food Eggs
	Males	Eggplant *Labu* squash
	General	Pork
Whyte 1974:63ff (Indonesia, Java)	Pregnant women	Sugarcane Certain plants with horizontal fruits
	Nursing mothers	Water and tea restricted for some time after birth
	Infants	Animal protein foods
	Adolescents	Cooling foods (many green, leafy vegetables and fruits)
Sri Kardjati et al. 1977:46ff (East Java)	Pregnant women and nursing mothers	Fresh fish *Kluwih* (kind of breadfruit) Bean sprouts Chilis Pineapple
Geertz 1961:86ff (East Java)	Pregnant women	Sugarcane *Kepel* (fruit with horizontal seeds) Eel Water and tea for some time after birth
	Nursing mothers	Strong seasoning
Zuidberg, 1978:107ff (West Java)	Pregnant women	Fruit
	Nursing mothers	Fruit
	Babies and children	Fish Meat

[a] Wherever possible, we have tried to identify taboos identified in West, Central, or East Java. Some sources, however, designate a taboo only as "Indonesian."

12. Social and nutritional context of "ethnic foods": Malay examples

Christine S. Wilson

Introduction: social roles of food

Food has always been more than something to still hunger (de Garine 1972: 143). A substance tinged with emotion from its associations with early care and nurturing, it is a focus of beliefs and myths regarding its properties (Frazer 1922:556) which may have arisen from intuitive recognition that what is eaten becomes incorporated into the tissues of the eater. Annual reappearance of a staple crop that depends upon weather and human care for its continuing existence may account for rites and propitiations carried out for its growth and fruitfulness.

For peoples in traditional and emergent societies, such staples continue to have central positions in the culture, as evidenced by their prominence in ceremonies honoring religious and life-cycle rites and the many ways in which foodstuffs are prepared from them. In much of Asia, rice is such a food. The polite greeting in several Asian tongues is, "Have you taken rice?" A meal lacking rice is not a true meal, and its absence causes subjective feelings of hunger. It is the only food other than the breast offered to Malay infants in the first weeks of life (personal observation). The overriding symbolic importance of such staples to their customary consumers led Jelliffe (1967:279) to term them "cultural superfoods." These "cultural superfoods" are usual components of feasts, accompanied by other, prestigious foods, especially meat. They are also, as suggested above, the principal ingredient of a variety of special foods served at lesser celebrations, such as religious and secular holidays during which sweets and other confections are "exchanged."

For Malays, food has many such social roles. It is conspicuous among gifts given by the groom's family to the bride at an engagement party. Special sweet cakes are exchanged between the families at the time of the wedding. Malay weddings also entail feasts prepared by many for many at the

Research on which this chapter is based was supported by National Institutes of Health grants GM 35,001-3 and AM-19152 to the author, and National Institutes of Health grant AI 10051 to the Department of Epidemiology and International Health, University of California, San Francisco, through the University of California International Center for Medical Research (UC ICMR) at the Institute for Medical Research, Kuala Lumpur, Malaysia.

homes of bride and groom. Circumcisions and funerals are marked by so-cially prescribed feasts. In Muslim Malaysia, the Islamic fasting month of *Ramadan*, in which food may not be taken in daylight hours, is broken by one obligatory feast that features seldom-eaten beef. Each day's fast through-out the month is ended by eating sweet foods exchanged between house-holds before the evening meal is served. The month ends with three days of social visiting, accompanied by consumption of delicacies at each house en-tered. Even on ordinary days, visitors to a Malay house are served a drink (tea or coffee) or a snack.

Malays also use food in magic and propitiation. Eggs bless a house-raising or a shadow play performance. Cakes and eggs are impaled on kites as of-ferings to the spirits at a kite-flying festival (Wilson 1970:272). For Malays, food, a subject that interests them, tells them who they are and helps pat-tern their lives.

Malay foods and collection of samples

The Malay cuisine or daily meal pattern, like that of much of Southeast Asia, is based on rice, fish, and coconuts (Wilson 1975:42), with side dishes of vegetables and sauces termed *lauk* and *sambal*, respectively. The fish, and sometimes vegetables as well, are often cooked in milk (*santan*) made from squeezing the essence from grated fresh coconuts seasoned with fresh and dry spices fried in oil to become a Malay curry. The menu is not lim-ited to curries and similar stews, however. The list of ingestibles includes a number of foods little known outside the region, most of which are part of the Malay diet.

These Malay foods were encountered during an ethnographic study of diet, nutrition, and health, and use of food within the culture in a coastal fishing village (*kampung*) in the state of Trengganu on the East Coast of the Malay Peninsula. Because of the nutritional emphasis of the study, food samples were collected for laboratory analysis by the Institute for Medical Research (IMR) in Kuala Lumpur, which has made similar analyses of many local Malaysian foods. Some of the foods described below were more com-mon to the East Coast region, but much that is consumed in Trengganu is sold in markets in Kuala Lumpur (the country's capital) and other parts of the country, as well as in other Southeast Asian countries.

The numbers of food samples collected in this study were limited by the distance of the study *kampung* (300 road miles) from the IMR laboratories, and unavailability of appropriate equipment for refrigerated transport of large numbers of fresh perishables and of preservatives, aside from those (salt, drying) used by *kampung* people. Results of analyses of some foods collected have not yet been reported. Other foods cited here that have not yet been analyzed should also be examined.

Pulut (glutinous rice)

Rice is not an unusual food to much of the world's population, but not many outside of Asia have tasted glutinous or sticky rice (called *pulut* in Malay/Indonesian), the type or rice used in Asian ceremonial meals. This variety contains varying amounts of soluble starch dextrins and maltose in the endosperm storage material (Burkill 1966:1623) that cause the cooked grains to stick together in a glutinous mass which is sweeter than ordinary rice. It is used for making the Malay *kueh* (cakes) *ketupat* and *tapai*, described below, as well as to prepare saffron- or turmeric-tinted yellow rice (*nasi kuning*; yellow is the royal color of Asia) for ceremonial occasions such as weddings, circumcisions, a new baby's naming ceremony, and *melenggang perut*, the ritual examination by the *bidan* (traditional midwife) of the position of the child in the womb at the seventh month of a first pregnancy. Packets of *nasi kuning* are given to women guests at a wedding, together with hard-boiled eggs dyed red, symbols of the bride's family's wish for future grandchildren. Smaller feasts following the naming and *melenggang perut* ceremonies feature yellow *pulut* and chicken curry. Four plates of this dyed *pulut*, decorated with sectioned, hard-cooked eggs, were part of the preliminary payment to the midwife for her services at the initial examination of the pregnant mother.

The most common *pulut* cakes, *ketupat*, are made as follows: For a quantity (several dozen), five *cupak* (quarts) of the rice are soaked, then steamed 20 minutes. The cooked rice is mixed with *santan* from six coconuts which have produced 1½ quarts of *santan*, and a handful of salt. Each cake, consisting of about four tablespoons of cooked rice and one tablespoon of *santan*, is folded in a palas leaf (*Licuala* spp.) in the shape of a cone, boiled again briefly, dried, then fried without additional oil, the fat from the coconut milk providing lubrication. The resulting product has a nutlike flavor. Thrice cooked, the cakes keep three days without refrigeration, and may be fried again briefly before eating to "refresh" them. *Ketupat* are made at least two times every year in each household for holiday exchanges with other families on *Hari Raya* (the feast day that ends the Islamic fasting month of *Ramadan*), or *Hari Raya Haji* (*Muharram*, the Prophet Muhammad's birthday). *Ketupat* are sometimes sold in coffee shops or to homemakers at other times of the year, when they are taken at breakfast or as snacks.

Boiled or steamed *pulut* is a special breakfast treat in more affluent households, sprinkled with fresh grated coconut mixed with a little sugar and salt.

Tapai, a substitute for alcoholic beverages

Pulut is also the base of *tapai*, the cake that, together with *ketupat*, is most popular at the annual religious holidays *Hari Raya* and *Hari Raya Haji*.

According to Burkill (1966:2318), *tapai* was at first the term for the yeast with which the cake is made. *Tapai* is prepared by steaming the *pulut* as is done for *ketupat*, then mixing it while still slightly warm with locally made yeast (*ragi*; see description below) and forming it into cakes that are placed in rubber tree leaves folded into triangles fastened with a coconut leaf rib. Usual recipes call for one cake of *ragi* for each *cupak* (quart) of rice. The leaf packets are placed in a closed container such as a large pot or bucket, covered with a *sarong* or cloth to keep out drafts, in the manner in which leavened bread is put to rise, and left two to three days before eating. According to people in the *kampung*, *tapai* is "sweet without addition of sugar," and thus a mystery. By sweetness they mean its mild though detectable taste of alcohol, although they are unaware that this prized fermented product contains a substance forbidden to them by their religion. The alcohol, although at a low level (probably about three percent; United States ICNND 1964:46), is evident to anyone more familiar with such substances. The cakes taste like *saki* (Japanese rice wine), or as though a little gin had been put in them.

A less expensive type of *tapai* is made from sliced, boiled tapioca (manioc, *Manihot utilissima*), prepared with *ragi* as was described for *tapai* made from *pulut*. (The leaf wrappings are usually omitted from tapioca *tapai*.)

In the late 1960s, *pulut* cost 60 cents Malay a cupak, $2.40 to $3.50 a *gantang* (gallon), whereas a *gantang* of ordinary rice was half that price. (The rate of exchange is approximately $2.50 Malay to $1.00 U.S., but the buying power of each dollar is about the same.) Tapioca was even cheaper, because it is planted and raised with less effort than that required by rice. *Tapai* from tapioca is made for sale commercially, in markets or shops, at all times of the year. *Tapai* made from *pulut* is served and exchanged only on the aforementioned religious holidays.

Ragi, kampung yeast

Ragi differs considerably from the dry yeast beads or pressed soft cakes sold in Western countries. Specimens obtained were hard, dusty, white, button-like cakes, an inch or so in diameter and 3/16-inch thick. Two of these cakes weighed 12.7 grams. They were locally reported to contain rice flour, curry spices, pepper, and coriander. According to Burkill (1966:2318), *Aspergillus* fungi as well as some *Saccharomyces* spores are introduced into the mixture, in part adventitiously, to make the product active.

Results of nutrient analysis of a sample of *ragi* by the Division of Nutrition for Medical Research are presented in Table 12.1. Nutrient levels in this sample were lower than those in yeast available in the United States for all components measured, except for carbohydrate (Watt and Merrill 1963:67).

Leavening ability of *ragi* was tested by the investigator using a standard U.S. bread recipe [which makes two loaves from one package of (U.S. com-

Table 12.1. *Village foods analyzed by the Institute for Medical Research*

Nutrient	*Ragi* (yeast preparation)	Cashew nut
Moisture (g)	13.00	3.68
Ash (g)	0.38	2.30
Crude protein (g)	8.56	22.35
Carbohydrate (by difference) (g)	77.22	23.67
Fat (g)	0.84	48.00
Iron (mg)	2.36	12.35
Calcium (mg)	26.66	49.37
Phosphorus (mg)	118.74	281.00
Calories (by bomb calorimetry) (mg)	372	668
Thiamine (mg)	0.26	0.67
Riboflavin (mg)	0.10	0.13
Nicotinamide (mg)	6.49	2.99

mercial) yeast], and two *biji* (pellets or wafers) of the yeast. Because the sponge did not rise well with one wafer of *ragi*, the dough was split, and the entire second *biji* of yeast was added to half the dough. The loaf that contained 1½ *biji* of *ragi* did not rise sufficiently before or after baking to make an edible product. It thus appears that *ragi* has less than half the leavening power of a like quantity of (U.S. commercial) dry yeast (Wilson 1970:343). It is used primarily to make *tapai* (see above).

Fruits of note

The Malay Peninsula has a wealth of fruits, native as well as introduced varieties (Allen 1967). Many of them, such as papaya, mango, pineapple, and guava, are found in other tropical regions and exported to temperate countries. The two discussed here are less familiar, have rather unusual properties and are much liked and prized in the *kampung*.

Durian

Durian (*Durio zibethinus*, Allen 1967:94), native to the Southeast Asia region, is believed to have originated in the Malay Peninsula or in Borneo (Burkill 1966:887). A member of the hibiscus family (hibiscus is the Malaysian national flower), it grows elsewhere in the tropics.

Perhaps no other fruit has been so written about, with so many conflicting reports or opinions. It is reputed to be an aphrodisiac. That rapid chemical changes take place in the pulp when the fruit falls has been known for years (Burkill 1966:888). The trees are usually planted, although some wild trees appear from seeds dropped by jungle animals that have eaten the fruit. Even cats and tigers are reported to like durian (Allen 1967:99). The trees are large, too tall to climb. The fruits are seasonal, becoming available in June and continuing until early October, in the peninsula. Impossible to pick, they are allowed to fall when they are fully ripe. People go in groups to the groves and camp outdoors all night, waiting for the large heavy fruits to drop. A small one bought at the beginning of the season weighed about 4¾ pounds. The thick green outer skin is a sphere of deep, sharp spines (which could inflict serious injury if stepped on accidentally), well designed to prevent the fruit from shattering when it falls, and not easy to open. Malays say, "If a durian falls on your head, the tree will die."

The "meat" or pulp of the fruit lies in discrete segments in which the seeds are embedded. Its color varies from yellowish-cream to rosy ecru. The aforementioned small fruit contained five such pulp segments, weighing a total of about one pound. The seeds may be eaten boiled or roasted. The skin is ashed and sometimes made into cakes. The meat may be preserved as a salted conserve or sweet jam, or made into cakes. Durian-flavored ice cream is made and sold commercially in Malaysia. Controversy, particularly among Europeans, centers most about the odor and taste. There is general agreement that a strong onion or garlic flavor predominates, with some undertones of soft cheese. The onion taste lingers in the mouth for several hours. Ability to taste some components of the flavor may be genetic. The odor clings to discarded skins, and chemical changes enhance a lingering smell, partially from decay, which characterizes whole *kampungs*, market areas, streets, and alleys while the fruit is available.

Malays say that durian is a "heating" food (Wilson 1970:283). Europeans who like it say that one feels hot after eating moderate amounts of the fruit. Some Malays believe it is dangerous to bathe after they have eaten durian, and some may eat little else in the peak season. Other Malays say it makes you feel hot, so that you *have* to bathe. People in the study *kampung* also believe drinking even a small amount of alcohol soon after eating durian is extremely dangerous, because both substances are considered "heating" and would wage war in the consumer. Religious prohibition against alcoholic beverages prevents their testing this hypothesis.

Laboratory studies made of the chemical changes in durian occurring over several days after the fruit falls showed the final breakdown products to be similar to those in alcoholic beverages believed to be the cause of hangover from overindulgence (Wilson 1970:348). Because of the rapidity of these chemical changes, the fruit can neither be eaten more than four or five days after falling, nor be shipped great distances. Timing of the chemical changes varies with variations in kinds of durian (Burkill 1966:888).

The great esteem in which the fruit is held, its almost supernatural value to these villagers, is indicated by admissions that, contrary to usual social practices, this food is not widely shared beyond members of immediate families. Its high energy content helps explain why other food may be limited to rice in a meal in which durian is the *pièce de résistance*. Of twenty families queried at the end of the durian season regarding eating practices and beliefs with respect to the fruit, one woman summed villagers' attitudes by saying, "There is never enough money when there is durian" (personal observation).

Ganjus *(cashew)*

Another fruit esteemed nearly as much as durian by people in this *kampung* is the cashew or *ganjus* [from the Brazilian name, *cajus*, for this tree, *Anacardium occidentale* (Burkill 1966:144)], also called *jambu golok* in the *kampung*. These trees, too, are planted, in villages and orchards on the East Coast. During the season the fruits are ripe, late March to June, nearly every household picks the fruit and roasts the nut for a snack several times a week.

As its name implies, the tree is also native to Malaysia. It originated in tropical America and was apparently brought by Portuguese traders to Goa and Malacca in the seventeenth century (Burkill 1966:145). A member of the Anacardiaceae family (Allen 1967:3), both mangoes and poison ivy are relatives. The cashew nut, the plant's seed, is external to the fruit and hangs below it as an appendage. In the study village, both the fruit and nut are eaten, and the young tender leaves are sometimes chewed, or eaten as a salad. It was said that pregnant women, particularly, like to eat the leaves. The roasted nut was analyzed by the IMR. The results, presented in Table 12.1, show the nut to have a good content of protein, iron, calcium, and thiamine.

The fruit is an excellent source of ascorbic acid (198 milligrams per 100 grams). The "fruit bat" or *keluang* (flying fox, *Pteropus vampyrus*; Medway 1969:10), a mammal which, like man, cannot manufacture vitamin C in its own body, also finds it an admirable solution to its obligate need for this vitamin. Flocks that come in the night vie with villagers to eat the fruit, and may "finish" a tree before morning.

The fruit, eaten by humans as a snack or cooked as a vegetable, contains an irritant present in the kernel tissues, and in the gum of the tree, called *getah* (rubber) by the *kampung* people and cardol by Burkill (1966:146), that blisters the skin and scratches the throat.

Cardol is anacardic acid. Chemically it is *o*-pentadecadienylsalicylic acid, or 2-hydroxy-6-pentadecadienylbenzoic acid, $C_{22}H_{32}O_3$ (*Merck Index* 1960). It is sparingly soluble in water, but freely soluble in alcohol, ether, and petroleum ether. Its structure was determined by Stadler, who isolated it in

Figure 12.1. Burning cashew nuts to drive off the toxic compounds.

1847. The oil of the nut is edible when the irritating substance and the stearic portion (about 17 percent) are removed. The rest of the oil is 80 percent oleic acid and 1.5 percent nonsaponifiable.

Heating destroys the irritating effects of cardol. *Kampung* people consider the *getah* in the shell of the nut a poison. It can be removed or destroyed by boiling or roasting. The latter process, they say, produces a tastier product. The shell (and the nut) is most often burned, in a pot over an outdoor fire. The eye-stinging cloud of white smoke which comes forth from the shell must disappear completely before the nut is safe to eat (Figure 12.1). When Malays prepare the fruits for cooking, they chop them fine, a practice that more readily exposes the cardol to heat inactivation. They are cooked *lemak* (in coconut milk, with chilis and onion) as part of a meal.

Despite the presence of orchards on the East Coast, and the popularity of the fruit and nut, commercial production of the cashew tree had not been attempted on a large scale in Malaysia by the mid-1970s. The juice, which is said to be diuretic when fermented, has been used as a flux in soldering metals, and can serve as marking ink. The gum from the tree is used in bookbinding in India, and can substitute for gum arabic (Burkill 1966:146). Malays treat diarrhea with a drink made from the tree bark. It acts as a cathartic by irritating the bowel (Burkill 1966:146).

Products of the sea

Turtle eggs

A number of places along the Malaysian East Coast have handmade signs in the form of a circle of reeds fastened atop a post or sapling to mark a "turtle beach," rented by a private individual from the government, where the big green sea turtles, known as *penyu* or *piun* (*Chelonia mydas*), come ashore at night each year in June, July, and August to dig a hole, lay their eggs, and go back to sea before morning. In return for a fee, and reservation of 10 percent of the eggs for hatching to preserve the species, renters may collect and sell the rest of the eggs.

The eggs, a little over an inch an diameter, are called *telur sotong*. Turtle eggs may have received the name *sotong* (cuttlefish) for their resemblance in taste and texture to the latter sea animal (Winstedt 1965:339). They have a soft shell, are salty, and will keep for several weeks. Soaking in fresh water for a few hours reduces the saltiness. In season, turtle eggs are sold by the dozen in East Coast markets. *Kampung* housewives hardboil them as they would fowl eggs. They are eaten as a snack, or as a side dish at meals. Individual turtles return to the same coastal sites every year, beaches well visited in season by local Malays and outsiders, where egg collecting is a social as well as a remunerative activity.

Belacan *and* budu *(prawn paste and fish paste)*

Southeast Asians preserve fish and other seafood by fermentation as well as by salting and drying. In Malaysia, small prawns or shrimp (*udang baring; Acetes erythraeus*) and various kinds of fresh sea fish are so processed (Burkill 1966:684). On the East Coast, prawns are netted close to shore by two or more boats working cooperatively, or by a *sungkur*, a close-meshed net fastened to two poles carried into the surf by two people, each holding one pole. In other parts of the peninsula, prawns are obtained by sunken tide nets. The nets collect animals additional to the sought-for shrimp. The whole catch is incorporated in *belacan*, fermented prawn paste.

On the East Coast in March and April, whole villages are redolent of the odor of drying prawns, particularly strong near the *bangsal* (fish-drying businesses), for *belacan* manufacture is a commercial rather than a cottage enterprise, although some housewives make their own *belacan*. The fresh contents of the net are dumped onto a mat laid on the ground, liberally sprinkled with salt, covered with another mat, and left to ferment for several days, a process that is fairly prompt in the tropical temperature. The resulting mass is pounded to a pulp in a large wooden mortar and allowed to dry in the sun before being pounded into a smooth paste for shipment or local sale. No precautions are taken to ensure that any part of the process is sanitary, and visible contamination from flies, airborne dirt, and other causes undoubtedly contributes to the fermentation.

The resulting product, smelling strongly of nitrogenous putrefaction compounds and very well liked, is eaten almost daily, usually mixed with ground chili peppers and onions, as a sauce or condiment accompanying rice. It is also an ingredient in curries, vegetable, and other cooked dishes.

Budu, or fermented fish paste, is make from *ikan bilis* [*Stolephorus indicus*, whitebait or anchovies (Scott 1959:26)], raw rice parched (fried without oil), tamarind, and brown sugar. A simpler recipe uses only the *bilis* and salt, one *gantang* (gallon) of fish to one *cupak* (quart) salt. The materials are left to ferment (decay) naturally for a month in a large covered pottery jar. The resulting sauce is a thick, grayish substance resembling Vietnamese *nuoc mam* in flavor, though not in color or texture.

In the study, *kampung budu* was made only at home. A similar product made in other parts of the country is known as *cencalok*. *Budu* is a relish taken with meals. Both *belacan* and *budu* provide salty, strong flavors to otherwise often bland meals. Malays do not add salt or other condiments to foods as they eat. According to Oliveiro (1955), *belacan* is high in protein and iron, and extremely high in calcium, 1552 milligrams per 100 grams, having almost no vitamins. *Budu* contains calcium and a little protein. Because the whole animal – including carapace or bones – is incorporated into these products, a usual serving of one to two teaspoons of these relishes is an alternative means toward meeting daily calcium needs in a society that does not consume dairy products.

Keropok

Another means by which fish is conserved in East Coast Malaysia is by mixing the meat with sago flour (*Metroxylon sagus*, called *sagu* by Malays) after the fish is deboned and before or after it is cooked. The mixture of fish and flour is rolled, sliced thin, and dried as chips (usually in the sun), which will keep almost indefinitely. A *kampung* housewife makes *keropok* to sell in the following manner: She buys, for example, 30 *ikan chonor* (lizard fish, *Surida timbil* or *S. myops* [Scott 1959:33–4]), a slender fish about 12 inches long, and a *cupak* (quart) of sago flour. After she has boiled, skinned, deboned, and beheaded the fish, she mixes, then pounds together the sago and fish meat, forming it into 14-inch rolls one inch in diameter. The product may be eaten in this form, cut in four- to six-inch lengths and fried in hot fat, or sliced thin by hand and sun-dried. The dry slices are "reconstituted" by frying in deep fat, producing a crisp, light cracker that resembles a potato chip in appearance and texture (Figure 12.2). "Fresh" rolls may be served as part of a meal. The chips are usually taken as snacks.

Keropok can be made from a variety of fish, the quality, flavor, and price varying accordingly. The best are those made from *ikan parang*, the dorab

Figure 12.2. Reconstituting *keropok* chips by frying in oil. Dried chips awaiting treatment are under the woman's elbow; fried chips fill the other two containers.

or wolf herring (*Chirocentrus dorab* [Scott 1959:19]), a large fish caught by drift net or line fishing. Good-quality dried *keropok* sold for three to four dollars per 100 chips in the early 1970s. Thrifty housewives make their own for the monsoon season when fresh fish are scarce because of rough seas.

Sweetmeats and other snacks

Malays eat many local snack items. Every housewife knows how to make most of them. Some women earn extra money selling *kueh* (cakes) and other snacks to housewives "lazy to cook" breakfast. Table 12.2 lists those most frequently eaten in this village, and outlines their ingredients (see Rosemary Firth 1943/1966:277ff, for further descriptions of similar cakes made in the state of Kelantan).

One particularly prized *kueh* is *dodol*. Kelantan women are said to make especially good *dodol*. Having a consistency between that of firm gelatin and soft caramel, with a flavor resembling the latter, *dodol* is sold in the main market in Khota Bahru in *kati* (1⅓ pounds) quantities, and by some *kueh* sellers in villages. It is made with glutinous rice pounded into flour,

Table 12.2. *Some cakes and other snacks made or sold in a Malay village*

Made of manioc

keretek or *repek ubi*	Dried crisp chips rolled in grated coconut
ketupat ubi	*Santan* and boiled manioc folded in a leaf cone
laksam (lasam)	Manioc flour steamed, rolled, and sliced, served with a sauce of *santan* containing pounded onions, black pepper, and dried fish topped with two to three kinds of chopped green leaves, *belacan*, and chilis; also made with rice flour
kueh badak	Fried cakes cut like doughnuts and rolled in grated coconut and sugar

Made of wheat flour

le(m)ping	Fried pancakes of flour, salt, sugar, coconut water or milk, sometimes soda or commercial yeast, and onions
kueh gulong	Pancake of flour, water, yellow food color; rolled around grated coconut and *santan*
kueh beriti	Round cakes baked in Malay oven; center filled with sugar and grated coconut
paun beriti	Same as above, fried
buah berjumpat	Round cakes, fried
kueh jumpat	Sugar, salt, soda, flour, *pisang putar* (a sticky banana), fried
kayu keramat	Long cakes, fried
kueh kacang	Fried cakes contained cooked, dried peas
kueh gandum	Flour, salt, *santan* or water, chopped onions, and sometimes dried fish, fried
kueh epok	Fish and grated coconut in a fried or pastry shell

Made of rice

nasi daging	Boiled rice mixed with cooked fish, *santan*, fenugreek, ginger, and salt
putu kueh	Pressed dry rice cakes with a little sugar
pulut kapit	Glutinous rice cooked or steamed with *santan* and pressed into compact squares with a weight; served with a sauce of pounded peanuts and chilis, and sometimes with small cubes of broiled meat, called *satay*
patikan	Cake of rice flour, sugar, and *santan;* colored with pandan and topped with "whipped" coconut milk

Other

pisang goreng	*Pisang putar* (see above), coated with a flour batter containing cumin and other spices and fried in deep fat
rujak keling	Cooked noodles, with sliced cooked *keropok*, sliced cucumber, bean sprouts, and hot chili sauce
mee goreng	Boiled noodles fried with chilis and onions
kerenpek	Sago flour and sugar pressed into dry cakes

coconut milk (*santan*), and *gula Malacca* (also called *manisan*, a brown sugar obtained from the palm inflorescence), and cooked and stirred in a *kuali* (a wide, shallow pan) until it thickens, a process that may take several hours (Allen 1967:219). A study village woman who came from Kelantan made *dodol* in quantity to sell. Using a huge *kawah* (cauldron) over an outdoor fire, she substituted 20 *kati* of tapioca (manioc) for rice flour, as it is less expensive, and used the milk from nine coconuts with 30 pieces of *manisan* (totaling 13 pounds). The latter were added gradually to the mixture.

Other cakes are made of rice flour or wheat flour. They may be fried in a *kuali* or baked in a Malay "oven," a brass pot with depressions to hold the batter and a tight-fitting cover with matching indentations. Burning fuel is placed above as well as below the "oven." *Kueh akak*, the rich cakes of rice flour, eggs, *santan*, and sugar made for weddings, are cooked in this manner. These cakes are also made at *Hari Raya* and *Hari Raya Haji*. Two *cupak* of rice pounded into flour, 10 kati of sugar, 40 eggs, and 5 coconuts produce 200 cakes at a cost of nine dollars, or 4.5 cents apiece (1970 figures).

Another rich cake served to wedding guests, *kueh kosidoh*, consists of one *kati* of wheat flour, one of sugar, a little powdered cloves, cinnamon, and mace, the milk from one coconut, and four eggs, which are mixed and stirred in a *kuali* over the fire until the paste reaches the consistency of mashed potatoes. It is shaped into an elaborate mound and served with bits of chopped fried onion (shallots) sprinkled on top.

Another sweetmeat, *cendol*, are small, soft, green pea-shaped balls which sometimes are served in a dish with a spoon with a sauce of *gula Malacca*, but more often are added to a sweet, iced syrup drink called *ayer batu* (*ayer batu* means ice). *Cendol* may be made of rice, sago, or green pea flour (Handy 1960:6). On the East Coast, they are made from rice flour, which is cooked with coconut milk until the mixture thickens; a leaf of pandan or green commercial food coloring is added. The boiled mixture is then pushed through 3/8-inch holes punched in a cigarette tin into a basin of cold water beneath to coagulate.

Two other common snacks are whole garlic or onions pickled in vinegar and sold in small plastic sacks, and chickpeas (*Cicer arietinium*) boiled with large quantities of salt, then dried. The latter are eaten as Westerners would consume peanuts. The plant does not grow in the peninsula (Burkill 1966: 537). The peas appear to be imported in the cooked, dried condition from the Middle East by Indian food merchants.

The most recent snack is probably *ice crem*, not the dairy-based product familiar to Western populations, although this, too, is made and sold commercially across the country. Rather *ice crem* is the pink-colored sugar syrup of *ayer batu* made from passion fruit juice mixed with sweetened condensed milk, then frozen in plastic sacks in the refrigerators of those shop owners who own such electric appliances.

Conclusion

Most of the foods described above are adjuncts to the main menu pattern. The fruits are seasonal; the seafood pastes or sauces, though eaten often, are not made frequently. Indeed, *belacan* (prawn paste) is also seasonal, because the small shrimp from which it is prepared "run" in March and April. Housewives replenish supplies from the fish-drying sheds or a local shop. Many of the cakes and other carbohydrate snack foods listed in Table 12.2 are taken as the first meal of the day or as midafternoon accompaniments to a drink of tea or coffee.

All the snack foods serve social roles, for visitors are expected to be offered some food item. Some of those described are exchanged on the religious holidays in the manner in which Western Christians exchange homemade baked goods at Christmas. All also serve nutrient roles, of which some have been indicated. The cakes all afford calories, and some protein and minerals. The fruits provide vitamins. Thus although the basic menu pattern of any population needs to be considered by researchers in order to understand resource management and to assess nutrient status, less widely used diet items should also be noted and examined. Such seemingly peripheral items are often highly valued by their consumers, and thus may tell much to the outside observer about the society as a whole.

13. Human diets: a biological perspective

Graham H. Pyke

No animals, human or otherwise, consume food items in the same proportions in which they are encountered. Rather all animals show some degree of selectivity, eating some items to greater or lesser extents than they occur. In other words, an animal that has encountered a food item may either eat the item or pass it by. In addition, an animal may stop consuming an item at any time or may continue until the item is totally consumed. Thus animals that are seeking food must frequently make dietary "choices" or "decisions." This does not, it should be added, imply anything about the nature, conscious or otherwise, of these choices or decisions.

General conceptual framework of dietary decisions

Animals make dietary decisions in response to various factors operating at the time. First, there are stimuli such as color or taste arising directly from the food. Second, there is the internal state of the animal (independent of past experience). For example, an animal may have a full or an empty stomach, or may be suffering from an illness or nutritional deficiency. Third, there are stimuli arising from an animal's social milieu. An animal may, for example, observe the feeding habits of other individuals or be influenced by interaction, direct or indirect, with other individuals. What we commonly think of as culture lies within this category of social stimuli. I shall return to this point later. Finally, an animal may be influenced by properties of the physical environment such as temperature and humidity.

An animal's past experience may also influence its dietary decisions. Such experience may be classified in the same manner as the above factors. It is convenient, however, to make a simple division on the basis of whether or not the experience is of a "social" nature, involving influences by and interactions with other individuals. Once again, cultural effects would be included in past experience of a social nature. Of course, it is possible, and I think likely, that the effects of past experience have physical representation in an animal's internal chemistry. If this is the case, then any such effects can be logically included in an animal's present internal state. In any case, the distinction between present state and past experience is indeed useful and will be maintained in this discussion.

It is possible that an animal's dietary decisions are precisely determined by the various factors outlined above and by past experience. In addition, given an exact knowledge of an animal's present and past history, it may be possible to predict the behavior of the animal only in a probabilistic sense. In other words, an animal might, all other things being equal, choose different options with different probabilities. In some instances, such probabilistic choices would in fact be expected. Trial-and-error learning, for example, requires a certain amount of trial or experimentation which, though possibly completely systematic, in some cases may be of a probabilistic nature. Unfortunately, it is difficult and perhaps impossible to differentiate between probabilistic decision making on the part of animals and ignorance on the part of a scientific observer.

Genes versus culture

In the past it was common to make the distinction between what is genetically determined and what is learned (Hinde 1970). This distinction seems to lose its usefulness, however, when it is realized that the learning process or the "rules" by which animals learn may be strongly influenced or even completely determined by an animal's genetic constitution (Pulliam and Dunford 1980). It is possible, in fact, that in some situations, given an exact knowledge of an animal's environment, the progress and outcome of the animal's learning might be precisely determined. As a particular result may be achieved in many ways, it is also possible that the outcomes of learning will have a more probabilistic form.

A more useful distinction appears to be between the influences of genes and of culture. There are, of course, many definitions of culture. For the purposes of this discussion, however, I define "cultural interactions" as interactions between individuals involving either observation or symbolic communication. Culture is then the outcome of such interactions. As illustrations of the use of this definition, consider the following examples: Suppose an animal learns that a particular kind of food is poisonous and growls every time its offspring attempt to eat such food. Suppose also that as a result of the growls the offspring do not eat the food. Finally suppose these offspring, upon reaching adulthood and having their own offspring, also growl whenever the next generation attempt to eat the poisonous food. The habits of growling by adults in the presence of the poisonous food and abstinence from eating the food by young and adults alike may spread through the population. This, by my definition, would be cultural change via cultural interactions. Alternatively, the acquisition of the dietary habit could be acquired through observation of adults by their offspring or by other forms of symbolic communication. These I would include as cultural interactions. On the other hand, suppose that the access of an animal to a food item is restricted by another individual, which chases the first animal away from the food item after it has consumed only a small portion of the item. In this case, the first animal may choose to go elsewhere rather than waste time gaining equally small portions of the food. This would be a social but not a cultural interaction. Assuming that this response to such an interaction with another individual is genetically programmed, the outcome of the interaction is genetic rather than cultural. There should also, of course, be genetic underpinnings of the cultural interactions. At some level, the responses to observation and symbolic communication *must* be genetically programmed. Thus cultural interactions and change should be viewed, I believe, as phenomena added to genetically programmed response systems. It is possible, as may be the case with humans, that these cultural phenomena mask and alter the underlying genetic basis so extensively that the genetic components assume negligible importance.

Predicting animal diets

Since 1966, a large and now rapidly growing number of attempts have been made to predict a number of aspects of animals' foraging behavior including their dietary choices (for reviews see Schoener 1971; Pyke, Pulliam, and Charnov 1977; Krebs 1978). These studies have all taken the following form: First it is assumed that those animals that forage most efficiently will leave most descendants in future generations. Then, assuming that the ability to forage efficiently (or to learn to forage efficiently) is heritable or genetically programmed, the population will *tend* through time to be made up of increasingly efficient individuals. This so far is simply a restatement of Darwin's theory of evolution by natural selection. Assuming, in addition, that this evolutionary process has been proceeding for a very long time with relatively little change in environmental conditions, then the average foraging behavior in the population should be such that the efficiency of foraging is approximately maximized. It is then necessary to decide the "currency" in which to measure or estimate foraging efficiency. In the case of nectar-feeding animals, for example, it is usually assumed that foraging efficiency is equivalent to the net rate of energy gain while the animal is foraging (Pyke 1980). This, it is argued, is reasonable because these animals typically do not do anything else while they seek nectar and because the nectar is essentially a sugar-water solution and hence simply an energy source. Whatever the currency of foraging efficiency, it is hypothesized that the animals will forage on average in such ways that this currency is maximized. Consequently this approach has become known as optimal foraging theory (Pyke et al. 1977).

Optimal foraging theory has proven quite successful in many but not all situations (Pyke et al. 1977; Krebs 1978). It has generated good understanding of the foraging of animals, such as nectar feeders, for which the currency of foraging efficiency seems simple and straightforward (e.g., Pyke

1978; Waddington and Holden 1979). It has had similar success in instances where animals foraged for food of constant chemical composition differing only in size and handling time (i.e., Werner and Hall 1974; Cowie 1977; Goss-Custard 1977; Krebs et al. 1977; Zach 1979). In such cases it may be realistic to hypothesize that the animals will maximize their rate of food gain. The optimal foraging approach has, however, been applied less often and with less success to more complicated situations. Herbivorous and omnivorous animals, for example, obtain essential nutrients as well as energy from most or all of their food and may often obtain very different combinations of these nutrients from different food types. For such animals, the ability to obtain a balanced diet may be the key to reproductive success, and hence part of the appropriate currency of foraging efficiency (Westoby 1974; Pulliam 1975). Humans, as omnivores, are likely to present similar difficulties to any extension of optimal foraging theory that includes them. Such difficulties may, however, become insignificant when compared with those stemming from the importance of culture in human lives.

Despite very recent attempts, a useful quantitative theory of cultural evolution has not yet been developed (e.g., Cavalli-Sforza and Feldman 1973a; Feldman and Cavalli-Sforza 1975; Pulliam and Dunford 1980). Consequently there exists at present no adequate quantitative theory combining biological and cultural evolution (see Cavalli-Sforza and Feldman 1973b; Ruyle 1973; Cavalli-Sforza 1974, 1975; Feldman and Cavalli-Sforza 1976; Durham 1976; Richerson and Boyd 1978). Without such a theory it will be most difficult to generate precise predictions concerning diets of any animal influenced by culture.

Dietary choices of nonhuman animals

I shall now return to the conceptual scheme outlined above for viewing diets of animals in general. I shall attempt to show that nonhuman animals are influenced by all the factors in the scheme including, in some cases, the effects of culture.

There are many studies showing that animals respond in an immediate fashion to properties of their food. Some animals exhibit selectivity in terms of size of food items (e.g., Hespenheide 1966; Labanick 1976; Thompson 1978; Pyke 1979). Color may also be important in some cases (Stiles 1976), as may odor (Drickamer 1972; Garcia and Brett 1977). It would be expected, in fact, that animals would use all their available senses to evaluate potential food items.

Rather few studies have explored the effect of physical factors such as temperature on dietary behavior. Hummingbirds increase their total daily intake of food when the ambient temperature decreases (Hainsworth 1978). Furthermore, the resulting increase in energy consumption is the same as the increase in energy requirements arising from the lower temperature (Hainsworth 1978). House (1972) found that the relative food values of two diets for fly larvae were inverted when the temperature changed from 15°C to 30°C. He did not, however, test the flies for dietary preference of one diet over the other.

That the dietary decisions of an animal are influenced by its internal state is shown by two kinds of study. The first line of evidence comes from studies that find that there are genetically based differences between individuals or populations in terms of feeding preferences. Arnold (1977), for example, demonstrated this for garter snakes by showing that naive, newborn snakes from different populations show different propensities to eat slugs (see also Burghardt 1977). Because the diet of female snakes does not apparently affect prey preferences of their offspring (Burghardt 1977), the differences between snake populations must be genetically based. This could be further confirmed by breeding the snakes from different populations under identical laboratory conditions and then testing for differences in feeding preference between populations. This sort of breeding experiment has in fact been carried out with a Tephritid fly (Huettel and Bush 1972) and the house mouse (Stockton and Whitney 1974). In both cases, genetically based differences in feeding preferences were clearly demonstrated (Huettel and Bush 1972; Stockton and Whitney 1974).

The second line of evidence comes from studies that show that an animal's state of hunger or health influences its dietary decisions in the absence of prior experience with the potential food items. Rats suffering from various dietary deficiencies, for example, will typically prefer a diet that corrects the deficiency, when given a choice (e.g., Scott and Verney 1949; Chan and Kare 1979). Also diabetic rats show different food preferences to normal rats (Peng and Evenson 1979). Finally, a number of studies have found that the time since an animal last fed has an influence on the animal's dietary decisions (e.g., Ivlev 1961; Gittelman 1978).

That past dietary experience influences an animal's feeding preferences has now been shown in a very large number of studies. Bees and nectar-feeding birds, for example, learn to associate color with food quality (e.g., Bene 1941). Rats and other vertebrates show taste and odor preferences that reflect the qualities of previous diet (e.g., Scott and Quint 1946; Warren and Pfaffmann 1959; Burghardt and Hess 1966; Garcia, Ervin, and Koelling 1966; Galef and Henderson 1972; Christensen, Caldwell, and Oberleas 1974). Phytophagous insects, such as butterfly larvae, sometimes show a preference for their previous food plant (e.g., Jermy, Hanson, and Dethier 1968; Hanson 1976). Such learning has in fact been found to occur in virtually all kinds of animals.

Animals are also influenced by interactions with other animals. Such interactions, which are usually referred to as "social interactions," may involve members of the same or of different species, and may range from relatively benign or neutral interactions to interactions that are quite aggressive or competitive in nature. Territorial defense and other forms of aggressive interaction, for example, are widespread among the animal world and may influence the behavior of animals in general and aspects of their dietary choices in particular (e.g., Feinsinger and Chaplin 1975). The presence of potential predators may also affect an animal's dietary behavior. An animal might, in the presence of a potential predator, make dietary decisions that involve reduced risk of becoming part of the predator's meal (e.g., Milinski and Heller 1978). Finally, some animals have been found to consume more food when in a group than when alone (Mugford 1977). These are examples of interactions that are social but not cultural in nature.

Of great interest in the context of the present discussions are studies of cultural interactions between animals. So far, however, most studies of this kind involve "observational learning" rather than symbolic communication. A variety of animals, including rats, cats, birds, monkeys, and apes, have been found to be influenced in their behavior in general and dietary habits in particular, by either direct visual observation of other conspecifics or by perceived qualities (e.g., odor, taste) of food obtained from other individuals (e.g., Fisher and Hinde 1950; Hinde and Fisher 1952; Klopfer 1957; John et al. 1968; Galef 1976; Jouventin, Pasteur, and Cambefort 1977; Mugford 1977). In some cases such observational learning may apparently lead to the development of traditions where different groups of individuals may have quite different food habits even though their environments are otherwise essentially the same. Traditions of this kind have been found in rats and Japanese macaques (Eibl-Eibesfeldt 1970). In the case of Japanese macaques the cultural spread of innovations has, in fact, been observed (e.g., Itani 1958; Kawamura 1959; Miyadi 1959; Kawai 1965). As would be expected, there are patterns to the cultural transmission, with the likelihood of one animal learning something from another, depending on the age, sex, and dominance status of the individuals involved (Itani 1958; Kawamura 1959; Miyadi 1959).

To date, there have been very few studies of symbolic communication in nonhuman animals. Frish (1967) discovered that honeybees transfer information concerning the distance and direction of a food source by means of a dance language. Savage-Rumbaugh, Rumbaugh, and Boysen (1978) reported that two chimpanzees were able to specify several foods accurately by symbolic name to one another when the identity of the food items was known by only one. These chimpanzees also spontaneously requested specific foods of one another by name (Savage-Rumbaugh et al., 1978). Epstein, Lanza, and Skinner (1980) found similar behavior in pigeons. Both the chimpanzees and the pigeons were unable, however, to transfer information without access to the symbols learned from the experimenters (Savage-Rumbaugh et al. 1978; Epstein et al. 1980). They were apparently unable to substitute their own symbols! Perhaps this is not surprising, given the extremely artificial and unnatural nature of the experimental situations. It is therefore necessary to pursue such studies of symbolic communication in more natural laboratory environments and in the field. However, given the impressive abilities thus far demonstrated, of chimpanzees and pigeons to communicate symbolically in laboratory environments, it seems likely that parallel behavior will be found under natural conditions.

Dietary choices of humans

In terms of the various factors influencing dietary decisions, humans appear to be qualitatively identical to nonhuman animals. Human food preferences are influenced by food properties such as taste and odor (e.g., Engen, Lipsitt, and Kayne 1963; Desor, Greene, and Maller 1973; Maller and Desor 1974; Lepkovsky 1977; Beauchamp and Maller 1977; Gershoff 1977), an individual's state of health (e.g., Davis 1928; Wilkins and Richter 1940), and social interactions with other individuals (e.g., Harper 1972). Though precise data seem lacking, it can also hardly be doubted that the physical environment exerts an influence as well. Such qualitative similarity seems hardly surprising, in fact, given the likely common evolutionary ancestry of all animals and the continuity of morphological and physiological traits across the animal kingdom.

In a more quantitative manner, however, humans are undoubtedly quite different, especially in terms of behavior, from other animals. Humans are very much cultural animals. It can hardly be doubted, in fact, that culture is much more important for humans than for other animals and that culture completely masks any influence of genes in many cases. It seems equally likely, however, that genes make some contribution to human behavior.

That human dietary choices are indeed influenced by genes is indicated by a number of studies. The strongest evidence comes from studies of humans that are sufficiently young that cultural influences have not had enough time to become important. Newborn infants, when offered sugar and water solutions, show taste preferences, as measured by voluntary volume intake, with respect to both sugar concentration and the kind of sugar used (Nisbett and Gurwitz 1970; Desor et al. 1973). These preferences may vary, furthermore, with an infant's sex and birth weight (Nisbett and Gurwitz 1970). In addition, Davis (1928) found that infants of weaning age, when offered a choice of simple natural foods, selected nutritionally optimal diets (see also Davis 1939; Sweet 1936). She also found that one child suffering from rickets, a bone disorder caused by vitamin D deficiency, voluntarily consumed cod liver oil, a rich source of vitamin D, until the disorder had disappeared (Davis 1928). A similar case history is provided by a 3½-year-old boy with deficient adrenal cortical tissue, who is believed to have kept himself alive for at least 2½ years by greatly increasing his salt intake. The boy died shortly after being placed in hospital on a standard, relatively low-salt diet (Wilkins and Richter 1940).

Differences between humans and nonhumans in terms of metabolism and sensory abilities must surely be genetically based. Furthermore, differences in these regards *between human individuals* may also be genetically based.

The ability to metabolize lactose, for example, appears to be genetically determined (Flatz, Saegudom, and Sanguanbhokhai 1969). The proportion of people in a population possessing this ability appears, in addition, to be correlated with the extent to which cow's milk has formed a major part of the diet of the population over many generations. Caucasians, for example, can usually metabolize lactose, whereas lactose intolerance is widespread in Thailand, where cow's milk has never been an important dietary component (Flatz et al. 1969). The ability to taste phenylthiocarbamide (PTC) is also genetically determined, being inherited as a simple dominant unit-factor in accordance with the primary Mendelian principle (Cohen and Ogdon 1949). To the extent that the abilities of humans to taste and smell various foods are genetically determined, so too must be their dietary preferences. In the light of the above studies, it also seems likely that there are further genetically based differences between individuals in terms of food preferences.

It is difficult to separate the effects of genes and culture in humans older than very young infants. One way of doing this is to compare monozygotic and dizygotic twins. If, in terms of some behavior, monozygotic twins tend to be more similar to each other than dizygotic twins (all else being equal), then there must be a genetic component to the behavior (Greene, Desor, and Maller 1975). Furthermore, the difference between the two levels of similarity can be used to estimate the magnitude of the genetic contribution. This approach has been applied to human dietary choices only once apparently (Greene et al. 1975). In this study, Greene et al. (1975) examined taste preferences of children aged between 9 and 15 years. They estimated that the heritability (i.e., genetic contribution) is essentially zero for preferences with respect to solutions of sucrose, or lactose, or sodium chloride (Greene et al. 1975). Thus culture appears to have completely overridden any genetic effects in this instance.

Some additional insight into genetic components of human dietary behavior could possibly be gained from studies of voluntary food intake of human adults under ad libitum food availability. Under such conditions, humans on an individual basis might voluntarily match their intakes of calories, protein, etc. with their expenditures, despite considerable variation between individuals in these expenditures. If this were the case then it would seem difficult not to conclude that humans have a genetically based ability to self-regulate certain aspects of their diet. So far, however, little evidence for such an ability has been found. Edholm et al. (1955), for example, found no correlation between the daily caloric expenditures of twelve military cadets and their daily caloric intakes. There was also no correlation when expenditures and intakes were determined over a two-week period (see Table 8 of Edholm et al. 1955). They did find, however, close agreement between a cadet's expenditure of calories on one day and his caloric intake two days later (Edholm et al., 1955).

Conclusion

Dietary decisions clearly involve cultural interactions in the case of some non-human animals and genetic effects in the case of humans. The exact nature and magnitudes of these interactions and effects, however, are far from clear. In fact, as the above discussion shows, there is an impressive lack of appropriate studies. It seems surprising and disappointing, for example, that Davis's (1928) study of voluntary food intake by very young human children has not been repeated or expanded. Equally surprising is the apparent complete lack of studies of how food *preferences* develop in humans from birth to adulthood. It is insufficient, it might be added, to document food habits and how they change. These aspects of diets are greatly affected by food availability. Attention must also be focused on dietary choices and preferences, as these are the fundamental determinants of dietary behavior. In the case of nonhumans, further studies of cultural interactions are also called for, especially studies of possible symbolic communication.

Why should we wish to explore and understand possible genetically based components of human dietary behavior? There are, it seems, two practical reasons. First, faced with an increasing array of artificial and unnatural foods, we must surely understand our innate *abilities* to choose a nutritionally balanced diet. If such abilities are as poor as their lack of attention might imply, then perhaps we should place further constraints on the cultural forces to which we subject ourselves. Second, in the same context, it would seem important to have a good knowledge of possible genetically based *constraints* on our dietary behavior. Perhaps, for example, our ability to choose a balanced diet is good in the presence of natural foods (as in the study of Davis 1928) and rather worse in the presence of less natural foods. Only when a full understanding of genetic and cultural determinants of human dietary behavior has been achieved can the world's food supply be properly managed.

Bibliography

Abel, M. G. 1954. Teaching nutrition in the melting pot of the Pacific. *Journal of the American Dietetic Association* 30:148–54.

Allen, B. J., Bourke, R. M., Clarke, L. J., Cogill, B., Pain, C. F., & Wood, A. W. 1980. Child malnutrition and agriculture on the Nembi plateau, Southern Highlands, Papua New Guinea. *Social Science and Medicine* 14D:127–32.

Allen, B. M. 1967. *Malayan fruits.* Donald Morgan Press Ltd., Singapore.

Anderson, E. N. 1980. 'Heating' and 'cooling' foods in Hong Kong and Taiwan. *Social Science Information* 9(2):237–68.

Anonymous. 1976. The miracle children: hospital feast for two saved in bush. *Daily Telegraph,* Wednesday, August 25:3.

Anonymous. 1980. Monster croc 'Is my father.' *The Sun,* Tuesday, July 22:14, 18.

Arnold, S. J. 1977. Polymorphism and geographic variation in the feeding behaviour of the garter snake *Thamnophis elegans. Science* 197:676–8.

Arnott, M. L. (Ed.) 1975. *Gastronomy: the anthropology of food and food habits.* Mouton, Paris.

Ashton, E. W. 1939. A sociological sketch of Sotho diet. *Transactions of the Royal Society of South Africa* 27:147–214.

Asian Development Bank 1980. *South Pacific agriculture – choices and constraints.* South Pacific Agriculture Survey. Australian National University Press, Canberra.

Asie du Sud-Est et Monde Insulindien 1978. Special issue: La cuisine: vocabulaire, activités, representations. IX(1–2):1–306.

Australia, Government of 1981. *The Australian Dairy Corporation and its Asian subsidiaries,* report of the Senate Standing Committee on Finance and Government Operations. Australian Government Publishing Service, Canberra.

Australia, Bureau of Agricultural Economics 1976. *Dairy products: situation and outlook.* Australian Government Publishing Service, Canberra.

Australia, Bureau of Agricultural Economics 1977. *Dairy products: situation and outlook.* Australian Government Publishing Service, Canberra.

Australia, Bureau of Agricultural Economics 1978. *Dairy products: situation and outlook.* Australian Government Publishing Service, Canberra.

Australia, Parliament of 1980. *Hansard* 20 March:866–7.

Australia Dairy Corporation 1979. *Annual report.* Australia Dairy Corporation, Melbourne.

Australia Dairy Corporation 1980. Annual report. Australia Dairy Corporation, Melbourne.

Australian Dairy Farmers Federation 1979. Dairy farmers mount urgent effort to save Asian milk company. Press release, 27 June.

Australian Financial Review 1970. Dairying's 10 year respite. 21 May:2.

Australian Financial Review 1970. Australian dairy products sales boom in Asia. 30 July:14.

Baer, E. 1978. Infant formula promotion in Malaysia, Part I:1-15; Part II:1-20, Interfaith Centre on Corporate Responsibility, New York, mimeographed.

Bailey, K. V. 1962a. Rural nutrition studies in Indonesia VII: field studies in Javanese infants. *Tropical and Geographical Medicine* 14:111-20.

Bailey, K. V. 1962b. The Gunung Kidul problem in perspective. *Tropical and Geographical Medicine* 14:238-58.

Bailey, K. V. 1963. Malnutrition in New Guinean children and its treatment with solid peanut foods. *Journal of Tropical Pediatrics* 9:35-43.

Bailey, K. V. 1965. Quantity and composition of breast milk in some New Guinea populations. *Journal of Tropical Pediatrics* 11:35-49.

Barrau, J. 1958. *Subsistence agriculture in Melanesia.* Bernice P. Bishop, Museum Bulletin No. 219, Honolulu.

Beauchamp, G. K., & Maller, O. 1977. The development of flavor preferences in humans: a review. In M. R. Kare & O. Maller (Eds.), *The Chemical Senses and Nutrition.* Academic Press, New York.

Beck, B. E. F. 1969. Colour and heat in south Indian ritual. *Man (N.S.)* 4:553-72.

Becroft, T. C. 1967a. Child-rearing practices in the Highlands of New Guinea: a longitudinal study of breast feeding. *Medical Journal of Australia* 2:598-601.

Becroft, T. C. 1967b. Child-rearing practices in the Highlands of New Guinea: general features. *Medical Journal of Australia* 2:810-3.

Becroft, T. C., & Bailey, K. V. 1965. Supplementary feeding trial in New Guinea Highland infants. *Journal of Tropical Pediatrics* 11:28-34.

Becroft, T. C., Stanhope, J. M., & Burchett, P. M. 1969. Mortality and population trends among the Kyaka Enga, Baiyer Valley. *Papua and New Guinea Medical Journal* 12:48-55.

Bell, F. L. S. 1931. The place of food in the social life of central Polynesia. *Oceania* II(2):117-35.

Bell, F. L. S. 1936. The avoidance situation in Tanga. *Oceania* VI(2):175-98; (3):306-22.

Bell, F. L. S. 1946. The place of food in the social life of the Tanga. Part I. The culture of the garden. *Oceania* XVII(2)139-72.

Bell, F. L. S. 1947. Part 2. The art of fishing. *Oceania* XVII(4):310-26.

Bell, F. L. S. 1947. Part 3. The raising of pigs. *Oceania* XVIII(1):36-59.

Bell, F. L. S. 1947. Part 4. Hunting and collecting. *Oceania* XVIII(3):233-47.

Bell, F. L. S. 1947. Part 5. Feasting and feeding. *Oceania* XIX(1):51-75.

Bene, F. 1941. Experiments on the colour preferences of black-chinned hummingbirds. *Condor* 43:237-42.

Bennett, J. W. 1943. Food and social status in a rural society. *American Sociological Review* 8:561-9.

Bennett, J. W., Smith, H. L., & Passin, H. 1942. Food and culture in southern Illinois – a preliminary report. *American Sociological Review* 7:645-60.

Beral, V., & Read, D. J. C. 1971. Insensitivity of respiratory centre to carbon dioxide in the Enga people of New Guinea. *Lancet* 2:1290-4.

Berg, A. 1973a. The economics of breast feeding. *Saturday Review of the Sciences,* May:29–32.

Berg, A. 1973b. *The nutrition factor: its role in national development.* The Brookings Institute, Washington D.C.

Berlin, B., Breedlove, D. E., & Raven, P. H. 1974a. *Principles of Tzeltal plant classification: an introduction to the botanical ethnography of a Mayan-speaking community of highland Chiapas.* Academic Press, New York.

Binns, C. W. 1976. Food volume, a limiting factor in nutrient intake in the Papua New Guinea Highlands. In K. Wilson & R. M. Bourke (Eds.), *Papua New Guinea Food Crops Conference Proceedings.* Department of Primary Industry, Port Moresby.

Blackburn, C. R. B., & Green, W. 1966. Precipitins against extracts of thatched roofs in the areas of New Guinea natives with chronic lung disease. *Lancet* 2:1396–7.

Blackburn, C. R. B. & Woolcock, A. J. 1971. Chronic disease of liver and lungs in New Guinea. *Journal of the Royal College of Physicians of London* 5:241–9.

Blackburn, C. R. B., Green, W. F., & Mitchell, G. A. 1970. Studies of chronic nontuberculous lung disease in New Guinea populations. *American Review of Respiratory Diseases* 102:567–74.

Blankhart, D. M., Ig. Tarwotjo, & Soetadi 1960. Measured weaning patterns in Indonesia. *Berita Departemen Kesehatan, Republic Indonesia* [Bulletin of the Department of Health, Indonesia] 9:15–58.

Boulding, E. 1977. *Women in the twentieth century world.* Sage Publications/Halsted Press, New York.

Bowers, N. 1968. The ascending grasslands: an anthropological study of ecological successions in a high mountain valley of New Guinea. Ph.D. dissertation, Department of Anthropology, Columbia University.

Brown, P. 1978. New Guinea: ecology, society and culture. *Annual Review of Anthropology* 7:262–91.

Brown, P., & Podolefsky, A. 1976. Population density, agricultural intensity, land tenure and group size in New Guinea Highlands. *Ethnology* 15:211–38.

Buchbinder, G. 1973. Maring microadaptation: a study of demographic, nutritional, genetic, and phenotypic variation in a Highland New Guinea population. Ph.D. dissertation, Department of Anthropology, Columbia University.

Buchbinder, G. 1977. Nutritional stress and postcontact population decline among the Maring of New Guinea. In L. Greene (Ed.), *Malnutrition, Behaviour and Social Organisation.* Academic Press, New York.

Bulmer, R. N. H. 1960a. Leadership and social structure among the Kyaka people of the Western Highlands of New Guinea. Ph.D. dissertation, Australian National University, Canberra.

Bulmer, R. N. H. 1960b. Political aspects of the *moka* ceremonial exchange system among the Kyaka people of the Western Highlands of New Guinea. *Oceania* 31(1):1–13.

Bulmer, R. N. H. 1965. The Kyaka of the Western Highlands. In P. Lawrence & M. J. Meggitt (Eds.), *Gods, ghosts and men in Melanesia: some regions of Australian New Guinea and the New Hebrides.* Oxford University Press, Melbourne.

Bulmer, R. N. H. 1967. Why is the cassowary not a bird? A problem of zoological taxonomy among the Karam of the New Guinea Highlands. *Man (N.S.)* 2(1): 5–25.

Bulmer, R. N. H., & Menzies, J. I. 1972. Karam classification of marsupials and rodents. Part I. *Journal of the Polynesian Society* 81:472–99.

Bulmer, R. N. H., & Menzies, J. I. 1973. Karam classification of marsupials and rodents. Part II. *Journal of the Polynesian Society* 82:86–107.

Bulmer, R. N. H., & Tyler, M. J. 1968. Karam classification of frogs. *Journal of the Polynesian Society* 77:333–85.

Bulmer, R. N. H., Menzies, J. I., & Parker, F. 1975. Karam classification of reptiles and fishes. *Journal of the Polynesian Society* 84:267–308.

Burchett, P. M. 1966. Amoebiasis in the New Guinea Western Highlands. *Medical Journal of Australia* 2:1079–81.

Burghardt, G. M. 1977. The ontogeny, evolution and stimulus control of feeding in humans and reptiles. In M. R. Kare & O. Maller (Eds.), *The Chemical Senses and Nutrition.* Academic Press, New York.

Burghardt, G. M., & Hess, E. H. 1966. Food imprinting in the snapping turtle, *Chelydra serpentina. Science* 151:108–9.

Burkill, I. H. 1966. *A dictionary of the economic products of the Malay Peninsula* (2nd ed.). Ministry of Agriculture and Cooperatives, Government of Malaysia, Kuala Lumpur.

Burman, D. 1976. Nutrition in early childhood. In D. S. McLaren & D. Burman (Eds.), *Textbook of paediatric nutrition.* Churchill Livingstone, Edinburgh.

Burridge, K. O. L. 1957. Race relations in Johore. *Australian Journal of Politics and History* 2(2):151–68.

Cassel, J. 1955. A comprehensive health program among South African Zulus. In B. D. Paul (Ed.), *Health, culture and community.* Russell Sage Foundation, New York.

Cassel, J. 1957. Social and cultural implications of food habits. *American Journal of Public Health* 47:732–40.

Castle, L. 1980. The economic context. In Asia Development Bank, *South Pacific agriculture – choices and constraints.* South Pacific Agriculture Survey, Australian National University Press, Canberra.

Cavalli-Sforza, L. 1974. The role of plasticity in biological and cultural evolution. *Annals of the New York Academy of Science* 231:43–59.

Cavalli-Sforza, L. 1975. Cultural and biological evolution. A theoretical inquiry. *Ateneo Parmense* 11:19–31.

Cavalli-Sforza, L., & Feldman, M. 1973a. Models for cultural inheritance. 1. Group mean and within group variation. *Theoretical Population Biology* 4:42–55.

Cavalli-Sforza, L., & Feldman, M. 1973b. Cultural versus biological inheritance: phenotypic transmission from parents to children. *Human Genetics* 25:618–37.

Cavannaugh, J. 1976. The Gogol wood chip project. In *Man and the biosphere report.* Australian Government Printing Office, Canberra.

Challis, R. L. 1970. The Pacific Islanders in urban environments. In R. M. Brown (Ed.), *New Zealand in the Pacific.* Institute of Public Administration, Wellington.

Chan, M. M., & Kare, M. R. 1979. Effect of vitamin B-6 deficiency on preference for several taste solutions in the rat. *Journal of Nutrition* 109:339–44.

Chang, K. C. (Ed.) 1977. *Food in Chinese culture: anthropological and historical perspectives.* Yale University Press, New Haven.

Chassy, J. P., van Veen, A. G., & Young, F. W. 1967. The application of social science research methods to the study of food habits and food consumption in an industrializing area. *American Journal of Clinical Nutrition* 20(1):56–64.

Chen, P. C. Y. 1970. Indigenous concepts of causation and methods of prevention in a rural Malay community. *Journal of Tropical Pediatrics* 16(2):33–42.

Chen, P. C. Y. 1972. Socio-cultural influences in vitamin A deficiency in a rural Malay community. *Journal of Tropical Medicine and Hygiene* 75(12):231–6.

Chen, P. C. Y. 1977. Food habits and malnutrition. *Medical Journal of Malaysia* 31: 170–5.

Chen, S. T. 1974. Protein–calorie malnutrition: a major health problem of multiple causation in Malaysia. *Southeast Asian Journal of Tropical Medicine and Public Health* 5:85–9.

Chen, S. T. 1975. Pneumonia and diarrhoea: killers of toddlers in developing countries. *Tropical and Geographical Medicine* 27:103–8.

Chen, S. T. 1976. Comparative growth of Malay, Chinese and Indian schoolchildren in Malaysia. *Southeast Asian Journal of Tropical Medicine and Public Health* 7:443–51.

Chen, S. T. 1979. Infant feeding practices in Malaysia. Department of Pediatrics, University of Malaya, Kuala Lumpur, mimeographed.

Chen, S. T., & Dugdale, A. E. 1972. Morbidity pattern amongst some primary school entrants in Malaysia. *Tropical and Geographical Medicine* 24:269–74.

Chetley, A. 1985. *Protecting Infant Health: A Health Worker's Guide to the International Code of Marketing of Breast Milk Substitutes*. International Organization of Consumers Unions in conjunction with International Baby Food Action Network, Penang, Malaysia.

Choice, 1980. The baby food scandal. February:42–6.

Chong, Y. H. 1969. *Food and nutrition in Malaysia*. Bulletin No. 14, Institute of Medical Research, Kuala Lumpur.

Chong, Y. H. 1976. Aspects of ecology of food and nutrition in Peninsular Malaysia. *Journal of Tropical Pediatrics* 22:239–56.

Christensen, C. M., Caldwell, D. F., & Oberleas, D. 1974. Establishment of a learned preference for a zinc-containing solution by zinc-deficient rats. *Journal of Comparative and Physiological Psychology* 87S:415–21.

Clarke, W. C. 1971. *Place and people: an ecology of a New Guinea community*. Australian National University Press, Canberra.

Clarke, W. C. 1976. The maintenance of agriculture and human habitats within the tropical forest ecosystem. In *Man and the Biosphere Report*. Australian Government Printing Office, Canberra.

Cleary, G. J., & Blackburn, C. R. B. 1968. Air pollution in native huts in the Highlands of New Guinea. *Archives of Environmental Health* 17:785–94.

Cleland, J. B., & Johnston, T. H. 1937/8. Notes on native names and uses of plants in the Musgrave Ranges region. *Oceania* 8:208–15, 328–42.

Clements, F. W., & Rogers, J. F. 1967. *You and your food*. A. H. & A. W. Reed, Sydney and Wellington.

Cobley, L. 1956. *An introduction to the botany of tropical plants*. Longmans & Green, New York.

Cohen, S. J., & Ogdon, D. P. 1949. Taste blindness to phenylthio-carbamide and related compounds. *Psychological Bulletin* 46:490–8.

Colson, A. C. 1971. *The prevention of illness in a Malay village: an analysis of concepts and behaviour*. Medical Behavioural Science Monograph, Series II, No. 1.

Conklin, H. C. 1954. The relation of Hanunoo culture to the plantworld. Ph.D. dissertation, Yale University, New Haven.

Corporate Examiner, The 1980. ICCR brief. New York, January.

Covarrubias, M. 1973. *Island of Bali*. Alfred A. Knopf, New York. (Originally published in 1936)

Cowie, R. J. 1977. Optimal foraging in great tits (*Parus major*). *Nature* 268: 137–9.

Cribb, A. B., & J. W. 1975. *Wild food in Australia*. Collins, Sydney.

Current Notes on International Affairs. 1969. Australia Indonesia joint venture. Opening of Indomilk factory in Jakarta. July:388–90.

Currier, R. L. 1966. The hot–cold syndrome and symbolic balance in Mexican and Spanish-American folk medicine. *Ethnology* 5(3):251–63.

Curson, P. H. 1973. The migration of Cook Islanders to New Zealand. *South Pacific Bulletin,* 2nd quarter:15–25.

Cussler, M. T., & Give, M. L. de 1942. The effect of human relations on food habits in the rural Southeast. *Applied Anthropology* 1(3):13–18.

Cussler, M. T., & Give, M. L. de 1943. Foods and nutrition in our rural Southeast. *Journal of Home Economics* 35:280–2.

Cussler, M. T., & Give, M. L. de 1952. *'Twixt the cup and the lip': psychological and socio-cultural factors affecting food habits*. Twayne Publishers, New York.

Damas, D. 1972. Central Eskimo system of food sharing. *Ethnology* 11:220–40.

Davidson, F. 1977. Coconut, breadfruit, taro, bananas and fish. *Health* 29(1):12–3.

Davidson, G. 1980. Asia Dairy: another aspect. *The Canberra Times* 2 July:2.

Davis, C. M. 1928. Self selection of diet by newly weaned infants. *American Journal of Diseases of Children* 36:651–79.

Davis, C. M. 1939. Results of the self-selection of diets by young children. *Canadian Medical Association Journal* 41:257–61.

Daws, G. 1974. *The shoal of time*. University of Hawaii Press, Honolulu.

de Garine, I. 1970. The social and cultural background of food habits in developing countries (traditional societies). In G. Blix (Ed.), *Food cultism and nutritional quackery: symposia of the Swedish Nutrition Foundation, VIII*. Almquist & Wiksells, Uppsala.

de Garine, I. 1972. The socio-cultural aspects of nutrition. *Ecology of Food and Nutrition* 1:143–63.

de Give, M. L., & Cussler, M. T. 1941. *Interrelations between the cultural pattern and nutrition. A study of a village of 300 inhabitants in the coastal plains area of a southeastern state*. U.S. Department of Agriculture Extension Service, Circular No. 366, 48 pp.

Dentan, R. K. 1968. *The Semai: a nonviolent people of Malaya*. Holt, Rinehart & Winston, New York.

Desor, J. A., Greene, L. S., & Maller, O. 1973. Taste in acceptance of sugars by human infants. *Journal of Comparative and Physiological Psychology* 84:496–501.

Deuel, H. 1955. Newer concepts of the role of fats and of the essential fatty acids in the diet. *Food Research* 20(1):81–96.

Djamour, J. 1965. *Malay kinship and marriage in Singapore*. Athlone Press, London.

Dornstreich, M. 1973. An ecological study of Gadio Enga (New Guinea) subsistence. Ph.D. dissertation, Department of Anthropology, Columbia University.

Douglas, M. 1966. *Purity and danger: an analysis of concepts of pollution and taboo*. Routledge & Kegan Paul, London.

Douglas, M. 1975. Deciphering a meal. In *Implicit meanings: essays in anthropology*. Routledge & Kegan Paul, London.

Douglas, W. H. 1976. Aboriginal categorisation of natural features. *Aboriginal Child at School* 4(5):51–64.

Drickamer, L. C. 1972. Experience and selection behaviour in the food habits of *Peromyscus:* use of olfaction. *Behavior* 41:269–87.

Dugdale, A. E. 1970. Breast feeding in a South East Asian city. *Far East Medical Journal* 6:23–4.

Dugdale, A. E. 1971. The effect of the type of feeding on weight gain and illness in infants. *British Journal of Nutrition* 26:423–32.

Duncan, L. S. W. 1971. Explanations for Polynesian crime rates. *Recent Law,* October:283–8.

Durham, W. H. 1976. The adaptive significance of cultural behavior. *Human Ecology* 4:89–121.

Dwyer, P. 1974. The price of protein: five hundred hours of hunting in the New Guinea Highlands. *Oceania* 44:278–93.

Edholm, O. G., Fletcher, J. G., Widdowson, E. M., & McCance, R. A. 1955. The energy expenditure and food intake of individual mean. *British Journal of Nutrition* 9:286–300.

Edmundson, W. C. 1976. *Land, food and work in East Java.* New England Monographs in Geography, No. 4. University of New England, Armidale.

Eggan, F., & Pijoan, M. 1943. Some problems in the study of food and nutrition. *American Indigena* 3:9–22.

Eibl-Eibesfeldt, I. 1970. Ethology: the biology of behaviour. Holt, Rinehart & Winston, New York.

Endicott, Karen. 1979. Batek Negrito sex roles. M.A. dissertation, Department of Prehistory and Anthropology, Australian National University, Canberra.

Endicott, Kirk. 1979. The impact of economic modernisation on the *Orang Asli* (Aborigines) of northern Peninsular Malaysia. In J. C. Jackson & M. Rudner (Eds.), *Issues in Malaysian development.* Heinemann Educational Books (Asia) Ltd., Singapore.

Engen, T., Lipsitt, L. P., & Kayne, H. 1963. Olfactory responses and adaptation in the human neonate. *Journal of Comparative Physiology* 56:73–7.

Epstein, R., Lanza, R. P., & Skinner, B. F. 1980. Symbolic communication between two pigeons (*Columba livia domestica*). *Science* 207:543–5.

FAO/WHO Ad Hoc Expert Committee. 1973. *Energy and protein requirements.* World Health Organization Technical Report Series, No. 522, Geneva.

Feachem, R. G. 1973. Environment and health in a New Guinea Highlands community. Ph.D. dissertation, University of New South Wales, Sydney.

Feachem, R. G. 1977. Environmental health engineering as human ecology: an example from New Guinea. In T. P. Bayliss-Smith & R. G. Feachem (Eds.), *Subsistence and survival: rural ecology in the Pacific.* Academic Press, London.

Feinsinger, P., & Chaplin, S. B. 1975. On the relationship between wing disc loading and foraging strategy in hummingbirds. *American Nature* 109:217–24.

Feldman, M., & Cavalli-Sforza, L. 1975. Models for cultural inheritance. II. A general linear model. *Annals of Human Biology* 2:215–26.

Feldman, M., & Cavalli-Sforza, L. 1976. Cultural and biological evolutionary processes. Selection for a trait under complex transmission. *Theoretical Population Biology* 9:238–59.

Files of the Colonial Office 1938. Department of Social Services Files CO/859. Public Records Office, London.

Finney, B. 1975. A Polynesian proletariat. In R. Force (Ed.), *Impact.* Bishop Museum Press, Honolulu.

Firth, Raymond. 1959. *Social change in Tikopia.* George Allen & Unwin, London.

Firth, Raymond. 1963. *We, the Tikopia: a sociological study of kinship in primitive Polynesia.* Beacon Press, Boston. (Originally published in 1936)

Firth, Raymond. 1966. *Malay fisherman: their peasant economy* (2nd ed.). The Norton Library, New York. (Originally published in 1946)

Firth, Raymond. 1967. *Primitive Polynesian economy.* Routledge & Kegan Paul, London. (Originally published in 1939)

Firth, Rosemary. 1966. *Housekeeping among Malay peasants.* Athlone Press, London. (Originally published in 1943)

Fisher, J., & Hinde, R. A. 1950. The opening of milk bottles by birds. *British Birds* 42:347-57.

Fisk, E. K. 1962. Planning in a primitive economy: some special problems of Papua New Guinea. *Economic Record* 38:84.

Fitzgerald, T. K. 1977a. Anthropological approaches to the study of food habits: some methodological issues. In T. K. Fitzgerald (Ed.), *Nutrition and anthropology in action.* van Gorcum, Assen/Amsterdam.

Fitzgerald, T. K. 1977b. A nutritional anthropologist discusses methodology. *Journal of the New Zealand Dietetic Association* 31(1):11-4.

Fitzgerald, T. K. 1978a. Migration and reciprocal changes in diet. *South Pacific Bulletin* 28(3):30-3.

Fitzgerald, T. K. 1978b. Pakeha and Polynesia: what these kids eat. *Education (N.Z.)* 1:15-17.

Fitzgerald, T. K. 1979. Southern folks' eating habits ain't what they used to be if they ever were. *Nutrition Today* 14(4):16-21.

Flatz, G., Saegudom, C., & Sanguanbhokhai, T. 1969. Lactose intolerance in Thailand. *Nature* 221:758-9.

Fook Gaik Sim n.d. *The promotion of sweetened condensed milk as infant food.* International Organization of Consumer Unions Regional Office for Asia and the Pacific, Penang.

Forster, R., & Ranum, O. (Eds.) 1979. *Food and drink in history. Selections from the Annales: economies, sociétés, civilisations,* Vol. 5. Trans. E. Forster & P. M. Ranum. John Hopkins University Press, Baltimore and London.

Fortes, M., & Fortes, S. L. 1936. Food in the domestic economy of the Tallensi. *Africa* 9:237-76.

Foster, G. M., & Anderson, B. G. 1978. *Medical anthropology.* Wiley, New York.

Frazer, J. G. 1922. *The golden bough: a study in magic and religion.* Macmillan Press, London.

Freedman, M. 1955. *A report on some aspects of food, health and society in Indonesia.* World Health Organization, MH/AS/219.55.

Freedman, M. 1958. Health education: how it strikes an anthropologist. *South Pacific Commission Quarterly Bulletin* April:52-6.

Freedman, R. L. 1977. Nutritional anthropology: an overview. In T. K. Fitzgerald (Ed.), *Nutrition and anthropology in action.* van Gorcum, Assen/Amsterdam.

Frisbie, J. 1961. *The Frisbies of the South Seas.* The Travel Book Club, London. (Originally published in 1959)

Frisch, K. V. 1967. *The dance language and orientation of bees.* Harvard University Press, Cambridge, Mass.

Galef, B. G., Jr. 1976. Social transmission of acquired behavior: a discussion of tradition social learning in vertebrates. *Advances in the Study of Behavior* 6: 77–100.

Galef, B. G., Jr., & Henderson, P. W. 1972. Mother's milk: a determinant of the feeding preferences of rat pups. *Journal of Comparative and Physiological Psychology* 78:213–9.

Garcia, J., & Brett, L. P. 1977. Conditioned responses to food odor and taste in rats and wild predators. In M. R. Kare & O. Maller (Eds.), *The chemical senses and nutrition.* Academic Press, New York.

Garcia, J. Ervin, F. R., & Koelling, R. A. 1966. Learning with prolonged delay of reinforcement. *Psychonomic Science* 5:121–2.

Geertz, C. 1960. *The religion of Java.* Free Press, New York.

Geertz, H. 1961. *The Javanese family: a study of kinship and socialization.* Free Press, New York.

George, S. 1979. *How the other half dies.* Penguin, Harmondsworth.

Gerrard, J. W. 1974. Breast feeding: second thoughts. *Pediatrics* 54:757–64.

Gershoff, S. N. 1977. The role of vitamins and minerals in taste. In M. R. Kare & O. Maller (Eds.), *The chemical senses and nutrition.* Academic Press, New York.

Gillison, A. N. 1976. A review of problems and techniques in restoring the tropical forest ecosystem. In *Man and the biosphere report.* Australian Government Printing Office, Canberra.

Gimlette, J. B. 1971. *Malay poisons and charm cures.* Oxford University Press, Kuala Lumpur. (Originally published in 1913)

Gittelman, S. H. 1978. Optimum diet and body size in backswimmers (*Heteroptera: Notonectidae, Pleidae*). *Entomological Society of America Annals* 71:737–47.

Golomb, L. 1978. *Brokers of morality: Thai ethnic adaptation in a rural Malaysian setting.* University Press of Hawaii, Honolulu.

Golson, J. 1976. The appearance of plant and animal domestication in New Guinea. In J. Garanger (Ed.), *La préhistoire Océanienne.* Centre National de la Recherche Scientifique, Paris.

Gordon, J. E., Wyon, J. B., & Ascoli, W. 1967. The second year death rate in less developed countries. *American Journal of the Medical Sciences* 254:357–80.

Goss-Custard, J. D. 1977. Responses of redshank, *Tringa totanus,* to absolute and relative densities of two prey species. *Journal of Animal Ecology* 46:867–74.

Goto, S., Sdao, M., Yano, K., & Takeuchi, I. Y. 1974. A survey of infant mortality rates in Sarawak. *South Asian Journal of Tropical Medicine and Public Health* 5:424–9.

Gould, R. A. 1967. Notes on hunting, butchering and sharing of game among the Ngatatjara and their neighbours in the West Australian desert. *Kroeber Anthropological Society Papers* 36:41–63.

Gould, R. A. 1969. Subsistence behaviour among the western desert Aborigines of Australia. *Oceania* 39(4):253–74.

Government of Malaysia 1979. Mid-term review of the Third Malaysia Plan 1976–1980, Kuala Lumpur.

Grant, L. 1984. Boycott ended, Nestle turns its attention to growth in U.S. *Los Angeles Times,* February 2:1–2.

Great Britain, Economic Advisory Council, Committee on Nutrition in the Colonial Empire. 1939. First report, Part I: *Nutrition in the Colonial Empire.* Cmd. 6050, His Majesty's Stationery Office, London.

Greene, L. A., Desor, J. A., & Maller, O. 1975. Heredity and experience: their relative importance in the development of taste preference in man. *Journal of Comparative and Physiological Psychology* 89:279-84.

Greiner, T. 1975. *The promotion of bottle feeding by multinational corporations: how advertising and the health professionals have contributed.* Cornell International Nutrition Monograph Series No. 2, Ithaca, New York.

Greiner, T. 1977. *Regulation and education: strategies for solving the bottle feeding problem.* Cornell International Nutrition Monograph Series No. 4, Ithaca.

Greiner, T. 1979. Breast feeding in decline: perspectives on the causes. In D. B. Jelliffe, E. F. Jelliffe, F. T. Sai, & P. Senanayake (Eds.), *Lactation, fertility and the working woman, Proceedings of the Joint International Planned Parenthood Federation/Union of Nutritional Sciences Conference, Italy, July 5-12, 1977.* International Planned Parenthood Federation, London.

Grossman, R. 1978. Women's place in the integrated circuit. *Pacific Research* 9:2-17.

Hainsworth, F. R. 1978. Feeding: models of costs and benefits in energy regulation. *American Zoologist* 18:701-14.

Haire, D. 1973. The cultural warping of childbirth. *Journal of Tropical Pediatrics and Environmental Child Health Monograph* 27:171-91.

Hallowell, A. I. 1954. *Culture and experience.* University of Pennsylvania Press, Philadelphia.

Hamilton, A. 1975. Aboriginal women: the means of production. In J. Mercer (Ed.), *The other half.* Penguin, Melbourne.

Handy, E. 1960. *My favourite recipes* (2nd ed.). M. P. H. Publications Snd. Bnd., Singapore.

Hanks, L. M. 1972. *Rice and man: agricultural ecology in Southeast Asia.* Aldine Atherton Inc., Chicago.

Hanson, F. E. 1976. Comparative studies in induction of food choice preferences in lepidopterous larvae. *Symposium of Biological Hunger* 16:71-7.

Harper, L. V. 1972. Social facilitation of feeding behavior in young *Homo sapiens. American Zoologists* 12:647.

Hauck, H. M. 1959. *Maternal and child health in a Siamese rice village: nutritional aspects.* Southeast Asia Program Data Paper No. 39, Ithaca, New York.

Hauck, H. M., and associates. 1956. *Aspects of health, sanitation, and nutritional status in a Siamese rice village.* Southeast Asia Program Data Paper No. 22, Cornell University Department of Asian Studies, Ithaca, New York.

Hauck, H. M., Sudsaneh, S., Hanks, J. R., and associates. 1958. *Food habits and nutrient intakes in a Siamese rice village.* Southeast Asia Program Paper No. 29, Cornell University Department of Asian Studies, Ithaca, New York.

Hawley, F., Pijoan, M., & Elkin, C. A. 1943. An inquiry into the food economy and body economy in Zia Pueblo. *American Anthropologist* 45:547-56.

Hays, T. E. 1979. Plant classification and nomenclature in Ndumba, Papua New Guinea Highlands. *Ethnology* 18:252-70.

Heath, J. 1978. Linguistic approaches to Nunggubuyu ethnozoology and ethnobotany. In L. R. Hiatt (Ed.), *Australian Aboriginal mythology: essays in honour of W. E. H. Stanner.* Australian Institute of Aborginal Studies, Canberra.

Hellman, E. 1936. Urban native food in Johannesburg. *Africa* 9:277-90.

Helsing, E. 1978. *Feeding practices in Europe: beliefs, motivations and possibilities for change.* Prepared for the International Symposium on Infant and Early Childhood Feeding, Michigan State University, October, 1979.

Helsing, E. 1979. Women's liberation and breast feeding. In D. B. Jelliffe, E. J. Jelliffe, F. T. Sai, & P. Senanyake (Eds.), *Lactation, fertility and the working woman, Proceedings of the Joint International Planned Parenthood Federation/Union of Nutritional Sciences Conference, Italy, July 5–12, 1977*. International Planned Parenthood Federation, London.

Hespenheide, H. A. 1966. The selection of seed size by finches. *Wilson Bulletin* 78: 190–7.

Hetzel, B. S., & Firth, H. J. 1978. *The nutrition of Aborigines in relation to the ecosystem of central Australia*. C.S.I.R.O., Melbourne.

Heywood, P. F. 1979. Nutrition problems of children in developing countries: their wider significance. *Proceedings of Nutrition Society of Australia* 4:12–19.

Hide, R. L. 1980. *Cash crop and food production in Chimbu*. History of Agriculture Working Paper No. 44, Port Moresby.

Hinde, R. A. 1970. *Animal behaviour: a synthesis of ethnology and comparative psychology* (2nd ed.). McGraw-Hill Kogakusha, Tokyo.

Hinde, R. A., & Fisher, J. 1952. Further observations on the opening of milk bottles by tits. *British Birds* 44:393–6.

Hipsley, E. H. 1969. *Metabolic studies in New Guineans: oxygen uptake and carbon dioxide excretion during fasting–resting exercising conditions*. South Pacific Commission Technical Paper No. 162, Noumea.

Hipsley, E. H., & Clements, F. W. (Eds.) 1950. *Report of the New Guinea Nutrition Survey Expedition 1947*. Government Printer, Sydney.

Hipsley, E. H., & Kirk, N. E. 1965. *Studies of dietary intake and the expenditure of energy by New Guineans*. South Pacific Commission Technical Paper No. 147, Noumea.

Hodge, J. V. 1972. The need for medical research in the South Pacific. *Association of Home Science Alumni Journal (N.Z.)* 41:27–9.

Hodgkinson, N. 1980. Asia Dairy story unfolds. *Canberra Times,* 25th June:8.

Hofvander, Y., Sjolin, S., & Vahlquist, B. 1979. Scandanavia. In D. B. Jelliffe, E. F. Jelliffe, F. T. Sai, & P. Senanyake (Eds.), *Lactation, fertility and the working woman, Proceedings of the Joint International Sciences Conference, Italy, July 5–12, 1977*. International Planned Parenthood, London.

Holmberg, A. 1969. *Nomads of the long bow: the Siriono of eastern Bolivia*. American Museum Science Books, Washington, D.C. (Originally published in 1950).

Holmes, S. 1956. Public health nutrition programmes in the Pacific Islands. *South Pacific Commission Quarterly Bulletin* April:13–15; 41–2.

House, H. L. 1972. Inversion in the order of food superiority between temperatures effected by nutrient balance in the fly larva *Agria housei* (Diptera: Sarcophagidae). *Canadian Entomologist* 104:1559–64.

Huettel, M. D., & Bush, G. L. 1972. The genetics of host selection and its bearing on sympatric speciation in Procecidochares (Diptera: Tephritidae). *Entomologia Experimentalis et Applicata* 15:465–80.

Hull, V. J. 1978. A study of birth interval dynamics in rural Java. In W. H. Mosley (Ed.), *Nutrition and Human Reproduction*. Plenum Press, New York.

Hull, V. J. 1979. Women, doctors and family health care: some lessons from rural Java. *Studies in Family Planning* 10(1/12):315–25.

Hull, V. J. 1983. The Ngaglik study: an inquiry into birth interval dynamics and maternal and child health in rural Java. *World Health Statistics Quarterly* 36(2): 100–18.

Hunn, E. S. 1977. *Tzeltal folk zoology: the classification of discontinuities in nature.* Academic Press, New York.

IBFAN News 1985. Minneapolis, December.

INFACT 1978. *INFACT Notes.* Infant Formula Action Coalition, Minneapolis.

INFACT 1980. *Newsletter* 1(2). Infant Formula Action Coalition, Minneapolis.

Irvine, F. R. 1957. Wild and emergency foods of Australian and Tasmanian Aborigines. *Oceania* 28(2):113–42.

Itani, J. 1958. On the acquisition and propagation of a new food habit in the troop of Japanese monkeys at Takasakyiyama. *Primates* 1:84–98.

Ivlev, V. S. 1961. *Experimental ecology of the feeding of fishes.* Yale University Press, New Haven, Conn.

Jain, A. K., & Bongaarts, J. 1981. Breast-feeding: patterns, correlates and fertility effects. *Studies in Family Planning* 12(3):79–99.

Jelliffe, D. B. 1967. Parallel food classifications in developing and industrialized countries. *American Journal of Clinical Nutrition* 20:279–81.

Jelliffe, D. B. 1968. *Infant nutrition in the subtropics and tropics.* World Health Organization, Geneva.

Jelliffe, D. B., & Jelliffe, E. F. P. 1975. Human milk, nutrition and the world resource crisis. *Science* 188:557–61.

Jelliffe, D. B., & Jelliffe, E. F. P. 1977. Breast is best: modern meanings. *New England Journal of Medicine* 297:912–15.

Jelliffe, D. B., & Jelliffe, E. F. P. 1978. *Human milk in the modern world.* Oxford University Press, Oxford.

Jelliffe, D. B., & Jelliffe, E. F. P. 1979. Adequacy of breastfeeding. *Lancet* 2:691–2.

Jensen, E. 1966. Iban birth. *Folk* 8–9:165–78.

Jermy, T., Hanson, T. E., & Dethier, V. G. 1968. Induction of specific food preference in lepidopterous larvae. *Entomologia Experimentalis et Aplicata* 11:211–30.

Jerome, N., Kandel, R., & Pelto, G. (Eds.) 1980. *Nutritional anthropology: contemporary approaches to diet and culture.* Redgrave, New York.

John, E. R. P., Chesler, P., Barlett, F., & Victor, I. 1968. Observational learning in cats. *Science* 159:1489–91.

Jouventin, P., Pasteur, G., & Cambefort, J. P. 1977. Observational learning of baboons and avoidance of mimics: exploratory tests. *Evolution* 31:214–18.

Kaberry, P. M. 1939. *Aboriginal women: sacred and profane.* Routledge, London.

Kahn, M. 1979. *The spectre of famine in Wamira, Milne Bay Province.* History of Agriculture Working Paper No. 25, University of Papua New Guinea and Department of Primary Industry, mimeographed.

Kahn, M. 1980. Taro irrigation: a descriptive account from Wamira, Papua New Guinea. *Oceania* 54:204–22.

Kawai, M. 1965. Newly acquired pre-cultural behaviour of the natural troop of Japanese monkeys on Koshima Island. *Primates* 6:1–30.

Kawamura, S. 1959. The process of subculture propagation among Japanese macaques. *Journal of Primatology* 2:43–60.

Kent, M. M. 1981. Breast-feeding in the developing world: current patterns and implications for future trends. *World Fertility Survey* Vol. 2. Population Reference Bureau, Inc.

Kera, R. T., & Maenu'u, L. P. 1976. The influence of land tenure and logging, replanting and protection of forests in the Solomon Islands. In *Man and the biosphere report.* Australian Government Printing Office, Canberra.

Klopfer, P. H. 1957. An experiment on empathic learning in ducks. *American Naturalist* 91:61-3.

Knobel, J. 1977. Breast-feeding and population growth. *Science* 198:1111-15.

Krebs, J. R. 1978. Optimal foraging. In J. R. Krebs & N. B. Davies (Eds.), *Behavioural ecology: an evolutionary approach.* Blackwell Scientific Publications, Oxford.

Labanick, G. M. 1976. Prey availability, consumption and selection in the cricket frog, *Acris crepitans* (Amphibia, Anura, Hylidae). *Journal of Herpetology* 10(4): 293-8.

Labouisse, H. R. 1978. The conquest of malnutrition. Inaugural ceremony of the Eleventh International Congress on Nutrition.

Lactation Review, The 1977. 2(3):1-11.

Lactation Review, The 1978. 3(1):1-7.

Laderman, C. 1981. Symbolic and empirical reality: a new approach to the analysis of food avoidance. *American Ethnologist* 8(3):468-93.

Laderman, C. 1983. *Wives and midwives: childbirth and nutrition in rural Malaysia.* University of California Press, Berkeley.

Lambert, J. N. 1978. *National nutrition survey.* National Printing Office, Port Moresby, mimeographed.

Lambert, J. N. n.d. Does cash cropping cause malnutrition? National Planning Office, Port Moresby, mimeographed.

Langley, D. 1947. Food consumption and dietary levels. In E. Hipsley & F. Clements (Eds.), *Report of the New Guinea Nutrition Survey Expedition,* Part 4, Canberra.

Lappé, F. M., & Collins, J. 1977. Food first: beyond the myth of scarcity. Houghton Mifflin, Boston.

Latham, M. C. 1977. Infant feeding in national and international perspective: an examination of the decline in human lactation and the modern crisis in infant and young child feeding practices. *Annals of the New York Academy of Sciences* 300:197-209.

Lea, D. A. M. 1972. Indigenous horticulture in Melanesia. In R. G. Ward (Ed.), *Man and the landscape in the Pacific Islands.* Oxford University Press (Clarendon Press), Oxford.

Lea, D. A. M. 1976. Human sustenance and the tropical forest. In *Man and the biosphere report.* Australian Government Printing Office, Canberra.

Ledogar, R. J. 1975. *Hunger for profits: U.S. food and drug multinationals in Latin America.* IDOC/North America Inc., New York.

Lepkovsky, S. 1977. The role of the chemical senses in nutrition. In M. R. Kare & O. Maller (Eds.), *The chemical senses and nutrition.* Academic Press, New York.

Lévi-Strauss, C. 1966. *The savage mind.* Weiderfeld & Nicholson, London.

Lévi-Strauss, C. 1969. *The raw and the cooked.* Jonathan Cape, London.

Levitt, D. 1981. *Plants and people: Aboriginal uses of plants on Groote Eylandt.* Australian Institute of Aboriginal Studies, Canberra.

Lindenbaum, S. 1977. The 'last course': nutrition and anthropology in Asia. In T. K. Fitzgerald (Ed.), *Nutrition and anthropology in action.* van Gorcum, Assen/Amsterdam.

Logan, M. H., & Morrill, W. T. 1979. Humoral medicine and informant variability: an analysis of acculturation and cognitive change amongst Guatemalan villagers. *Anthropos* 74:785-802.

Macpherson, C. 1977. Polynesians in New Zealand: an emerging eth-class. In D. Pitt (Ed.), *Social class in New Zealand.* Longman Paul, Aukland.

Maiden, J. H. 1889. *The useful native plants of Australia (including Tasmania).* Facsimile edition, Compendium, Melbourne.

Majnep, I. S., & Bulmer, R. N. H. 1977. *Birds of my Kalam country.* University of Auckland Press, Auckland.

Malaysia, Government of 1973. *Mid term review of the second Malaysia plan 1971–75.* Government Press, Kuala Lumpur.

Malcolm, L. A. 1969. Child mortality and disease pattern: recent changes in the Bundi area. *Papua New Guinea Medical Journal* 12:13–17.

Malcolm, L. A. 1970. Growth, malnutrition, and mortality of the infant and toddler in the Asai Valley of the New Guinea Highlands. *American Journal of Clinical Nutrition* 23:1090–5.

Malcolm, L. A. 1979. Protein–energy malnutrition and growth. In F. Falkner and J. M. Turner (Eds.), *Human growth,* Vol. 3, *Neurobiology and Nutrition.* Plenum, New York.

Malinowski, B. 1935. *Coral gardens and their magic,* Vol. 1. Allen & Unwin, London.

Maller, O., & Desor, J. A. 1974. The effects of taste on ingestion by human newborns. In J. Bosma (Ed.), *Oral sensation and perception: development in the fetus and infant.* U.S. Government Printing Office, Washington, D.C.

Man and the biosphere 1976. *Report on ecological effects of increasing human activities on tropical and subtropical forest ecosystems.* Australian Government Printing Office, Canberra.

Manderson, L. 1981a. Traditional food beliefs and critical life events in Peninsular Malaysia. *Social Science Information* 20:947–75.

Manderson, L. 1981b. Humoral medical theory and traditional food classification in Peninsular Malaysia. *Ecology of Food and Nutrition* 11:81–93.

Manderson, L. 1981c. Roasting, smoking, and dieting in response to birth: Malay confinement in cross-cultural perspective. *Social Science and Medicine* 15B:509–20.

Manderson, L. 1982. Bottle feeding and ideology in colonial Malaya: the production of change. *International Journal of Health Services* 12(4):597–616.

Mann, L. 1977. Some effects of foreign investment: the case of Malaysia. *Bulletin of Concerned Asian Scholars* 9(4):2–14.

Margulies, L. 1975. Baby formula abroad: exporting infant malnutrition. *Christianity and Crisis,* 11 October:1–4.

Margulies, L. 1977. A critical essay on the role of promotion in bottle feeding. *PAG (Protein Advisory Group)* 7(3–4):73–83.

Margulies, L. 1978. Death and business get their market. *Business and Society Review* 25:43–9.

Martin, M. A. 1978. Les vegetaux dans l'alimentation et la médecine dans le Cambodge d'après 1975. *Asie du Sud-Est et Monde Insulindien* IX(1–2):209–18.

Maude, A. 1973. Land shortage and population pressure in Tonga. In H. Brookfield (Ed.), *The Pacific in transition.* Arnold, New York.

Mauss, M. 1969. *The gift.* Cohen & West, London.

McArthur, M. 1960. Food consumption and dietary levels of groups of Aborigines living on naturally occurring foods. In C. P. Mountford (Ed.), *Records of the American–Australian Scientific Expedition to Arnhem Land.* Melbourne University Press, Melbourne.

McArthur, M. 1962. *Malaya-12. Assignment Report June 1958 – November 1959,* World Health Organization, WPR/449/62.

McArthur, M. 1974. Pigs for the ancestors: a review article. *Oceania* 45:87–123.

McArthur, M. 1977. Nutrition research in Melanesia: a second look at the Tsembaga. In T. P. Bayliss-Smith & R. G. Feachem (Eds.), *Subsistence and survival: rural ecology in the Pacific.* Academic Press, London.

McCarthy, D. D. (Ed.) 1956. *New Zealand medical research in the South West Pacific.* Coulls Somerville, Wilkie Ltd., Dunedin.

McCarthy, F. D., & McArthur, M. 1960. The food quest and the time factor in Aboriginal economic life. In C. P. Mountford (Ed.), *Records of the American-Australian Scientific Expedition to Arnhem Land,* Vol 2. Melbourne University Press, Melbourne.

McComas, M., Fookes, G., Taucher, G., & Falkner, F. 1982/1985. *The dilemma of Third World nutrition: Nestle and the role of infant formula.* Nestle S.A.

McCullough, J. M. 1973. Human ecology, heat adaptation, and belief systems: the hot-cold syndrome of Yucatan. *Journal of Anthropological Research* 29(1):32–6.

McDonald, H. 1980. *Suharto's Indonesia.* Fontana, Melbourne.

McKay, D. A. 1971. Food, illness, and folk medicine: insights from Ulu Trengganu, West Malaysia. *Ecology of Food and Nutrition* 1(2):67–72.

McKay, D. A., Lim, R. K. H., Notaney, K. H., & Dugdale, A. G., 1971. Nutritional assessment by comparative growth achievement of Malay children below school age. *Bulletin of the World Health Organization* 45(2):233–42.

McKay, S. R. 1960. Growth and nutrition of infants in the western highlands of New Guinea. *Medical Journal of Australia* 1:452–9.

McKeown, T. 1979. *The role of medicine: dream, mirage or nemesis?* Princeton University Press, Princeton, N.J.

McKnight, D. 1973. Sexual symbolism of food among the Wik-Mungkun. *Man (N.S.)* 8(2):194–209.

McLean, D. 1972. Australia and the expansion of capitalism in Indonesia. *Review of Indonesian and Malayan Affairs* 6(2):29–69.

McPherson, H. J. 1965. Investigation of ophthalmological conditions in Kelantan. *Medical Journal of Malaya* 20:26.

Mead, M. 1943. Dietary patterns and food habits. *Journal of the American Dietetic Association* 19:1–5.

Mead, M. 1955. *Cultural patterns and technical change.* New American Library (Mentor Books), New York.

Mead, M. 1963. *Sex and temperament in three primitive societies.* Morrow, New York. (Originally published in 1935)

Medway, Lord 1969. *The wild mammals of Malaya and offshore islands including Singapore.* Oxford University Press, Kuala Lumpur.

Meehan, B. 1977. Hunters by the seashore. *Journal of Human Evolution* 6:363–70.

Meehan, B. 1982a. *Shell bed to shell midden.* Australian Institute of Aboriginal Studies, Canberra.

Meehan, B. 1982b. Ten fish for one man: some Anbarra attitudes towards food and health. In J. Reid (Ed.), *Body, land and spirit: health and healing in an Aboriginal society.* University of Queensland Press, St. Lucia.

Meggitt, M. J. 1958. The Enga of the New Guinea Highlands: some preliminary observations. *Oceania* 28:253–330.

Mehmet, O. 1983. Managed industrialization: poverty redressa; policies in Malaysia. In S. Arief & J. K. Sundaram (Eds.), *Malaysian Economy and Finance.* South East Asia Research and Development Institute, Rosecons, Australia, pp. 36–49.

Merck Index of Chemicals and Drugs, The 1960. (2nd ed.). Merck & Co., Rahway, N.J.

Milinski, M., & Heller, R. 1978. Influence of a predator on the optimal foraging behaviour of sticklebacks (*Gasterosteus aculeatus* L.). *Nature* 275:624–3.

Miller, C. Baner, A., & Denning, H. 1952. Taro as a source of thiamine, riboflavine and niacin. *Journal of the American Dietetic Association* 28(5S):435–8.

Miller, F. J. (Trans.) 1921. *Ovid's Metamorphoses.* Loeb Classical Library, Heineman, London.

Miyadi, D. 1959. On some new habits and their propagation in Japanese monkey groups. *Proceedings, XV International Congress of Zoology,* pp. 857–60.

Moerman, M. 1968. *Agricultural change and peasant choice in a Thai village.* University of California Press, Berkeley.

Morgane, P. J., & Jacobs, H. L. 1969. Hunger and satiety. *World Review of Nutrition and Dietetics* 10:100–213.

Morphy, H. 1980. Painting their land. Paper presented at Land Rights Symposium, Australian Institute of Aboriginal Studies biennial meeting, 21–22 May.

Mugford, R. A. 1977. Eternal influences on the feeding of carnivores. In M. R. Kare & O. Maller (Eds.), *The chemical senses and nutrition.* Academic Press, New York.

Murrai, M., Pen, F., & Miller, D. 1958. *Some tropical South Pacific Island foods.* University of Hawaii Press, Honolulu.

Murrell, T. G. C., & Walker, P. D. 1978. Pig-bel – azoonosis? *Journal of Tropical Medicine and Hygiene* 81:231–5.

Nash, M. 1965. *The golden road to modernity: village life in contemporary Burma.* Wiley, New York.

Needham, R. (Ed.) 1973. *Right and left: essays on dual symbolic classification.* University of Chicago Press, Chicago.

Nestle S. A. 1978. *Nestle infant food policy.* Infant and Dietetic Department, Nestle Products Technical Assistance Co. Ltd., Switzerland.

Nestle S. A. 1979a. Personal communication from Bernard Bersier, Senior Vice President, form letter with enclosure.

Nestle S. A. 1979b. *The infant formula controversy: a Nestle view.* The Nestle Company Inc., White Plains, Ga.

Nietschmann, B. 1973. *Between land and water: the subsistence ecology of the Miskito Indians, Eastern Nicaragua.* Seminar Press, New York.

Nisbett, R. E., & Gurwitz, S. B. 1970. Weight, sex and the eating behaviour of human newborns. *Journal of Comparative and Physiological Psychology* 73:245–53.

Norgan, N., Ferro-Luzzi, A., & Durnin, J. 1974. The energy and nutrient intake and the energy expenditure of 204 New Guinean adults. *Philosophical Transactions of the Royal Society, Series B* 268:309–48.

Ohtsuka, R. 1977a. The sago eaters: an ecological discussion with special reference to the Oriomo Papuans. In J. Allen, J. Golson, and R. Jones (Eds.), *Sunda and Sahul.* Academic Press, New York.

Ohtsuka, R. 1977b. Time–space use of the Papuans depending on sago and game. In H. Watanabe (Ed.), *Human activity system.* University of Tokyo Press, Tokyo.

O'Laughlin B. 1974. Mediation of contradiction: why Mbum women do not eat chicken. In M. Z. Rosaldo & L. Lamphere (Eds.), *Women, culture and society.* Stanford University Press, Stanford.

Oliveiro, C. J. 1955. The nutritive value of foods. *Proceedings of the Alumni Association of Malaya* 8:105-29.

Oliver, D. L. 1974. *Ancient Tahitian society.* Australian National University Press, Canberra.

Oomen, H. A. P. C. 1971. Ecology of human nutrition in New Guinea: evaluation of subsistence patterns. *Ecology of Food and Nutrition* 1:3-18.

Oomen, H. A. P. C., & Corden, M. W. 1970. *Metabolic studies in New Guineans: nitrogen metabolism in sweet potato eaters.* South Pacific Commission Technical Paper No. 163, Noumea.

Oomen, H. A. P. C., & Malcolm, S. H. 1965. *Nutrition and the Papuan child: a study in human welfare.* South Pacific Commission Technical Paper No. 118, Noumea.

Oomen, H. A. P. C., Spoon, W., Heesterman, J. E., Ruinard, J., Luyken, R., & Slump, S. 1961. The sweet potato as the staff of life of the highland Papuan. *Tropical and Geographical Medicine* 13:55-66.

Ortner, S. 1974. Is female to male as nature is to culture? In M. Z. Rosaldo & L. Lamphere (Eds.), *Women, culture and society.* Stanford University Press, Stanford.

PAG Bulletin (Protein Advisory Group) 1973. Breast feeding and weaning practices in developing countries and the factors influencing them. 3(4):24-9.

PAG Bulletin (Protein Advisory Group) 1977a. Infant feeding in the less developed countries: an industry viewpoint. 7(3-4):62-72.

PAG Bulletin (Protein Advisory Group) 1977b. Women in food production, food handling and nutrition. 7(3-4):40-9.

Pagezy, H. 1978. Orientation des recherches en anthropologie biologique et en anthropologie de l'alimentation effectives depuis 1974 en Asie du Sud-Est et dans l'Ocean Indien. *Asie du Sud-Est et Monde Insulindien* IX(1-2):31-40.

Parish, W. L., & Whyte, M. K. 1978. *Village and family in contemporary China.* University of Chicago, Chicago.

Passmore, R., Nichol, B. M., & Rao, M. N. 1974. *Handbook of nutritional requirements.* World Health Organization, Geneva.

Peng, Y.-S., & Evenson, J. K. 1979. Food preference and protein intake of normal and diebetic rats fed diets varying in protein quality and quantity. *Journal of Nutrition* 109:1952-61.

Peng Khor Kok. 1983. *Recession and the Malaysian economy.* Institut Masyarakat, Malaysia.

Peters, F. E. 1958. *The chemical composition of South Pacific foods.* South Pacific Commission Technical Paper No. 115, Noumea.

Peters, W. 1960. Studies on the epidemiology of malaria in New Guinea. *Transactions of the Royal Society of Tropical Medicine and Hygiene* 54:242-60.

Peterson, N. 1973. Camp site location amongst Australian hunter-gatherers: archaeological and ethnographic evidence for a key determinant. *Archaeology and Physical Anthropology in Oceania* 8(3):173-93.

Peterson, N. 1978. The importance of women in determining the composition of residential groups in Aboriginal society. In F. Gale (Ed.), *Woman's role in Aboriginal society* (3rd ed.). Australian Institute of Aboriginal Studies, Canberra.

Petros-Barvazian, A., & Carballo, M. 1979. Lactation, reproduction and fertility. In D. B. Jelliffe, E. F. Jelliffe, F. T. Sai, and P. Senanayake (Eds.), *Lactation, fertility and the working woman, Proceedings of the Joint International Planned parenthood Federation/Union of Nutritional Sciences Conference, Italy, July 5–12, 1977.* International Planned Parenthood Federation, London.

Pijoan, M. 1942a. Food availability and social function. *New Mexico Quarterly Review* 12:418–23.

Pijoan, M. 1942b. Cyanide poisoning from choke-cherry seeds. *American Journal of the Medical Sciences* 204:550–3.

Pijoan, M., & Elkin, C. A. 1943. Secondary anemia due to prolonged and exclusive milk feeding among Shoshone Indians. *Journal of Nutrition* 27:67–75.

Pimental, D. et al. 1973. Food production and the energy crisis. *Science* 182:443–9.

Pitt, J. 1979. Immunological aspects of human milk. In D. Raphael (Ed.), *Breastfeeding and food policy in a hungry world.* Academic Press, New York.

Pollock, N. 1978. Takapoto. La Prosperité, retour aux îles. *Journal de la Société des Océanistes* 60(34):133–5.

Pollock, N. J. 1979. Work, wages and shifting cultivation on Niue. *Pacific Studies* 2: 132–43.

Poole, R. C. 1973. Introduction. In C. Lévi-Strauss, *Totemism.* Trans. R. Needham. Penguin, Harmondsworth.

Poorwo 1962. Malnutrition in Indonesia. In A. Burgess and R. Dean (Eds.), *Malnutrition and food habits.* Tavistock, London.

Popkin, B. M., & Solon, F. S. 1976. Income, time, the working mother and child nutriture. *Journal of Tropical Pediatrics and Environmental Child Health* 22: 156–65.

Popkin, B., Bilsborrow, R. E., & Akin, J. S. 1982. Breast-feeding patterns in low-income countries. *Science* 218:1082–93.

Poston, R. N. 1979. Nutrition and immunity. In R. J. Jarrett (Ed.), *Nutrition and disease.* Croom Helm, London.

Powdermaker, H. 1932. Feasts in New Ireland: the social function of eating. *American Anthropologist* 34:236–47.

Prior, I. 1976. Nutritional problems in The Pacific Islands. The 1976 Muriel Bell Memorial Lecture, Otago.

Pulliam, H. R. 1975. Diet optimization with nutrient constraints. *American Naturalist* 109:765–8.

Pulliam, H. R., & Dunford, C. 1980. Programmed to learn: an essay on the evolution of culture. Columbia University Press, New York.

Pura, 1984. *Asian Wall Street Journal.* December 10:13–14.

Pyke, G. H. 1978. Optimal foraging in hummingbirds: testing the marginal value theorem. *American Zoologist* 18:739–52.

Pyke, G. H. 1979. Optimal foraging in fish. In R. H. Stroud & H. Clepper (Eds.), *Predatory-prey systems in fisheries management,* Sport Fishing Institute, Washington D.C.

Pyke, G. H. 1980. Optimal foraging in nectar-feeding birds and coevolution with their plants. In A. C. Kamil & T. D. Sargent (Eds.), *Foraging Behaviour.* Garland Press, New York.

Pyke, G. H., Pulliam, H. R., & Charnov, E. L. 1977. Optimal foraging: a selective review of theory and tests. *Quarterly Review of Biology* 52:137–54.

Rajalakshmi, R. 1969. *Applied nutrition.* Harshad Desai Unity Printers, Baroda.

Ramanamurthy, P. S. V. 1969. Physiological effects of 'hot' and 'cold' foods in human subjects. *Journal of Nutrition and Dietetics* 6:187–91.

Rampal, I. 1977. Nutritional status of primary school children; a comparative rural and urban study 1976. *Medical Journal of Malaysia* 32:6–16.

Ransley, G. 1975. Patrol report. *Ningerum* May–June 1975.

Raphael, D. 1973. The role of breast feeding in a bottle oriented world. *Ecology of Food and Nutrition* 2:121–6.

Raphael, D. (Ed.) 1979. *Breastfeeding and food policy in a hungry world.* Academic Press, New York.

Rapp, R. 1978. Family and class in contemporary America: notes toward an understanding of ideology. *Science and Society* 42:278–300.

Rappaport, R. 1968. *Pigs for the ancestors: ritual in the ecology of a New Guinea people.* Yale University Press, New Haven.

Read, M. H. 1938. Native standards of living and African culture change. Illustrated by examples from the Ngoni Highlands of Nyasaland. *Africa* 11(3): Suppl. 56 pp.

Reeder, L. G. 1972. Migration, socio-cultural mobility and cardiovascular disease. In J. M. Stanhope & J. S. Dodge (Eds.), *Migration, and Related Social and Health Problems in New Zealand and the Pacific.* Proceedings, Epidemiology Unit, Wellington Hospital, November 2–3.

Reid, J. C., & Mununggur, D. 1977. We are losing our brothers: sorcery and alcohol in an Aboriginal community. *Medical Journal of Australia* 2 (Special suppl.):1–5.

Rence, G. 1980. Land, trustees and timber. *Pacific Perspective* 8:18–19.

Richards, A. I. 1932. *Hunger and work in a savage tribe.* Routledge, London.

Richards, A. I. 1939. *Land, labour and diet in Northern Rhodesia. An economic study of the Bemboi tribe.* Oxford University Press, Oxford.

Richards, A. I., & Widdowson, E. M. 1936. A dietary study in north-eastern Rhodesia. *Africa* 9:166–96.

Richerson, P. J., & Boyd, R. 1978. A dual inheritance model of the human evolutionary process. 1. Basic postulates and a simple model. *Journal of Social and Biological Structures* 1:127–54.

Riggs, N. V. 1954. The occurrence of macrozamin in the seeds of cycads. *Australian Journal of Chemistry* 7:123–4.

Robinson, K. 1983. Women and work in an Indonesian mining town. In L. Manderson (Ed.), *Women's Work and Women's Roles: Economics and Everyday Life in Indonesia, Malaysia and Singapore.* Development Studies Centre Monograph No. 32. Australian National University Press, Canberra.

Robinson, K. 1985. The Soroako nickel project: a healthy development? *International Journal of Health Services* 15(2):301–19.

Rogers, D., & Miner, M. 1963. Amino acid profile of manioc leaf protein in relation to nutritive value. *Economic Botany* 17:211–16.

Roheim, G. 1950. *Psychoanalysis and anthropology.* International Universities Press, New York.

Rose, R. J. 1960. *Maori-European standard of health.* Special Report No. 1, Medical Statistics Branch, Department of Health, Wellington, April.

Ross, E. B. 1978. Food taboos, diet and hunting strategy: the adaptation to animals in Amazon cultural ecology. *Current Anthropology* 19(1):1–16.

Roth, W. E. 1901–10. *North Queensland Ethnography Bulletins 1–18.* Nos. 1–8 published by the Home Secretary's Department, Brisbane; Nos. 9–18 in Records of the Australian Museum 6–8.

Rowland, M. G. M., Paul, A. A., & Whitehead, R. G. 1981. Lactation and infant nutrition. *British Medical Bulletin* 37:77–82.

Rudder, J. 1978/9. Classification of the natural world among the Yolngu, Northern Territory, Australia. *Ethnomedizin* 5:349–60.

Ruddle, K., Johnson, D., Townsend, P. K., & Rees, J. D. 1978. *Palm sago: a tropical starch from marginal lands.* Australian National University Press, Canberra.

Ruyle, E. E. 1973. Genetic and cultural pools: some suggestions for a unified theory of biocultural evolution. *Human Ecology* 1:201–15.

Sahlins, M. 1962. *Moala: culture and nature on a Fijian Island.* University of Michigan Press, Ann Arbor.

Sahlins, M. 1972. *Stone age economics.* Aldine-Atherton, Chicago.

Sai, F. T. 1979. International Planned Parenthood perspectives. In D. B. Jelliffe, E. F. Jeliffe, F. T. Sai, & P. Senanayake (Eds.), *Lactation, fertility and the working woman, Proceedings of the Joint International Planned Parenthood Federation/Union of Nutritional Sciences Conference, Italy, July 5–12, 1977.* International Planned Parenthood Federation, London.

Salmond, G. C. 1975. *Maternal and infant care in Wellington: a health care consumer study.* Special Report No. 45, Department of Health, Wellngton.

Savage-Rumbaugh, E. S., Rumbaugh, D. M., & Boysen, S. 1978. Symbolic communication between two chimpanzees (*Pan troglyodytes*). *Science* 201:641–4.

Schieffelin, E. 1977. *The sorrow of the lonely and the burning of the dancers.* University of Queensland Press, St. Lucia.

Schlegel, S. A., & Guthrie, H. A. 1973. Diet and the Tiruray shift from swidden to plow farming. *Ecology of Food and Nutrition* 2:181–91.

Schneider, D. 1957. Typhoons on Yap. *Human Organization* 16(2):10–15.

Schoener, T. W. 1971. Theory of feeding strategies. *Annual Review of Ecology and Systematics* 11:369–404.

Schuphan, W. 1970. Control of plant proteins: the influence of genetics and ecology of food plants. In R. Lawrie (Ed.), *Proteins as human food.* Butterworth, London.

Schuster, D. 1979. *Urbanization in the Pacific.* Miscellaneous Work Paper No. 3, Pacific Islands Program, University of Hawaii, Honolulu.

Scott, E. M., & Quint, E. 1946. Self-selection of diet. III. Appetites for B vitamins. *Journal of Nutrition* 32:285–92.

Scott, E. M., & Verney, E. L. 1949. Self selection of diet. IX. The appetite for thiamine. *Journal of Nutrition* 37:81–91.

Scott, J. S. 1959. *An introduction to the sea fishes of Malaya.* Ministry of Agriculture, Federation of Malaya, Kuala Lumpur.

Scragg, R. F. R. 1969. Mortality changes in rural New Guinea. *Papua New Guinea Medical Journal* 12:73–83.

Scrimshaw, N. S. 1976. Strengths and weaknesses of the committee approach: an analysis of past and present recommended dietary allowances for protein in health and disease. *New England Journal of Medicine* 294:136–42, 198–203.

Scrimshaw, N. S. & Underwood, B. 1980. Timely and appropriate complementary feeding of the breast-fed infant – an overview. *U.N. University Food and Nutrition Bulletin* 2:19–22.

Scrimshaw, N. S., Taylor, C. E., & Gordon, J. E. 1968. *Interaction of nutrition and infection.* Monograph Series No. 57, World Health Organization, Geneva.

Sebrell, W., & Harris, R. 1967. *The vitamins: chemistry, physiology, pathology, methods.* Vol. 1 (2nd ed.). Academic Press, New York.

Shankman, P. 1979. Island economics and multi-national investment. *Anthropological Resource Centre Newsletter* 3(1):1.

Shaw, B. D. 1980. Child nutrition and health under rapid social and economic change in Papua New Guinea: the need for an integrated approach. Development Studies Centre, Australian National University, Canberra, mimeographed.

Simoons, F. 1961. *Eat not this flesh.* University of Wisconsin, Madison.

Simpson-Hebert, M., & Huffman, S. 1981. The contraceptive effect of breastfeeding. In *Studies in Family Planning,* Vol. 12, No. 4, pp. 125–33.

Simson, S. 1975a. Crisis raises pressure for change in dairy scheme. *Australian Financial Review* October 20:2.

Simson, S. 1975b. Australian's troubled dairy industry. *Australian Financial Review* December 29:2.

Simson, S. 1977a. Joint ventures boost dairy sales in Asia. *Australian Financial Review* March 23.

Simson, S. 1977b. Asia Dairy runs into severe problems on supply. *Australian Financial Review* September 15.

Sinnett, P. F. 1975. *The People of Murapin.* Classey, Oxford.

Sinnett, P. F. 1977. Nutritional adaptation among the Enga. In T. Bayliss & R. Feachem (Eds.), *Subsistence and survival: rural ecology in the Pacific.* Academic Press, New York.

Skeat, W. W., & Blagden, C. O. 1906. *Pagan races of the Malay Peninsula.* Macmillan, London.

Somare, M. 1973. New Guinea's eight point plan. *Pacific Perspectives* 2(1):3.

South Pacific Commission 1981. *Statistical summary.* Noumea.

Specht, R. L. 1958a. The climate, geology, soils and plant ecology of the northern portion of Arnhem Land. In R. L. Specht & C. P. Mountford (Eds.), *Records of the American–Australian Scientific Expedition to Arnhem Land,* Vol. 3. Melbourne University Press, Melbourne.

Specht, R. L. 1958b. An introduction to the ethno-botany of Arnhem Land. In R. L. Specht and C. P. Mountford (Eds.), *Records of the American–Australian Scientific Expedition to Arnhem Land,* Vol. 3. Melbourne University Press, Melbourne.

Spiro, M. E. 1977. *Kinship and marriage in Burma.* University of California Press, Berkeley.

Sri Kardjati, Kusin, J. A., & de With, C. 1977. *Geographical distribution and prevalence of nutritional deficiency diseases in East Java, Indonesia,* East Java Nutrition Studies Report I, University of Airlangga and Royal Tropical Institute, Surabaya and Amsterdam.

Stack, C. 1974. *All our kin.* Harper & Row, New York.

Stiles, F. G. 1976. Taste preferences, colour preferences, and flower choice in hummingbirds. *Condor* 78:10–26.

Stockton, M. D., & Whitney, G. 1974. Effects of genotype, sugar and concentration on sugar preference of laboratory mice (*Mus musculus*). *Journal of Comparative and Physiological Psychology* 86:62–8.

Stokes, J. 1981. Anindilyakwa phonology from phoneme to syllable. In B. Waters (Ed.), *Australian phonologies: collected papers.* Work Papers of SIL-AAB, Series A, Vol. 5, Summer Institute of Linguistics, Darwin.

Strathern, M. 1972. *Women in between. Female roles in a male world: Mount Hagen.* Seminar Press, London.

Sun (Sydney), The 1972. Milking dairymen. 25 September.

Sundaram, J. K. 1983. Malaysia's new economic policy and "national unity": development and inequality 25 years after independence. In S. Arief & J. K. Sundaram (Eds.), *Malaysian Economy and Finance.* South East Asia Research and Development Institute, Rosecons, Australia, pp. 3–25.

Suskind, R. M. (Ed.) 1977. *Malnutrition and the immune response.* Raven Press, New York.

Sweet, C. 1936. Voluntary food habits of normal children. *Journal of the American Medical Association* 107:765–7.

Talbot, N. T. 1972. Incidence and distribution of helminth and arthropod parasites of indigenous owned pigs in Papua New Guinea. *Tropical Animals Health Production* 4:182–90.

Tambiah, S. J. 1969. Animals are good to think and good to prohibit. *Ethnology* 8(4):425–59.

Tan, M., Djamadias, Suharso, Yulfita Rhardjo, Sutedjo, & Sunardjo. 1970. *Social and cultural aspects of food patterns and food habits in five rural areas in Indonesia.* National Institute of Economic and Social Research and Directorate of Nutrition, Department of Health, Jakarta.

Tarwotjo & Suhadi Hardjo 1964. *The role of fish in Indonesian child diet and methods to improve traditional fish processing. Proceedings A-A Congress of Pediatrics,* Jakarta.

Taylor, W. R. 1964. Fishes of Arnhem Land. In R. L. Specht (Ed.), *Records of the American–Australian Scientific Expedition to Arnhem Land,* Vol. 4. Melbourne University Press, Melbourne.

Tempo 1976a. Susu untuk bayi: kenapa dilarang? 28 February:13–14.

Tempo 1976b. Tetap bisa dimimum, asal . . . 28 February:14.

Tempo 1976c. Giliran susu bubuk. 27 March:16.

Tempo 1977a. Foremost exit tapi bawan bakal seru, 2 April:50–1.

Tempo 1977b. Botol sampayne sudan dibuka tapi sugiri bilang tunggu dulu, 14 May: 49–50.

Teoh, S. K. 1975. Breast feeding in a rural area in Malaysia. *Medical Journal of Malaysia* 29:175–9.

Terra, G. 1964. Significance of leaf vegetables, especially of cassave, in tropical nutrition. *Tropical and Geographical Medicine* 16(2):97–108.

Thompson, D. J. 1978. Prey size selection by larvae of the damselfly, *Ischnura elegans* (Odonata). *Journal of Animal Ecology* 47:769–85.

Thomson, A. M., & Black, A. E. 1975. Nutritional aspects of human lactation. *WHO Bulletin* 53:163–77.

Thomson, D. F. 1949. *Economic structure and the ceremonial exchange cycle in Arnhem Land.* Macmillan, Melbourne.

Tindale, N. B. 1925. Natives of Groote Eylandt and of the west coast of the Gulf of Carpentaria, Part 1. *South Australian Museum Records* 2:61–102.

Tindale, N. B. 1926. Natives of Groote Eylandt and of the west coast of the Gulf of Carpentaria, Part 2. *South Australian Museum Records* 3:103–34.

Tongue, R. K. 1974. *The English of Singapore and Malaysia.* Eastern Universities Press, Singapore.

Tonkin, S. L. 1974. Polynesian child health: effects on education. In D. Bray & C. Hill (Eds.), *Polynesian and Pakeha in New Zealand education,* Vol. II. Heinemann, Auckland.

Townsend, P. 1969. Subsistence and social organization in a New Guinea society. Ph.D. dissertation, Department of Anthropology, University of Michigan.

Townsend, P., Liao, S., & Konlande, J. 1973. Nutritive contributions of sago ash used as a native salt in Papua New Guinea. *Ecology of Food and Nutrition* 2: 91–7.

Tudge, C. 1979. *The famine business.* Penguin, Harmondsworth.

Turnbull, C. 1972. *The mountain people.* Simon & Schuster, New York.

Turner, D. H. 1974. *Tradition and transformation: a study of the Groote Eylandt area Aborigines of northern Australia.* Australian Institute of Aboriginal Studies, Canberra.

United Nations 1962. *Population Bulletin of the United Nations,* No. 6.

United States, National Research Council, Committee of Food Habits 1943. *The problem of changing food habits, National Research Council Bulletin 108.* National Academy of Science, Washington, D.C.

United States, National Research Council, Committee of Food Habits 1945. *Manual for the study of food habits, National Research Council Bulletin 111.* National Academy of Science, Washington, D.C.

United States, Interdepartmental Committee on Nutrition for National Defense (ICNND) 1964. *Federation of Malaya, Nutrition Survey, September–October 1962.* ICCND, Bethesda, Maryland.

Van Esterik, P. 1977. Lactation, nutrition and changing cultural values: infant feeding practices in rural and urban Thailand. In G. Means (Ed.), *Development and underdevelopment in South-East Asia.* Canadian Society for Asian Studies, Ottawa.

Vavra, Z. 1972. *Labor force projections by race, sex and age for western Malaysia: 1970–1975.* The Christian Michelsen Institute, Bergen.

Venkatachalam, P. S. 1962. *A study of the diet, nutrition and health of the people of the Chimbu area (New Guinea Highlands).* Monograph No. 4, Department of Public Health, Port Moresby.

Vines, A. P. 1970. *An epidemiological sample survey of the highlands, mainland and islands regions of the territory of Papua New Guinea.* Department of Public Health, Port Moresby.

Waddell, E. 1972. *The mound builders: agricultural practices, environment, and society in the central highlands of New Guinea,* American Ethnological Society Monograph No. 53, University of Washington Press, Seattle.

Waddington, K. D., & Holden, L. R. 1979. Optimal foraging: on flower selection by bees. *American Naturalist* 114:179–96.

Waddy, J. A. 1982. Biological classification from a Groote Eylandt Aborigine's point of view. *Journal of Ethnobiology* 2:63–77.

Waddy, J. A. 1984. Classification of plants and animals from a Groote Eylandt Aboriginal point of view. Ph.D. dissertation, Macquarie University, North Ryde, N.S.W.

Wade, N. 1974. Bottle-feeding: adverse effects of a Western technology. *Science* 184: 45–8.

Waiko, J. 1977. The people of Papua New Guinea, their forests and their aspirations.

In J. Winslow (Ed.), *The Melanesian environment, Ninth Waigani Seminar, 1975.* Australian National University Press, Canberra.

Ward, R. G., & Hau'ofa, E. 1980. Summary and epilogue. In Asian Development Bank, *South Pacific agriculture – choices and constraints.* South Pacific Agriculture Survey, Australian National University Press, Canberra.

Warner, W. L. 1958. *Black civilization: a social study of an Australian tribe.* Harper, New York. (Originally published in 1937)

Warren, R. P., & Pfaffmann, C. 1959. Early experiences and taste aversion. *Journal of Comparative and Physiological Psychology* 52:263–6.

Wasserstrom, R. 1979. Infant formula. *Anthropology Resource Centre Newsletter* 3(2):5.

Waterlow, J. C. 1979. Adequacy of breastfeeding. *Lancet* 2:897–8.

Waterlow, J. C., & Thomson, A. M. 1979. Observations on the adequacy of breast-feeding. *Lancet* 2:238–42.

Watt, B. K., & Merrill, A. L. 1963. *Composition of foods – raw, processed, prepared, Agriculture Handbook No. 8.* Agricultural Research Service, U.S. Department of Agriculture, Washington D.C.

Watt, R. 1980. Forestry. In Asian Development Bank, *South Pacific agriculture – choices and constraints.* South Pacific Agriculture Survey, Australian National University Press, Canberra.

Weiner, A. B. 1977. *Women of value, men of renown.* University of Queensland Press, St. Lucia.

Wellin, E. 1955a. Water boiling in a Peruvian town. In B. D. Paul (Ed.), *Health, culture, and community.* Russell Sage Foundation, New York.

Wellin, E. 1955b. Maternal and infant feeding practices in a Peruvian village. *Journal of the American Dietetic Association* 31:889–94.

Werner, E. E., & Hall, D. J. 1974. Optimal foraging and the size selection of prey by the bluegill sunfish (*Lepomis macrochirus*). *Ecology* 55:1042–52.

Westoby, M. 1974. An analysis of diet selection by large generalist herbivores. *American Naturalist* 108:290–304.

Wheatcroft, W. 1975. The legacy of Afekan: cultural symbolic interpretation of religion among the Tifalmin of New Guinea. Ph.D. dissertation, Department of Anthropology, University of Chicago.

White, K. J. 1976. Planned developments in Lowland rainforests in Papua New Guinea. In *Man and the Biosphere Report,* Australian Government Printing Office, Canberra.

White, M. K. 1978. Breastfeeding and dental caries. *La Leche League News* 20:53–5.

White, N. 1979. Tribes, genes and habitats: genetic diversity among Aboriginal populations in Northern Territory of Australia. Ph.D. dissertation, La Trobe University.

Whitehead, R. G., Rowland, M. G. M., Hutton, M., Prentice, A. M., Muller, E., & Paul, A. 1978. Factors influencing lactation performance in rural Gambian mothers. *Lancet* 2:178–81.

Whiting, M., & Morton, J. 1966. *Tropical plant foods with exceptional nutritional value. Proceedings of the Seventeenth International Horticultural Congress,* Vol. 4, pp. 99–105.

Whyte, R. O. 1974. *Rural nutrition in monsoon Asia.* Oxford University Press, Kuala Lumpur.

Wilcocks, C., & Manson-Bahr, P. E. C. 1972. *Manson's tropical diseases.* Baillers Tindall, London.

Wilkins, L. & Richter, C. P. 1940. A great craving for salt by a child with cortico-adrenal insufficiency. *Journal of the American Medical Association* 114:866–8.

Williams, N. M. 1982. A boundary is to cross: observations on Yolngu boundaries and permission in Australia. In N. Williams and E. S. Hunn (Eds.), *Resource managers: North American and Australian hunter-gatherers,* Westview Press, for the American Association for the Advancement of Science, Boulder, Colo.

Willis, M. F., & Wannan, J. S. 1966. Some aspects of the epidemiology of lepto-spirosis in New Guinea. *Medical Journal of Australia* 1:129–36.

Wilson, C. S. 1970. Food beliefs and practices of Malay fishermen: an ethnographic study of diet on the east coast of Malaya. Unpublished Ph.D. dissertation. University of California, Berkeley.

Wilson, C. S. 1973a. Food habits: a selected annotated bibliography. *Journal of Nutrition Education* 5(1), Suppl. 1:41–72.

Wilson, C. S. 1973b. Food taboos of childbirth – the Malay example. *Ecology of Food and Nutrition* 2:267–73.

Wilson, C. S. 1975. Rice, fish and coconuts – the bases of Southeast Asian flavours. *Food Technology* 29(6):42–4.

Wilson, C. S. 1979. Food – custom and nurture. An annotated bibliography on socio-cultural and biocultural aspects of nutrition. *Journal of Nutrition Education* 11(4), Suppl. 1:211–64.

Wilson, M. 1981. Bottle babies and managed mothers. *Science for the People* 3(1): 17–29.

Winick, M. (Ed.) 1979. *Hunger disease: studies by the Jewish physicians in the Warsaw ghetto.* Wiley, New York.

Winikoff, B. 1978. Nutrition, population and health: some implications for policy. *Science* 200:895–902.

Winstedt, R. O. 1965. *An unabridged Malay–English dictionary* (6th ed.). Merican (Malaysia), Kuala Lumpur.

Woolcock, A. J., & Blackburn, C. R. B. 1967. Chronic lung disease in the territory of Papua New Guinea: an epidemiological study. *Australasian Annals of Medicine* 16:11–19.

Woolcock, A. J., Blackburn, C. R. B., Freeman, M. H., Zylstra, W., & Spring, S. R. 1970. Studies of chronic (nontuberculous) lung disease in New Guinea populations. *American Review of Respiratory Disease* 102:575–90.

Woolcock, A. J., Colman, M. H., & Blackburn, C. R. B. 1972. Factors affecting normal values for ventilatory lung function. *American Review of Respiratory Disease* 106:692–709.

Wong, H. B. 1975. The role of the medical and health professionals in promoting desirable policies and practices. *PAG Bulletin (Protein Advisory Group)* 5(1): 16–19.

World Health Organization (WHO) 1966. *The health aspects of food and nutrition. A manual for developing countries in the Western Pacific Region of WHO.* WHO Western Pacific Regional Office, Manila.

World Health Organization (WHO) 1973. *Energy and protein requirements.* World Health Organization Technical Report Series No. 522, Rome.

World Health Organization 1979. *Breastfeeding.* Geneva.

World Health Organization 1981. *International code of marketing of breast-milk substitutes.* Geneva.

Worsley, P. M. 1961. The utilization of food resources by an Australian Aboriginal tribe. *Acta Ethnographica* 10:153–90.

Young, M. W. 1971. *Fighting with food: leadership, values, and social control in a Massim society.* Cambridge University Press, Cambridge.

Young, M. W. 1977. Bursting with laughter: obscenity, values and social control in a Massim society. *Canberra Anthropology* 1(1):75–87.

Young, M. W. 1983. *Magicians of manumanua: living myth in Kalauna.* University of California Press, Berkeley.

Young, P. 1985. Press conference of International Baby Foods Conference, Mexico City, February 2–5.

Yusof, Z. H. A., & Yusof, K. 1974. *Some socio-economic and medical aspects of Malay mortality in urban rural areas.* Occasional Papers No. 1, Malaysian Center for Developmental Studies, Kuala Lumpur.

Zach, R. 1979. Shell dropping – decision making and optimal foraging in Northwestern crows. *Behaviour* 68:106–17.

Zainal Abidin bin Ahmad 1947. The various significations of the Malay word *sejuk.* *Journal of the Malayan Branch, Royal Asiatic Society* XX(Part II):41–4.

Zeidenstein, G. 1977. *Including women in development efforts. The president's report.* Population Council Annual Report, New York.

Zuidberg, L. (Ed.) 1978. *Family planning in rural West Java: the Serpong Projects.* Nabrink & Son, Amsterdam.

Index